Enhancing Firm Sustainability Through Governance

CORPORATIONS, GLOBALISATION AND THE LAW

Series Editor: Janet Dine, *Director, Centre for Commercial Law Studies, Queen Mary, University of London, UK*

This uniquely positioned monograph series aims to draw together high quality research work from established and younger scholars on what is an intriguing and under-researched area of the law. The books will offer insights into a variety of legal issues that concern corporations operating on the global stage, including interaction with the World Trade Organization (WTO), international financial institutions and nation states, in both developing and developed countries. While the underlying foundation of the series will be that of company law, broadly-defined, authors are encouraged to take an approach that draws on the work of other social sciences, such as politics, economics and development studies and to offer an international or comparative perspective where appropriate. Specific topics to be considered will include corporate governance, corporate responsibility, taxation and criminal liability, amongst others. The series will undoubtedly offer an important contribution to legal thinking and to the wider globalisation debate.

Titles in the series include:

Transnational Corporations and International Law
Accountability in the Global Business Environment
Alice de Jonge

The Corporate Objective
Andrew Keay

Secured Credit and the Harmonisation of Law
The UNCITRAL Experience
Gerard McCormack

A Legal Framework for Emerging Business Models
Dynamic Networks as Collaborative Contracts
Emily M. Weitzenboeck

Directors' Duties and Shareholder Litigation in the Wake of the Financial Crisis
Edited by Joan Loughrey

Governance of Distressed Firms
David Milman

The Nature of Corporate Governance
The Significance of National Cultural Identity
Janet Dine and Marios Koutsias

Corporate Social Responsibility in Contemporary China
Jingchen Zhao

Enhancing Firm Sustainability Through Governance
The Relational Corporate Governance Approach
Francesco de Zwart

Enhancing Firm Sustainability Through Governance

The Relational Corporate Governance Approach

Francesco de Zwart

Lecturer, Adelaide Law School, The University of Adelaide, Australia

CORPORATIONS, GLOBALISATION AND THE LAW

Edward Elgar PUBLISHING

Cheltenham, UK • Northampton, MA, USA

Published by
Edward Elgar Publishing Limited
The Lypiatts
15 Lansdown Road
Cheltenham
Glos GL50 2JA
UK

Edward Elgar Publishing, Inc.
William Pratt House
9 Dewey Court
Northampton
Massachusetts 01060
USA

A catalogue record for this book
is available from the British Library

Library of Congress Control Number: 2015933460

This book is available electronically in the **Elgar**online
Law subject collection
DOI 10.4337/9781784715526

MIX
Paper from responsible sources
FSC® C013056
FSC www.fsc.org

ISBN 978 1 78471 551 9 (cased)
ISBN 978 1 78471 552 6 (eBook)

Typeset by Servis Filmsetting Ltd, Stockport, Cheshire
Printed and bound in Great Britain by T.J. International Ltd, Padstow

To
My Wife, Professor Melissa de Zwart
and
My Daughters, Brontë and Emily de Zwart
Thanks for Loving
and to
My old Articles of Clerkship Principal and Friend
Ian Renard AM

Contents

Figures

Tables

Preface

Begun in 2007, the 'relational corporate governance approach' presented in this book is an original contribution in what today is a crowded research space.

Much earlier than the GFC, corporate collapses such as those of Enron and WorldCom in the US and HIH Insurance in Australia, culminating in measures such as the US's *Sarbanes-Oxley Act* of 2002 and the New York Stock Exchange *Corporate Governance Rules of 2003*, had already put governance practices under the microscope. Consequently, a huge body of legal, economic and econometric literature has grown examining developments in corporate governance codes and their constituent individual governance variables.

This book represents the first stage of the relational approach and lays the foundations for an on-going project. The relational approach is a hybrid. Based on theory and with a springboard from empirical studies, it is both theoretical in explanation and operational in application.

The relational approach is a tool which complements and enhances the explanatory power of the existing principal 'law and economics' theories and models of the firm. It maps the effectiveness of corporate governance variables in use in corporate governance codes and laws around the world and assesses reform proposals in the field. The approach can be used by regulators, policy-makers, law reformers and corporate actors and their advisors as a diagnostic tool to analyse the governance health of individual companies and the governance actions required to remedy sub-optimal governance and management arrangements. The principal aim of the relational approach is to describe and evaluate the *interrelationships* between the most significant fields of corporate governance study and practice and the governance variables to which these fields give rise. In this way, the relational approach can be used to make predictions in relation to the relative importance of governance variables *inter se* in reducing (or increasing) agency costs and enhancing (or reducing) the long-term efficiency and survival of the for-profit firm.

The relational approach is built from an artificial environment that simulates the real world sphere of corporate governance and is comprised of the four Key Fields drawn from the Social Science Research Network (http://www.ssrn.com/) electronic library database: (1) application of the principal theories of the firm to the relational approach; (2) 'autopsies' of the Enron (and Hastie Group) corporate collapses; (3) comparative international and national corporate governance codes; and (4) empirical studies of the effectiveness of governance variables. From these Key Fields a 'weighing mechanism' is constructed comprising four theoretical components.

First, the relational approach introduces a new definition of relational corporate governance known as the 'three relational axes of good governance'. These three relational axes act like a set of scales to theoretically 'weigh' the competing interests of those 'inside' the corporation and those 'outside'. Second, the relational approach establishes a set of eight 'governance factors' which are the principal or central themes underlying the four Key Fields. These eight governance factors are the eight most common themes in the relational approach's simulated representation of real-world corporate governance. The theoretical 'weighing' of the governance factors in the three relational axes of good governance is already completed and presented for the reader. Thus the *interrelationships* between the eight governance factors are presented in two diagrams called 'interrelationship schemes', one for the shareholder (primacy) model and the other representing the stakeholder model.

For application to real-world governance practice from these interrelationship schemes, the relational approach constructs – for each of 39 governance variables – a 'relational effect path' that seeks to explain which governance factors are affected by each governance variable and the direction of the effect.

The interrelationships depicted in a relational effect path for each governance variable are then displayed in operational tables. The Coverage Table (Table 3.1) summarises the relational effect path for each governance variable. In the Relational Proximity Table (Table 3.2), each governance variable is ranked in order of descending relative importance on a new rating scale known as 'relational proximity' or '*rprox*'. The greater the number of governance factors affected by a governance variable in either direction, then the greater is the relative importance of that variable in affecting agency costs and the long-term efficiency and survival/sustainability of the for-profit corporation.

The significant fields of research in this book – comprising the four Key Fields – are growing constantly. And so, too, must the relational approach grow. But even in a book this size, it is not possible to list all the theoretical literature, empirical studies, codes and other works which affect the relational approach. So additional references, updates to the research, modifications and additions to the governance variables – and eventually even new Key Fields – will be available electronically on the relational approach companion website (http://www.relationalcorporate governance.org).

Dr Francesco de Zwart
1 December 2014

Table of cases

Case	Page
Dodge v Ford Motor Co (1919) 204 Mich 459, 507; 170 NW 668; 684 (per Ostrander J, Steere, Fellows, Stone and Brooke JJ concurring), available at http://au.westlaw.com (accessed 16 May 2008)	7
Walker v Wimborne [1976] HCA 7; (1976) 137 CLR 1 (3 March 1976)	7, 42, 96, 102
Wyong Shire Council v Shirt [1980] HCA 12 (1 May 1980); (1980) 146 CLR 40, available at http://www.austlii.edu.au/au/cases/cth/HCA/1980/12.html (accessed 6 March 2015)	30

Table of statutes

Statute	Page
Corporations Act 2001 (Cth), available at http://www.austlii.edu.au/au/legis/cth/consol_act/ca2001172/index.html#s9 (accessed 6 March 2015)	7, 30, 42, 56, 58, 96–97, 101–103, 123, 282–283, 286, 300–301
Emergency Economic Stabilization Act of 2008, (US), H.R. 1424, Troubled Assets Relief Programme ('TARP'), available at http://frwebgate.access.gpo.gov/cgi-bin/getdoc.cgi?dbname=110_cong_bills&docid=f:h1424enr.txt.pdf (accessed 6 March 2015), ('EESA'). For further information on TARP and the EESA, see House Committee on Financial Services at http://financialservices.house.gov/ (accessed 6 March 2015). For a description of the EESA's passage through the House, Senate and President's signature *see* http://www.govtrack.us/congress/bill.xpd?bill=h110-1424 (accessed 6 March 2015)	1
Sarbanes-Oxley Act of 2002, (US), PL 107-204, 2002 HR 3763, 30 July 2002, 116 Stat 745, available at http://international.westlaw.com.proxy.library.adelaide.edu.au (accessed 19 November 2012), ('SOX')	39–40, 46, 49–50, 60–62, 164, 219, 224, 230, 238–239, 274–275, 285
Securities Exchange Act of 1934, (US), June 6, 1934, Chapter 404, Title I, Sec. 1, 48 Stat. 881 (as Amended Through P.L. 111–72, Approved 13 October 2009), available at http://www.sec.gov/about/laws/sea34.pdf (accessed 6 March 2015), ('SEA')	164

Table of government and regulatory body reports, codes, rules and publications

Australian Securities Exchange (ASX) (AUSTRALIA)

Report, Code, Rule or Publication	Page
ASX 2003 Best Practice Recommendations The original ASX best practice recommendations were contained in the ASX Corporate Governance Council, *Principles of Good Corporate Governance and Best Practice Recommendations,* Australian Securities Exchange, March 2003 ('ASX 2003 Best Practice Recommendations').	52, 54, 96, 151–152, 176–182
ASX Draft Recommendations Proposed changes to the ASX 2003 Best Practice Recommendations were the subject of public comment. See ASX Corporate Governance Council, *Principles of Good Corporate Governance and Best Practice Recommendations, Exposure Draft of Changes*, Australian Securities Exchange, 2 November 2006 ('ASX Draft Recommendations').	152

<table>
<tr><th>Report, Code, Rule or Publication</th><th>Page</th></tr>
<tr><td>ASX 2007–10 Revised Principles
The ASX 2003 Best Practice Recommendations were revised on 2 August 2007. See ASX Corporate Governance Council, Corporate Governance Principles and Recommendations, Second Edition, Australian Securities Exchange, 2 August 2007. These Principles and Recommendations were further amended in June 2010. See ASX Corporate Governance Council:

• Corporate Governance Principles and Recommendations with 2010 Amendments, June 2010 ('ASX 2007-10 Revised Principles');
• Revised Corporate Governance Principles and Recommendations (Second Edition, August 2007);
• Marked-Up Amendments dated 30 June 2010 to the Second Edition of the Corporate Governance Principles and Recommendations ('ASX 2010 Marked-Up Amendments'); and
• Summary Table of the 30 June Changes to the Second Edition of the Corporate Governance Principles and Recommendations ('ASX 2010 Summary Table').

These documents are available at http://www.asxgroup.com.au/corporate-governance-council.htm (accessed 6 March 2015).</td><td>52, 54, 56, 58, 96–98, 151, 153, 176–182, 326

52, 54, 56, 58, 96–98, 151, 153, 176–182, 326

153

153, 182

153, 182</td></tr>
<tr><td>ASX 2014 Principles and Recommendations
The ASX 2007–10 Revised Principles were revised and replaced by the Third Edition of the Principles and Recommendations which were released on 27 March 2014 and (at p 7) took effect for a company's financial year commencing on or after 1 July 2014 ('ASX 2014 Principles and Recommendations').

For a comparison of the ASX 2007–10 Revised Principles and the ASX 2014 Principles and Recommendations, see Translation Table, Corporate Governance Council Recommendations (New to Old) and (Old to New), ('CGC Recommendations Translation Tables').

These documents are available at http://www.asx.com.au/regulation/corporate- governance-council.htm (accessed 6 March 2015).</td><td>38, 40, 42, 52, 54, 56, 60, 97-99, 102, 151, 153, 176–183, 253, 323, 326, 330

182</td></tr>
</table>

Report, Code, Rule or Publication	Page
Australian Securities Exchange, ASX Listing Rules, General Rule 3.1, Continuous Disclosure, 01/01/2003, p 301, available at http://www.asx.com.au/ListingRules/chapters/Chapter03.pdf, p 302, (accessed 02/02/09)	39–40
Australian Securities Exchange, ASX Listing Rules, Rule 4.10.3, available at http://www.asx.com.au/ListingRules/chapters/Chapter04.pdf (accessed 26/08/10)	323

Financial Reporting Council (UK)

Report, Code, Rule or Publication	Page
Financial Reporting Council (FRC), *The Combined Code on Corporate Governance,* June 2006, London ('UK Combined Code')	151–152, 171–175, 226
Financial Reporting Council (FRC), *The UK Approach to Corporate Governance*, November 2006, London ('FRC UK Governance Approach 2006')	146, 171
Financial Reporting Council (FRC), *The UK Approach to Corporate Governance,* October 2010, London ('FRC UK Governance Approach 2010')	146
Financial Reporting Council (FRC), *The UK Corporate Governance Code*, June 2010, as amended in September 2012, London ('UK Corporate Governance Code 2010–12')	151–152, 171–175

Report, Code, Rule or Publication	Page
Financial Reporting Council (FRC), *The UK Corporate Governance Code*, September 2014, London, ('UK Corporate Governance Code 2014')	42, 60, 151–152, 171–175, 183, 252–253, 330
For the 2014 amendments to the UK Corporate Governance Code 2010–12 *see* Financial Reporting Council (FRC), *Feedback Statement – Revisions to the UK Corporate Governance Code,* September 2014, London.	151–152
Other documents published by the FRC: • *Good Practice Suggestions from The Higgs Report,* London ('Higgs Report Suggestions'); • *Guidance on Board Effectiveness,* 2010, London; • *Feedback Statement, Revisions to the UK Corporate Governance Code and Guidance on Audit Committees,* September 2012, London ('FRC Feedback Statement 2012'); • *Challenges for Audit Committees Arising from Current Economic Conditions,* November 2009, London; • *The UK Stewardship Code,* September 2012, London; • *Audit Firm Governance Code,* January 2010, London; • *Guidance on Audit Committees,* September 2012, London; • *Internal Control: Guidance to Directors,* (formerly known as the Turnbull Guidance), originally published in 1999 and last revised in 2005, London; and • *Going Concern and Liquidity Risk: Guidance for Directors of UK Companies,* 2009, London. FRC documents are available at http://www.frc.org.uk/ (accessed 6 March 2015).	

Other Government And Regulatory Bodies

Report, Code, Rule or Publication	Page
Australian Government, Corporations and Markets Advisory Committee (CAMAC), *Executive Remuneration, Report*, April 2011, available at http://www.camac.gov.au/camac/camac.nsf/byHeadline/PDFFinal+Reports+2011/$file/Executive_remuneration_report_April11.pdf (accessed 6 March 2015)	300
Australian Government, Corporations and Markets Advisory Committee, *The Social Responsibility of Corporations, Report,* December 2006, Sydney, available at http://www.camac.gov.au (accessed 6 March 2015), ('CAMAC Social Responsibility Report')	93–95, 100–101
Australian Government, Productivity Commission, *Executive Remuneration in Australia*, Productivity Commission Inquiry Report No 49, 19 December 2009, available at http://www.pc.gov.au/__data/assets/pdf_file/0008/93590/executive-remuneration-report.pdf, (accessed 2 January 2013)	300
Business Roundtable, *Principles of Corporate Governance 2005, A White Paper by Business Roundtable*, November 2005, Washington, DC ('Business Roundtable Principles 2005') The 2005 Principles were updated in April 1010 and June 2012. For the current Principles, see Business Roundtable, *Principles of Corporate Governance 2012,* June 2012, Washington, DC ('Business Roundtable Principles 2012') available at http://businessroundtable.org/uploads/studies-reports/downloads/BRT_Principles_of_Corporate_Governance_-2012_Formatted_Final.pdf (accessed 27 March 2013)	151–152 151–152, 165–168

Report, Code, Rule or Publication	Page
California Public Employees' Retirement System (CalPERS), *Global Principles of Accountable Corporate Governance*, Sacramento, California, available at http://www.calpers-governance.org/docs-sof/principles/2011-11-14-global-principles-of-accountable-corp-gov.pdf, updated 14 November 2011 (accessed 14 August 2013). For the current *Global Principles*, see California Public Employees' Retirement System (CalPERS), *Global Principles of Accountable Corporate Governance*, 19 May 2014, Sacramento, California, available at http://www.calpers-governance.org/docs-sof/principles/2014-05-calpers-global-principles-accountable-corp-gov.pdf. (accessed 13 March 2015), ('CalPERS Global Governance Principles 2014')	151–152, 165–168
The Committee on the Financial Aspects of Corporate Governance, *Report of the Committee on the Financial Aspects of Corporate Governance,* 1 December 1992, London: Gee & Co Ltd ('Cadbury Report')	3, 28, 151–152, 171–175, 326
Commonwealth Association for Corporate Governance, *Principles for Corporate Governance in the Commonwealth, Towards Global Competitiveness and Economic Accountability*, Final Version, November 1999, ('CACG Guidelines'), available at http://www.ecseonline.com/PDF/CACG%20Guidelines%20-%20Principles%20for%20Corporate%20Governance%20in%20the%20Commonwealth.pdf (accessed 6 March 2015)	6–27, 60, 151, 154–157, 359, 361
The Conference Board, Inc., *Commission on Public Trust and Private Enterprise,* 9 January 2003, available at http://www.conference-board.org/publications (accessed 6 March 2015), Part 2: 'Corporate Governance: Principles, Recommendations and Specific Best Practice Suggestions', ('Conference Board Principles')	151–152, 165–168

Report, Code, Rule or Publication	Page
The International Bank for Reconstruction and Development/The World Bank and Organisation for Economic Co-operation and Development, *Global Corporate Governance Forum: 1 Focus: Corporate Governance and Development*, Stijn Claessens (author), Washington, DC,2003. See also The International Bank for Reconstruction and Development/The World Bank and Organisation For Economic Co-operation and Development, *Global Corporate Governance Forum: 2 Toolkit: Developing Corporate Governance Codes of Best Practice, User Guide*: *Volume 1 Rationale,* Washington, DC 2005 ('WB-OECD Global Corporate Governance Forum')	26
International Corporate Governance Network, *ICGN Statement on Global Corporate Governance Principles,* July 8, 2005, ICGN Annual Conference, London, ('ICGN Statement'). The *Principles* in the ICGN Statement were updated in 2009 and appear as Part C *International Principles of Accountable Corporate Governance* of the CalPERS Global Governance Principles 2014 above available at http://www.calpers-governance.org/docs-sof/principles/2014-05-calpers-global-principles-accountable-corp-gov.pdf. (accessed 13 March 2015)	60, 151, 154–157, 359, 361
Investment & Financial Services Association Limited (IFSA), *Blue Book, IFSA Guidance Note No. 2.00, Corporate Governance: A Guide for Fund Managers and Corporations*, 6th edn, June 2009, available at, http://www.fsc.org.au/downloads/file/IFSAGuidanceNotes/2GN_2_Corporate_Governance_2009.pdf ('IFSA Blue Book') (accessed 6 March 2015)	151, 153, 176–182

<table>
<tr><th>Report, Code, Rule or Publication</th><th>Page</th></tr>
<tr><td>IOSCO, Technical Committee of the International Organization of Securities Commissions in consultation with the OECD, Board Independence of Listed Companies, Final Report, March 2007, available at http://www.iosco.org/library/pubdocs/pdf/IOSCOPD238.pdf ('IOSCO Report'), 26 (accessed 6 March 2015)</td><td>290, 310–311</td></tr>
<tr><td>IOSCO, International Organization of Securities Commissions, Technical Committee And Emerging Markets Committee Of The International Organization Of Securities Commissions, Survey On The Regulation Of Non-Audit Services Provided By Auditors To Audited Companies, March 2007, available at http://www.iosco.org/library/pubdocs/pdf/IOSCOPD241.pdf (accessed 6 March 2015)</td><td>125, 280</td></tr>
<tr><td>New York Stock Exchange, Final NYSE Corporate Governance Rules, ('NYSE Final Rules'), approved by SEC 4 November 2003 (except s 303A.08) and 30 June 2003 (s 303A.08). The Rules (as amended from time to time) comprise section 303A.00 of the NYSE Listed Company Manual. See section 303A.00 Corporate Governance Standards (approved 25 November 2009), available at http://nysemanual.nyse.com/lcm/ (accessed 6 March 2015). Subsequent amendments have been made to:

• Section 303A.00 – Corporate Governance Standards (approved 22 August 2013)
• Section 303A.02 – Corporate Governance Standards (approved 11 January 2013)
• Section 303A.05 – Corporate Governance Standards (approved 11 January 2013)
• Section 303A.07 – Audit Committee Additional Requirements (approved 22 August 2013)

These Rule amendments are available at http://nysemanual.nyse.com/lcm/ (accessed 6 March 2015).</td><td>42, 49–50, 60, 151–152, 164–169, 183, 219, 224–225, 238-239, 269, 274, 285, 292, 330</td></tr>
</table>

Report, Code, Rule or Publication	Page
Organisation for Economic Co-Operation and Development (OECD), *OECD Principles of Corporate Governance 2004,* 2004, OECD Publications Service, Paris ('OECD Principles') *see* http://www.oecd.org/document/49/0,3343,en_2649_34813_31530865_1_1_1_37439,00.html (accessed 6 March 2015).	4, 26, 28, 38, 40, 42, 52-53, 60, 99, 151, 153–158, 165–169, 172–175, 177–181, 261–262, 326–327, 329–330, 359, 361
Ramsay, Ian, *Independence of Australian Company Auditors: Review of Current Australian Requirements and Proposals for Reform,* Report to the Minister for Financial Services and Regulation, Commonwealth of Australia, October 2001 (as printed in March 2002), available at http://archive.treasury.gov.au/contentitem.asp?ContentID=296 (accessed 6 March 2015)	282
Treadway Commission, *Report of the National Commission on Fraudulent Financial Reporting,* National Commission on Financial Reporting (US), 1987.	117

Administrators' Report

Report	Page
PPB Advisory, *Hastie Group Limited and Specific Subsidiaries, Report by Joint and Several Administrators Pursuant to Section 439A of the Corporations Act 2001*, 21 January 2013, available at http://www.ppbadvisory.com/creditor-information/v/281/hastie-group/2nd-creditor-meeting ('*Administrators' Report*'), (accessed 6 March 2015)	2, 10–11, 37-38, 40, 42–43, 56-57, 107, 109–111, 113, 115–118, 122–123, 128–130, 132, 138, 361

1. The challenge of corporate governance

1.1 THE GLOBAL FINANCIAL CRISIS AND FAILURES OF CORPORATE GOVERNANCE

The world-wide crisis in financial markets and, in particular, the repercussions on equities markets around the world consequent on the 'credit crunch' of 2008–09 and beyond has once again focused attention on corporate governance. Indeed, the fallout from the Global Financial Crisis (GFC) continues to have dramatic regulatory, social, economic and political effects around the world.[1]

The crux of the GFC is widely acknowledged as a combination of failures in regulatory supervision, 'gate-keeping' by intermediaries, greed and fundamental failings of *internal* corporate governance.[2] Yet, pre-GFC corporate collapses such as those of Enron and WorldCom in the US,[3] HIH Insurance in Australia[4] and collapses in other countries painted a

---

[1] Julia Black, 'Paradoxes and Failures: "New Governance" Techniques and the Financial Crises' (2012) 75(6) *MLR* 1037. See especially 1037–41. For the largest government 'bailout' in history, see the US government's Troubled Assets Relief Programme ('*TARP*'). A component of TARP is enacted under the *Emergency Economic Stabilization Act of 2008*, H.R. 1424, accessed 3 February 2015 at http://frwebgate.access.gpo.gov/cgi-bin/getdoc.cgi?dbname=110_cong_bills&docid=f:h1424enr.txt.pdf ('EESA'). For further information on TARP and the EESA, see House Committee on Financial Services at http://financialservices.house.gov/ (accessed 6 March 2015). For a description of the EESA's passage through the House, Senate and President's signature, see http://www.govtrack.us/congress/bill.xpd?bill=h110-1424 (accessed 6 March 2015).

[2] Black, ibid.

[3] The Enron collapse is examined in detail in Chapter 5.

[4] For a discussion of the corporate collapses of HIH Insurance and One.Tel in Australia and the regulatory responses to corporate collapses in various jurisdictions, see Jennifer G Hill, 'Regulatory Responses to Global Corporate Scandals' (2005) 23 *Wisconsin International Law Journal* 367; Sydney Law School Research Paper No 06/35; Vanderbilt Law and Economics Research Paper No 06-04, accessed 3 February 2015 at SSRN: http://ssrn.com/abstract=886104.

similar picture. More recently, collapses such as that of the Hastie Group in Australia in 2012[5] prompt this book to examine what lessons from these collapses have failed to be learnt? And what measures could have been taken – prospectively – to avoid the abyss?

Flowing from this, the following questions are posed by this book:

- What behaviours of corporate actors such as the individual directors, the CEO and management were present in these collapses and what are the consequences of these behaviours for firm survival or (in today's parlance) sustainability?
- What is the regulatory corporate governance environment which applies to these companies and how do individual corporate governance measures, mechanisms and processes (called 'governance variables') operate in the real world to enhance or reduce the effects of these behaviours?
- What are the 'core' or 'central' failures in governance variables that arise in corporate collapses?
- How do these governance variables interact with each other, that is, what are the **relationships** between governance variables?
- And which corporate governance variables are relatively more important – again, in the real world – in determining the survival or sustainability of the publicly-traded for-profit corporation?

These key questions at the heart of corporate governance discourse are the focus of this book. It proposes a diagnostic tool to prospectively analyse and assess the governance 'health' of individual companies and to both predict and enhance firm survival.

---

[5] See PPB Advisory, *Hastie Group Limited and Specific Subsidiaries, Report by Joint and Several Administrators Pursuant to Section 439A of the Corporations Act 2001*, 21 January 2013, accessed 3 February 2015 at http://www.ppbadvisory.com/creditor-information/v/281/hastie-group/2nd-creditor-meeting ('*Administrators' Report*'). The collapse of the Hastie Group is examined in detail in Chapter 5.

1.2 SEPARATION OF OWNERSHIP FROM MANAGEMENT AND THE ROLE OF CORPORATE GOVERNANCE

1.2.1 The Balancing of Interests of 'Insiders' and 'Outsiders'

The corporate governance sphere – indeed, on some views, the corporation itself[6] – involves a balancing exercise between corporate 'insiders' such as the directors, CEO and management with 'outsiders' such as shareholders or investors, employees, lenders, suppliers, regulators and, increasingly, social and environmental interests. The insider and outsider designations flow from the traditional separation of ownership (shareholders) from management or control (directors) in publicly-traded companies. One of the most influential definitions of corporate governance by Sir Adrian Cadbury in 1992 emphasises this separation:

> [c]orporate governance is the system by which companies are directed and controlled. Boards of directors are responsible for the governance of their companies. The shareholders' role in governance is to appoint the directors and the auditors and to satisfy themselves that an appropriate governance structure is in place. The responsibilities of the board include setting the company's strategic aims, providing the leadership to put them into effect, supervising the management of the business and reporting to shareholders on their stewardship. The board's actions are subject to laws, regulations and the shareholders in general meeting.[7]

---

[6] For a detailed discussion, see the papers relating to the 'nexus of contracts' theory and the 'anti-contractarian' views of the firm from the symposium on contractual freedom in corporate law held on 9 and 10 December 1988 at Columbia Law School, published at (1989) 89 *Colum L Rev* 1395.

[7] The Committee on the Financial Aspects of Corporate Governance and Gee and Co Ltd, *Report of the Committee on the Financial Aspects of Corporate Governance*, 1 December 1992, London: Burgess Science Press ('Cadbury Report'), Para 2.5. For an earlier discussion of the definitions in this section, see Francesco de Zwart (90% author) and George Gilligan, 'Comparative Corporate Governance Schemes and their Relevance for the Sporting Sector', Monash University Department of Business Law and Taxation, Working Paper No 16 (November 2008), accessed 3 February 2015 at http://ssrn.com.abstract=1295682, 6–7.

For the development of corporate governance, see Brian R Cheffins, 'The History of Corporate Governance', *Oxford Handbook Of Corporate Governance*, Mike Wright, Donald Siegel, Kevin Keasey and Igor Filatotchev, eds., Oxford University Press, 2013; University of Cambridge Faculty of Law Research Paper No. 54/2011; ECGI – Law Working Paper No. 184/2012, (December 1, 2011), accessed 24 April 2015 at SSRN: http://ssrn.com/abstract=1975404.

In another influential definition, written more than ten years later, the OECD explained the meaning and purpose of corporate governance in a manner which classifies governance variables as measures or mechanisms which seek to punish or deter management misconduct or which seek to align the interests of insiders with outside shareholders:

> [c]orporate governance involves a set of relationships between a company's management, its board, its shareholders and other stakeholders. Corporate governance also provides the structure through which the objectives of the company are set, and the means of attaining those objectives and monitoring performance are determined. Good corporate governance should provide proper incentives for the board and management to pursue objectives that are in the interests of the company and its shareholders and should facilitate effective monitoring.[8]

For a long time now, various theories and models of the Anglo-American corporate firm, international and national corporate governance codes and an ever-increasing body of theoretical literature and empirical studies have sought to explain the interaction between these corporate insiders and outsiders. Again, the book begins with these theories and models.

1.2.2 Separation of Ownership, 'Nexus of Contracts', Agency Costs and the Shareholder Model

The well-known theories and models relating to the separation of ownership and management of the corporation are the 'nexus of contracts', agency theory, the shareholder (primacy) model (and its related shareholder wealth-maximisation principle), the stakeholder model and the director primacy model.

Statement of the nexus theory

Bainbridge explains the nexus of contracts theory as follows:

For the development of US corporate governance, see Brian R Cheffins, 'The History of Modern U.S. Corporate Governance: Introduction', *Edward Elgar's Corporate Governance in the New Global Economy Series*, 2011; University of Cambridge Faculty of Law Research Paper No. 29/2012, accessed 24 April 2015 at SSRN: http://ssrn.com/abstract=2192151.

[8] Organisation for Economic Co-Operation and Development, *OECD Principles of Corporate Governance 2004*, 2004, OECD Publications Service, Paris ('OECD Principles'), Preamble, p 11. See http://www.oecd.org/document/49/0,3343,en_2649_34813_31530865_1_1_1_37439,00.html (accessed 3 February 2015).

> [n]exus of contracts theory visualizes the firm not as an entity, but as an aggregate of various inputs acting together to produce goods or services. Employees provide labor. Creditors provide debt capital. Shareholders initially provide equity capital and subsequently bear the risk of losses and monitor the performance of management. Management monitors the performance of employees and coordinates the activities of all the firm's inputs. The firm is seen as simply a legal fiction representing the complex set of contractual relationships between these inputs.[9]

According to Easterbrook and Fischel and, separately, Bratton, the effect of the nexus of contracts theory is to discourage management misconduct in the publicly-owned and traded corporation.[10] In short, welfare-reducing terms of the contract (or, more accurately, the various contracts or relationships) between the various actors cause a reduction in market price and, therefore, return on investment causing investors to seek more profitable investments. For publicly-traded firms, the 'market for corporate control' acts in conjunction with the nexus of contracts theory to further discourage management misconduct.

The market for corporate control operates as part of the efficient market hypothesis to punish management which engages in value- or performance-reducing behaviour. Cunningham explains that the efficient market hypothesis operates on the assumption that share prices can accurately reflect the corporation's value[11] so that a (lower) share price will reflect poor performance and, by proxy, poor management leaving the firm open to, among other things, hostile takeover and removal of management.[12] Cunningham also notes that the market for corporate control

---

[9] Stephen M Bainbridge, 'In Defense of the Shareholder Wealth Maximization Norm' A Reply to Professor Green" (1993) 50 *Washington & Lee Law Review* 1423, accessed 3 February 2015 at SSRN: http://ssrn.com/abstract=303780, 1426–7 (footnote omitted).

[10] Frank H Easterbrook and Daniel R Fischel, 'The Corporate Contract' (1989) 89 *Colum L Rev* 1416, 1430 and 1430–1 and William W Bratton, 'The "Nexus Of Contracts" Corporation: A Critical Appraisal' (1989) 74 *Cornell L Rev* 407, 417 and 418.

[11] Easterbrook and Fischel, ibid, 1430–1 and Lawrence A Cunningham, 'Behavioral Finance and Investor Governance' (2002) 59 *Washington & Lee Law Review* 767, accessed 3 February 2015 at SSRN: http://ssrn.com/abstract=255778, 3. The author cites Donald C Langevoort, 'Theories, Assumptions and Securities Regulation: Market Efficiency Revisited' (1992) 140 *U Pa L Rev* 85. See also, Eugene F Fama, Michael C Jensen, Lawrence Fisher and Richard Roll, 'The Adjustment of Stock Prices to New Information' (1969) 10 *International Economic Review* 1–22, accessed 3 February 2015 at SSRN: http://ssrn.com/abstract=321524.

[12] Easterbrook and Fischel, above n 10, 1430–1 and Cunningham, ibid.

is assisted by other governance measures – in particular, 'reputational constraints' (and consequences) relating to individual managers.[13]

Agency theory

Commentators such as Jensen and Meckling have sought to explain the separation effect in terms of agency (costs) theory.[14] Examined in detail in Chapter 4, this theory posits that, when making decisions, insiders or 'agents' *should* act on behalf of the outsiders or 'principals'. However, the agent's own self-interest in 'shirking', empire building, compensation, perks and other advantages may cause directors, CEOs and managers to deviate from what is in the shareholders' best interests. As a result, the shareholders incur costs to 'monitor' and 'bond' with the directors/managers as well as other 'residual' costs.[15]

For Jensen and Meckling, thus, the for-profit corporation (and even a non-profit organisation) is effectively a nexus of contracts:[16]

> which is also characterized by the existence of divisible residual claims on the assets and cash flows of the organization which can generally be sold without permission of the other contracting individuals.[17]

Thus, the agency (cost) relationship between 'insider-managers' and 'outsider-shareholders' underpins the nexus model. In the shareholder (or shareholder primacy) model of corporate governance, the shareholders are the only residual claimants.[18] Thus, it is the residual nature of

---

[13] Cunningham, above n 11, 3.

[14] See discussion in section 4.2.3.1 of Chapter 4.

[15] The classic formulation is found in Michael C Jensen and William H Meckling, 'Theory of the Firm: Managerial Behavior, Agency Costs and Ownership Structure' in Michael C. Jensen, *A Theory of the Firm: Governance, Residual Claims and Organizational Forms*, Cambridge, MA: Harvard University Press, December 2000; (1976) 3(4) *Journal of Financial Economics*, accessed 3 February 2015 at SSRN: http://ssrn.com/abstract=94043, 5–6.

[16] Jensen and Meckling, ibid, 8–9. For further discussion of the nexus of contracts theory of the firm and corporate law, see Stephen M Bainbridge, 'The Board of Directors as Nexus of Contracts: A Critique of Gulati, Klein & Zolt's "Connected Contracts" Model', UCLA, School of Law Research Paper No 02-05, January 2002, accessed 3 February 2015 at SSRN: http://ssrn.com/abstract=299743, 9–11 and Bainbridge, above n 9, 1426–7.

[17] Jensen and Meckling, above n 15, 8–9.

[18] Gerard J Charreaux, 'Corporate Governance Theories: From Micro Theories to National Systems Theories' (January 2004), Universite de Bourgogne Fargo Working Paper No 1040101, accessed 3 February 2015 at SSRN: http://ssrn.com/abstract=486522, 8; Amir N Licht, 'The Maximands of Corporate Governance: A Theory of Values and Cognitive Style' (November 2003), ECGI – Law

the shareholders' position which defines the shareholder as the central element of the shareholder primacy model and its related shareholder wealth-maximisation principle which follows.

1.2.3 The Shareholder Wealth-maximisation Principle

For Roe, the interests of shareholders and managers are aligned in part by managerial 'belief' in the shareholder wealth-maximisation principle (which he calls a 'soft control').[19] In United States corporate (case) law, the origin of the shareholder wealth-maximisation principle is often said to arise from the decision in *Dodge v Ford Motor Co*.[20] The correctness of this principle, at least as having been derived from *Dodge v Ford Motor Co*, has been challenged.[21] Despite this, the principle permeates much of US corporate law, including, as one example, the fiduciary duties of directors.[22]

In the case of Australian law, a similar situation exists. Subsection 181(1)(a) of the Corporations Act provides that a director's powers and duties must be exercised 'in good faith in the best interests of the *corporation*.'[23] While expressed to be owed to the corporation, it is well-known from the Australian High Court's decision in *Walker v Wimborne*[24] that this means, in the general case and apart from situations of insolvency or near insolvency of the corporation, that the duties must be exercised for the benefit of its shareholders as a whole.[25]

Working Paper No 16/2003, accessed 3 February 2015 at SSRN: http://ssrn.com/abstract=469801 and (2004) 29(3) *Delaware Journal of Corporate Law* 649–746, accessed 3 February 2015 at SSRN: http://ssrn.com/abstract=764025, 4. For a discussion of the nature of agency costs and residual claims in different forms of organisation, see Eugene F Fama and Michael C Jensen, 'Separation of Ownership and Control' in Michael C Jensen, *Foundations Of Organizational Strategy*, Cambridge, MA: Harvard University Press, 1998 and (1983) 26 *Journal of Law and Economics* 301, accessed 3 February 2015 at SSRN: http://ssrn.com/abstract=94034.

19 Mark J Roe, 'Political Preconditions To Separating Ownership from Corporate Control' (2000) 53 *Stanford Law Review* 539, accessed 3 February 2015 at SSRN: http://ssrn.com/abstract=165143, 554–5.

20 *Dodge v Ford Motor Co* (1919) 204 Mich 459, 507; 170 NW 668; 684 (per Ostrander J, Steere, Fellows, Stone and Brooke JJ concurring).

21 Lynn A Stout, 'Why We Should Stop Teaching Dodge v. Ford' (September 2007), UCLA School of Law, Law-Econ Research Paper No 07-11, accessed 3 February 2015 at SSRN: http://ssrn.com/abstract=1013744.

22 Douglas G Baird and M Todd Henderson, 'Other People's Money' (2008) 60 *Stanford Law Review* 1309, Symposium Issue, 2008, accessed 3 February 2015 at SSRN: http://ssrn.com/abstract=1017615.

23 Corporations Act 2001 (Cth), section 181(1)(a) (emphasis added).

24 *Walker v Wimborne* [1976] HCA 7; (1976) 137 CLR 1 (3 March 1976).

25 Ibid (1976) 137 CLR 1, 7 (per Mason J).

1.3 'CORE' AREAS OF CORPORATE GOVERNANCE AND CORPORATE FAILURES

In Chapter 6, the 'relational approach' proposed by this book identifies a 'model' or comparative scheme in table-form which can be used as a benchmark in the comparison of all cross-border and national governance codes. The chapter assesses the position and relative importance of governance variables from this comparative scheme to identify – as a measure of continuity and relative importance – a smaller 'core' set of governance variables for the international/cross-border sector and each of the national sectors of the US, UK and Australia. Looking ahead to Chapter 6, these core governance variables are:

- timely/regular disclosure of information;
- questions and voting in meetings;
- interested or conflicted director disclosure;
- employee/management/director incentive and participation schemes;
- timely disclosure of material information including remuneration policies;
- independent/external audit;
- quality and integrity of information;
- board functions and independence – compliance with statutory and legal duties on organisation/directors;
- principal board responsibilities – corporate governance compliance;
- principal board responsibilities – selection and monitoring of key management;
- principal board responsibilities – fair and open election of directors;
- principal board responsibilities – interested director or management conflicts or transactions;
- principal board responsibilities – reporting, audit, financial/operational control, risk management and internal audit;
- independence from management – non-executive/independent directors; and
- independence from management – responsibilities of board sub-committees delineated and disclosed.[26]

These core governance variables are in turn used to construct the central elements of the relational approach in this book. For present purposes, however, it is illustrative for the separation of ownership from

---

[26] See discussion in section 6.8.1 below.

management to identify which of these governance variables are central to the pre- and post-GFC corporate collapses of Enron and the unfolding story of the Hastie Group.

1.3.1 Multiple Failures in Core Governance Variables

In Chapter 5, a detailed examination of the Enron corporate collapse is juxtaposed with that of the Hastie Group. But an overview of the Enron and Hastie facts is illustrative for introductory purposes of the challenges posed for any system of corporate governance.

Enron was the seventh largest US company at the time of its collapse. Indeed, Gordon observes that:

> The Enron case has seemed particularly disturbing because the case represents a failed stress test for many institutions of US shareholder capitalism, circa 1990s. As with most catastrophes, many separate systems simultaneously failed: *auditing and accounting, executive compensation, internal monitoring by the board, and external monitoring by securities analysts.*[27]

The Enron share price remained high despite the close attention of institutions and analysts.[28] For Gordon, the complexity of the company's structure and off-balance sheet transactions caused information asymmetry problems obscuring its true (and much lower) value.[29] Each of Enron's traders was a separate profit centre causing 'phantom' profits to be recorded.[30] Off-balance sheet entities – in particular 'Special Purpose Entities' (SPEs) – caused the valuation and solvency of those entities to be problematic.[31]

By contrast, danger signs for the Hastie Group were prominent. After listing on the ASX, Hastie Group Limited ('HST') acquired a number

---

27 Jeffrey N Gordon, 'Governance Failures of the Enron Board and the New Information Order of Sarbanes-Oxley', Columbia Law and Economics Working Paper No 216; Harvard Law and Economics Discussion Paper No 416 (March 2003), accessed 3 February 2015 at SSRN: http://ssrn.com/abstract=391363, 3 (emphasis added).

28 See discussion in section 5.2.1.1 of Chapter 5.

29 Jeffrey N Gordon, 'What Enron Means for the Management and Control of the Modern Business Corporation: Some Initial Reflections' (2002) *69 University of Chicago Law Review* 1233, accessed 3 February 2015 at SSRN: http://ssrn.com/abstract=305343, 6.

30 Douglas G. Baird and Robert K. Rasmussen, 'Four (or Five) Easy Lessons From Enron' (2002) 55 *Vanderbilt Law Review* 1787, accessed 3 February 2015 at SSRN: http://ssrn.com/abstract=358442, 118.

31 Ibid, 120–122.

of businesses – many overseas – emerging with '7,000 employees, turnover in excess of $1.8b, construction work-in-progress (WIP) of $2.9 [billion] and assets employed of nearly $1 [billion]'.[32] The Group then experienced a dramatic decline in profitability which required five profit downgrades from November 2010 to May 2012.[33] The company was required to enter a moratorium agreement with its bankers[34] and then raised $158 million to repay debt.[35] Large write-downs were made against its major assets including goodwill, receivables and work-in-progress totaling $254 million[36] and trading in Hastie Group shares were suspended twice, the latter accompanied by accounting irregularities of $20 million.[37] The Group was placed into administration on 28 May 2012.[38]

Enron director independence was undermined by various factors. Branson is critical of high fees and consulting contracts for directors.[39] But share and option holdings were argued to reduce the quality of monitoring[40] as was Enron's director compensation policy.[41] Internal decision-making at Enron was typified by familiarity between board members and deference to management[42] while the ultra-competitive culture at Enron undermined risk-management controls by stifling dissent and driving misconduct in the pursuit of profit.[43] In the Hastie collapse, too, there were significant inadequacies in the Hastie audit committee, monitoring and control including that 'the Audit and Risk Committee . . . was largely inactive'[44] as well as inadequate operational management processes,

---

32 Administrators' Report, above n 5, section 2.5.1, p 12 of 99.

33 Ibid, Timeline of Key Events Leading Up To the Administration of the Hastie Group, p 17 of 99.

34 Ibid.

35 Ibid, section 2.5.2, p 13 of 99.

36 Ibid.

37 Ibid.

38 Ibid, section 2.1, p 10 of 99.

39 Douglas M Branson, 'Enron – When All Systems Fail: Creative Destruction or Roadmap to Corporate Governance Reform?' (2003) 48 *Villanova Law Review* 989; Villanova Law/Public Policy Research Paper No 2003-13, accessed 3 February 2015 at SSRN: http://ssrn.com/abstract=473205, 1003.

40 Stuart L Gillan and John D Martin, 'Financial Engineering, Corporate Governance, and the Collapse of Enron', U of Delaware Coll. of Bus. and Econ. Ctr. for Corp. Governance Working Paper No 2002-001 (November 2002), accessed 3 February 2015 at SSRN: http://ssrn.com/abstract=354040, 23–4.

41 Ibid, 24.

42 See discussion in section 5.2.2.2 below.

43 See discussion in section 5.2.2.3.2 below.

44 Administrators' Report, above n 5, section 2.5.3, p 14 of 99.

reporting systems and interrogation and control by the board in relation to management.[45]

The Enron collapse was typified by significant earnings manipulation[46] again stemming from the use of off-balance sheet SPEs to hide debt and minimize tax.[47] CEO, executive and director compensation – particularly in the form of equity and share options – exacerbated earnings manipulation.[48] At Hastie too, the Administrators found significant culture problems in Hastie financial results and forecasts including that 'there appears to have been a general culture of ignoring bad news . . .' and 'the Board, prior to the appointment of the interim CEO . . . appeared not to have "an enquiring mind" as to [the] reliability of financial statements and overall reporting'.[49]

Significant, too, in the Enron collapse was the undermining of external auditor independence leading to a massive audit failure by Enron's auditors, Arthur Andersen. This was said to be principally on account of the significant amount of non-audit tax services,[50] Andersen's role as both internal and external auditor[51] and the practice of Enron hiring former Andersen employees.[52] The Administrators have also raised issues in relation to the Hastie Group audit querying the auditor's compliance with a number of Australian Auditing Standards.[53]

Even from this brief overview, there are important similarities and differences in the two collapses for drawing out themes and tensions for regulators, policy-makers, law reformers and corporate actors. These are examined in detail in Chapter 5.

1.3.2 Key Fields and Research Questions in Firm Sustainability

In the relational approach, there are four 'Key Fields' which represent a simulation of the 'real world' sphere of corporate governance discourse. In other words, these are the four areas which will be examined in order to

---

45 Ibid. See also, section 7.9, p 61 of 99 and section 7.9.5, p 65 of 99.

46 See discussion in section 5.2.3 below.

47 See discussion in section 5.2.3.1 below.

48 See discussion in section 5.2.3.2.1 below.

49 Administrators' Report, above n 5, section 2.5.3, p 14 of 99.

50 See discussion in section 5.2.4.2 below.

51 Matthew J Barrett, 'Enron and Andersen – What Went Wrong and Why Similar Audit Failures Could Happen Again', accessed 3 February 2015 at SSRN: http://ssrn.com/abstract=794831, 159.

52 Ibid, 160.

53 Administrators' Report, above n 5, section 7.11, p 67 of 99.

construct the relational approach to examining the governance health and sustainability of the corporation:

1. Application of the Principal Theories of the Firm to the Relational Approach;
2. 'Autopsies' of the Enron and Hastie Corporate Collapses;
3. Comparative Corporate Governance Codes; and
4. Empirical Studies of the Effectiveness of Governance Variables.

How are the Key Fields selected?

The four Key Fields are the most significant and influential areas of corporate governance discourse measured by the number of articles and/or working papers. Thus it is important to explain how the four Key Fields were selected in order to substantiate the legitimacy of decisions taken regarding the identity of the governance variables examined in the book and the structure and components of the relational approach.

The Key Fields are selected from the single most current and voluminous collection of works in the very wide expanse of corporate governance – the e-library of the Social Science Research Network (SSRN).[54] A search was undertaken in 2007 using the general 'corporate governance' search term. Of course, it is not possible even in a work this size to discuss all these works. The works chosen were selected for relevance and impact. Thus a qualitative element was added to the selection process by discussing works that are important or representative in hypothesising the actual real world behaviour of governance variables.

Because of considerations of scope and size, it was necessary to exclude from this initial collection on SSRN – and thereafter – works relating to the perceived effects of various areas of governance inquiry including, principally:

- accounting and auditing principles, standards and governing or regulatory bodies;
- governance of private firms and semi-government, non-profit or voluntary firms/organisations;
- the fiduciary duties of directors under the laws of equity or statute; and

[54] See http://www.ssrn.com (accessed 3 February 2015). References in this book to working papers from the SSRN website will bear the date of posting and/or revision of the papers as signified in the suggested citation by SSRN.

- detailed theories, examinations and applications of principles of corporate social responsibility or CSR except interests that affect or influence the stakeholder model as described in Chapter 4.

In 2012, the next stage of review of SSRN literature was undertaken to update the works within the four Key Fields. Again, the general 'corporate governance' search term was used. The works chosen were selected for relevance and impact from a sample of 250 works with the highest download figures over the preceding three years, the lowest with approximately 395 downloads. The next review of SSRN literature took place from 20 December 2013 to 6 January 2014 again using the 'corporate governance' search term. Again, the works chosen were selected for relevance and impact from a sample of 200 works with the highest download figures spanning the previous two years with the lowest download figure of 277 downloads. The final review took place from 9–14 October 2014 encompassing 100 works spanning the previous year with the lowest download figure of 155 downloads.

The book now introduces each Key Field as the structural foundation of the relational approach. Each component of the relational approach – and the governance variables themselves – are identified after examination of one or more Key Fields.

1.3.2.1 Key Field No 1 – Application of the principal theories of the firm to the relational approach

Key Field No 1 examines the application of the pre-eminent theories and models of the firm to the relational approach. Key Field No 1 demonstrates how the relational approach adds explanatory power to these theories.

The key questions in section 1.1 asked what behaviours of the individual directors, CEO and management were present in corporate collapses and what are the consequences of these behaviours for firm sustainability? So this Key Field asks:

- How do the pre-eminent theories and models seek to balance the competing interests between corporate insiders and outsiders?
- And how does the relational approach help to explain the operation of these theories and models?

1.3.2.2 Key Field No 2 – 'Autopsies' of the Enron and Hastie corporate collapses

The following Key Field No 2 describes how these theories are undermined in the case of corporate collapses like Enron and Hastie. This Key Field provides a detailed examination of the commentator views on the Enron corporate collapse as a pre-GFC example of corporate failure. Then juxtaposed is the relational approach's own comparison of the Hastie collapse from the post-GFC period. The key questions in section 1.1 seek the 'core' features of these collapses. Thus, the relational approach asks:

- What are the structural features of the Enron and Hastie corporate collapses in pre- and post-GFC times and how did they operate at the relevant time?
- And what lessons do they provide for a diagnostic approach or tool for regulators, policy-makers, law reformers and corporate actors and their advisors relating to the sustainability of the corporation?

1.3.2.3 Key Field No 3 – Comparative corporate governance codes

Two key questions in section 1.1 ask what is the regulatory corporate governance environment for corporations and which governance variables are relatively more important in determining the sustainability of the firm? Originally springing from a number of collapses last century including Enron, this Key Field examines the multitude of governance variables in the real world in which they operate. The Key Field examines codes for the international/cross-border sector and the US, UK and Australia.

Thus, Key Field No 3 asks:

- Which governance variables have developed over time and across sectors (international/cross-border and national) to form the central planks of governance codes and schemes?

1.3.2.4 Key Field No 4 – Empirical studies on the effectiveness of governance variables

The relational approach's key questions ask how individual governance variables operate in the real world to enhance or reduce the effects of corporate actors such as the board, individual directors, the CEO and management. Key Field No 4 thus examines a wide range of empirical and other studies which examine the effects of governance variables on shareholder wealth measures such as firm value/share price, firm operating performance/profit and the probability of earnings manipulation. The largest Key Field, it asks:

- What is the effectiveness of individual corporate governance variables in affecting the long-term efficiency and sustainability of the corporation?

- What factors intervene to reduce the operation and effectiveness of these corporate governance variables?
- And what is the relative importance of individual corporate governance variables *inter se* in reducing (or increasing) agency costs and enhancing (or reducing) the long-term efficiency and sustainability of the for-profit firm?

1.4 RELATIONAL CORPORATE GOVERNANCE

Based on the underlying interrelationships, themes and tensions in these four Key Fields, the approach proposed for regulators, policy-makers, law reformers, corporate actors and their advisors in this book is called 'relational corporate governance'. It is based on identifying, describing and predicting the nature, behaviour and interrelationships between corporate governance variables. It is critical to the understanding of governance variables that they do not operate in isolation but have a significant 'zone of effect'. They affect the operation of other governance variables as well as other managerial and governance structures within the corporation.

The key goals or aims of relational corporate governance drawn from the four Key Fields above are to:

(1) introduce a new definition of 'corporate governance' that weighs or balances the aims, behaviours and positional conflict of insiders and outsiders. This is known as the 'three relational axes of good governance' and is introduced in Chapter 2;[55]
(2) create a 'simulated corporate governance environment' which represents the 'real world' sphere of corporate governance. These are the four Key Fields introduced above;
(3) Identify, describe and map diagrammatically the interrelationships, themes and tensions underpinning these four Key Fields. These are the eight 'governance factors' introduced below and the 'interrelationship schemes' between these factors presented in Chapter 2.[56] The governance factors and interrelationship schemes are combined to create a 'relational effect path' for each governance variable;
(4) Create a comparative table or scheme system upon which to compare across sectors and over time the governance variables utilised in the major US, UK, Australian and international/cross-border for-profit

[55] See the discussion in sections 2.3.1–2.3.3 below.
[56] See Figures 2.6 and 2.7.

corporate governance codes or schemes. These are the Governance Code Tables and Commonality Tables of Chapter 6; and

(5) As an over-arching aim, to propose an approach or tool for regulators, policy-makers, law reformers and corporate actors to predict, measure and enhance the relative importance of governance variables *inter se* in reducing (or increasing) agency costs and enhancing (or reducing) the long-term efficiency and sustainability of the for-profit firm.

1.5 AGENCY COSTS AND SUSTAINABILITY IN THE RELATIONAL APPROACH

A very good argument can be put that reducing agency costs *causes* the long-term efficiency and sustainability of the for-profit firm to be enhanced. If, as suggested by Jensen and Meckling, agency costs are reflected in the market price of shares,[57] then reducing these costs on a long-term basis by the employment of governance variables could lead to long-term and sustained market value improvement.

Indeed, the express purpose of many of the empirical studies of the effectiveness of governance variables in the book is just this. For example, many of these studies seek to show that a collection of governance variables, or particular individual variables, enhance the monitoring of management and thus reduce agency costs. This, these studies argue, in turn enhances sustainability measures or proxies such as the firm's cost of capital, firm value and firm operating performance. In other studies, the agency cost:sustainability relationship may not be the express purpose but is the underlying tenor of the study. Indeed, this is also one of the underlying assumptions of the relational approach proposed in this book.

Thus the relational approach, being theoretical, will first *assume* in Chapters 2–6 that hypotheses can be made about governance variables in reducing (or increasing) such agency costs and that, in turn, the long-term efficiency and survival or sustainability of the for-profit firm may be enhanced (or diminished). Then, in Chapters 7–10, the book will examine empirical studies which reveal the real-world effects of governance variables on shareholder wealth measures such as firm value/share price, firm operating performance/profit and the probability of earnings manipulation. In future stages, the agency cost:sustainability relationship in this approach can be empirically tested.

---

[57] See discussion in section 4.2.3 below.

1.6 OVERVIEW OF THE BOOK

1.6.1 Overview of the Relational Corporate Governance Approach

The approach for regulators, policy-makers, law reformers and corporate actors presented in the relational approach aims to evaluate and map on a 'first principles' basis the insider and outsider forces on the corporation and the nature, behaviour, effect and, consequently, relative importance of 39 corporate governance variables which arise in international and national corporate governance best practice and discourse.

1.6.2 Introduction to Relational Approach Chapters

Chapter 2 constructs the principal components of the relational approach and introduces the 39 governance variables. It begins with an overview of the argued micro- and macro-economic benefits of 'good' corporate governance. Then follows detailed analysis and justification for the four components. The 'three relational axes of good governance' – the theoretical weighing mechanism – are presented in descriptive and diagram form. These act as a set of scales to weigh the objectives, behaviours and positional conflict of insiders versus outsiders. The eight governance factors are the 'backbone' of the relational approach. They represent the most significant and recurring themes or aims underpinning the four Key Fields and, therefore, the 39 governance variables drawn from those Fields. The third component – the two interrelationship schemes – represents the hypothesized interrelationships between the eight governance factors. These schemes are used later in the book to construct the fourth component – a relational effect path for each governance variable. This path depicts the number and identity of governance factors affected by each governance variable and the direction of the effect. The chapter culminates with a diagram of the overall relational corporate governance approach in Figure 2.8.

The hypothesised interrelationships between the governance variables and governance factors depicted in the relational effect paths are summarised in Chapter 3 in two operational tables. Table 3.1 displays the number and identity of each governance factor affected by a governance variable and the direction of the effect. Table 3.2 arranges the 39 governance variables in order or groups of descending relative importance (known as 'relational proximity rating') in affecting agency costs and the long-term efficiency and sustainability of the firm.

Chapters 4–10 cover a vast territory. They examine the four significant areas that simulate 'real-world' corporate governance discourse – the four Key Fields.

Chapter 4 contains an analysis and application of the principal theories and models of the firm explained in terms of the relational approach. The chapter shows that the relational approach adds explanatory power, components and examples to the currently pre-eminent theories of the firm – the 'nexus of contracts', agency theory, the shareholder (primacy) model, the stakeholder model and the director primacy model.

In Chapter 5, the theory in the preceding chapter is translated into a real-world case study of the behaviour of governance variables in one of the largest corporate collapses ever – the pre-GFC corporate collapse of Enron. Juxtaposed with this is the relational approach's own analysis of the post-GFC collapse of the Hastie Group. This chapter seeks to show three things. First, to extract the themes and tensions of the Enron collapse to support the identification, structure and articulation of the eight governance factors. Second, to identify the intervening factors or problems which reduced the effectiveness of the governance variables examined in the book. Finally, to show how these governance variables behaved in the multitude of governance failures of the Enron and Hastie corporate collapses.

The Enron corporate collapse (and others) spawned a large number of corporate governance codes of 'best-practice'. Chapter 6 is thus a comparative analysis of these and subsequent international and national corporate governance codes. The aim of Chapter 6 is two-fold. First, to produce a 'model' or comparative scheme in table-form which can be used as a benchmark or comparison for all governance codes. Second, to identify a smaller 'core' set of variables from international and national codes for justifying the selection of the themes and tensions in the three relational axes of good governance and the governance factors.

There follows the first of four parts on the Empirical Studies Key Field No 4.

In Chapter 7, the governance variables are examined to determine their effectiveness in reducing agency costs and increasing the long-term efficiency and sustainability of the firm. This is the first chapter which presents a relational effect path for each governance variable – this path sets out the number and identity of governance factors affected by the relevant governance variable and the direction of the effect. The relational effect paths are critical for two reasons:

- first, they are an interpretation/translation of the empirical studies into the components of the relational approach; and

- second, to determine the relative importance of a governance variable *vis-à-vis* other governance variables in reducing (increasing) agency costs and enhancing (reducing) the long term efficiency and sustainability of the firm. This is examined by proxies relating to firm operating performance/profit and firm value/share price. The greater the number of governance factors affected by a governance variable, the greater is that variable's relative importance relative to other variables.

Thus, Chapter 7 examines 'overall' governance (as a function of *multiple* governance variables), the strength of the national shareholder protection regime and 'Board Factors I' – director independence and the proportion of non-executive/independent directors.

Then, for Chapter 8, the governance variables examined are:

- 'Board Factors II' – board size and outside board positions of independent directors; and
- other firm-specific variables – anti-takeover mechanisms such as staggered board elections, audit subcommittee presence, independence and expertise, 'block' and institutional shareholdings and division in the CEO/Chairperson roles.

Again, a relational effect path is presented for each governance variable and firm efficiency and sustainability is measured by firm operating performance and firm value.

In Chapter 9, the proxy for long-term efficiency and sustainability is earnings manipulation or management. Increases in earnings management represent increases in the agency costs of outside shareholders and therefore a fall in firm sustainability. The governance variables examined include many identified previously – but now assessed against the probability of earnings management/manipulation.

The purpose of Chapter 10 is to present the fourth and final part of the Empirical Studies Key Field No 4. The corporate governance effects of director, CEO and management compensation are examined with respect to the governance variables. The chapter constructs the relational effect paths for the compensation-related governance variables including director/CEO pay levels, equity/option holdings of directors and management and short-term options for directors and outside directors on the audit committee.

The relational approach concludes in Chapter 11 with observations and analysis relating to the interrelationships and relational proximity of the 39 governance variables. Links are drawn in relation to the themes and tensions underpinning the four Key Fields. Comparisons of the relational approach's findings on the relational proximity rating of governance variables are made against the current state of research in those Fields. Chapter 11 concludes with observations on the structure, explanatory power and scope of the relational approach as well as areas for future research.

2. The framework of the relational corporate governance approach

2.1 APPROACH TO THE RELATIONAL CORPORATE GOVERNANCE FRAMEWORK

The purpose of this chapter is to show how the relational corporate governance approach and its constituent components determine the relational proximity of governance variables. To do so, the additional purpose of this chapter is to construct the principal components of the relational approach and to introduce the 39 governance variables. This includes the following theoretical components introduced in the previous chapter:

- the 'three relational axes of good governance' – the theoretical weighing mechanism which weighs the objectives, behaviours and positional conflict of insiders versus outsiders;
- the eight 'governance factors' – the most significant and recurring themes and tensions underpinning the four Key Fields; and
- the two 'interrelationship schemes' which represent the hypothesised relationships between the governance factors under the shareholder primacy model and the stakeholder model of corporate governance – these are used to construct a 'relational effect path' for each governance variable.

The relational approach's principal terms and components are defined in Table A.2 of Appendix 2, *Glossary of Relational Corporate Governance Approach Terms and Components*.

In short, each relational effect path depicts the number and identity of the governance factors affected by each governance variable and the direction of the effect. The more governance factors affected by a governance variable, then the greater is its relational proximity relative to other governance variables in affecting agency costs (in either direction) and the long-term efficiency and sustainability of the firm.

The relational approach seeks to add to the relevant literature on the operation of economic actors in Anglo-American firms where there is a separation between ownership and management. These firms operate in a dense financial market typified by a large number of widely-dispersed shareholders.[1] The firms have unitary boards such as those operating in the United States, United Kingdom and Australia.[2]

Using the Relational Corporate Governance Approach in Figure 2.1

A walk through Figure 2.1 sets out how the relational approach works from the perspective of the reader and sets out how the components are combined to predict the relational proximity (relative effect) of governance variables on the sustainability of the firm.

Figure 2.1 depicts how the components and tables which comprise the relational approach are constructed. As can be seen from the figure, all these components and tables originate from an examination of the four Key Fields on the left-hand side of the diagram. The four Key Fields simulate the 'real world' sphere of corporate governance available to the reader in the first stage of the relational approach. They are:

1. Application of the principal theories of the firm to the relational approach;
2. 'Autopsies' of the Enron and Hastie corporate collapses;
3. Comparative corporate governance codes; and
4. Empirical studies of the effectiveness of governance variables.

The articles, working-papers and other works comprising these Key Fields are drawn from the SSRN platform.[3] These four Key Fields contain the 39 governance variables which are examined in the relational approach.[4] These are the 39 governance and management structures, mechanisms,

---

[1] Brian R Cheffins, 'Does Law Matter?: The Separation of Ownership and Control in the United Kingdom', September 2000, ERSC Centre for Business Research, University of Cambridge, Working Paper No 172, accessed 5 February 2015 at SSRN: http://ssrn.com/abstract=245560. For a discussion of the determinants and 'path dependence' of corporate structure ('diffused' *versus* 'concentrated') and governance in different countries, see Lucian A Bebchuk and Mark J Roe, 'A Theory of Path Dependence in Corporate Ownership and Governance' (1999) 52 *Stanford Law Review* 127–170, accessed 24 April 2015 at SSRN: http://ssrn.com/abstract=202748.

[2] Turnbull tells us that such a board structure exists for most listed companies in the US, UK, Canada and Australia. See Shann Turnbull, 'Why Unitary Boards Are Not Best Practice: A Case for Compound Boards', November 2000, accessed 5 February 2015 at SSRN: http://ssrn.com/abstract=253803, 2.

[3] See http://www.ssrn.com. See discussion in section 1.3.2 above.

[4] These governance variables are set out in Table 2.1.

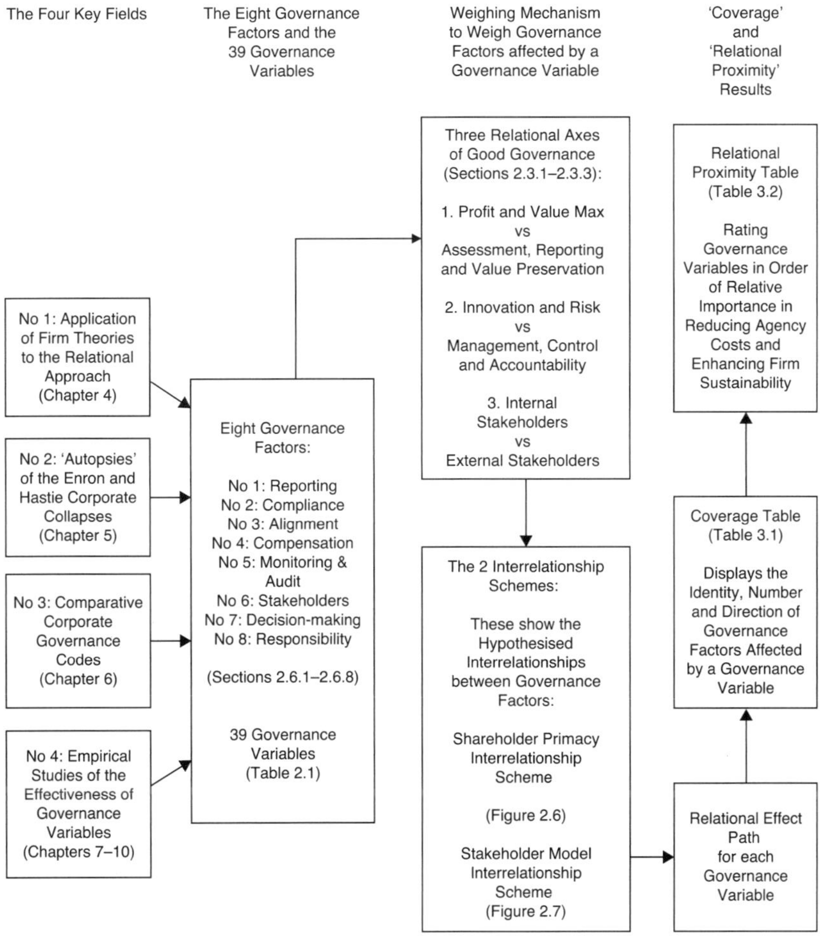

Figure 2.1 Relational corporate governance approach

processes and protocols which seek to deter or punish management misconduct or which align the interests of the management with those of the outside dispersed shareholders.[5]

As the relational approach is based on predicting the interrelationships between these 39 governance variables, the aim at this point is to identify what those interrelationships are. These interrelationships are represented by the eight governance factors. Themes and considerations from each

[5] See discussion in section 1.2.1 above.

of the four Key Fields are brought forward from the later chapters to construct each of the governance factors:

1. **Reporting** – Transparency, timing and integrity of financial and other reports;
2. **Compliance** – Corporate governance and legal compliance;
3. **Alignment** – Alignment of management and shareholder interests;
4. **Compensation** – Board, CEO and management compensation and incentives;
5. **Monitoring & Audit** – Internal and external/audit monitoring quality;
6. **Stakeholders** – Identification, participation and protection of stakeholder interests;
7. **Decision-making** – Quality of board, CEO and management decision-making; and
8. **Responsibility** – Delineation and disclosure of powers, duties and lines of responsibility.

These governance factors provide the factors, themes or considerations which are relevant to any decision to employ individual governance variables. The legitimacy of observations and conclusions derived from the relational approach are dependent on the governance factors.

The aim now is to determine – by hypothesis – how these 39 governance variables affect each other. This aim is achieved by proxy. The interrelationships between the 39 governance variables must be the interrelationships between the eight governance factors which underpin those governance variables. To determine the interrelationships between the governance factors, the relational approach uses the weighing mechanism of the three relational axes of good governance also constructed in this chapter.[6] The interrelationships produced by this weighing are already calculated and presented for the reader – these are the two interrelationship schemes.

The examination of the individual governance factors then moves to the construction of these two interrelationship schemes. These two schemes are diagrams setting out the hypothesised interrelationships between all of the eight governance factors. There are two schemes – one based on the shareholder primacy model[7] and the other based on the stakeholder model[8] of corporate governance.

---

[6] See discussion in sections 2.3.1–2.3.3 below.

[7] See Figure 2.6.

[8] See Figure 2.7.

Next to be determined is how the employment (or omission) of each governance variable affects each other governance variable. The relational approach recognises at this time the pre-eminence of the shareholder primacy model of corporate governance.[9] Thus, the Shareholder Primacy Interrelationship Scheme diagram is the basis of a relational effect path produced for each governance variable in Chapters 7–10. These paths depict the identity, number and direction of the governance factors affected by each of the 39 governance variables. In short, the greater the number of governance factors affected by a governance variable – in the manner set out in the Shareholder Primacy Interrelationship Scheme – then the greater is that governance variable's relative importance compared to other governance variables in reducing agency costs and enhancing the long-term efficiency and sustainability of the firm.

The final step is to present the results of the relational effect path for each governance variable in two operational tables. Each of the 39 relational effect paths are summarised in the Coverage Table (Table 3.1). Then the Relational Proximity Table (Table 3.2) ranks and groups the governance variables in order of descending relative importance in affecting the governance factors and, thus, the long-term efficiency and sustainability of the firm.

The Benefits of 'Good' Corporate Governance

Having presented the challenge for corporate governance in Chapter 1, Chapter 2 begins with an overview of the most observable force in terms of governance phenomena – the argued benefits of 'good' corporate governance.

2.2 OVERVIEW OF THE FIRM-SPECIFIC (MICRO) AND MACRO-ECONOMIC BENEFITS OF 'GOOD' CORPORATE GOVERNANCE

Here, the principal firm-specific benefits of the adoption of good governance variables are summarised as:

- reducing firm cost of capital;
- increasing firm value and operating performance; and
- stakeholder interest identification, participation and protection.

---

9 See discussion in section 4.3.2 below.

These reflect the research of Claessens (writing on behalf of The World Bank and the OECD) who summarised the developmental effects of good governance for businesses (in other words, the employment of governance variables) as including improved access to capital, reduced capital costs, managerial improvement (with consequent improvement in results) and enhanced stakeholder relationships.[10]

Claessens identifies increased investment, growth and employment as some of the *macro-economic* benefits flowing from the firm-specific benefits.[11] These macro-economic benefits or effects represent the cumulative effects that are said to arise from the adoption of firm-specific governance variables.

Support for this research can also be found in various other statements of the firm-specific and macro-economic aims and consequential effects of the adoption of good governance variables in the for-profit sphere. The OECD sees corporate governance as essential for various reasons largely related to market confidence, efficiency and development resulting in a lower cost of capital.[12]

Related to this in terms of global movements, the OECD also recognised the importance of 'internationally accepted principles' of good governance in attracting long-term foreign investment.[13] The Commonwealth Association for Corporate Governance (CACG) similarly identified enhanced profits and efficiency for organisations, sustained

---

[10] The International Bank for Reconstruction and Development/The World Bank and Organisation For Economic Co-operation and Development, *Global Corporate Governance Forum: 1 Focus: Corporate Governance and Development*, Stijn Claessens (author), 2003, Washington, DC, at p 14. For an earlier working-paper version of the discussion in section 2.2 by de Zwart, see Francesco de Zwart (90% author) and George Gilligan, 'Comparative Corporate Governance Schemes and their Relevance for the Sporting Sector', Monash University Department of Business Law and Taxation, Working Paper No 16 (November 2008), accessed 5 February 2015 at http://papers.ssrn.com/sol3/papers.cfm?abstract_id=1295682, 8–9.

[11] Claessens, ibid. More recently, in 2012, Claessens and Yurtoglu confirm this analysis and conclusion but with some caveats. See Stijn Claessens and Burcin Yurtoglu, 'Corporate Governance in Emerging Markets: A Survey' (15 January 2012), accessed 5 February 2015 at SSRN: http://ssrn.com/abstract=1988880.

[12] Organisation for Economic Co Operation and Development, *OECD Principles of Corporate Governance 2004*, 2004, OECD Publications Service, Paris ('*OECD Principles*'), Preamble, p 11, accessed 5 February 2015 at http://www.oecd.org/corporate/ca/corporategovernanceprinciples/31557724.pdf.

[13] Ibid, p 13.

competitiveness for national economies and organisations and market 'stability' and 'credibility' as related to good governance.[14]

2.3 THE COMPONENTS OF THE RELATIONAL APPROACH

As depicted above, the theoretical weighing mechanism of the relational approach and its results are comprised of four components – the three relational axes of good governance, the eight governance factors, the two interrelationship schemes and the relational effect path for each governance variable.

The three relational axes of good governance are like a set of scales for weighing the objectives (Axis No 1), behaviours (Axis No 2) and positional conflict (Axis No 3) of the insiders and outsiders.[15]

The eight governance factors are the 'backbone' of the relational approach and so are critical to the theoretical components and the operational tables.[16] The governance factors represent the most significant recurring themes or aims underpinning the four Key Fields and thus the 39 governance variables to which the Fields give rise.

The hypothesised or predicted interrelationships between the eight governance factors are set out in the interrelationship schemes. The number of, and manner and direction in which, these factors are affected or influenced by the governance variables are depicted in relational effect paths. These paths determine the relative importance – known as the 'relational proximity rating' – of those variables in affecting the shareholder wealth measures. This chapter now turns to examine in detail the theoretical components.

---

14 Commonwealth Association for Corporate Governance, *Principles for Corporate Governance in the Commonwealth, Towards Global Competitiveness and Economic Accountability*, Final Version, November 1999 ('CACG Guidelines'), p 3, accessed 5 February 2015 at http://www.ecseonline.com/PDF/CACG%20Guidelines%20-%20Principles%20for%20Corporate%20Governance%20in%20the%20Commonwealth.pdf.

15 See Figures 2.2 and 2.3.

16 See the Coverage Table in section 3.3.1 and the Relational Proximity Table in section 3.3.2.1 below.

2.3.1 The Three Relational Axes of Good Governance

Drawing on the definitions of corporate governance from the Cadbury Report and OECD described in Chapter 1,[17] the definition of relational corporate governance seeks to balance the competing aims, behaviours and interests of insiders such as the directors, CEO and management with traditional outsiders such as shareholders and other wider stakeholders:

1. **Objectives Axis**
   On one axis, the freedom of a company's management to pursue (profit-maximising) objectives (value enhancement) at one end is balanced against the interests of the shareholders (owners) in monitoring management's performance (performance assessment and reporting) and seeing that a company's resources are not dissipated (value preservation).
2. **Behaviours Axis**
   On another axis, 'entrepreneurism' and 'innovation' (risk-taking) are balanced against risk management, 'control' and 'accountability' (responsibility).
3. **Positional Conflict Axis**
   Lastly, the interests of those 'within' the company such as the board, CEO and executives/management (internal stakeholders) are balanced against the interests of those 'outside' the company such as shareholders/investors, employees, lenders, suppliers, government legislators and regulators and social interests including the environment and the general public (external stakeholders).

2.3.2 The Purpose and Interrelationship of the Three Relational Axes

The three relational axes of good governance, while represented separately in the above definition, are employed simultaneously in balancing or weighing the governance factors in the relational approach. The three relational axes are represented separately because each has a separate purpose. But while the three relational axes are employed simultaneously, they do not all operate in the same manner or – in terms of three-dimensional space – on the same plane.

---

[17] See discussion in section 1.2.1 above. For an earlier working paper version of the three relational axes of good governance devised by de Zwart, see de Zwart (90% author) and Gilligan, above n 10, 7–8.

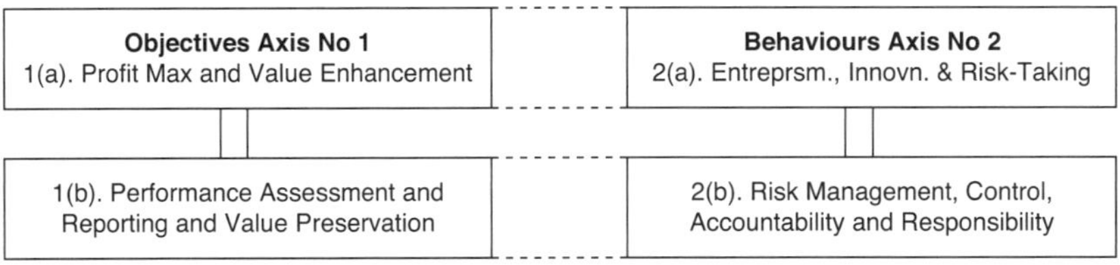

Figure 2.2 The functional purpose – Objectives Axis No 1 and Behaviours Axis No 2

Objectives Axis No 1 and Behaviours Axis No 2

Diagrammatically, as shown in Figure 2.2, Relational Axes Nos 1 and 2 *do* operate on the same plane of three-dimensional space. While there is clearly some overlap between these Axes, they are not identical. On the one hand, Objectives Axis No 1 is cast in terms of functional objectives – for example, profit maximisation, value enhancement and value preservation. On the other hand, Behaviours Axis No 2 denotes functional behaviours such as innovation, risk-taking, risk management and control.

Axes 1(a) and 2(a) represent the aim/objective and behavioural drivers of firm profitability and value and, therefore, long-term efficiency and sustainability. By contrast – and this is not meant in a negative sense – Axes 1(b) and 2(b) represent the checks and balances which are equally necessary to attain or enhance these efficiency and sustainability outcomes.

Positional Conflict Axis No 3

The third Axis is quite different. It is known as the 'Positional Conflict Axis No 3'. It is not concerned with functions or activities. Instead, it represents the positional conflict between different stakeholders – insiders and outsiders – and, in addition, between the insiders and outsiders *inter se*. Thus, again represented three-dimensionally, this Axis 'hovers' above Axes Nos 1 and 2 for the purpose of demarcating or delineating the parties or interests to be protected by those Axes. This is depicted in Figure 2.3.

2.3.3 The Weighing Process of the Three Relational Axes

The three relational axes are *not* the product of the weighing process of the relational approach. Instead, they are a conceptual means of describing the three-dimensional scales where the weighing process in relation to the eight governance factors must take place.

The weighing process of the three relational axes is akin to the weighing

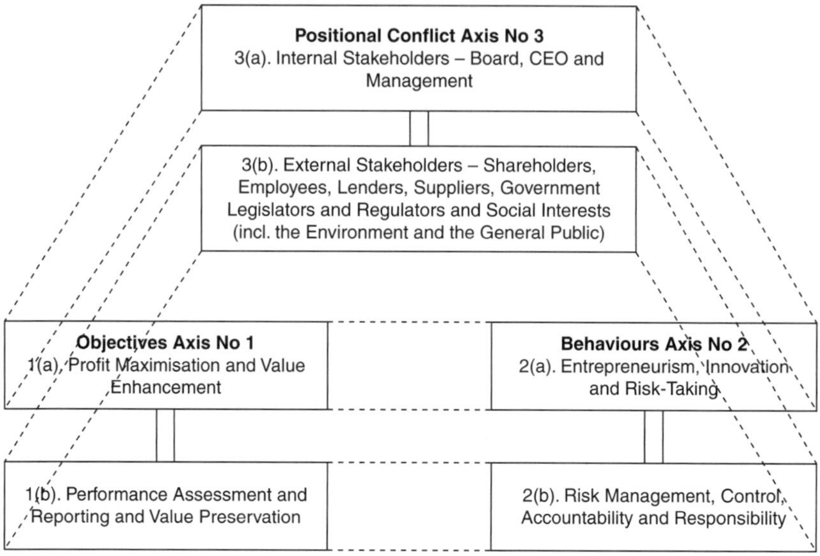

Figure 2.3 The positional purpose – Positional Conflict Axis No 3

of factors that takes place in the breach of duty stage of negligence law. As is well-known, the standard of care under negligence law principles (under the common law and statutes such as the *Corporations Act* 2001) requires a director to exercise reasonable care to avoid foreseeable harm in the management of all aspects of the corporation. In negligence law, the precautions a 'reasonable' director must take to protect the company from foreseeable harm are determined by the 'calculus of negligence'. This is a combination of considerations/factors including the probability of the harm occurring, its likely seriousness or gravity, the burden of taking precautions and any competing social justifications for the impugned conduct.[18] These factors – both legally and in an economic sense – determine the relative importance of the various areas of external foreseeable harm facing the corporation.

The relational approach is akin to treating management misconduct as merely a type of foreseeable harm – in this case internal – facing the company. But instead of weighing three factors, the relational approach

[18] *Wyong Shire Council v Shirt* [1980] HCA 12 (1 May 1980); (1980) 146 CLR 40; [1980] HCA 12, para [14]; (1980) 146 CLR 40, 48, per Mason J (as he then was), accessed 5 February 2015 at http://www.austlii.edu.au/au/cases/cth/HCA/1980/12.html.

weighs eight governance factors to determine the relative importance of governance variables in counteracting agency costs and enhancing the long-term sustainability of the firm.

In relation to the type of internal harm that the relational approach adopts as foreseeable, Jensen and Meckling's seminal agency theory principle introduced in Chapter 1 is again adopted. The most influential theory in modern corporations law, it posits that rational managers will seek to maximise their own interests at the expense of shareholders by engaging in value-reducing behaviours such as 'shirking', 'empire building', over-compensation and (over) perquisites.[19]

The relational approach is that the precautions to avoid or reduce agency costs are the governance variables themselves. These are the structures, mechanisms, processes and protocols that deter and punish director, CEO and management misconduct or which align the interests of those insiders with the interests of outside shareholders. It is to the governance variables that the relational approach now turns.

2.4 INTRODUCTION TO THE GOVERNANCE VARIABLES

The 39 governance variables are the governance and management structures which seek to punish or deter director, CEO and management misconduct or which align the interests of those insiders with the interests of outside shareholders. They are critical to the relational approach because the approach is constructed on the basis that the governance variables affect one another – the operation of each governance variable is affected by the 'zone of effect' of each other governance variable. This zone of effect is represented by the relational effect path of that governance variable. The strength or otherwise of a governance variable's zone of effect is thus measured by its relational proximity rating – its relative importance compared to other governance variables.

Section references for the analysis of empirical studies and the relational effect path for each governance variable are set out in the right-hand column of the following Table 2.1. Relational effect path references are in **bold** type. The 39 governance variables are defined in Table A.1 of Appendix 1, *Glossary of Governance Variables* and named and abbreviated in Table 2.1.

---

19 See discussion in section 1.2.2 above.

Table 2.1 Summary of governance variables

No	Governance Variable	Abbreviation (Alphabetical)	Section Ref.
1.	Audit Committee – Accounting Expertise – Earnings Manipulation Reduction Effect	**AudAccEarn**	9.2.1.1.1 **9.2.1.1.2**
2.	Audit Committee – Presence, Operation and Frequency	**AudCom**	5.2.2.2 **8.4.2** 8.4.3.1
3.	Audit Committee – Financial Expertise (Accounting)	**AudExpAcc**	**8.4.4**
4.	Audit Committee – Non-Accounting Expertise – 'Free Rider' Effect	**AudFree**	**9.2.1.1.2**
5.	Audit Committee – Independence in Combination with Frequency of Meeting – Reduction in Earnings Manipulation Effect	**AudIndFreq**	6.2.3.1.2 **9.2.1**
6.	Audit Committee – Independence – Information Flow and Decision Quality 'Trade-off'	**AudIndInfo**	6.2.3.1.2 **8.4.3**
7.	Audit Committee – Independence – Monitoring Effect	**AudIndMon**	5.2.2.2 6.2.3.1.2 6.2.3.1.4 **8.4.3**
8.	Audit Committee – Short Term Options Granted to Outside Directors – Reduction in Monitoring Effect	**AudShortOpts**	5.2.2.1 5.2.3.2.1 6.2.3.1.4 **10.2.5.1**
9.	Block Shareholding – Other Shareholder Agency Costs	**BlockCosts**	**8.5.1–8.5.2**
10.	Block Shareholding – Monitoring Effect	**BlockMon**	**8.5.1–8.5.2**
11.	Board – Attendance Level (High)	**BrdAttend**	7.3.1.2 **7.3.2.1.2**
12.	Board and Committee (Non-Audit) Size – Earnings Manipulation Effect	**BrdCmEarn**	5.2.3 **9.2.2**
13.	Board and Committee Size	**BrdCmSize**	**8.2.2.2**
14.	Board Independent Director: Executive Director Proportion – Information Flow and Decision Quality 'Trade-off'	**BrdIndInfo**	6.2.3.1.2 **7.3.2.1.3**

No	Governance Variable	Abbreviation (Alphabetical)	Section Ref.
15.	Board Independent Director: Executive Director Proportion – Monitoring Effect	**BrdIndMon**	5.2.2.1 6.2.3.1.2 6.2.3.1.4 **7.3.2.1.1–7.3.2.1.2**
16.	Board – Annual Review	**BrdReview**	**7.3.2.1.2**
17.	Board – Director Skills 'Mix'	**BrdSkills**	**7.3.1.2.1**
18.	Compensation Committee – Presence, Operation and Frequency	**CompCom**	5.2.2.2 **10.2.4.1**
19.	Director/CEO Compensation Levels	**DirCEO$**	5.2.2.1.1 5.2.3.2 6.2.3.1.4 **10.2.4**
20.	Duality of CEO/Chair Positions – CEO Dismissal Probability	**DualDismiss**	**8.6.3**
21.	Duality of CEO/Chair Positions – Probability of Earnings Manipulation	**DualEarn**	**9.2.1.1.3**
22.	Duality of CEO/Chair Positions – Effect on Strategic Decision-making	**DualStrat**	**8.6.3**
23.	Duality of CEO/Chair Positions – Monitoring and Decision-Quality 'Trade-off'	**DualTrade**	**8.6.1–8.6.2**
24.	Equity/Option Plans and Holdings of Directors/Executives – Incentive/'Alignment' Effect (excludes short-term options)	**EqOptIncent**	5.2.2.1 5.2.3.2.1 6.2.3.1.4 **10.2.4**
25.	Equity/Option Plans and Holdings of Directors/Executives – 'Entrenchment' Effect (excludes short-term options)	**EqOptEntrch**	5.2.2.1 5.2.3.2.1 6.2.3.1.4 **10.2.4**
26.	External/Independent Audit Function	**ExtAudEarn**	5.2.4 **9.2.3.3**
27.	National Governance/ Shareholder Protection Regime	**NationGov**	5.2.1.1 6.3.1 7.3.1.3 **7.3.1.3.2**
28.	Nominating Committee – Presence, Operation and Frequency	**NomCom**	5.2.2.2 **7.3.1.2.2**
29.	Nominating Committee – Independence Proportion	**NomInd**	5.2.2.2 6.2.3.1.2 **7.3.1.2.2**

Table 2.1 (continued)

No	Governance Variable	Abbreviation (Alphabetical)	Section Ref.
30.	Non-Audit Services of External Auditor	**NonAuditS**	5.2.4.2 **9.2.3.2–9.2.3.3**
31.	Other Anti-Takeover Mechanisms (excludes staggered board elections)	**OtherATMs**	5.2.1.1 8.3.1 **8.3.1.1**
32.	Outside Board Positions of Independent Directors	**OutBrdPos**	6.2.3.1.2 **8.2.3.1**
33.	Outside/External Board Advisers	**OutBrdAdv**	**7.3.2.1.2**
34.	Reputational Constraints – 'Disclosure Standards'	**ReputDiscl**	5.2.5.1 6.2.3.1.4 **10.4.1**
35.	Reputational Constraints – 'Transparent Reporting'	**ReputRep**	5.2.5.1 6.2.3.1.4 **10.4.1**
36.	Staggered Board Elections	**StagBrdElect**	8.3.1 **8.3.1.1**
37.	Short-Term Option Holdings/ Plans of Directors and Executives	**ShortTOpts**	5.2.2.1 5.2.3.2.1 6.2.3.1.4 **10.2.5.1**
38.	Transparency and Timing of Reporting – Monitoring Effect	**TransTimeMon**	5.2.1.1 5.2.3 5.2.5.1 6.2.3.1.3 **9.1.2.1**
39.	Transparency and Timing of Reporting – Information Flow Reduction Effect	**TransTimeRedn**	5.2.3 5.2.5.1 6.2.3.1.3 **9.1.2.1**

2.5 PRINCIPAL CONSIDERATIONS IN THE SELECTION OF THE GOVERNANCE FACTORS

2.5.1 The Governance Factors are Drawn from the Key Fields

The governance factors represent the eight principal themes or factors that underpin the four Key Fields and thus the 39 individual governance variables to which these Fields give rise. In other words, the eight governance factors represent the considerations which are drawn from – and link – each of these four Key Fields.

In turn, the interrelationships between the governance factors are brought together and summarised in the interrelationship schemes depicted in Figures 2.6 and 2.7. These schemes are then used to construct for each governance variable an individual relational effect path showing the identity, number and direction of governance factors affected by each governance variable. In this chapter, the relational approach justifies the principal considerations that have been adopted in the identification, structure and articulation of the governance factors.

2.5.2 What is a Governance Factor?

As noted above, a governance factor is an underlying and recurring theme derived from within the four Key Fields. In other words, it is, *in itself*, an object, purpose or end of 'good governance'. It may also be considered to be an intermediate step or combination of steps to achieve such an object, purpose or end or to avoid harming good governance outcomes. For example, improving the quality of board, CEO and management decision-making (Decision-making Factor No 7) is clearly an object, purpose or end of good governance. That end is also assisted by improving the transparency, timing and integrity of financial and other reports (Reporting Factor No 1) and the delineation and disclosure of powers, duties and lines of responsibility (Responsibility Factor No 8). Similarly, alignment of management and shareholder interests (Alignment Factor No 3) is another end of good governance. It can be achieved, in one way, by the design of board, CEO and management compensation and incentives (Compensation Factor No 4).

But in the determination of what precisely constitutes a governance factor, it is important to articulate just what is an 'underlying theme' of the Key Fields.

2.5.3 Governance Factors Must Be Distinguished From Governance Variables

In selecting the governance factors, it is important not to mistake for a governance factor what is really a governance variable. For example, some would submit that the independence of directors from management is a 'theme' of contemporary corporate governance. It certainly is a focus. This is reflected in Chapter 6's demonstration that 'independence from management' including 'non-executive/independent directors' is a 'core' feature of global/cross-border and national (US, UK and Australian) corporate governance codes.[20] But such independence is not, *in itself*, an object, purpose or end of 'good governance'.

Instead, director independence (or the proportion of independent directors) serves as an argued *means* to affect, attain or enhance some (or all) of the themes constituting the governance factors themselves. Examples include Alignment Factor No 3,[21] Monitoring & Audit Factor No 5[22] and Decision-making Factor No 7.[23]

2.6 THE GOVERNANCE FACTORS AND RECURRING THEMES AND TENSIONS FROM THE KEY FIELDS

The principal considerations in the selection of the eight governance factors are now presented in numerical order. The order is *not* a reflection of the relative importance of the factor. For some of the factors, a table is presented to describe the Key Field from which the theme is taken and the source of the theme within that Key Field. The aim of the tables is to demonstrate that the governance factors are recurring or universal themes throughout one or more of the Key Fields.

2.6.1 Reporting Factor No 1: Transparency, Timing and Integrity of Financial and Other Reports

Intuitively, Reporting Factor No 1 is, or should be, a critical component of virtually all corporate governance regimes as it provides or constitutes the means by which any meaningful assessment of (inside) managerial performance may be undertaken by (outside) shareholders or other stakeholders as demonstrated in Table 2.2.

Thus, the themes represented in Reporting Factor No 1 are properly to be considered recurring in all four of the Key Fields and so significant in the relational approach.

This significance is also reflected in the three relational axes of good governance. There, Objectives Axis 1(b) (Performance Assessment and Reporting and Value Preservation) and Behaviours Axis 2(b) (Risk

---

20 See discussion in section 6.8.1 below.

21 Alignment of Management and Shareholder Interests. See discussion in section 2.6.3 below.

22 Internal and External/Audit Monitoring Quality. See section 2.6.5 below.

23 Quality of Board, CEO and Management Decision-making. See discussion in section 2.6.7 below.

Table 2.2 Reporting factor No 1

No	Source of Theme, Consideration or Factor	Description	Section
Key Field No 1 – Application of the Principal Theories of the Firm to the Relational Approach			
1.	The market for corporate control operates as part of the efficient market hypothesis to remove management which engages in value or performance-reducing behaviour.[1]	• The efficient market hypothesis itself assumes that share prices reflect all publicly available information.[2]	4.2.2
		• Problems of imperfect knowledge (or information asymmetry),[3] bounded rationality of investors[4] and the timing (lag) of market adjustments[5] can disrupt this management-disciplining mechanism.	4.2.2
Key Field No 2 – Autopsies of the Enron and Hastie Corporate Collapses			
1.	• Enron Off-balance sheet 'Special Purpose Entities' or 'SPEs'	• failure of both timely and adequate information to the market.	5.2.1.1 5.2.3.1
	• Concealment of Enron debt and 'self-hedging' arrangements	• undermining of the market for corporate control and efficient market hypothesis.	5.2.1.1 5.2.3.1
	• Recognition of income in trading between Enron-owned entities[6]		5.2.1.1
	• Other Enron earnings management arrangements[7]		5.2.3
	• By contrast, Hastie group danger signs were prominent including standstill arrangements with bankers, equity raising of $A158 million, large write-downs to goodwill, trade and other receivables and charges against EBIT of $A 55 million increased to $A 88 million and shares suspended on two occasions[8]		5.2.1.1

Table 2.2 (continued)

No	Source of Theme, Consideration or Factor	Description	Section
	• But the Hastie Board was criticised by the Administrators over its financial reporting suggesting Hastie's books and records were deficient and did not accurately explain the Group's financial position and performance and may have been materially misstated.[9]		5.2.5.1
Key Field No 3 – Comparative Corporate Governance Codes			
1.	International/cross-border and national (US, UK and Australian) corporate governance codes examined in Chapter 6	• Core feature of 'timely/ regular disclosure of material information'.	6.8.1
2.	OECD Principles[10]	• Entire Principle V devoted to Reporting Factor No 1.[11]	6.2.2
		• Principle V.C. includes reference to the Monitoring & Audit Factor No 5's independent audit.[12]	6.2.2
3.	ASX 2014 Principles and Recommendations:[13] • Principle 4 • Principle 5	• Requirement to 'Safeguard integrity in corporate reporting'[14]	6.6.1
		• Requirement to '[m]ake timely and balanced disclosure' of 'all material matters concerning . . . a material effect on the price or value of [the entity's] securities'.[15]	6.6.1
		• Disclosure requirements not limited to financial reporting but extend to 'financial position, performance, ownership and governance'[16] which 'allows investors to assess the impact of the information'.[17]	6.6.1

No	Source of Theme, Consideration or Factor	Description	Section
		• This is the basis of the ASX (and other relevant jurisdiction) Listing Rule continuous disclosure obligations[18]	6.6.1
4.	SOX[19] Reform Provisions	1. 'Responsibility for Accuracy of Financial Reports' – sections 302 and 304. 2. 'Transparency and Timing' – sections 401, 402, 403, 408 and 409. 3. Provisions designed to reduce the incidence of earnings manipulation – sections 404 and 406[20] and sections 201–204 and 206[21]	
Key Field No 4 - Empirical Studies of the Effectiveness of Governance Variables			
1.	Empirical Studies:	• Transparency and timeliness of reporting principally remedies the 'information asymmetry' problem arising in agency theory which creates 'agency risk' for shareholders.	9.1.1
	• Ashbaugh-Skaife, Collins and LaFond[22] and Patel and Dallas[23]	• agency risk and the cost of equity capital reduces with increased transparency and timeliness of financial reporting[25] and	9.1.1
	• Hermalin and Weisbach[24]	• corporate governance effects of increasing transparency is a higher quality of board monitoring (which must be balanced against the costs of exposing management to greater scrutiny)	9.1.2

Notes:

1. See discussion in section 1.2.2 above.
2. Lawrence A Cunningham, 'Behavioral Finance and Investor Governance' (2002) 59 *Washington & Lee Law Review* 767, accessed 5 February 2015 at SSRN: http://ssrn.com/abstract=255778, 3. The author cites Donald C Langevoort, 'Theories, Assumptions and Securities Regulation: Market Efficiency Revisited' (1992) 140 *U Pa L Rev* 85. See also, Eugene F Fama, Michael C Jensen, Lawrence Fisher and Richard

Table 2.2 (continued)

Roll, 'The Adjustment of Stock Prices to New Information' (1969) 10 *International Economic Review* 1–22, accessed 24 April 2015 at SSRN: http://ssrn.com/abstract=321524.

3. George W Dent, Jr, 'Academics in Wonderland: The Team Production and Director Primacy Models of Corporate Governance', June 2007, Case Legal Studies Research Paper No 07-21, accessed 5 February 2015 at SSRN: http://ssrn.com/abstract=995186, 18–19 of 72.
4. Ibid.
5. Ibid, 19 of 72.
6. See discussion in section 5.2.1.1 below.
7. See discussion in section 5.2.3 below.
8. See PPB Advisory, *Hastie Group Limited and Specific Subsidiaries, Report by Joint and Several Administrators Pursuant to Section 439A of the Corporations Act 2001*, 21 January 2013, accessed 5 February 2015 at http://www.ppbadvisory.com/creditor-information/v/281/hastie-group/2nd-creditor-meeting ('Administrators' Report') (accessed 22 February 2013), section 2.5.2, p 13 of 99 and Timeline of Key Events, p 17 of 99. See discussion in section 5.2.1.1 below.
9. Administrators' Report, ibid, section 7.9.5, p 65 of 99, section 7.10, p 66 of 99 and section 7.13.2, p 71 of 99.
10. Organisation for Economic Co-Operation and Development, *OECD Principles of Corporate Governance 2004*, 2004, OECD Publications Service, Paris ('*OECD Principles*'), Preamble, p 11, accessed 5 February 2015 at http://www.oecd.org/corporate/ca/corporategovernanceprinciples/31557724.pdf02_Chapter2.docx.
11. Ibid, Principle V, p 22.
12. Ibid, Principle V.C., p 22.
13. ASX Corporate Governance Council, Corporate Governance Principles and Recommendations, Third Edition, which were released on 27 March 2014 and (at p 7) took effect for a company's financial year commencing on or after 1 July 2014 ('ASX 2014 Principles and Recommendations'). See also *Translation Table, Corporate Governance Council Recommendations (New to Old) and (Old to New)* ('CGC Recommendations Translation Tables'). These documents are available at http://www.asx.com.au/regulation/corporate-governance-council.htm (accessed 5 February 2015).
14. Ibid, Principle 4, p 21.
15. Ibid, Principle 5, p 24.
16. Ibid.
17. Ibid.
18. Australian Securities Exchange, ASX Listing Rules, General Rule 3.1, Continuous Disclosure, 14 April 2014, p 301 accessed 5 February 2015 at http://www.asx.com.au/regulation/rules/asx-listing-rules.htm.
19. PL 107-204, 2002 HR 3763, July 30, 2002, 116 Stat 745, available at http://www.sec.gov/about/soa2002.pdf ('SOX').
20. 'Internal Controls and Finance Code of Ethics'.
21. 'Auditors and Non-Audit Services'.
22. Hollis Ashbaugh-Skaife, Daniel W Collins and Ryan LaFond, 'Corporate Governance and the Cost of Equity Capital', December 2004, accessed 5 February 2015 at SSRN: http://ssrn.com/abstract=639681, 1.
23. Sandeep A Patel and George S Dallas, 'Transparency and Disclosure: Overview of Methodology and Study Results - United States', October 2002, accessed 5 February 2015 at SSRN: http://ssrn.com/abstract=422800, 4 of 29.
24. Benjamin E Hermalin and Michael S Weisbach, 'Transparency and Corporate Governance', January 2007, accessed 5 February 2015 at SSRN: http://ssrn.com/abstract=958628, 1 and 19.
25. Hollis Ashbaugh-Skaife, Daniel W Collins and Ryan LaFond, 'Corporate Governance and the Cost of Equity Capital', December 2004, accessed 5 February 2015 at SSRN: http://ssrn.com/abstract=639681, 2–3.

Management, Control, Accountability and Responsibility) represent the checks and balances contemplated in the weighing process of the governance factors. As the above discussion demonstrates, the considerations represented in Reporting Factor No 1 are thus a fundamental (theoretical) condition for the effective operation of those two Axes.

2.6.2 Compliance Factor No 2: Corporate Governance and Legal Compliance

Corporate governance and legal compliance are critical as an overriding requirement of *all* other governance factors. Thus all governance variables utilised by a company must be consistent with the rule of law. The overriding nature of the compliance factor is represented in Figure 2.4.

Table 2.3 demonstrates that Compliance Factor No 2 is a significant theme arising from the Key Fields.

Thus, the themes represented in Compliance Factor No 2 are properly to be considered recurring in all four of the Key Fields and so are classified as a governance factor.

2.6.3 Alignment Factor No 3: Alignment of Management and Shareholder Interests

Alignment Factor No 3 is a prominent theme in the entirety of the Key Field No 1 – the application of the principal theories of the firm to the relational approach. The alignment of management and shareholder interests is one of the principal aims underlying two of the four main theories and

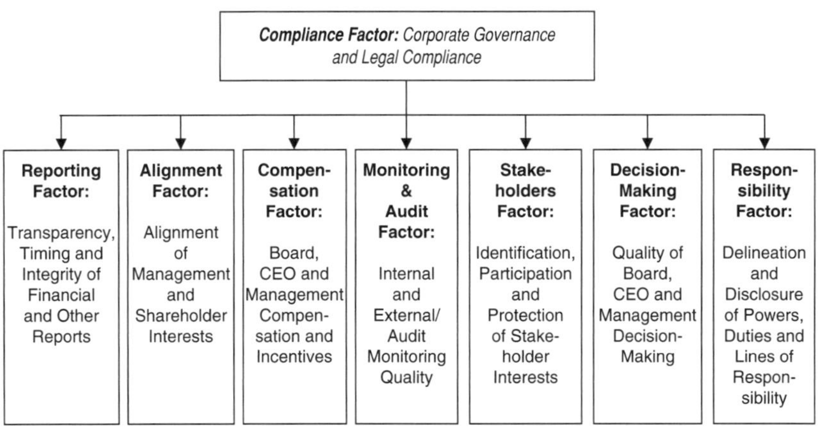

Figure 2.4 Compliance factor No 2: Interrelationships

Table 2.3 Compliance factor No 2

No	Source of Theme, Consideration or Factor	Description	Section
Key Field No 1: Application of Principal Theories of the Firm to the Relational Approach			
1.	• Tension between the shareholder primacy model and the associated shareholder wealth-maximisation principle vis-à-vis stakeholder model of corporate governance.	• Compliance Factor requires that shareholder primacy is currently the pre-eminent or overriding theory in Australia on account of the Australian High Court decision in *Walker v Wimborne* and section 181(1)(a) *Corporations Act 2001* (Cth).	1.2.3
Key Field No 2 –Autopsies of the Enron and Hastie Corporate Collapses			
1.	• US legally-mandated accounting standards and rules relating to Enron	• Significant failures in corporate governance and legal compliance	5.2.3
		• Argued that standards and rules were adequate but Enron's non-compliance was central to the relevant accounting fraud and earnings manipulation (Catanach and Rhoades).[1]	5.2.3
	• Australian Accounting Standards and Rules relating to the Hastie Group	• Hastie Board was criticised by the Administrators over its financial reporting suggesting Hastie's books and records were deficient and did not accurately explain the Group's financial position and performance and may have been materially misstated.[2]	5.2.5.1
Key Field No 3 – Comparative Corporate Governance Codes			
1.	• *Corporations Act* 2001 (Cth) and common law, equitable and statutory duty of directors.	• 'Imported' into relational approach by the Compliance Factor No 2	2.6.2
2.	• Comparative Corporate Governance Codes Key Field No 3 including the OECD Principles, NYSE Final Rules, the UK	• Core features are the principal board functions and responsibilities of *both* 'compliance with statutory and legal duties'	6.8.1

No	Source of Theme, Consideration or Factor	Description	Section
	Corporate Governance Code 2014[3] and ASX 2014 Principles and Recommendations.	and 'corporate governance compliance'.[4]	
Key Field No 4: Empirical Studies of the Effectiveness of Governance Variables			
1.	• Studies of the 'strength' of the national shareholder protection and governance regime	• Increases in the level of national shareholder protection and governance regime (to a certain point) improve firm performance • Common law regimes appear to provide the highest level of protection vis-à-vis civil code countries.	7.3.1.3 7.3.1.3.1

Notes:
1. See Anthony H Catanach and Shelley C Rhoades, 'Enron: A Financial Reporting Failure?' (2003) 48(4) *Villanova Law Review* 1057, accessed 5 February 2015 at http://ssrn.com/abstract=418920, 18. See discussion in section 5.2.3 below.
2. See PPB Advisory, *Hastie Group Limited and Specific Subsidiaries, Report by Joint and Several Administrators Pursuant to Section 439A of the Corporations Act 2001*, 21 January 2013, accessed 5 February 2015 at http://www.ppbadvisory.com/creditor-information/v/281/hastie-group/2nd-creditor-meeting ('Administrators' Report') (accessed 22 February 2013), section 7.9.5, p 65 of 99, section 7.10, p 66 of 99 and section 7.13.2, p 71 of 99.
3. Financial Reporting Council (FRC), *The UK Corporate Governance Code*, September 2014, London, available at http://www.frc.org.uk/ (accessed 5 February 2015) ('UK Corporate Governance Code 2014').
4. See discussion in section 6.8.1 below.

models of the firm and corporate governance examined in Chapter 4 – agency theory[24] and the shareholder primacy model.[25]

The seminal work of Fama and Jensen is the key consideration in the adoption of Alignment Factor No 3. The authors characterise the key feature of the dispersed shareholding public company to be a separation of ownership from management of the firm.[26] In this respect, for Jensen

[24] See discussion in sections 4.2.3 and 4.2.3.1–4.2.3.2 below.

[25] See discussion in sections 4.3.1–4.3.2.1 below.

[26] Eugene F Fama and Michael C Jensen, 'Separation of Ownership and Control', in Michael C Jensen, *Foundations of Organizational Strategy*,

and Meckling, agency costs include monitoring costs on behalf of the shareholder:[27]

> [i]f both parties to the relationship are utility maximizers, there is good reason to believe that the agent will not always act in the best interests of the principal. The *principal* can limit divergences from his interest by establishing appropriate incentives for the agent and by incurring monitoring costs designed to limit the aberrant activities of the agent.[28]

Thus, the alignment of management and shareholder interests – whether by way of incentive, monitoring or disciplinary devices – is a key feature of agency cost theory. If we assume that shareholders are the only 'residual claimants' of the corporation, then Alignment Factor No 3 is also a key feature of the shareholder primacy model of corporate governance.[29]

This can be demonstrated by a number of examples. First, the Shareholder Primacy Interrelationship Scheme depicted in Figure 2.6 below displays Alignment Factor No 3 as an 'umbrella' or 'guiding principle' over all other governance factors except Compliance Factor No 2.[30] This is depicted in Figure 2.5.

A real-world example of this relates to the ongoing debate relating to director, CEO and management compensation. Hill and Yablon explain that the 'alignment' principle encapsulated in Alignment Factor

---

Cambridge, MA: Harvard University Press, 1998, and (1983) 26 *Journal of Law and Economics* 301, accessed 5 February 2015 at SSRN: http://ssrn.com/abstract=94034.

[27] Michael C Jensen and William H Meckling, 'Theory of the Firm: Managerial Behavior, Agency Costs and Ownership Structure' in Michael C. Jensen, *A Theory of the Firm: Governance, Residual Claims and Organizational Forms*, Cambridge, MA: Harvard University Press, December 2000; (1976) 3(4) *Journal of Financial Economics* 305–60, accessed 5 February 2015 at SSRN: http://ssrn.com/abstract=94043, 5–6.

The description of the problems raised by the separation of ownership from control is, of course, much earlier including the work of Adolph A Berle and Gardiner C Means, *The Modern Corporation and Private Property*, The Macmillan Company, first published in 1932. See William W Bratton, 'Berle and Means Reconsidered at the Century's Turn' (2001) 26(3) *Journal of Corporation Law* 737–770, accessed 24 April 2015 at SSRN: http://ssrn.com/abstract=291081, especially pp. 753–759. See also Charles R T O'Kelley, 'Berle and the Entrepreneur' (2010) 33(4) *Seattle University Law Review* 1141, accessed 24 April 2015 at SSRN: http://ssrn.com/abstract=1579220.

[28] Ibid, 5 (emphasis in original).

[29] See discussion in section 4.3.2 below.

[30] See discussion in section 2.6.2 below.

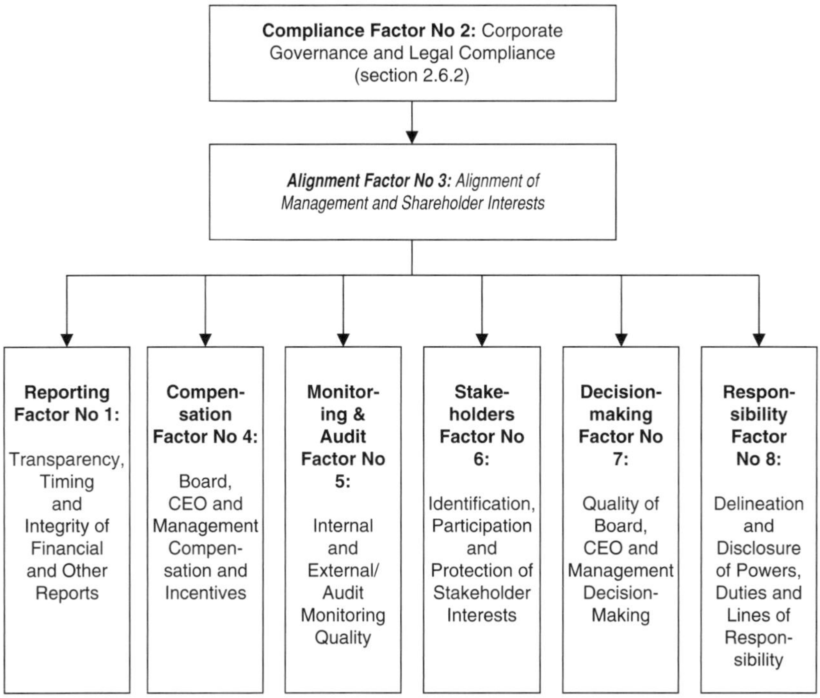

Figure 2.5 Shareholder primacy model 'umbrella'

No 3 serves as one of several theoretical approaches upon which such compensation and incentives *should* be designed.[31]

Yet the Enron corporate collapse demonstrates, as one aspect of that failure, the misalignment of management and shareholder interests in a number of areas. First, in the link between earnings manipulation and the short-term nature of CEO, executive and director compensation.[32] Contributing to this misalignment was the lack of both director[33] and auditor[34] independence with the consequent reduction in the quality of

[31] Jennifer J Hill and Charles M Yablon, 'Corporate Governance and Executive Remuneration: Rediscovering Managerial Positional Conflict', Vanderbilt Law and Economics Research Paper No 03-02 (2002) 25 *University of New South Wales Law Journal* 294, accessed 5 February 2015 at SSRN: http://ssrn.com/abstract=375240, 13. See discussion in section 10.1.2 below.

[32] See discussion in section 5.2.3.2 below.

[33] See discussion in sections 5.2.2.1–5.2.2.3 below.

[34] See discussion in section 5.2.4 below.

board monitoring on behalf of shareholders. One remedial response to the collapse was the SOX reforms. These reforms sought to enhance the alignment of directors and management with outside shareholders in provisions relating to both directors and management[35] and earnings manipulation.[36]

2.6.4 Compensation Factor No 4: Board, CEO and Management Compensation and Incentives

As explained by Jensen and Meckling in the preceding section, managerial compensation and incentive devices play a critical role in the firm theories contained in Key Field No 1 as one of the principal mechanisms to reduce agency costs.[37]

A prominent example of the significance of Compensation Factor No 4 comes from the Enron and Hastie Collapses Key Field No 2. That collapse demonstrates the argued link between earnings manipulation and the short-term nature of CEO, executive and director compensation.[38] Gillan and Martin explain that, at Enron, there were substantial shareholdings amongst directors as well as option holdings by all but one outside director.[39] In addition, financial arrangements with directors – consulting fees, related entity transactions and donations – resulted in a 'true' independence proportion closer to 43 per cent.[40] For Gillan and Martin, these arrangements and the share and option holdings of directors 'may have attenuated any inclination to aggressively monitor management's practices'.[41]

The Comparative Corporate Governance Codes Key Field No 3 also demonstrates the importance of Compensation Factor No 4. Many of the governance codes in this Field were developed in response to the Enron and other collapses.[42] Not surprisingly, Chapter 6 of this book identifies 'employee/management/director incentive and participation schemes' as a core feature of global/cross-border and national (US, UK and Australian)

---

35 See Table 6.4 US National Corporate Governance Codes below.

36 Ibid.

37 Jensen and Meckling, above n 27, 5.

38 See discussion in section 5.2.3.2 below.

39 Stuart L Gillan and John D Martin, 'Financial Engineering, Corporate Governance, and the Collapse of Enron', U of Delaware Coll. of Bus. and Econ. Ctr. for Corp. Governance Working Paper No 2002-001 (November 2002), accessed 5 February 2015 at SSRN: http://ssrn.com/abstract=354040, 22.

40 Ibid, 23–24.

41 Ibid, 24.

42 See discussion in section 6.1.3.2 below.

corporate governance codes.[43] In addition, the 'timely disclosure of material information *including remuneration policies*' is also identified as a core governance code feature in that chapter.[44]

Finally, compensation and incentives of board members, CEOs and management figure prominently in Part 4 of the Empirical Studies Key Field No 4. These empirical studies are analysed in the entirety of Chapter 10.

2.6.5 Monitoring & Audit Factor No 5: Internal and External/Audit Monitoring Quality

Internal and external audit monitoring quality is a wide concept in the relational approach. As its terms indicate, it includes, on the one hand, notions of internal audit and, on the other hand, third-party 'independent' audit. But Monitoring & Audit Factor No 5 is not limited to internal and external audit. Its terms deliberately extend to consider matters including financial and other internal controls, risk assessment, reporting and management procedures, governance and ethical codes of conduct or guidelines (as control devices). Critically, Monitoring & Audit Factor No 5 extends to the nature, operation and quality (strength) of the board and management's inquiry, supervisory and monitoring duties. And this in turn extends to all aspects of the firm's financial, operational and governance activities and obligations.

Monitoring & Audit Factor No 5 is a significant theme emerging from all four Key Fields as set out in Table 2.4.

The interrelationship between Monitoring & Audit Factor No 5 and Reporting Factor No 1

Significantly, the interrelationship between Monitoring & Audit Factor No 5 and Reporting Factor No 1 is **reflexive**. In other words, these two Factors inform or affect each other in a continuous cycle. Thus, in practical terms of the weighing process of the relational approach, governance variables which affect one of these factors will be very likely to affect the other.

2.6.6 Stakeholders Factor No 6: Identification, Participation and Protection of Stakeholder Interests

The themes encapsulated in Stakeholders Factor No 6 are the 'other side of the coin' to those of Alignment Factor No 3 – Alignment of

---

43 See discussion in section 6.8.1 below.

44 Ibid.

Table 2.4 Monitoring & audit factor No 5

No	Source of Theme, Consideration or Factor	Description	Section
Key Field No 1: Application of Principal Theories of the Firm to the Relational Approach			
1.	• Agency theory	• Agency costs of the principal-agent relationship include **monitoring costs** on behalf of the shareholder (Jensen and Meckling[1]) which are 'designed to limit the aberrant activities of the agent' (Jensen and Meckling[2])	4.2.3–4.2.3.2
		• Effective decision-making structure which reduces agency costs divides decision 'initiation' and 'implementation' ('decision management') from 'ratification' and '**monitoring**' ('decision control')[3] the latter function being undertaken of behalf of the shareholders by a board of directors (Fama and Jensen[4])	4.2.3.2
Key Field No 2 –Autopsies of the Enron and Hastie Corporate Collapses			
1.	• Audit failure by the auditing firm of Arthur Andersen.	• Coffee considers the Enron collapse to be, primarily, a failure of the relevant auditors.[5] • End of one of the world's largest and most reputable accounting firms, Arthur Andersen (Barrett)[6]	5.2.4.1–5.2.4.2
2.	• Non-audit services of the audit firm	• Chapter 5 examines the effect of non-audit services on the quality of monitoring	5.2.4.2

No	Source of Theme, Consideration or Factor	Description	Section
Key Field No 3 – Comparative Corporate Governance Codes			
1.	• International/ cross-border and national (US, UK and Australian) governance codes	• External and independent audit is a core feature of practically every modern international/cross-border and national (US, UK and Australian) corporate governance code[7]	6.8.1
		• US' SOX[8] reforms and, flowing from this, the NYSE Final Rules[9] both devote considerable attention to the external audit.[10]	Table 6.4 US National Corporate Governance Codes
Key Field No 4: Empirical Studies of the Effectiveness of Governance Variables			
1.	• Independent audit function	• Independence or freedom from influence of the third-party auditor is a continuing theme in governance study and discourse.[11]	9.2.3.1–9.2.3.3
2.	• Independence of directors or the proportion of independent directors	• Studies examine whether increased independence enhances **monitoring** quality and, in turn, firm profitability and firm value	7.3.2.1–7.3.2.1.7
3.	• Proportion of insider/ management equity ownership	• Empirical studies examine whether these variables enhance **monitoring** quality and decision-making and, in turn, firm profitability and firm value	7.3.2.1.5
	• Board skills 'mix'		7.3.1.2–7.3.1.2.1
	• Board size		8.2.1–8.2.2
	• Outside board positions of independent directors		8.2.3
	• Anti-takeover mechanisms		8.3
	• The market for corporate control		8.3.1
	• Presence, independence (proportion),		9.2.1–9.2.2

Table 2.4 (continued)

No	Source of Theme, Consideration or Factor	Description	Section
Key Field No 4: Empirical Studies of the Effectiveness of Governance Variables			
	time and financial expertise of the audit sub-committee		
	• Division in the CEO/ Chairperson roles		8.6
4.	• Non-Audit services of the audit firm	• Chapter 9 examines the effect of non-audit services on earnings 'management' or 'manipulation'.	9.2.3.1–9.2.3.3

Notes:

1. Michael C Jensen and William H Meckling, 'Theory of the Firm: Managerial Behavior, Agency Costs and Ownership Structure' in Michael C. Jensen, *A Theory of the Firm: Governance, Residual Claims and Organizational Forms*, Cambridge, MA: Harvard University Press, December 2000; (1976) 3(4) *Journal of Financial Economics* 305–60, accessed 5 February 2015 at SSRN: http://ssrn.com/abstract=94043, 5–6.
2. Ibid, 5.
3. Eugene F Fama and Michael C Jensen, 'Separation of Ownership and Control', in Michael C Jensen, *Foundations of Organizational Strategy*, Cambridge, MA: Harvard University Press, 1998, and (1983) 26 *Journal of Law and Economics* 301, accessed 5 February 2015 at SSRN: http://ssrn.com/abstract=94034, 4–5 and 9.
4. Ibid, 14 and 16.
5. John C Coffee, Jr, 'Understanding Enron: It's About the Gatekeepers, Stupid', Columbia Law & Economics Working Paper No 207, July 2002, accessed 5 February 2015 at SSRN: http://ssrn.com/abstract=325240, 5.
6. See the examination of Andersen's role in Matthew J Barrett, 'Enron and Andersen – What Went Wrong and Why Similar Audit Failures Could Happen Again', in Nancy B. Rapoport and Bala G. Dharan (eds), *Enron: Corporate Fiascos and their Implications*, St Paul, MN: Foundation Press, 2004, pp 155–68, accessed 5 February 2015 at SSRN: http://ssrn.com/abstract=794831.
7. See discussion in section 6.8.1 below.
8. PL 107-204, 2002 HR 3763, July 30, 2002, 116 Stat 745, available at http://www.sec.gov/about/laws/soa2002.pdf ('SOX').
9. New York Stock Exchange, *Final NYSE Corporate Governance Rules* ('NYSE Final Rules'), approved by SEC 4 November 2003 (except s 303A.08) and 30 June 2003 (s 303A.08). The Rules (as amended from time to time) comprise section 303A.00 of the NYSE Listed Company Manual. See section 303A.00 Corporate Governance Standards (approved 25 November 2009), available at http://nysemanual.nyse.com/lcm/ (accessed 5 February 2015). Subsequent amendments have been made to:

    - Section 303A.00 – Corporate Governance Standards (approved 22 August 2013)
    - Section 303A.02 – Corporate Governance Standards (approved 11 January 2013)
    - Section 303A.05 – Corporate Governance Standards (approved 11 January 2013)
    - Section 303A.07 – Audit Committee Additional Requirements (approved 22 August 2013)

    These Rule amendments are also available at http://nysemanual.nyse.com/lcm/.

Table 2.4 (continued)

10. See SOX, above n 8 of this Table 2.4, Title II – Auditor Independence, sections 201–209 and NYSE Final Rules, ibid, sections 303A.06 (Audit Committee) and 303A.07 (Audit Committee Additional Requirements).
11. See, for example, Coffee, above n 5 of this Table 2.4 and Lawrence A Cunningham, 'Beyond Liability: Rewarding Effective Gatekeepers' (2007) 92 *Minnesota Law Review* 323, accessed 5 February 2015 at SSRN: http://ssrn.com/abstract=1022360.

Management and Shareholder Interests. Stakeholders Factor No 6 is among the most rapidly expanding areas of new-millennium and current governance discourse.[45]

Table 2.5 sets out the principal considerations and real world examples which illustrate the significance of Stakeholders Factor No 6. These considerations are drawn principally from Key Field No 1 (Application of Principal Theories of the Firm to the Relational Approach) and Key Field No 3 (Comparative Corporate Governance Codes).

Thus, the Stakeholders Factor No 6 is significant in terms of the theoretical underpinnings of the relational approach. This finds traction in the three relational axes of good governance, in particular, Positional Conflict Axis No 3.[46] The underlying tension in the Positional Conflict Axes 3(a) and 3(b) is a weighing of the interests of internal and external stakeholders.

2.6.7 Decision-making Factor No 7: Quality of Board, CEO and Management Decision-making

Decision-making Factor No 7 is a fundamental theme both underpinning and arising from Key Fields Nos 1–4 and, indeed, the nature of the for-profit corporation.[47] This is depicted in Table 2.6.

As a real world example, Table 2.6 also demonstrates the extensive variety of factors which commentators in the 'autopsies' of the Enron and Hastie corporate collapses (*Key Field No 2*) have examined in relation to

[45] See discussion in sections 4.4–4.4.2.3 below.
[46] See discussion in sections 2.3.1–2.3.3 above.
[47] For a detailed discussion, see the papers relating to the nexus of contracts theory and the anti-contractarian views of the firm from the symposium on contractual freedom in corporate law held on 9 and 10 December 1988 at Columbia Law School published at (1989) 89 *Colum L Rev* 1395.

Table 2.5 Stakeholders factor No 6

No	Source of Theme, Consideration or Factor	Description	Section
Key Field No 1 – Application of Principal Theories of the Firm to the Relational Approach			
1.	• Tensions between the principal and rival models – the shareholder primacy model vis-à-vis the stakeholder model.[1] • Stakeholder model requires 'that managers should make decisions that take account of the interests of *all* the stakeholders in a firm' (Jensen)[2]	• Perceived shortcomings in the shareholder model form the basis of the stakeholder model.[3] • Licht explains that the shareholder model's assumption of a single residual claimant (i.e., the shareholder) is flawed and 'unrealistic'[4] • Satisfying a wide range of stakeholder needs is argued to be necessary to enhance the long-term survival or sustainability of the for-profit corporation[5] • Relationships with stakeholders are 'intangible assets' of the firm which are beyond the firm's 'direct control'[6] and preservation of these intangible assets is dependent on addressing and satisfying such stakeholder interests (Capasso)[7]	4.4.1 4.4.1 4.4.1.1 4.4.1.1
Key Field No 3 – Comparative Corporate Governance Codes			
1.	• OECD Principles[8]	• These devote an entire Principle to the factor of Stakeholder Participation.[9]	6.2.2
2.	• Principle 3 of the ASX 2003 Best Practice Recommendations[10] was amended in the ASX 2007–10 Revised Principles[11]	• Principle 3 was amended in the ASX 2007–10 Revised Principles to provide for acknowledgement of stakeholder interests.[12] • This writer argues that the ASX 2007–10 Revised Principles constituted a *composite* shareholder-stakeholder governance model. Now see ASX 2014 Principles and Recommendations, Principle 3, *Act ethically and responsibly*, which relates to the purpose and content of a code of conduct.	4.4.1.3 and 6.6.1 4.4.1.3 and 6.6.1

No	Source of Theme, Consideration or Factor	Description	Section
3.	• Australian Government's Corporations and Markets Advisory Committee ('CAMAC') Report issued in December 2006 entitled *The Social Responsibility of Corporations.*[13]	• Aspects of the Report examine the relevance of stakeholder interests in enhancing the long-term efficiency and survival/ sustainability of the for-profit corporation.	4.4.1.1
Key Field No 4 – Empirical Studies of the Effectiveness of Governance Variables			
1.	• National regime and firm-specific governance variable empirical studies	• Growing number of studies on influence of stakeholder interests[14]	

Notes:

1. See discussion in sections 4.4–4.4.2.3 below.
2. Michael C Jensen, 'Value Maximization, Stakeholder Theory, and the Corporate Objective Function' in J Andriof, *et al* (eds), *Unfolding Stakeholder Thinking*, Sheffield: Greenleaf Publishing, 2002; (2001) 14(3) *Journal of Applied Corporate Finance* 8–21; (2001) 7 *European Financial Management* 297–317 and M Beer and N Norhia (eds), *Breaking the Code of Change*, Cambridge, MA: Harvard Business Press, 2000, accessed 5 February 2015 at SSRN: http://ssrn.com/abstract=220671, 8.
3. See, for example, Alberto Chilosi and Mirella Damiani, 'Stakeholders vs. Shareholders in Corporate Governance' (2007) 4(4) *The Icfai Journal of Corporate Governance* 7–45, accessed 5 February 2015 at SSRN: http://ssrn.com/abstract=975293.
4. Amir N Licht, 'The Maximands of Corporate Governance: A Theory of Values and Cognitive Style' (2004) 29(3) *Delaware Journal of Corporate Law* 649–746, 652, accessed 5 February 2015 at SSRN: http://ssrn.com/abstract=764025.
5. See discussion in section 4.4.1.1 below.
6. Arturo Capasso, 'Stakeholder Theory and Corporate Governance: The Role of Intangible Assets', accessed 5 February 2015 at SSRN: http://ssrn.com/abstract=610661, 8.
7. Ibid, 9.
8. Organisation for Economic Co-Operation and Development, *OECD Principles of Corporate Governance 2004*, 2004, OECD Publications Service, Paris ('*OECD Principles*'), Preamble, p 11, accessed 5 February 2015 at http://www.oecd.org/corporate/ca/corporategovernanceprinciples/31557724.pdf02_Chapter2.docx.
9. Ibid, Principle IV, p 21.
10. The original ASX best practice recommendations were contained in the ASX Corporate Governance Council, *Principles of Good Corporate Governance and Best*

Table 2.5 (continued)

Practice Recommendations, Australian Securities Exchange, March 2003 ('ASX 2003 Best Practice Recommendations').

11. The ASX 2003 Best Practice Recommendations were revised on 2 August 2007. See ASX Corporate Governance Council, *Corporate Governance Principles and Recommendations, Second Edition*, Australian Securities Exchange, 2 August 2007. These Principles and Recommendations were further amended in June 2010. See ASX Corporate Governance Council, *Corporate Governance Principles and Recommendations with 2010 Amendments*, June 2010 ('ASX 2007–10 Revised Principles'). These documents are available at http://www.asxgroup.com.au/corporate-governance-council.htm (accessed 5 February 2015).
12. ASX 2007–10 Revised Principles, ibid, Revised Principle 3, p 22. Now see ASX Corporate Governance Council, Corporate Governance Principles and Recommendations, Third Edition ('ASX 2014 Principles and Recommendations'), Principle 3, *Act ethically and responsibly*, which relates to the purpose and content of a code of conduct.
13. Corporations and Markets Advisory Committee, *The Social Responsibility of Corporations, Report*, December 2006, Australian Government, Sydney, accessed 5 February 2015 at http://www.camac.gov.au ('CAMAC Social Responsibility Report').
14. See, for example, Meredith A Jones, Shelley D Marshall, Richard James Mitchell and Ian Ramsay, 'Company Directors' Views Regarding Stakeholders', University of Melbourne Legal Studies Research Paper No 270, October 2007, accessed 5 February 2015 at SSRN: http://ssrn.com/abstract=1023259.

the (diminished) quality of decision-making which contributed to those collapses. These are examined in detail in Chapter 5.

In practical terms, Decision-making Factor No 7 is closely aligned to Monitoring & Audit Factor No 5. In other words, these themes should normatively inform and shape each other. Thus, in real-world terms, as the monitoring process within the corporation identifies that some action is required, so then is the decision-making process engaged. In turn, decision-making action should again normatively engage the monitoring and evaluation/assessment functions in a continuous cycle.

2.6.8 Responsibility Factor No 8: Delineation and Disclosure of Powers, Duties and Lines of Responsibility

Responsibility Factor No 8 is represented in the three relational axes of good governance. It provides the legal, constitutional (in the company law sense) and organisational/operational authority for the actions of individuals within, and organs (such as the board and subcommittees) of, the corporation. The themes encapsulated in Responsibility Factor No 8 are critical to the effectiveness and efficiency of many of the other governance factors – in particular, Decision-making Factor No 7, Monitoring & Audit Factor No 5 and, through the interrelationships discussed above in relation to both those Factors, Reporting Factor No 1.

Table 2.6 Decision-making factor No 7

No	Source of Theme, Consideration or Factor	Description	Section
Key Field No 1: Application of Principal Theories of the Firm to the Relational Approach			
1.	• Key feature of the dispersed shareholding public company[1]	• Separation of ownership from management of the firm (Fama and Jensen).[2]	1.2.2
		• Agency relationship between inside managers who act on behalf of outside shareholders giving rise to agency costs (Jensen and Meckling).[3]	1.2.2
		• Shareholders (the owners) cannot interfere in the day-to-day **decision-making** of the company which is vested in the board of directors and management (Bainbridge).[4]	1.2.2
		• Effective decision-making structure which reduces agency costs divides decision 'initiation' and 'implementation' ('decision management') from 'ratification' and 'monitoring' ('decision control')[5] the latter function being undertaken of behalf of the shareholders by a board of directors (Fama and Jensen[6])	4.2.3.2
Key Field No 2 – Autopsies of the Enron and Hastie Corporate Collapses			
1.	• Director independence • Share and option holdings • Board member familiarity and deference	• Commentators examine whether these variables enhance or reduce the quality of **decision-making** in the Enron collapse thus	5.2.2.1 5.2.2.1–5.2.2.1.2 5.2.2.2

Table 2.6 (continued)

No	Source of Theme, Consideration or Factor	Description	Section
	• The independence of committees	contributing to Enron's failure	5.2.2.2
	• Risk management and the (in)adequacy of reports		5.2.2.3.1
	• The effects on risk management of the risk-taking culture at Enron		5.2.2.3.2
2.	• Poor management and monitoring of Hastie acquisitions	Administrators concluded that the acquisition strategy resulted in a number of effects including: • inaccurate and inadequate financial reporting and **consequently poor decision making by the Board**.[7]	5.2.2.3.1
Key Field No 3: Comparative Corporate Governance Codes			
1.	• Section 198A of the *Corporations Act*.[8]	• Reinforces **decision-making** division between shareholders (owners) and directors (controllers)	1.2.2
2.	• ASX 2007–10 Revised Principles[9]	• Devotes the entire Revised Principle 3 to 'Promote ethical and responsible **decision-making**'.[10] Now see ASX 2014 Principles and Recommendations, above, Principle 3, *Act ethically and responsibly*, which relates to the purpose and content of a code of conduct.	4.4.1.3 and 6.6.1
Key Field No 4: Empirical Studies of the Effectiveness of Governance Variables			
1.	• Proportion of insider/ management equity ownership	• Empirical studies examine whether these variables enhance	7.3.2.1.5

No	Source of Theme, Consideration or Factor	Description	Section
	• Board skills 'mix' • Board size • Outside board positions of independent directors • Anti-takeover mechanisms • The market for corporate control • Presence, independence (proportion) time and financial expertise of the audit sub-committee • Division in the CEO/ Chairperson roles	monitoring quality and **decision-making** and, in turn, firm profitability and firm value	7.3.1.2 8.2.1–8.2.2.2 8.2.3 8.3 8.3.1 9.2.1–9.2.1.1.2 8.6

Notes:

1. For a detailed discussion, see the papers relating to the nexus of contracts theory and the anti-contractarian views of the firm from the symposium on contractual freedom in corporate law held on 9 and 10 December 1988 at Columbia Law School published at (1989) 89 *Colum L Rev* 1395.
2. Eugene F Fama and Michael C Jensen, 'Separation of Ownership and Control', in Michael C Jensen, *Foundations of Organizational Strategy*, Cambridge, MA: Harvard University Press, 1998, and (1983) 26 *Journal of Law and Economics* 301, accessed 5 February 2015 at SSRN: http://ssrn.com/abstract=94034, 4–5 and 9.
3. Michael C Jensen and William H Meckling, 'Theory of the Firm: Managerial Behavior, Agency Costs and Ownership Structure' in Michael C. Jensen, *A Theory of the Firm: Governance, Residual Claims and Organizational Forms*, Cambridge, MA: Harvard University Press, December 2000; (1976) 3(4) *Journal of Financial Economics* 305–60, accessed 5 February 2015 at SSRN: http://ssrn.com/abstract=94043, 5–6.
4. Stephen M Bainbridge, 'The Board of Directors as Nexus of Contracts: A Critique of Gulati, Klein & Zolt's "Connected Contracts" Model', UCLA, School of Law Research Paper No 02-05, January 2002, accessed 5 February 2015 at SSRN: http://ssrn.com/abstract=299743, 2. The author cites Adolph A Berle and Gardiner C Means, *The Modern Corporation and Private Property*, 1932, pp 84–9. For an examination of the merits of group decision-making in the context of a corporate board *cf* individual decision-making, see Stephen M Bainbridge, 'Why a Board? Group Decisionmaking in Corporate Governance' (2002) 55 *Vanderbilt Law Review* 1–55, accessed 5 February 2015 at SSRN: http://ssrn.com/abstract=266683.
5. Eugene F Fama and Michael C Jensen, 'Separation of Ownership and Control', in Michael C Jensen, *Foundations of Organizational Strategy*, Cambridge, MA: Harvard University Press, 1998, and (1983) 26 *Journal of Law and Economics* 301, 4–5 and 9.
6. Ibid, 14 and 16.
7. PPB Advisory, *Hastie Group Limited and Specific Subsidiaries, Report by Joint and Several Administrators Pursuant to Section 439A of the Corporations Act 2001*, 21

Table 2.6 (continued)

January 2013, accessed 5 February 2015 at http://www.ppbadvisory.com/creditor-information/v/281/hastie-group/2nd-creditor-meeting ('Administrators' Report'), section 7.9.2, p 62 of 99.

8. *Corporations Act* 2001 (Cth), s 198A (Replaceable Rule) See http://www.austlii.edu.au/au/legis/cth/consol_act/ca2001172/s198a.html (accessed 5 February 2015).
9. See ASX Corporate Governance Council, *Corporate Governance Principles and Recommendations with 2010 Amendments*, June 2010 ('ASX 2007–10 Revised Principles').
10. Ibid, Revised Principle 3.

For example, to operate effectively, the decision-making powers and responsibilities within different organs of the company – such as the board and subcommittees – and different levels of management or individual office-holders must be delineated (constitutionally or otherwise). Thus, in practice, Decision-making Factor No 7 is closely aligned with Responsibility Factor No 8 and these factors inform each other reflexively. Equally, the delineation and disclosure of particular powers, duties and lines of responsibility are integral to the effectiveness of any monitoring system within the corporation. Therefore, Responsibility Factor No 8 is an important element of Monitoring & Audit Factor No 5. Support for this argument is provided by a conceptual analysis of 'accountability' in multi-level governance in the public and democratic sphere by Bovens.[48] Bovens defines 'accountability' in terms also relevant to the corporate context:

> [a]ccountability is *a relationship between an actor and a forum, in which the actor has an obligation to explain and to justify his or her conduct, the forum can pose questions and pass judgement, and the actor may face consequences*.[49]

Bovens' concept is important to the weighing process contemplated by the three relational axes of good governance. That is, that there is an 'actor' who has an 'obligation'. Without the ability to effectively attribute an 'obligation' (or alternatively in terms of Behaviours Axis 2(b), 'responsibility') *for a particular duty, power or function* to an actor (whether, for example, individual officeholder, executive, key-position employee, board or sub-committee), there is no accountability or responsibility. Thus, for example, if there is no accountability or responsibility, Decision-making

[48] Mark Bovens, 'Analysing and Assessing Accountability: A Conceptual Framework' (2007) 13(4) *European Law Journal* 447–68, available at SSRN: http://ssrn.com/abstract=992006.

[49] Ibid, 450 (emphasis in original).

Factor No 7 and Monitoring & Audit Factor No 5 and, in turn, Reporting Factor No 1 would be critically undermined.

The following Table 2.7 demonstrates that the Responsibility Factor No. 8 is a fundamental theme arising from each of the Key Fields Nos 1–4.

Thus, Responsibility Factor No 8 is a recurring theme as it is integral to the effective operation of other governance factors – in particular, Decision-making Factor No 7, Monitoring & Audit Factor No 5 and Reporting Factor No 1.

2.7 INTERRELATIONSHIPS BETWEEN GOVERNANCE FACTORS – THE INTERRELATIONSHIP SCHEMES

2.7.1 The Two Interrelationship Schemes

The Interrelationship Schemes are a synthesis of the individual interrelationships examined in sections 2.6.1–2.6.8 above. In practical terms, the Interrelationship Schemes are a diagrammatic representation of possible or hypothesised interrelationships identified between the eight governance factors. Again, there are two Interrelationship Schemes – one based on the shareholder primacy model and one based on the stakeholder model of corporate governance.

Shareholder primacy interrelationship scheme

The tensions between the shareholder primacy principle and the stakeholder model are reflected in Alignment Factor No 3 and Stakeholders Factor No 6. Indeed, as explained in section 2.6.3 above, Alignment Factor No 3 is an 'umbrella' or 'guiding' principle over all other governance factors – except Compliance Factor No 2.[50] In such a case, the interrelationship scheme represents the shareholder primacy model as reflected by Alignment Factor No 3's 'guiding principle' role.

Stakeholder interrelationship scheme

Where, by contrast, the interrelationship scheme is to reflect the stakeholder model, then the reverse will be the case. Stakeholders Factor No 6 will then constitute the 'umbrella' or 'guiding principle' in the design and implementation of governance variables over the other governance factors. This is again with the exception of

50 See discussion in section 2.6.3 above.

Table 2.7 Responsibility factor No 8

No	Source of Theme, Consideration or Factor	Description	Section
Key Field No 1: Application of the Principal Theories of the Firm to the Relational Approach			
1.	• Separation of widely-dispersed shareholders from management of the corporation	• An effective decision-making structure to reduce agency costs **typically divides** decision 'initiation' and 'implementation' ('decision management') from 'ratification' and 'monitoring' ('decision control') (Fama and Jensen)[1]	4.2.3.2
		• Latter function is undertaken on behalf of shareholders by a board of directors (Fama and Jensen)[2]	4.2.3.2
Key Field No 2: Autopsies of the Enron and Hastie Corporate Collapses			
1.	• Attendance of the Chairman and separate CEO at Enron committees including 'executive', 'finance' and 'audit'	• Undermining of Enron board's monitoring function (Gillan and Martin)[3]	5.2.2.2
Key Field No 3: Comparative Corporate Governance Codes			
1.	• International (OECD, ICGN and CACG) and National (US, UK, and Australian) governance codes	• Core feature is that 'responsibilities of board sub-committees [be] delineated and disclosed'.	6.8.1
2.	• SOX reforms relating to directors and management and earnings manipulation[4] including:		
	○ Section 301	• Enhances lines of responsibility in relation to auditor appointment, compensation and oversight and conduct of the audit	
	○ Section 302	• Delineates responsibility in relation to the certification of annual and quarterly reports by the CEO and CFO.	

No	Source of Theme, Consideration or Factor	Description	Section
	❍ Section 304	• Enhances lines of responsibility by requiring that the CEO or CFO reimburse the company for bonuses, incentive payments and trading profits on an accounting restatement.	
	❍ Section 404	• Enhances lines of responsibility by requiring that an internal control report be included in the company's annual report including management's responsibility for the establishment and maintenance of internal controls and management assessment of the effectiveness of these controls.	
Key Field No 4 – Empirical Studies of the Effectiveness of Governance Variables			
1.	• Division in CEO and Chairperson roles	• Available studies find no significant effect on *firm value* in **dividing these roles** (Weir, Laing and McKnight)[5] and (Larcker, Ormazabal and Taylor)[6]	8.6.1
		• **Dividing these roles** 'is significantly positively correlated with better contemporaneous and subsequent *operating performance*' (Bhagat and Bolton)[7]	8.6.1

Notes:

1. Eugene F Fama and Michael C Jensen, 'Separation of Ownership and Control', in Michael C Jensen, *Foundations of Organizational Strategy*, Cambridge, MA: Harvard University Press, 1998, and (1983) 26 *Journal of Law and Economics* 301, 4–5 and 9.
2. Ibid (1983) 26 *Journal of Law and Economics* 301, 310–11, accessed 5 February 2015 at SSRN: http://ssrn.com/abstract=94034, 14 and 16.
3. Stuart L Gillan and John D Martin, 'Financial Engineering, Corporate Governance, and the Collapse of Enron', U of Delaware Coll. of Bus. and Econ. Ctr. for Corp.

Table 2.7 (continued)

Governance Working Paper No 2002-001 (November 2002), accessed 5 February 2015 at SSRN: http://ssrn.com/abstract=354040, 25.

4. See PL 107-204, 2002 HR 3763, July 30, 2002, 116 Stat 745, available at http://www.sec.gov/about/laws/soa2002.pdf ('SOX') and discussion in section 6.4.2 below.
5. C Weir, D Laing and P J McKnight, 'An Empirical Analysis of the Impact of Corporate Governance Mechanisms on the Performance of UK Firms', accessed 5 February 2015 at SSRN: http://ssrn.com/abstract=286440, 19.
6. David F Larcker, Gaizka Ormazabal and Daniel J Taylor, 'The Market Reaction to Corporate Governance Regulation', (2011) 101(2) *Journal of Financial Economics* 431–448, 433; Rock Center for Corporate Governance at Stanford University Working Paper Series No 82 (October 14, 2010).
7. Sanjai Bhagat and Brian J Bolton, 'Corporate Governance and Firm Performance' (June 2007), accessed 5 February 2015 at SSRN: http://ssrn.com/abstract=1017342, 5 (emphasis in original).

Compliance Factor No 2 and, this time, Alignment Factor No 3 so that 'other' stakeholder interests do not necessarily rank over those of the shareholder-stakeholders.

2.7.2 The Direction of the 'Effect' in the Interrelationship Schemes

An arrow connecting two (or more) governance factors in Figures 2.6 and 2.7 below depict an hypothesised interrelationship between the relevant governance factors. In practical terms, this represents a hypothesis that one governance factor affects another governance factor in the direction of the arrow. A 'two-way' arrow hypothesises that the relevant governance factors affect each other. Again, such an interrelationship is described as reflexive.

Two principal assumptions relate to the interrelationship schemes. First, consistent with reality, it is not possible – in isolation – to determine the governance factor 'first' affected by a particular governance variable. Take, for example, the Board skills 'mix' variable – '[BrdSkills] (+)'.[51] [BrdSkills] (+) variable's relational effect path is positive (+) and is presented as beginning with Monitoring & Audit Factor No 5 and Decision-making Factor No 7. Each of these governance factors has a reflexive relationship with the other.[52] Here, it is not possible to identify which governance factor is affected first. Secondly, while a particular governance variable may impact a particular governance factor significantly,

[51] Board – Director Skills 'Mix' – see discussion in section 7.3.1.2.1 below.

[52] See Figure 7.2 [BrdSkills] (+) variable relational effect path in section 7.3.1.2.1 below.

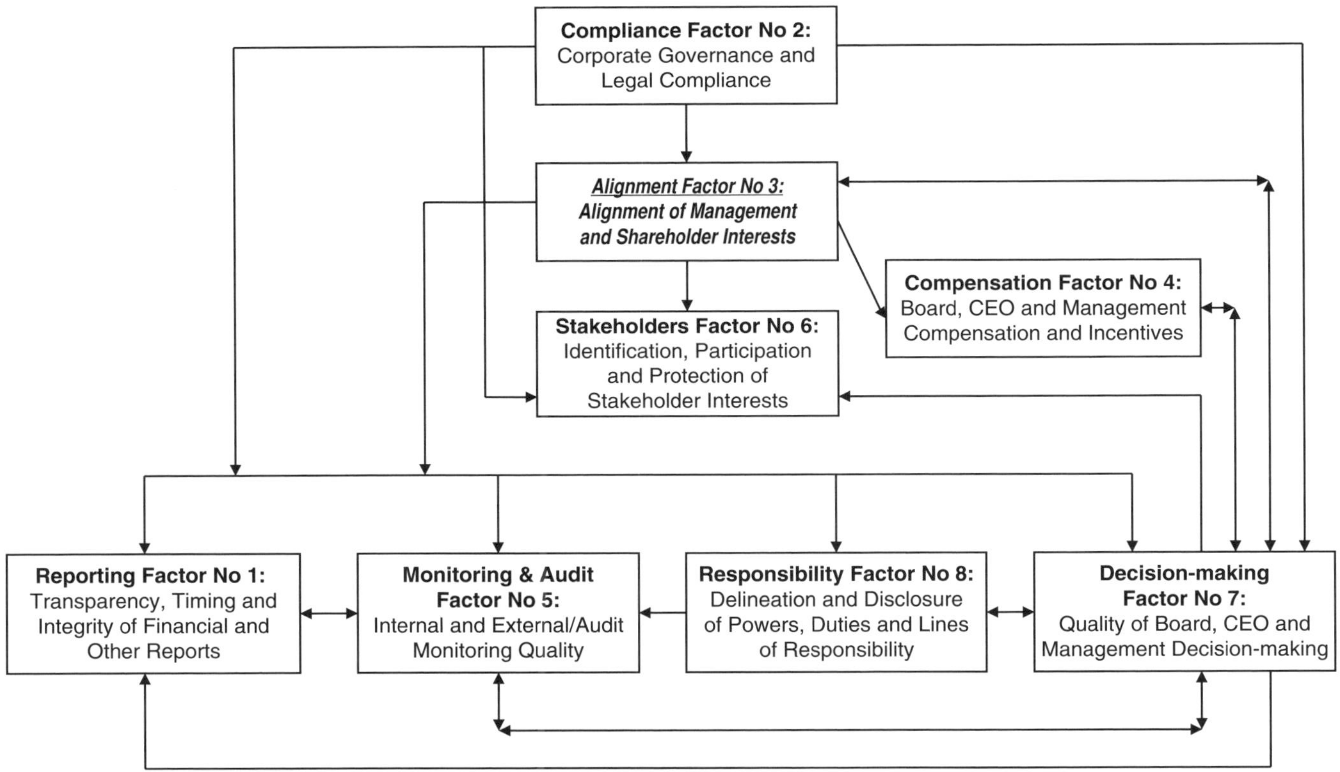

Figure 2.6 Shareholder primacy interrelationship scheme

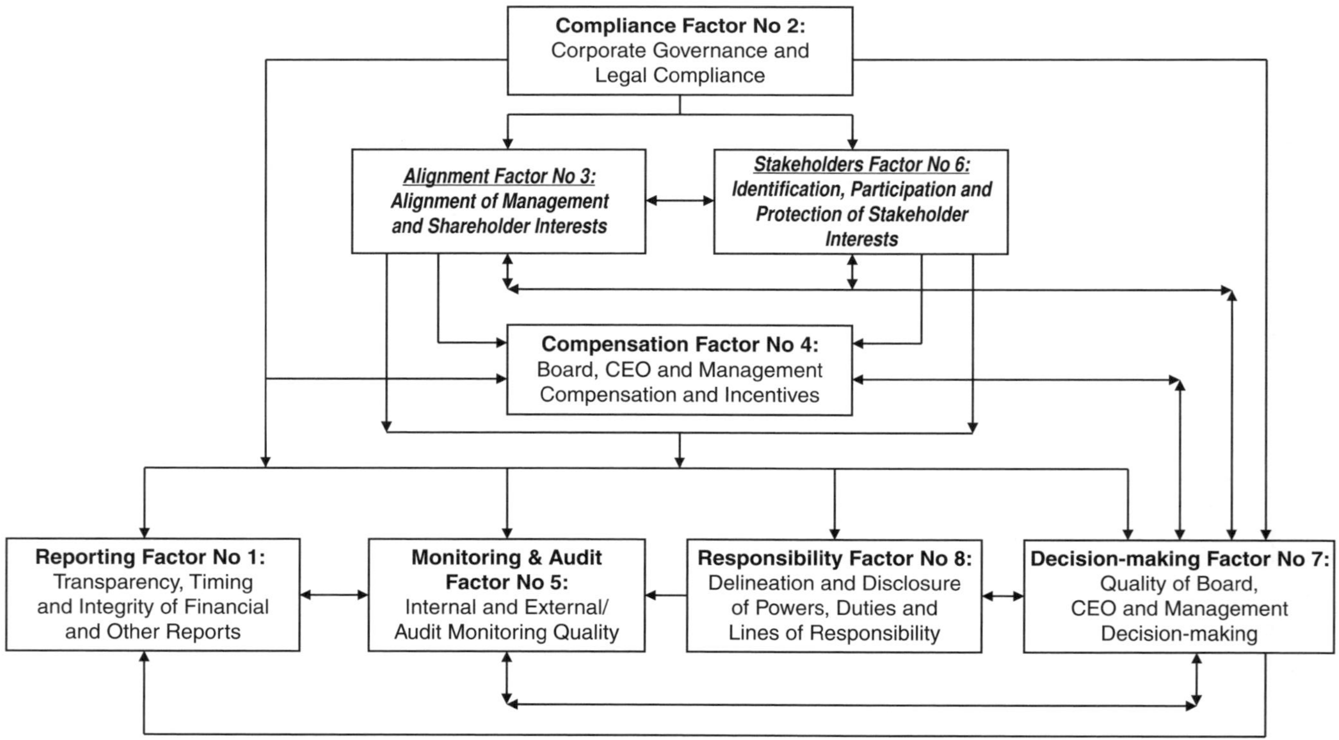

Figure 2.7 Stakeholder model interrelationship scheme

the flow-on or 'ripple-effect'[53] of that governance variable may not be of the same order, magnitude or direction (positive or negative). Thus, in the identification of the 'start' of a relational effect path for a governance variable, the relational approach will begin with the governance factor(s) and direction of effect identified by the relevant empirical studies relating to that governance variable in Chapters 7–10.

2.8 CONCLUSION – THE RELATIONAL CORPORATE GOVERNANCE FRAMEWORK

The 'Relational Corporate Governance Framework' of the approach in this book is depicted in Figure 2.8. The Framework brings together all the theoretical components introduced in Chapters 1 and 2. As shown in the diagram, all the components of the relational approach are ultimately drawn from the four Key Fields that form the base of the pyramid-like structure of the Framework.

In the next chapter, the relational approach presents the governance variables in practice – the results of the empirical studies of the effectiveness of governance variables comprising Key Field No 4. These studies are used to construct a relational effect path for each governance variable in Chapters 7–10. Each relational effect path is summarised in the Coverage Table (Table 3.1). In the Relational Proximity Table (Table 3.2), this 'Coverage' is converted to a measure of the relative importance of each governance variable in affecting agency costs and the long-term efficiency and survival of the firm. These operational results tables are presented in Chapter 3.

---

53 This term is taken from the term used by Professor Jane Stapleton to describe the flow-on effects of negligently inflicted 'pure' economic loss in the tort of negligence. See Jane Stapleton, 'Duty of Care and Economic Loss: A Wider Agenda' (1991) 107 *Law Quarterly Review* 249, 255.

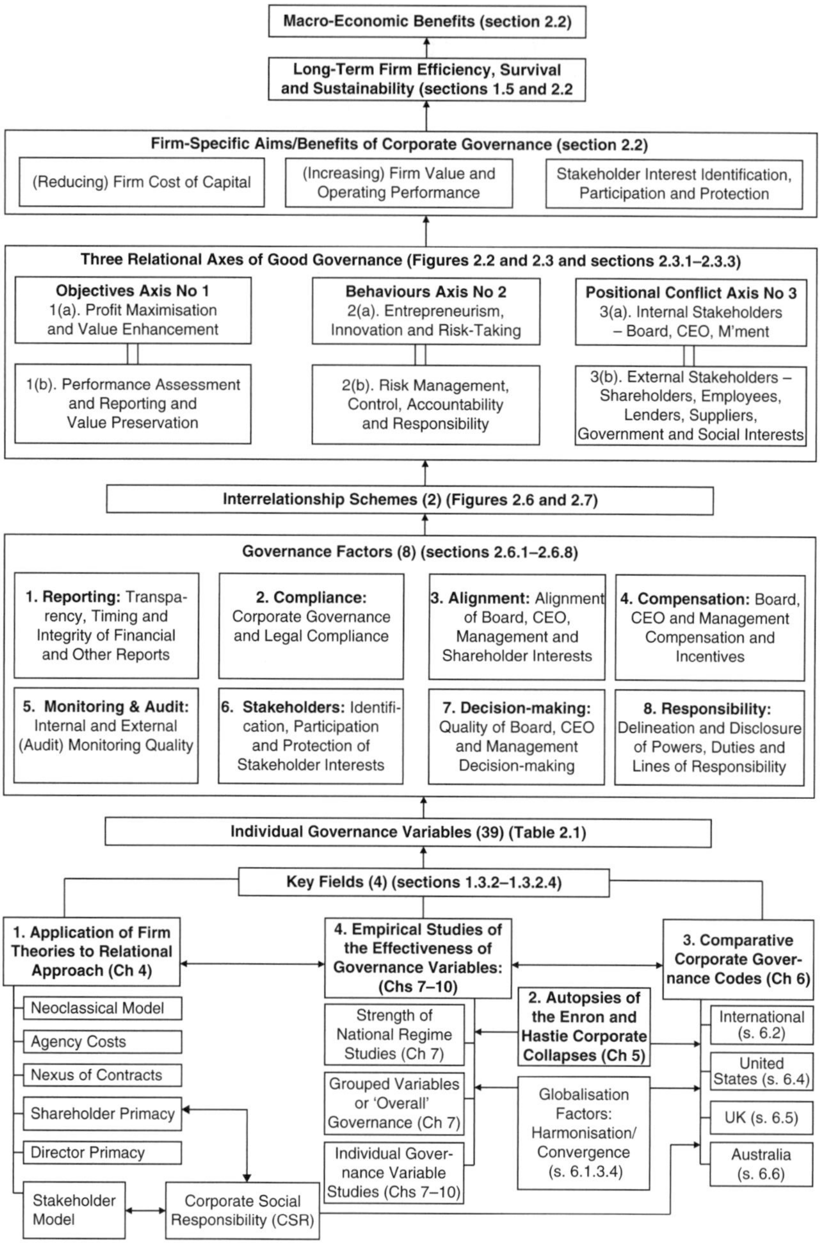

Figure 2.8 The relational corporate governance framework

3. Governance variables in practice

3.1 PURPOSE AND APPROACH OF CHAPTER 3

This chapter presents the results of the empirical studies of the effectiveness of governance variables comprising Key Field No 4 and examined in Chapters 7–10 of the relational approach. Those chapters combine the results of these empirical studies with the shareholder primacy interrelationship scheme[1] to present a relational effect path for each governance variable. This path depicts the identity and number of the governance factors affected by a governance variable and the direction of the effect.

The results of the relational approach are contained in two operational Tables – the Coverage Table[2] and, ultimately, the Relational Proximity Table.[3] The aim of these Tables is to present the results of the assessment of the relative importance or 'relational proximity' of individual governance variables in reducing (or increasing) agency costs and enhancing (or reducing) the long-term efficiency and survival or sustainability of the for-profit firm in a transparent manner. Similarly visible is the relational approach's assessment of the interrelationships between individual governance factors and, in turn, the 39 governance variables in achieving these ends. Thus, the results for the relational effect path for each governance variable are presented ahead of the Key Fields to add explanation and analysis to those Fields.

3.2 OPERATIONAL MEASURES OF THE RELATIONAL APPROACH – GOVERNANCE VARIABLE 'COVERAGE' AND 'RELATIONAL PROXIMITY RATING'

Generally speaking, the empirical studies of governance variables in Chapters 7–10 have been conducted in a manner suitable to the means

1 See Figure 2.6.
2 See Table 3.1.
3 See Table 3.2.

and ends of the particular authors. These studies are not generally configured in a manner directed to ascertaining the effect of those variables on all eight governance factors. In many cases, the effect of the variables in the studies is directed to only one or two themes within the governance factors – such as the quality of board monitoring, the quality of decision-making or the risk of earnings manipulation. Indeed, even when these studies are directed to particular governance factors, there are often conflicting or statistically insignificant results. So the starting points for the 39 relational effect paths are the empirical studies presented in Chapters 7–10.[4] And the interrelationships between governance variables and governance factors beyond the bounds of the particular studies are hypothesised relationships.

The way in which these hypothesised relationships are constructed was explained in Figure 2.1 in Chapter 2. In short, the interrelationships between the governance factors are already calculated and presented for the reader – these are the two Interrelationship Schemes in Figures 2.6 and 2.7. The pre-eminence of the shareholder primacy model of corporate governance dictates that the shareholder primacy interrelationship scheme in Figure 2.6 be used to construct the relational effect paths. The interrelationship scheme sets out the way in which governance factors are linked to one or more other governance factors. The interrelationship scheme 'start' point is nominated by the relational approach.[5] This is a factor suggested by the empirical study relating to the effectiveness of the relevant governance variable in Chapters 7–10. This empirical study also suggests the direction of the effect (+/−) on the governance factors. Thus, a relational effect path for each governance variable depicts the identity and number of the governance factors affected by a governance variable and the direction of the effect.

The hypothesised effect of a governance variable on a governance factor set out in a relational effect path is known as governance variable 'coverage'. In other words, this coverage is represented diagrammatically in the relational effect path of a governance variable. As the name suggests, this path is summarised and displayed in the Coverage Table (Table 3.1).

The coverage of governance variables summarised in the Coverage Table is then converted into a measure of relative importance in affecting agency costs and firm sustainability. That measure is known as the 'relational proximity rating' of a governance variable and is depicted on a scale from +/− 100.00 to 0.00 '*rprox*' units in the Relational Proximity

---

4 See discussion in section 2.7.2 above.

5 Ibid.

Table 3.1 Coverage Table: Hypothesised significant coverage effect and direction of interrelationship between governance variables and governance factors

No	Governance Variable (Table 2.1) & (Table A.1 of Appendix 1)	Relational Effect Path Reference	Direction of Effect (+) (+/−) (−)	Governance Factor (Sections 2.6.1–2.6.8)								Total Governance Variable Coverage
				1	2	3	4	5	6	7	8	
1.	AudAccEarn	9.2.1.1.2	+	•	•	•	•	•		•		+6
2.	AudCom	8.4.2	+	•	•	•	•	•		•		+6
3.	AudExpAcc	8.4.4	+	•	•	•	•	•		•		+6
4.	AudFree	9.2.1.1.2	−	•	•	•	•	•		•		−6
5.	AudIndFreq	9.2.1	+	•		•	•	•	•	•	•	+7
6.	AudIndInfo	8.4.3	−	•				•		•	•	−4
7.	AudIndMon	8.4.3	+	•		•	•	•	•	•	•	+7
8.	AudShortOpts	10.2.5.1	−	•		•	•	•	•	•	•	−7
9.	BlockCosts	8.5.1–2	−	•		•	•	•	•	•		−6
10.	BlockMon	8.5.1–2	+	•		•	•	•	•	•		+6
11.	BrdAttend	7.3.2.1.2	+	•		•	•	•	•	•	•	+7
12.	BrdCmEarn	9.2.2	+/−	•	•	•	•	•		•		+/−6
13.	BrdCmSize	8.2.2.2	+/−	•	•	•	•	•		•		+/−6
14.	BrdIndInfo	7.3.2.1.3	−	•				•		•	•	−4
15.	BrdIndMon	7.3.2.1.1–2	+	•		•	•	•	•	•	•	+7
16.	BrdReview	7.3.2.1.2	+	•		•	•	•	•	•	•	+7
17.	BrdSkills	7.3.1.2.1	+	•		•	•	•	•	•	•	+7
18.	CompCom	10.2.4.1	+/−	•		•	•	•	•	•	•	+/−7
19.	DirCEO$	10.2.4	+/−	•		•	•	•	•	•	•	+/−7
20.	DualDismiss	8.6.3	−	•		•	•	•	•	•	•	−7
21.	DualEarn	9.2.1.1.3	−	•		•	•	•	•	•	•	−7
22.	DualStrat	8.6.3	−	•				•		•	•	−4

Table 3.1 (continued)

No	Governance Variable (Table 2.1) & (Table A.1 of Appendix 1)	Relational Effect Path Reference	Direction of Effect (+) (+/−) (−)	Governance Factor (Sections 2.6.1–2.6.8)								Total Governance Variable Coverage
				1	2	3	4	5	6	7	8	
23.	DualTrade	8.6.1–2	+/−	●		●	●	●	●	●	●	+/−7
24.	EqOptIncent	10.2.4	+	●		●	●	●	●	●	●	+7
25.	EqOptEntrch	10.2.4	−	●		●	●	●	●	●	●	−7
26.	ExtAudEarn	9.2.3.3	+	●		●	●	●	●	●	●	+7
27.	NationGov	7.3.1.3.2	+	●	●	●	●	●	●	●	●	+8
28.	NomCom	7.3.1.2.2	+/−	●		●	●	●	●	●	●	+/−7
29.	NomInd	7.3.1.2.2	+	●		●	●	●	●	●	●	+7
30.	NonAuditS	9.2.3.2–3	−	●		●	●	●	●	●	●	−7
31.	OtherATMs	8.3.1.1	−	●	●	●	●	●	●	●	●	−8
32.	OutBrdPos	8.2.3.1	−	●		●	●	●	●	●		−6
33.	OutBrdAdv	7.3.2.1.2	+	●		●	●	●	●	●	●	+7
34.	ReputDiscl	10.4.1	+	●	●	●	●	●	●	●	●	+8
35.	ReputRep	10.4.1	+	●	●	●	●	●	●	●	●	+8
36.	StagBrdElect	8.3.1.1	−	●	●	●	●	●	●	●	●	−8
37.	ShortTOpts	10.2.5.1	−	●		●	●	●	●	●	●	−7
38.	TransTimeMon	9.1.2.1	+	●	●	●	●	●	●	●	●	+8
39.	TransTimeRedn	9.1.2.1	−	●				●		●	●	−4

Table (Table 3.2). The relational proximity rating of a governance variable is calculated by starting with the coverage (measured from +/− 1 up to +/− 8) produced by that governance variable and then dividing by the total number of governance factors (that is, again 8). Finally, that resultant figure is expressed as a percentage by multiplying by 100. The ultimate Relational Proximity Table then groups the 39 governance variables in descending order of relational proximity in affecting agency costs and the long-term efficiency and sustainability of the firm.

3.3 THE HYPOTHESISED COVERAGE EFFECT ON GOVERNANCE FACTORS BY INDIVIDUAL GOVERNANCE VARIABLES

3.3.1 The Coverage Table

The Coverage Table (Table 3.1) displays the governance factors affected (and the direction of that effect) by the operation of individual governance variables. In this way, the *interrelationships* between individual agency cost-reducing (or increasing) governance variables is depicted in table-form by identifying multiple governance factors hypothesised to be affected by a relevant governance variable.

3.3.1.1 Operation of the Coverage Table

A dot marking ('•') in any column representing a governance factor in the Coverage Table denotes some significant hypothesised effect on that governance factor by an individual governance variable. In addition, the effect on a governance factor which is displayed in the Coverage Table can be direct or indirect. It may be indirect because that governance variable affects – as an intermediate step – other governance variables or governance factors as displayed in the relational effect paths in Chapters 7–10.

By contrast, the absence of such a dot marking indicates that there is *no* effect on that governance factor. Again, a dot marking will be absent where the effect of a particular governance variable on a governance factor is so insignificant that it may properly be ignored. Otherwise, the relative importance of such a governance variable will be skewed towards the upper end of the rating scale. Possible refinements of this aspect of the relational approach – dependent on empirical testing – are discussed in Chapter 11.

3.3.1.2 Direction of effect and 'dual direction' governance variables

A positive direction or relationship ('+') signifies that the particular governance variable enhances the attainment of the particular governance

Table 3.2 Relational Proximity Table: Hypothesised relative importance of governance variables in the sustainability of the firm

Relational Proximity Groups	Relational Proximity Group 8			Relational Proximity Group 7	
Total Governance Variable Coverage (Table 3.1)	+ 8	+/− 8	− 8	+ 7	+/− 7
Relational Proximity Rating*	+ 100.00	+/−100.00	− 100.00	+ 87.50	+/− 87.50
	TransTimeMon		OtherATMs	AudIndFreq	DualTrade
	NationGov		StagBrdElect	AudIndMon	NomCom
	ReputDiscl			BrdAttend	CompCom
	ReputRep			BrdIndMon	DirCEO$
				BrdReview	
				BrdSkills	
				ExtAudEarn	
				NomInd	
				OutBrdAdv	
				EqOptIncent	

Relational Proximity Groups	Relational Proximity Group 4			Relational Proximity Group 3	
Total Governance Variable Coverage (Table 3.1)	+ 4	+/− 4	− 4	+ 3	+/− 3
Relational Proximity Rating*	+ 50.00	+/− 50.00	− 50.00	+ 37.50	+/− 37.50
			AudIndInfo		
			BrdIndInfo		
			DualStrat		
			TransTimeRedn		

Note:
* Calculated by ('Total Governance Variable Coverage') divided by (total number of Governance Factors = 8) x 100.

factor and, consequently, results in a hypothesised reduction in agency costs between insiders and outsiders of the corporation. By contrast, a negative directional marker or relationship ('−') denotes a hypothesised diminution in the attainment of that governance factor or an increase in such agency costs.

Some hypothesised relationships between governance variables and governance factors are displayed as both positive and negative ('+/−'). This denotes a relationship whose direction, all other things being equal,

	Relational Proximity Group 6			Relational Proximity Group 5		
− 7	+ 6	+/− 6	− 6	+ 5	+/− 5	− 5
− 87.50	+ 75.00	+/− 75.00	− 75.00	+ 62.50	+/− 62.50	− 62.50
DualDismiss DualEarn NonAuditS AudShortOpts EqOptEntrch ShortTOpts	AudAccEarn AudCom AudExpAcc BlockMon	BrdCmEarn BrdCmSize	AudFree BlockCosts OutBrdPos			

	Relational Proximity Group 2			Relational Proximity Group 1		
− 3	+ 2	+/− 2	− 2	+ 1	+/− 1	− 1
− 37.50	+ 25.00	+/− 25.00	− 25.00	+ 12.50	+/− 12.50	− 12.50

cannot be determined (even hypothetically) in isolation but which depends on the presence or absence of other structural determinants. These determinants are described in the relational approach as intervening or confounding variables.

One consequence of denoting a governance variable as '+/−' may be to reduce the explanatory and predictive power of the relational approach. But this also reflects the reality of the complexity of the interrelationships between governance factors and therefore needs to be reflected in the relational approach. Even so, only six governance variables have a 'dual' directional marker:

- Board and Committee (Non-Audit) Size – Earnings Manipulation Effect: **[BrdCmEarn] (+/−)**;[6]
- Board and Committee Size: **[BrdCmSize] (+/−)**;[7]
- Compensation Committee – Presence, Operation and Frequency: **[CompCom] (+/−)**;[8]
- Director/CEO Compensation Levels: **[DirCEO$] (+/−)**;[9]
- Duality of CEO/Chair Positions – Monitoring and Decision-Quality 'Trade-off': **[DualTrade] (+/−)**;[10] and
- Nominating Committee – Presence, Operation and Frequency: **[NomCom] (+/−)**.[11]

To reduce the incidence of 'dual-direction' governance variables, the relational approach has where practicable separated 'dual-direction' individual governance variables into their positive and negative aspects resulting in two separate governance variables. For example, in the case of independent outside directors, there is a suggested positive effect (that is, a reduction in agency costs) on account of the monitoring quality[12] of such directors. Thus, the **[BrdIndMon]** variable is positive **(+)**.[13] This effect is separated from the argued negative effect (that is, an increase in agency costs) of a reduction in the quality of the 'manager-specific' and 'firm-specific' information flow to the board.[14] Thus, the **[BrdIndInfo]** variable is negative **(−)**.[15] The governance variable coverage of each such governance variable is then assessed separately with a consequential improvement in explanatory and predictive power.

3.3.1.3 Partial coverage of governance factors

The relational approach in its present form cannot differentiate between, on the one hand, a significant hypothesised effect and, on the other hand, a small (but not negligible) hypothesised effect. In the absence of empirical

---

6 See discussion in section 9.2.2 below.

7 See discussion in section 8.2.2.2 below.

8 See discussion in section 10.2.4.1 below.

9 See discussion in section 10.2.4 below.

10 See discussion in sections 8.6.1–8.6.2 below.

11 See discussion in section 7.3.1.2.2 below.

12 See, for example, Bernard S Black and Woochan Kim, 'The Effect of Board Structure on Firm Value in an Emerging Market: IV, DiD, and Time Series Evidence from Korea', Finance Working Paper No 179/2007 (June 2007), accessed 9 February 2015 at: http://ssrn.com/abstract=968287, 5.

13 See discussion in sections 7.3.2.1.1–7.3.2.1.2 below.

14 See discussion in section 7.3.2.1.3 below.

15 Ibid.

testing, the relational approach cannot accurately reflect the *partial* coverage of (or effect on) a governance factor by a governance variable. In other words, all dot markings have been assigned the value of one (1) coverage unit in the relational approach. An alternative method to improve the descriptive and predictive accuracy of the relational approach would be to accord a different weighting to individual governance factors based on empirical testing. This is further discussed in the improvements to the relational approach in Chapter 11.

3.3.2 The Hypothesised Relative Importance of Governance Variables – The Relational Proximity Table

3.3.2.1 Hypotheses in relation to the relational proximity of governance variables

In the Relational Proximity Table (Table 3.2), the *total* coverage of governance factors by a governance variable is used to make a hypothesis of the relative importance of that governance variable in affecting agency costs and firm sustainability. This is known as relational proximity and is expressed as a numerical rating from +/−100.00 *rprox* to (conceivably) 0.00 *rprox*.

The *higher* the total coverage and therefore relational proximity rating of a particular governance variable, the *greater* is the hypothesised effect of that governance variable in reducing (or increasing) total agency costs between insiders and outsiders of the for-profit firm. And, in turn, the *greater* is the effect of that governance variable in enhancing (or reducing) the long-term efficiency and survival/sustainability of such firms. Observations and analysis of the results and interrelationships displayed in the Relational Proximity Table (Table 3.2) are set out in the following chapters relating to the Key Fields.

In the following Chapter 4, this book examines the application of the principal theories and models of the firm to the relational approach. The purpose is to show how the relational approach adds explanatory power and components to these principal theories – the 'nexus of contracts', agency theory, the shareholder (primacy) model, the stakeholder model and the director primacy model. Importantly, the weighing mechanism of the relational approach is shown to be a theoretical representation of the nexus.

4. Key Field No 1: The application of the principal theories of the firm to the relational approach

4.1 PROBLEMS ARISING FROM THE SEPARATION OF OWNERSHIP FROM MANAGEMENT

This chapter examines Key Field No 1 – *the Application of the Principal Theories of the Firm to the Relational Approach.* More particularly, the chapter first examines the theoretical basis of the relational approach and, in particular, the governance theory or model underpinnings of the 'weighing mechanism' introduced in Chapters 1 and 2 comprising:

- the three relational axes of good governance;[1]
- the eight governance factors;[2] and
- the two interrelationship schemes.[3]

This chapter will demonstrate that the weighing mechanism or process constitutes the relational approach's *theoretical* representation of the nexus.

As part of the weighing of insider and outsider interests, the relational approach seeks to complement and add explanatory power to five of the existing principal 'law and economics' theories and models of the firm – the nexus of contracts, agency theory, the shareholder primacy model, the stakeholder model and the director primacy model. These principal theories and their interrelationship with the weighing mechanism of the three relational axes of good governance, the eight governance factors (that is, the eight recurring or underpinning aims or purposes which 'good governance' seeks to achieve drawn from the four Key Fields) and the two interrelationship schemes will thus be examined here.

---

1 See discussion in sections 2.3.1–2.3.3 above.
2 See the discussion in sections 2.6.1–2.6.8 above for eight governance factors.
3 See Figures 2.6 and 2.7 in Chapter 2.

Separation Theories and Agency Costs

As part of this purpose, this chapter examines the separation of ownership from management in the paradigm dispersed-shareholding public corporation and the consequent competing interests of inside and outside corporate actors as the basis of problems which give rise to agency costs.[4] These agency costs (which include monitoring costs[5]), in turn, call for the application of countervailing governance variables as incentive devices which monitor, limit and punish management misconduct.[6]

The relational approach does not intend to examine in detail all theories of the firm or the effects of the separation of ownership from management within those models. This has been done, and continues to be done, by other commentators.[7] Again, the five principal theories of the firm have been selected because they are the most examined or numerous in the SSRN collection of literature.

The second purpose of this chapter is to demonstrate that the relational approach adds explanatory power to the principal theories of the firm comprising Key Field No 1. This is achieved using both theoretical analysis and diagrammatic representation.

Thirdly, the chapter will demonstrate that the relational approach is aligned with the nexus of contracts theory in terms of seeking to avoid or minimise welfare or value-reducing charter (constitution) terms or management behaviour which – under that theory – in the long-term, is both inefficient and harmful to the survival or sustainability of the corporation.

Fourthly and critically, the relational approach considers arguments that maximising stakeholder interests is critical for the sustainability of

---

[4] Michael C Jensen and William H Meckling, 'Theory of the Firm: Managerial Behavior, Agency Costs and Ownership Structure' in Michael C Jensen, *A Theory of the Firm: Governance, Residual Claims and Organizational Forms*, Cambridge, MA: Harvard University Press, December 2000; (1976) 3(4) *Journal of Financial Economics*, accessed 3 March 2015 at SSRN: http://ssrn.com/abstract=94043, 5–6.

[5] Jensen and Meckling, ibid, 5–6.

[6] Ibid, 5.

[7] See, for example, Thomas Wuil Joo, 'Theories and Models of Corporate Governance' in H. Kent Baker, Ronald Anderson (eds), *Corporate Governance: A Synthesis Of Theory, Research, And Practice*, Hoboken, NJ: John Wiley & Sons, 2010; UC Davis Legal Studies Research Paper No 213, accessed 3 March 2015 at SSRN: http://ssrn.com/abstract=1543397 and Charles R T O'Kelley, 'Coase, Knight, and the Nexus-of-Contracts Theory of the Firm: A Reflection on Reification, Reality, and the Corporation as Entrepreneur Surrogate' (2011–2012) 35(4) *Seattle University Law Review* 1247–1270, (March 6, 2012), accessed 23 April 2015 at SSRN: http://ssrn.com/abstract=2017237.

the corporation. As part of this, the chapter examines problems arising from the identity and priority of stakeholder interests *inter se* and against the shareholder wealth-maximisation principle. The relational approach assists in answering some of these questions by applying its own overriding goal – to minimise long-term agency costs to facilitate continual survival of the firm.

4.2 THE NEXUS OF CONTRACTS FOUNDATIONS OF THE THREE RELATIONAL AXES OF GOOD GOVERNANCE AND GOVERNANCE FACTORS

Figure 4.1 is a diagram of the **Weighing Mechanism** of the relational approach. The relational approach hypothesises that this Weighing Mechanism is a *theoretical* representation of the voluntary contracts or obligations comprising the nexus of contracts theory. This theory characterises the corporation as an intersection of voluntary obligations (or contracts or relationships) between the various corporate actors, in particular outside shareholders *inter se* and between such shareholders and inside managers.[8]

The relational approach submits that, complementary to the nexus of contracts theory, the relational approach enhances the explanatory and predictive power of this theory by identifying and weighing the inter-relational themes (that is, the three relational axes of good governance and the eight governance factors) that underpin the voluntary obligations among corporate actors. These voluntary obligations are typified by the corporation's charter or constitution[9] as well as the 'off-the-rack' set of 'contractual' terms supplied by the 'default' rules of corporate law (such as the duties of directors) supplied by the legislature and the courts.[10]

---

[8] Frank H Easterbrook and Daniel R Fischel, 'The Corporate Contract' (1989) 89 *Colum L Rev* 1416, 1418 and 1428 and Stephen M Bainbridge, 'In Defense of the Shareholder Wealth Maximization Norm: A Reply to Professor Green' (1993) 50 *Washington & Lee Law Review* 1423, accessed 3 March 2015 at SSRN: http://ssrn.com/abstract=303780, 1426–7 (footnote omitted). See also Leo E Strine and Travis J Laster, 'The Siren Song of Unlimited Contractual Freedom', Harvard Law School John M. Olin Center Discussion Paper No. 789, (August 1, 2014) accessed 23 April 2015 at SSRN: http://ssrn.com/abstract=2481039.

[9] See Easterbrook and Fischel, ibid.

[10] This term is used by Easterbrook and Fischel, above n 8, 1444. These sources of the 'default' rules are considered by C A Riley, 'Contracting Out of Company

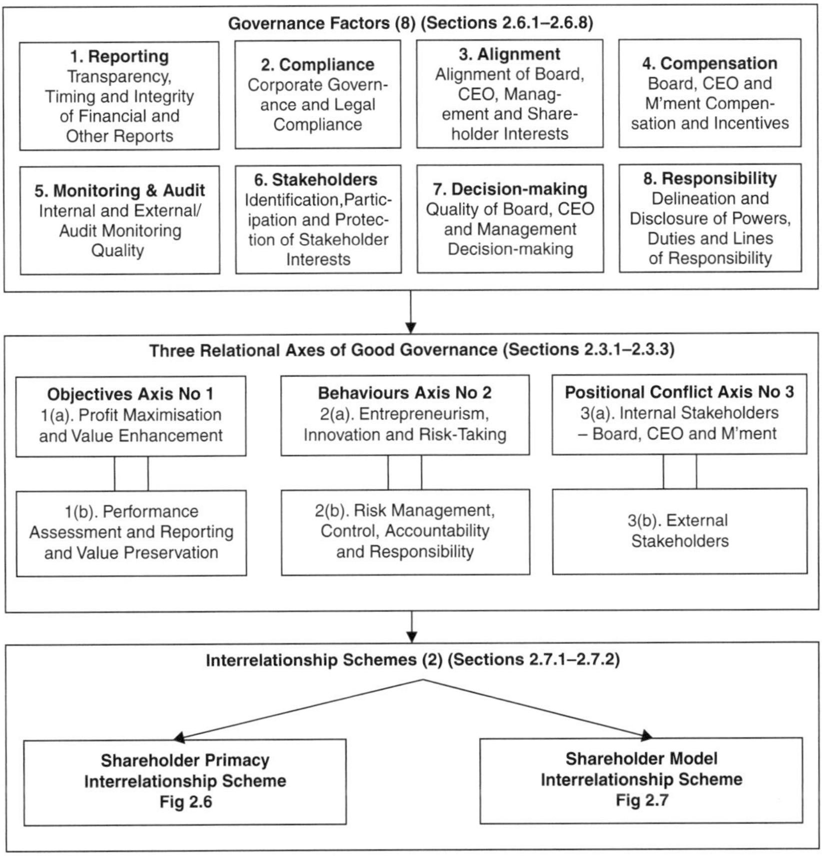

Figure 4.1 Weighing Mechanism of the relational approach

4.2.1 'Neoclassical' Model Shortcomings are Unsuitable for the Relational Approach

Hart explains that the 'neoclassical' model treats a firm as comprising:

> . . . a set of feasible production plans. A manager presides over this production set, buying and selling inputs and outputs in a spot market and choosing the plan that maximizes owners' welfare. Welfare is usually represented by profit, or, if profit is uncertain so that profit-maximization is not well defined, by

---

Law: Section 459 of the Companies Act 1985 and the Role of the Courts' (1992) 55 *Modern L Rev* 782, 787.

expected net present value of future profit (possibly discounted for risk) or by market value.[11]

However, the neoclassical model is of limited utility to the relational approach. Hart explains that the neoclassical model cannot resolve issues of competing interests among corporate actors, that is, that it does not address issues of structure – the size, extent or boundaries of the firm – nor how conflicts of interest between suppliers of equity, management and employees are resolved.[12] Important in this respect is the relational approach's purpose – to weigh the competing interests of corporate actors to achieve long-term efficiency and/or survival or sustainability of the corporation.

4.2.2 Relational Approach is Aligned with Nexus of Contracts Theory

Bainbridge's explanation of the nexus of contracts theory emphasised it as 'a legal fiction representing the complex set of contractual relationships between' input providers such as employees, creditors, shareholders and management.[13] The market for corporate control acts together with the nexus of contracts to punish management misconduct which reduces firm value. The market for corporate control itself assumes that markets are efficient and that the share price reflects all public information relating to the firm. Management misconduct[14] causes the share price to fall. At this time, the theory posits, an external hostile takeover will be launched which will remove the incumbent management. In practice, asymmetric information problems reduce the effectiveness of this mechanism.

---

[11] O Hart, 'An Economist's Perspective on the Theory of the Firm' (1989) 89 *Colum L Rev* 1757, 1758 (footnote omitted).

[12] Hart, ibid, 1758. See also Riley, above n 10, 783 and William W Bratton, 'The "Nexus of Contracts" Corporation: A Critical Appraisal' (1989) 74 *Cornell L Rev* 407, 407 and 413.

[13] Bainbridge, 'In Defense of the Shareholder Wealth Maximization Norm: A Reply to Professor Green', above n 8, 1426–7 (footnote omitted).

[14] Opportunistic behaviour arises due to information asymmetry problems. For example, Ashbaugh-Skaife, Collins and LaFond explain the managerial misbehaviour problems associated with separation of ownership from management in terms of 'information asymmetry' that creates 'agency risk' for shareholders. See Hollis Ashbaugh-Skaife, Daniel W Collins and Ryan LaFond, 'Corporate Governance and the Cost of Equity Capital' (December 2004), accessed 3 March 2015 at SSRN: http://ssrn.com/abstract=639681, 1.

The combined effect of the efficient market hypothesis and 'reputational constraints'

As introduced above, the market for corporate control is a component of the efficient market hypothesis to discipline insider-managers that engage in value or performance-reducing behaviour. As a theme already introduced above, an underpinning assumption of the efficient market hypothesis is that a corporation's value is accurately reflected in the stock price[15] with low stock prices reflecting underperforming stock (and management) thus inviting hostile takeover.[16] As Zeitoun and Osterloh explain, this use of hostile takeovers gives management an incentive to act in favour of outside shareholders lest the management be replaced when the stock price falls.[17]

While the efficient market hypothesis assumes that share prices reflect all publicly available information relating to the firm (or perfect knowledge), it is not, however, without difficulties. Dent describes two important problems that arise in reality. The first is an 'information problem' which casts doubt on the accuracy of all information released to the market and, compounding this, the problem that:

> [e]ven if public information is accurate, investors have limited capacity to process it. Investors act with bounded rationality; that is, they expend resources to analyze information only to the point where it seems that the profits from analysis exceed the costs.[18]

Thus, Dent argues, companies tend to have corporate governance arrangements (such as constitutions) that are 'familiar to institutional investors,

---

15 Lawrence A Cunningham, 'Behavioral Finance and Investor Governance' (2002) 59 *Washington & Lee Law Review* 767, accessed 3 March 2015 at SSRN: http://ssrn.com/abstract=255778, 3. The author cites Donald C Langevoort, 'Theories, Assumptions and Securities Regulation: Market Efficiency Revisited' (1992) 140 *U Pa L Rev* 85.

16 Cunningham, ibid.

17 Hossam Zeitoun and Margit Osterloh, 'Firm Governance and the Role of Top Management', working paper, University of Zurich-Institute for Organization and Administrative Science, Zurich, 23 April 2008, 4. The authors cite H G Manne, 'Mergers and the Market for Corporate-Control' (1965) 73(2) *Journal of Political Economy*, 110–20 and Michael C Jensen and R S Ruback, 'The Market for Corporate-Control – the Scientific Evidence' (1983) 11(1–4) *Journal of Financial Economics* 5–50.

18 George W Dent, 'Academics in Wonderland: The Team Production and Director Primacy Models of Corporate Governance', Case Legal Studies Research Paper No 07-21 (June 2007), accessed 3 March 2015 at SSRN: http://ssrn.com/abstract=995186, 18–19 of 72 (footnote omitted).

that facilitate[d] pricing relative to other companies, that [are] backed by a developed body of precedents and judges familiar with the arrangement' with little variance. This flows from the fact that market participants have considerable reliance on ratings agencies and advisors to assess corporate governance arrangements.[19]

The second problem identified by Dent is that 'markets take time' – that '[t]he investor's difficulty escalates when the correction of the mispricing of a stock may take a long time'.[20]

Putting these problems aside, Cunningham also notes that the efficient market hypothesis is assisted by other governance measures. In particular, Cunningham identifies reputational constraints (and consequences) relating to individual managers as significant.[21] Indeed, the reputational constraints on outside directors are emphasised by Fama and Jensen as an important aspect of the recommended division between 'decision management' and 'decision control' discussed below.[22]

To this end, the relational approach includes the individual Governance Variables of **[ReputDiscl] (+)**[23] (Reputational Constraints – 'Disclosure Standards', +100.00 *rprox*) and **[ReputRep] (+)**[24] (Reputational Constraints – 'Transparent Reporting', +100.00 *rprox*). These governance variables divide the reputational constraints concept into constituent components that reflect Singh's proposition[25] that the reputational constraints aspect of the market for corporate control in turn depends on two elements – 'disclosure standards' and 'transparent reporting'.

---

19 Ibid, 19 of 72 (footnotes omitted). For a discussion of the role of ratings agencies and other financial market intermediaries in the Enron corporate collapse, see section 5.2.4.3.2 below.

20 Ibid, 19 of 72.

21 Cunningham, above n 15, 3.

22 Eugene F Fama and Michael C Jensen, 'Separation of Ownership and Control' in Michael C Jensen, *Foundations of Organizational Strategy*, Cambridge, MA: Harvard University Press, 1998 and (1983) 26 *Journal of Law and Economics* 301–26, accessed 3 March 2015 at SSRN: http://ssrn.com/abstract=94034, 19. See discussion in section 4.2.3.2 below.

23 See discussion in section 10.4.1 below.

24 Ibid.

25 Ravi Singh, 'Board Independence and the Design of Executive Compensation', EFA 2005 Moscow Meetings Paper; Harvard NOM Working Paper No 673741 (September 2006), accessed 3 March 2015 at SSRN: http://ssrn.com/abstract=673741, 1.

4.2.2.1 Market for corporate control reflected in governance factors and governance variables

Thus, to reflect an important condition of the operation of nexus theory, the relational approach reproduces as governance factors and governance variables individual components of the market for corporate control.

For example, governance factors such as Reporting Factor No 1, Compliance Factor No 2, Alignment Factor No 3, Monitoring & Audit Factor No 5 and Responsibility Factor No 8 assist in maintaining the functioning of the market for corporate control by reducing information asymmetry.

In the case of the 39 governance variables examined in this relational approach, the market for corporate control is represented by governance variables also seeking to reduce information asymmetry. For example, the variables **[NationGov] (+)**,[26] **[ReputDiscl] (+)**,[27] **[ReputRep] (+)**[28] and **[TransTimeMon] (+)**[29] together account for all of the four variables accorded the highest positive Coverage/Rating of +8/+100.00 *rprox*.

In addition, the information asymmetry-countervailing governance variables of **[AudIndFreq] (+)**,[30] **[AudIndMon] (+)**,[31] **[BrdAttend] (+)**,[32] **[BrdIndMon] (+)**[33] and **[ExtAudEarn] (+)**[34] account for five out of a total of ten governance variables accorded the next highest positive Coverage/Rating of +7/+87.50 *rprox*.

On the negative side, the market for corporate control may also be adversely affected by governance variables such as **[StagBrdElect] (−)**[35] and

---

[26] National Governance/Shareholder Protection Regime – see discussion in section 7.3.1.3.2 below.

[27] Reputational Constraints – 'Disclosure Standards' – see discussion in section 10.4.1 below.

[28] Reputational Constraints – 'Transparent Reporting' – see discussion in section 10.4.1 below.

[29] Transparency and Timing of Reporting – Monitoring Effect – see discussion in section 9.1.2.1 below.

[30] Audit Committee – Independence in Combination with Frequency of Meeting – Reduction in Earnings Manipulation Effect – see discussion in section 9.2.1 below.

[31] Audit Committee – Independence – Monitoring Effect – see discussion in section 8.4.3 below.

[32] Board – Attendance Level (High) – see discussion in section 7.3.2.1.2 below.

[33] Board Independent Director: Executive Director Proportion – Monitoring Effect – see discussion in sections 7.3.2.1.1–7.3.2.1.2 below.

[34] External/Independent Audit Function – see discussion in section 9.2.3.3 below.

[35] Staggered Board Elections – see discussion in section 8.3.1.1 below.

[Other ATMs] (−)[36] each of which has a Coverage/Rating of −8/−100.00 *rprox*.

The significance of the positive +100.00 *rprox* scores is that insider actions which reduce or adversely affect the transparency and timing of information (**[TransTimeMon] (+)**) or the effectiveness of the management-disciplining mechanism of the market for corporate control will significantly increase agency costs and significantly reduce the long-term efficiency and sustainability of the for-profit corporation.

Also, taking the negative −100.00 *rprox* scores of the **[StagBrdElect] (−)** and **[OtherATMs] (−)** governance variables, insider actions which again reduce the effectiveness of the market for corporate control – such as staggered board elections and other anti-takeover mechanisms – will again significantly increase these agency costs and significantly reduce such efficiency and sustainability of the corporation.

In summary, the interests of (inside) management *vis-à-vis* (outside) shareholders and the discouragement of management misconduct are two underpinning themes of the nexus of contracts. As explained further below, these themes are reflected in the design of the three relational axes of good governance, the governance factors and, consequently, the interrelationship schemes.[37] Thus, the relational approach is aligned with the nexus of contracts theory in terms of seeking to avoid or diminish value-reducing behaviour which, in the long-term, is both inefficient and harmful to the survival or sustainability of the firm.

4.2.3 The Components of the Relational Approach and Agency Costs

In order to assist regulators, policy-makers, law reformers and corporate actors, the relational approach's governance variables are aligned with, and complementary to, agency theory. Jensen and Meckling suggest that the bestowal of discretion in insiders may prompt managerial misconduct (again, such as shirking, empire-building, overcompensation and perquisites) giving rise to agency costs[38] (which include monitoring costs[39]) that reduce the economic welfare of the outsiders and are reflected in the market price of shares.[40]

---

[36] Other Anti-Takeover Mechanisms (excludes staggered board elections) – see discussion in section 8.3.1.1 below.

[37] See Figures 2.6 and 2.7 in chapter 2.

[38] Jensen and Meckling, above n 4, 5–6.

[39] Ibid.

[40] Ibid, 11. For further discussion of agency costs, see Mark J Roe, 'The Institutions of Corporate Governance', Harvard Law and Economics Discussion

In the relational approach, the various structures, mechanisms, processes and protocols – that is, the governance variables themselves – must be utilised to discipline managers or to align their interests with those of outsiders.[41] Thus, governance variables such as **[AudCom] (+)**[42] (Audit Committee – Presence, Operation and Frequency, +75.00 *rprox*), **[BrdAttend] (+)**[43] (Board – Attendance Level (High), +87.50 *rprox*), **[BrdIndMon] (+)**[44] (Board Independent Director: Executive Director Proportion – Monitoring Effect, +87.50 *rprox*), **[CompCom] (+/−)**[45] (Compensation Committee – Presence, Operation and Frequency, +/− 87.50 *rprox*), **[ExtAudEarn] (+)**[46] (External/Independent Audit Function, +87.50 *rprox*) and **[TransTimeMon] (+)**[47] (Transparency and Timing of Reporting – Monitoring Effect, +100.00 *rprox*) in theory go toward reducing such monitoring costs.

Significantly for the design of the relational approach, the agency cost relationship between 'insider-managers' and 'outsider-shareholders' underpins the nexus model. To align the relational approach in this respect, components of the approach – in particular, the governance factors – are similarly underpinned by the agency costs concept. It is to these components that this chapter now turns.

4.2.3.1 Governance factors and interrelationship schemes are based on agency costs theory

General agency costs theory The purpose of the relational approach is to make hypotheses in relation to the relative importance of governance variables in affecting (positively or negatively) agency costs. This chapter has also explained that the three relational axes of good governance, the weighing of the governance factors and the interrelationship schemes are a theoretical representation of the intersection of the voluntary obligations comprising the nexus of contracts. Thus, putting these two notions together here, the chapter demonstrates that the governance factors are based on – and further explain – the agency costs theory and its associated

---

Paper No 488 (August 2004) (Revised 17 March 2008), accessed 3 March 2015 at SSRN: http://ssrn.com/abstract=612362, 3–4.

41 Jensen and Meckling, above n 4, 5.

42 See discussion in section 8.4.2 below.

43 See discussion in section 7.3.2.1.2 below.

44 See discussion in sections 7.3.2.1.1–7.3.2.1.2 below.

45 See discussion in section 10.2.4.1 below.

46 See discussion in section 9.2.3.3 below.

47 See discussion in section 9.1.2.1 below.

classification of those costs. Thus, too, the interrelationship schemes which depict the interrelationships between the governance factors[48] are based on agency costs theory.

According to Jensen and Meckling, the agency costs of the nexus or set of contracts or relationships comprising the corporation include monitoring costs on behalf of the shareholder:[49]

> [i]f both parties to the relationship are utility maximizers, there is good reason to believe that the agent will not always act in the best interests of the principal. The *principal* can limit divergences from his interest by establishing appropriate incentives for the agent and by incurring monitoring costs designed to limit the aberrant activities of the agent.[50]

Indeed, for Hermalin and Weisbach, governance mechanisms – in the terminology of the relational approach, the governance variables – 'are simply restrictions on these contracts imposed by an outside authority'.[51]

Monitoring costs require countervailing governance variables For example, the need (or cause) for such monitoring costs and, therefore, countervailing governance variables such as **[AudCom] (+)**,[52] **[BrdAttend] (+)**,[53] **[BrdIndMon] (+)**,[54] **[CompCom] (+/−)**,[55] **[ExtAudEarn] (+)**[56] and **[TransTimeMon] (+)**[57] is explained in more detail by Evans and Evans who point to the dispersed nature of shareholdings and informational imbalance between principal and agent.[58]

---

48 As demonstrated in Chapter 2, the Interrelationship Schemes in Figures 2.6 and 2.7 are a composite of the individual relationships between governance factors analysed in sections 2.6.1–2.6.8 above.

49 Jensen and Meckling, above n 4, 5–6.

50 Ibid, 5 (emphasis in original).

51 Benjamin E Hermalin and Michael S Weisbach, 'A Framework for Assessing Corporate Governance Reform' (6 February 2006), accessed 3 March 2015 at SSRN: http://ssrn.com/abstract=881581, 1.

52 Audit Committee – Presence, Operation and Frequency, +75.00 *rprox* – see section 8.4.2 below.

53 Board – Attendance Level (High), +87.50 *rprox*, – see section 7.3.2.1.2 below.

54 Board Independent: Executive Director Proportion – Monitoring Effect, +87.50 *rprox* – see sections 7.3.2.1.1–7.3.2.1.2 below.

55 Compensation Committee – Presence, Operation and Frequency, +/− 87.50 *rprox* – see section 10.2.4.1 below.

56 External/Independent Audit Function, +87.50 *rprox* – see section 9.2.3.3 below.

57 Transparency and Timing of Reporting – Monitoring Effect, +100.00 *rprox* – see section 9.1.2.1 below.

58 Robert T Evans and John P Evans, 'The Influence of Non-Executive Director Control and Rewards on CEO Remuneration: Australian Evidence',

Immediately, then, the effect of this monitoring costs concept in terms of the relational approach can be seen as giving rise to more than half the governance factors – Reporting Factor No 1, Compliance Factor No 2, Alignment Factor No 3, Monitoring & Audit Factor No 5 and Responsibility Factor No 8.[59] Important, too, in the above description of managerial misbehaviour is the pursuit by management of 'perks' and over-compensation. This is specifically addressed in the relational approach by Compensation Factor No 4 and Alignment Factor No 3.[60]

Other agency costs include 'bonding' costs and 'residual' losses Other agency costs include costs incurred by the agent for bonding with the principal (bonding costs[61]) and any loss (residual loss) arising where the (agent) manager fails to act in the shareholder's wealth-maximising interests[62] (for example, a takeover bid at an overvaluation or the sale of a business asset of the corporation at an undervaluation).

For Jensen and Meckling, monitoring, bonding and residual costs together help to explain the market price of shares.[63] As the shareholdings of the company become more diffused (that is, the shareholdings of the original or founding manager-shareholders dilute with the result that 'residual claims' of these manager-shareholders decrease), the gap between the interests of outside shareholders and inside managers increases as the manager-shareholders seek additional perquisites in turn causing monitoring (and consequential agency) costs to increase.[64]

4.2.3.2 'Decision management' and 'decision control' dichotomy reflected in governance factors

Thus, for Fama and Jensen, the separation (and dispersed nature) of the residual claimants from the decision-making management gives rise to a decision-making structure which, *to be effective and reduce agency costs,*

EFMA 2002 London Meetings, accessed 3 March 2015 at SSRN: http://ssrn.com/abstract=263050, 3–4.

59 The governance factors are constructed in sections 2.6.1–2.6.8 below.

60 Ibid.

61 Jensen and Meckling, above n 4, 5.

62 Ibid, 5–6. For a discussion of the merits and problems of the concept of shareholder wealth-maximisation, see Petra Joerg, Claudio F Loderer, Lukas Roth and Urs Waelchli, 'Shareholder Value: Principles, Declarations, and Actions', ECGI – Finance Working Paper No 95/2005 (5 August 2008), accessed 3 March 2015 at SSRN: http://ssrn.com/abstract=1099936.

63 Jensen and Meckling, above n 4, 11. For further discussion of agency costs, see Roe, above n 40, 3–4.

64 Jensen and Meckling, above n 4, 11–12.

typically divides decision 'initiation' and 'implementation' ('decision management') from 'ratification' and 'monitoring' ('decision control'),[65] the latter function being undertaken on behalf of shareholders by a board of directors.[66] This critical 'decision control' function of the board – and its significance for the governance factors – is taken up below in discussing the director primacy model.[67]

For present purposes, this chapter notes here that the constituent components of Fama and Jensen's dichotomy between 'decision management' and 'decision control' are reflected in a number of the governance factors. Primarily, Responsibility Factor No 8[68] is a reflection of this recommended division. Other governance factors illustrating the division of functions include Decision-making Factor No 7 and Monitoring & Audit Factor No 5.[69]

4.2.4 Director Primacy Model Reflected in the Governance Factors

The director primacy model places the board at the *precise* nexus of the various voluntary obligations or relationships representing the corporation.[70] Bainbridge states that (unavoidable) agency costs are 'the *inevitable* consequence of vesting discretion in someone other than the residual claimant'.[71] In this way, Bainbridge explains that the benefits of discretion

---

65 Fama and Jensen, above n 22, 4–5 and 9.

66 Ibid, 14 and 16.

67 Stephen M Bainbridge, 'The Board of Directors as Nexus of Contracts: A Critique of Gulati, Klein & Zolt's "Connected Contracts" Model', UCLA, School of Law Research Paper No 02-05 (January 2002), accessed 3 March 2015 at SSRN: http://ssrn.com/abstract=299743, 27; Stephen M Bainbridge, 'Director Primacy: The Means and Ends of Corporate Governance', UCLA, School of Law Research Paper No 02-06 (February 2002), accessed 3 March 2015 at SSRN: http://ssrn.com/abstract=300860, 8 and 17 and Stephen M Bainbridge, 'The Geography of Revlon-Land' (2013) 81 *Fordham Law Review*, Forthcoming; UCLA School of Law, Law-Econ Research Paper No 12-13 (July 23, 2012), accessed 3 March 2015 at SSRN: http://ssrn.com/abstract=2115769.

68 The governance factors are constructed in sections 2.6.1–2.6.8 above.

69 Ibid.

70 Bainbridge, 'The Board of Directors as Nexus of Contracts: A Critique of Gulati, Klein & Zolt's "Connected Contracts" Model', above n 67, 27. See also Bainbridge, 'Director Primacy: The Means and Ends of Corporate Governance', above n 67, 8 and 17 and Stephen M Bainbridge, 'Preserving Director Primacy by Managing Shareholder Interventions', *Research Handbook on Shareholder Power and Activism*, Forthcoming; UCLA School of Law, Law-Econ. Research Paper No. 13-09 (August 27, 2013), accessed 24 April 2015 at SSRN: http://ssrn.com/abstract=2298415.

71 Bainbridge, 'The Board of Directors as Nexus of Contracts: A Critique of Gulati, Klein & Zolt's "Connected Contracts" Model', above n 67, 34

must be balanced with accountability in the exercise of that discretion.[72] In terms of the relational approach's own three relational axes of good governance – Behaviours Axis No 2(a) and 2(b)[73] – 'entrepreneurism' and 'innovation' (risk-taking) is balanced against risk management, 'control' and 'accountability' (responsibility).

How then is this balance achieved? For Bainbridge, it is through the *board itself*. The author sees the board as an 'institutional restraint on agency costs' which it achieves by establishing a monitoring structure throughout each level of the company with itself at the top and with a 'multi-membership' of directors which is 'inherently harder for misbehaving subordinates to suborn than would be a single autocrat'.[74]

4.2.4.1 Board-dependent variables have a high governance factor coverage and relational proximity rating

Adopting Bainbridge's model, the relational approach displays a significant Board-Governance Factor relationship structure that also flows through to the relevant governance variables. Thus, board-dependent or board-influenced governance variables will have a *relatively* high governance variable coverage[75] and relational proximity rating in the Relational Proximity Table[76] in comparison to other governance variables. Thus, board-dependent governance variables with a *positive* effect on reducing agency costs will have a (relatively) high relational proximity.

(emphasis added). The phenomenon of discretion being vested in the agent arises due to the problem of 'incomplete contracts' – see Maria Maher and Thomas Andersson, 'Corporate Governance: Effects on Firm Performance and Economic Growth' (February 2000), accessed 3 March 2015 at SSRN: http://ssrn.com/abstract=218490, 3.

[72] Bainbridge, 'The Board of Directors as Nexus of Contracts: A Critique of Gulati, Klein & Zolt's "Connected Contracts" Model', above n 67, 34.

[73] See discussion in sections 2.3.1–2.3.3 above.

[74] Bainbridge, 'The Board of Directors as Nexus of Contracts: A Critique of Gulati, Klein & Zolt's "Connected Contracts" Model', above n 67, 31. See also Bainbridge, 'Director Primacy: The Means and Ends of Corporate Governance', above n 67, 25–8.

For the discussion of a suggestion that, instead of natural persons, board services could be performed by partnerships, corporations and other firms, see Stephen M Bainbridge and M Todd Henderson, 'Boards-R-Us: Reconceptualizing Corporate Boards', University of Chicago Coase-Sandor Institute for Law & Economics Research Paper No. 646; UCLA School of Law, Law-Econ Research Paper No. 13-11, (July 10, 2013), accessed 24 April 2015 at SSRN: http://ssrn.com/abstract=2291065.

[75] See the full Coverage Table (Table 3.1) in section 3.3.1 above.

[76] See the full Relational Proximity Table (Table 3.2) in section 3.3.2.1 above.

For example, the **[AudCom] (+)**,[77] **[AudAccEarn] (+)**[78] and the **[AudExpAcc] (+)**[79] variables all have a relational proximity of +75.00 *rprox*. These comprise three out of the four variables with this rating. Further, director-related variables such as **[AudIndFreq] (+)**,[80] **[AudIndMon] (+)**,[81] **[BrdAttend] (+)**,[82] **[BrdIndMon] (+)**,[83] **[BrdReview] (+)**,[84] **[BrdSkills] (+)**,[85] **[NomInd] (+)**[86] and **[EqOptIncent] (+)**[87] have a relational proximity of +87.50 *rprox*. These comprise eight out of the ten variables with this rating.

Not surprisingly on the negative side, the board-dependent governance variable of **[StagBrdElect] (−)**[88] is one of the two governance variables with the highest *negative* coverage/rating of −8/−100.00 *rprox* while **[AudShortOpts] (−)**,[89] **[EqOptEntrch] (−)**[90] and **[ShortTOpts] (−)**[91] comprise three out of the six governance variables with the next-highest negative coverage/rating of −7/−87.50 *rprox*.

---

[77] Audit Committee – Presence, Operation and Frequency – see discussion in section 8.4.2 below.

[78] Audit Committee – Accounting Expertise – Earnings Manipulation Reduction Effect – see discussion in section 9.2.1.1.2 below.

[79] Audit Committee – Financial Expertise (Accounting) – see discussion in section 8.4.4 below.

[80] Audit Committee – Independence in Combination with Frequency of Meeting – Reduction in Earnings Manipulation Effect – see discussion in section 9.2.1 below.

[81] Audit Committee – Independence – Monitoring Effect – see discussion in section 8.4.3 below.

[82] Board – Attendance Level (High) – see discussion in section 7.3.2.1.2 below.

[83] Board Independent Director: Executive Director Proportion – Monitoring Effect – see discussion in sections 7.3.2.1.1–7.3.2.1.2 below.

[84] Board – Annual Review – see discussion in section 7.3.2.1.2 below.

[85] Board – Director Skills 'Mix' – see discussion in section 7.3.1.2.1 below.

[86] Nominating Committee – Independence Proportion – see discussion in section 7.3.1.2.2 below.

[87] Equity/Option Plans and Holdings of Directors/Executives – Incentive/'Alignment' Effect (excludes short-term options) – see discussion in section 10.2.4 below.

[88] Staggered Board Elections – see discussion in section 8.3.1.1 below.

[89] Audit Committee – Short Term Options Granted to Outside Directors – Reduction in Monitoring Effect – see discussion in section 10.2.5.1 below.

[90] Equity/Option Plans and Holdings of Directors/Executives – 'Entrenchment' Effect (excludes short-term options) – see discussion in section 10.2.4 below.

[91] Short-Term Option Holdings/Plans of Directors and Executives – see discussion in section 10.2.5.1 below.

4.3 APPLICATION OF THE SHAREHOLDER PRIMACY AND STAKEHOLDER MODELS TO THE RELATIONAL APPROACH

4.3.1 The Relational Approach and the Shareholder Primacy Model

Agency costs theory and the shareholder model are not co-extensive. While often combined in the same breath, the former is much broader and, as Jensen and Meckling describe, arises in any situation where discretion is vested in an agent to maximise the welfare of a principal.[92] Similarly, the shareholder model, while incorporating an agency theory component, looks beyond agency costs. In this section, we are *not* concerned with the entirety of the shareholder model. Instead, this chapter is concerned to identify the *distinguishing feature* of the shareholder model which gives rise to governance (and equally, in this case, agency theory) considerations – that the outside shareholders are the *only* residual claimants and that inside managers must act to maximise the welfare of those outside shareholders.[93]

4.3.2 Shareholder Primacy – The Precedence of the Shareholders' Residual Claims are Reflected in the Governance Factors

Jensen and Meckling consider that the corporation is, in addition to a nexus of contracts, also comprised of the shareholders' 'divisible residual claims on the assets and cash flows of the organization'.[94] In the shareholder primacy model of corporate governance, the shareholders are the only residual claimants.[95] Then, at this point, the shareholder

---

[92] Jensen and Meckling, above n 4, 6–7.

[93] For a discussion of the 'balance of power' between shareholders and management, see Jennifer G Hill, 'The Shifting Balance of Power between Shareholders and the Board: News Corp's Exodus to Delaware and Other Antipodean Tales' (January 2008), Sydney Law School Research Paper No 08/20, accessed 3 March 2015 at SSRN: http://ssrn.com/abstract=1086477. For a discussion of two different models of shareholder primacy, see David Millon, 'Radical Shareholder Primacy' (2014) 10(4) *University of St. Thomas Law Journal* 1013; Washington & Lee Legal Studies Paper No. 2014-17, (July 28, 2014) accessed 23 April 2015 at SSRN: http://ssrn.com/abstract=2473189.

[94] Jensen and Meckling, above n 4, 8–9. See discussion in section 1.2.2 above.

[95] Gerard J Charreaux, 'Corporate Governance Theories: From Micro Theories to National Systems Theories' (January 2004), Universite de Bourgogne Fargo Working Paper No 1040101, accessed 3 March 2015 at SSRN: http://ssrn.com/abstract=486522, 8 and Amir N Licht, 'The Maximands

wealth-maximisation principle aligns[96] the interests of shareholders and managers as follows in the next section.

4.3.2.1 The 'default standard' of the shareholder wealth-maximisation principle

In this respect, Rhee explains the (well-known) purpose of the shareholder wealth-maximisation principal *in terms of agency theory and the nexus of contracts*. The principle acts as a 'default standard' that supplies the necessary rule governing the agent's behaviour in the 'contract' between shareholders and managers.[97]

The relational approach – through its alignment with the nexus of contracts and agency theories – is able to similarly adopt the operation of this default rule concept of shareholder primacy when (of course) in the relevant shareholder primacy mode.[98]

4.4 THE INFLUENCE OF STAKEHOLDER THEORY IN THE RELATIONAL APPROACH

The stakeholder model posits that the shareholders are not the only residual claimants of the corporation. Thus, the stakeholder model argues, the management of a corporation should, in performing its duties, take into account the interests of others affected by the corporation's actions. In this way, this Chapter will now go on to examine the stakeholder model as an additional and significant influence on the three relational axes of good governance and, in particular, limb 3(b) of Positional Conflict Axis No 3.[99] Of course, the stakeholder model's influence is also reflected in Stakeholders Factor No 6 – *Identification, Participation and Protection of Stakeholder Interests*.

The next section begins by identifying perceived problems with the shareholder primacy model to highlight arguments by commentators that

---

of Corporate Governance: A Theory of Values and Cognitive Style' (November 2003), ECGI – Law Working Paper No 16/2003, available at SSRN: http://ssrn.com/abstract=469801 and (2004) 29(3) *Delaware Journal of Corporate Law* 649–746, accessed 3 March 2015 at SSRN: http://ssrn.com/abstract=764025, 4.

96 See discussion in section 1.2.3 above.

97 Robert J Rhee, 'Corporate Ethics, Agency, and the Theory of the Firm' (2008) 3(2) *Journal of Business & Technology Law* 1101, accessed 3 March 2015 at SSRN: http://ssrn.com/abstract=1083478, 1109–10.

98 See discussion in section 4.4.1.2 below.

99 See Figure 2.3 in Chapter 2.

satisfying a wide range of stakeholder needs is – consistent with the relational approach's over-arching purpose – *necessary* to enhance the long-term survival or sustainability of the for-profit corporation.

4.4.1 Shortcomings of the Shareholder Primacy Model

Perceived shortcomings in the shareholder primacy model form the basis of its main rival, the stakeholder model.[100] While a detailed criticism of the shareholder primacy model is beyond the scope of this book, Licht explains that the shareholder model's assumption of a single residual claimant (that is, the shareholder) is flawed and 'unrealistic'.[101]

Accordingly, Jensen explains that the stakeholder model requires 'that managers should make decisions that take account of the interests of *all* the stakeholders in a firm'.[102] In terms of the composition of limb 3(b) of Positional Conflict Axis No 3,[103] Maher and Andersson note that:

> [o]ther stakeholders may include contractual partners such as employees, suppliers, customers, creditors, and social constituents such as members of the community in which the firm is located, environmental interests, local and national governments, and society at large.[104]

---

[100] See, for example, Alberto Chilosi and Mirella Damiani, 'Stakeholders vs. Shareholders in Corporate Governance' (20 March 2007), accessed 3 March 2015 at SSRN: http://ssrn.com/abstract=975293 and Dan Awrey, William Blair and David Kershaw, 'Between Law and Markets: Is There a Role for Culture and Ethics in Financial Regulation?', LSE Legal Studies Working Paper No 14/2012 (5 October 2012), accessed 3 March 2015 at SSRN: http://ssrn.com/abstract=2157588.

[101] Amir N Licht, 'The Maximands of Corporate Governance: A Theory of Values and Cognitive Style', above n 95, 4.

[102] Michael C Jensen, 'Value Maximization, Stakeholder Theory, and the Corporate Objective Function', in J. Andriof, *et al* (eds), *Unfolding Stakeholder Thinking*, Sheffield: Greenleaf Publishing, 2002. Also published in (2001) 14(3) *Journal of Applied Corporate Finance* 8–21; (2001) 7 *European Financial Management* 297–317 and in M. Beer and N. Norhia (eds), *Breaking the Code of Change*, Cambridge, MA: Harvard Business Press, 2000 (October 2001), accessed 3 March 2015 at SSRN: http://ssrn.com/abstract=220671, 8 (emphasis in original).

[103] See Figure 2.3 in Chapter 2.

[104] Maher and Andersson, 'Corporate Governance: Effects on Firm Performance and Economic Growth', above n 71, 5. See also Corporations and Markets Advisory Committee, *The Social Responsibility of Corporations, Report*, December 2006, Australian Government, Sydney, accessed 3 March 2015 at http://www.camac.gov.au ('CAMAC Social Responsibility Report').

Thus, a wide net of stakeholder interests[105] are envisaged by the stakeholder model. But how does the stakeholder model enhance the long-term efficiency and survival of the firm?

4.4.1.1 Arguments that maximising stakeholder interests is critical for the sustainability of the corporation

In this section, the relational approach considers arguments that the maximisation of stakeholder interests within the rubric of the stakeholder model is *necessary* to achieve the long-term sustainability of the for-profit firm. As this outcome is parallel or co-extensive with the over-arching purpose of the relational approach, then *one* implication of these arguments is that the stakeholder model's additional underpinning influence on Positional Conflict Axis No 3 and Stakeholders Factor No 6 *should* be significant. And this should be irrespective of the current status of the shareholder primacy principle.

In the stakeholder model, the necessity for the recognition and the taking into account by management of stakeholder interests (for example, by consultation and participation) is not merely an ethical or moral call. Instead, according to Licht, and important for the foundations of Positional Conflict Axis No 3 and Stakeholders Factor No 6, the *continual* balancing or 'maximisation' of these various interests is critical to the future sustainability of the firm.[106] Bainbridge, too, while a strong advocate of the shareholder model, impliedly acknowledges this argument.[107]

While a detailed examination of the principles of corporate social responsibility or CSR is beyond the scope of this book, the CAMAC Social Responsibility Report describes the 'compliance', 'philanthropic' and 'business' approaches 'each being directly or indirectly linked to corporate benefit (which includes avoidance of detriment)'.[108] In addition, the CAMAC Social Responsibility Report describes two further approaches – 'social primacy' and 'social obligation' – that 'are not

---

[105] For a discussion of a model or approach to create or increase 'stakeholder value' and the governance mechanisms in dealings with various stakeholders, see Gerard J Charreaux and Philippe Desbrieres, 'Corporate Governance: Stakeholder Value versus Shareholder Value' (1998) 1(2) *Revue Finance Contrôle Stratégie* 57–88 (June 1998), accessed 3 March 2015 at SSRN: http://ssrn.com/abstract=262902.

[106] Licht, 'The Maximands of Corporate Governance: A Theory of Values and Cognitive Style', above n 95, 4–5.

[107] Bainbridge, 'In Defense of the Shareholder Wealth Maximization Norm', above n 8, 1443 (footnote omitted). See also Bainbridge, 'Director Primacy: The Means and Ends of Corporate Governance', above n 67, 52.

[108] CAMAC Social Responsibility Report, above n 104, p 34.

necessarily linked to corporate benefit'.[109] In the case of the 'business' approach, CAMAC explains that compliance with 'environmental and other societal laws' is justified on the grounds of the long-term value of the corporation.[110]

Immediately, it is observed that enhancing firm value and risk management are aspects of Objectives Axis limb 1(a) and Behaviours Axis limb 2(b) respectively of the three relational axes of good governance. CAMAC describes this 'business' approach as compatible with enhancing 'shareholder interests'. CAMAC provides various examples of how the observance of CSR principles enhances firm value, operating profits, risk management and, ultimately, firm sustainability.[111] The relational approach submits that this process is very closely akin to that of the firm-specific aims and effects of good governance described in section 2.2 above.

Relationships with stakeholders are vital to sustainability Capasso highlights the importance of relationships with stakeholders as 'intangible assets' of the firm which are beyond the firm's 'direct control'[112] and these are particularly important for firms:

> whose critical factors for success are represented by the professional capabilities of the staff, but also in those firms owing their competitive advantage to their belonging either to an industrial district or to a network of interdependent firms.[113]

Capasso therefore stresses that the preservation of these intangible assets is – in an echo of Stakeholders Factor No 6 – dependent on addressing and satisfying such stakeholder interests.[114]

4.4.1.2 Comparison of the influence of shareholder primacy and the stakeholder model on the governance factors

How would the competing guiding principles – shareholder primacy and the stakeholder model – affect the operation of the governance factors? The influence of the shareholder primacy principle – including the

---

[109] Ibid.
[110] Ibid, p. 40 (footnote omitted).
[111] Ibid, pp. 40–52 and the footnotes therein.
[112] Arturo Capasso, 'Stakeholder Theory and Corporate Governance: The Role of Intangible Assets', accessed 3 March 2015 at SSRN: http://ssrn.com/abstract=610661, 8. Capasso, at 11, calls these relationships 'relational assets'.
[113] Ibid, 8–9.
[114] Ibid, 9.

Corporations Act's s 181(1)(a)[115] – in the relational approach is readily apparent. Alignment Factor No 3[116] is drawn squarely from this principle's pre-eminent position (on account of the Australian High Court's decision in *Walker v Wimborne*[117]) in Key Field No 1 (the Application of the Principal Theories of the Firm to the Relational Approach). The tensions between the shareholder primacy principle and its main rival – the stakeholder model – are also reflected in Stakeholders Factor No 6. Indeed, Alignment Factor No 3 is an 'umbrella' or 'guiding' principle over all other governance factors except Compliance Factor No 2.[118] In such a case, the relational approach is in shareholder primacy mode. This was represented in Figure 2.5.

Where, by contrast, the relational approach is in stakeholder mode, then the reverse will be the case. Stakeholders Factor No 6 and Alignment Factor No 3 will then together constitute the 'umbrella' or 'guiding' principles on the grounds that the interests of 'other' stakeholders do not necessarily rank over those of the shareholder-stakeholders. Again, only Compliance Factor No 2 ranks above them on account of its overriding nature.[119]

4.4.1.3 ASX 2007–10 and 2014 Governance Codes acknowledge stakeholder interests

In relation to Stakeholders Factor No 6 of the relational approach, Principle 3 of the ASX 2003 Best Practice Recommendations[120] was amended in the ASX 2007–10 Revised Principles to provide for acknowledgement of stakeholder interests. Revised Principle 3 of the ASX 2007–10 Revised Principles was expressed in part in terms of stakeholder theory:

---

115 See discussion in section 1.2.3 above.

116 The eight governance factors are constructed in sections 2.6.1–2.6.8 above.

117 See discussion in section 1.2.3 above.

118 See also Charreaux, above n 95, 6 (emphasis added), who explains that governance structures and mechanisms have a 'disciplinary perspective' – again, in terms of the shareholder model – which:

> . . . *constitute a means of forcing the managers to 'maximize' the shareholder value*. This perspective has particularly dominated the studies relating to the board of directors, the annual shareholder's meeting, the remuneration systems for managers, the legal and accounting regulations and takeovers as well.

119 See discussion in section 2.6.2 above.

120 The original ASX best practice recommendations were contained in the ASX Corporate Governance Council, *Principles of Good Corporate Governance and Best Practice Recommendations*, Australian Securities Exchange, March 2003 ('ASX 2003 Best Practice Recommendations').

> To make ethical and responsible decisions, companies should not only comply with their legal obligations, *but should also consider the reasonable expectations of their stakeholders including: shareholders, employees, customers, suppliers, creditors, consumers and the broader community in which they operate.*[121]

Also, Revised Principle 3.1 of the ASX 2007–10 Revised Principles required companies to establish and disclose a code of conduct for various matters including 'the practices necessary to take into account their legal obligations and the *reasonable expectations of their stakeholders*'.[122] It is submitted that, consequent on the introduction of these changes and ignoring the effect of Corporations Act s 181(1)(a) discussed above,[123] the ASX 2007–10 Revised Principles would have constituted a *composite* shareholder-stakeholder governance model.[124]

Principle 3 of the ASX 2014 Principles and Recommendations[125] continues to require companies to 'Act ethically and responsibly' with reference to stakeholder expectations:

> Investors and other stakeholders expect listed entities to act ethically and responsibly . . . with honesty, integrity and in a manner that is consistent with the reasonable expectations of investors and the broader community.[126]

---

[121] ASX Corporate Governance Council, *Corporate Governance Principles and Recommendations with 2010 Amendments*, June 2010, Australian Securities Exchange ('ASX 2007–10 Revised Principles'), Revised Principle 3, p 22 (emphasis added). See also CAMAC Social Responsibility Report, above n 104, Para [3.5], p 95.

[122] ASX 2007–10 Revised Principles, ibid, Revised Recommendation 3.1, p 22. In its suggestions for the contents of such a code, Box 3.1 of the ASX 2007–10 Revised Principles seeks to include themes relating to *both* the shareholder (primacy) model and the stakeholder model (at p 23).

[123] See discussion in section 1.2.3 above and section 4.4.1.2 above.

[124] For a discussion of the movement towards stakeholderism in various Anglo-American jurisdictions, see Andrew R Keay, 'Moving Towards Stakeholderism? Constituency Statutes, Enlightened Shareholder Value and All That: Much Ado About Little?' (4 January 2010), accessed 3 March 2015 at SSRN: http://ssrn.com/abstract=1530990. See also Andrew R Keay, 'Stakeholder Theory in Corporate Law: Has It Got What It Takes?' (4 January 2010), accessed 3 March 2015 at SSRN: http://ssrn.com/abstract=1531065.

[125] ASX Corporate Governance Council, *Corporate Governance Principles and Recommendations*, Third Edition, which were released on 27 March 2014 and (at p 7) took effect for a company's financial year commencing on or after 1 July 2014 ('ASX 2014 Principles and Recommendations'). See also *Translation Table, Corporate Governance Council Recommendations (New to Old) and (Old to New)* ('CGC Recommendations Translation Tables'). These documents are available at http://www.asx.com.au/regulation/corporate-governance-council.htm (accessed 3 March 2015).

[126] ASX 2014 Principles and Recommendations', ibid, Principle 3, p 19.

While this explicit reference to the word 'stakeholders' is the only one, there is a reference to investors and the broader community. Additionally, Principle 3's reference to being a 'good corporate citizen' includes reference to typical groups of stakeholders – workers, suppliers and customers and the environment. [127]

ASX 2007–10 and 2014 Governance Codes do not prioritise stakeholder-shareholder interests Again, as generally structured or operated, the relational approach is in shareholder primacy mode as described in section 4.4.1.2 above – but may be 'switched' to stakeholder mode. However, the ASX 2007–10 Revised Principles and ASX 2014 Principles and Recommendations give no further guidance on *how, or in what priority, the various stakeholder interests should be balanced amongst themselves or against the shareholder value-maximisation principle*. The ASX 2014 Principles and Recommendations make reference to 'value over the longer term' and 'building long-term value for its investors' with no further guidance.[128]

This, of course, is a very relevant consideration if, when the relational approach is switched to stakeholder mode, it is necessary to utilise Stakeholders Factor No 6[129] in conjunction with Alignment Factor No 3[130] as the 'umbrella' or 'guiding' factors. It is to this problem that the relational approach now turns.

4.4.2 Perceived Problems and Suggested Solutions in Balancing Competing Stakeholder Interests

The relational approach considers in this section the most controversial, if not difficult, problem faced by the stakeholder model – the balancing of shareholder and other stakeholder interests (that is, on the assumption that *no* pre-eminence is given to the former[131]).

Here, this chapter highlights Jensen's 'many masters' problem that may reduce the ability to satisfy in total all such interests simultaneously.

---

127 Ibid.

128 Ibid.

129 The governance factors are constructed in sections 2.6.1–2.6.8 above.

130 Ibid.

131 This assumption is, on purpose, expressed differently to any assumption that the relevant interests rank equally. Such an equal ranking pre-supposes that some form of weighing has already taken place which, in the absence of any model, is unsupportable. It is the determination of this ranking between the relevant shareholder and stakeholder interests that this section seeks to examine.

Further, and accepting this problem, the chapter examines proposals for how a stakeholder model may work in practice and highlights possible difficulties including Bainbridge's problem of 'managerial sin'.

4.4.2.1 Balancing and priority of stakeholder interests

In terms of the weighing of competing interests, of ongoing difficulty for Licht and, separately, Bainbridge, in connection with the stakeholder model is how the balancing of interests should be performed in practice and the order of precedence.[132] In the relational approach, this problem is represented by the question of the weighting accorded to Stakeholders Factor No 6 *vis-à-vis* Alignment Factor No 3. These quandaries are neither solved by the OECD Principles[133] nor the ASX 2014 Principles and Recommendations.[134]

The 'many masters' problem of stakeholder interests Similarly, Jensen highlights the 'many masters' problem that could mean *no* stakeholder's interest is fully satisfied and which could lead to 'managerial confusion' and (importantly for the purposes of the relational approach) undermine future efficiency and sustainability.[135] In this respect, Jensen also describes the impossibility of simultaneously maximising more than one interest with resultant (again) managerial confusion and lack of objective, again undermining sustainability.[136]

Indeed, similar to Jensen, Maher and Andersson note that one problem with the stakeholder model is that 'it is difficult, if not impossible, to ensure that corporations fulfil these wider objectives'[137] and suggest that insiders 'may use "stakeholder" reasons to justify poor company performance'.[138] In the end, the authors appear to suggest a combination of aspects of the

---

132 Licht, 'The Maximands of Corporate Governance: A Theory of Values and Cognitive Style', above n 95, 63–4, 67 and 79. Bainbridge, 'In Defense of the Shareholder Wealth Maximization Norm', above n 8, 1435–6, calls this the 'two masters' problem.

133 Organisation for Economic Co-Operation and Development, *OECD Principles of Corporate Governance 2004*, 2004, OECD Publications Service, Paris ('OECD Principles'). See http://www.oecd.org/document/49/0,3343,en_2649_34813_31530865_1_1_1_37439,00.html (accessed 3 March 2015).

134 See discussion in section 4.4.1.3 above.

135 Jensen, 'Value Maximization, Stakeholder Theory, and the Corporate Objective Function', above n 102, 9.

136 Ibid, 10–11.

137 Maher and Andersson, above n 71, p 5.

138 Ibid, 6.

two principal models as a solution to perceived weaknesses.[139] Bainbridge also highlights the problem of 'managerial sin':

> management could freely pursue its own self-interest by playing shareholders off against nonshareholders. When management's interests coincide with those of shareholders, management could justify its decision by saying that shareholder interests prevailed in this instance, and vice-versa.[140]

How, then, should the difficulties described by these authors be addressed? This chapter concludes the examination of the stakeholder model with a discussion of this question.

4.4.2.2 In-practice approaches to implementation of the stakeholder model

Maximising stakeholder (including shareholder) interests essential to sustainability In this section, the relational approach will *assume* that maximising in an ongoing sense the various stakeholder interests (including but not limited to shareholder-stakeholders) of the corporation is essential to the long-term existence/sustainability of the firm.[141] This assumption, in effect, equates the maximisation (in the long term) of all stakeholder needs with the purpose of 'good' corporate governance. Therefore, and here accepting the problems of how the competing stakeholder interests are to be weighed, how could such a model work in practice?

One way is through the use of 'non-shareholder constituency statutes'. These are provisions which *expressly* limit, in favour of particular stakeholders, the shareholder wealth-maximisation principle (or relevant provisions of the relevant companies' statute) and these are also considered by CAMAC.[142]

Another method to address the problem of the weighing of competing corporate stakeholder interests requires, on some views, little or no amendment to existing corporations' legislation. Bainbridge, for one, does *not overstate* this balancing problem, suggesting that non-shareholder

---

139 Ibid, 6–7.

140 Bainbridge, 'In Defense of the Shareholder Wealth Maximization Norm', above n 8, 1438.

141 In fact, the argument that maximising such stakeholder interests is for the long-term benefit of shareholders could be argued *solely* under the shareholder primacy principle.

142 CAMAC Social Responsibility Report, above n 104, Para [3.8.3], pp 99–102.

interests can often be catered for *even in difficult cases* – with the 'business judgement rule' in the US providing a viable defence for directors in most cases where shareholder 'wealth' is diminished.[143]

While a detailed examination of Australia's comparative Corporations Act s 180(2)[144] is beyond the scope of this first stage of the relational approach, CAMAC considers various proposals for legislative change in this respect[145] and these include '*an amended business judgment defence*'.[146] Ultimately, CAMAC views amendment to current law and statutory provisions as unnecessary as these 'are sufficiently broad to enable corporate decision-makers to take into account the environmental and other social impacts of their decisions . . .'.[147] CAMAC further observes that such amendments to require or permit directors to consider specific stakeholder interests could introduce uncertainty.[148]

Again, the CAMAC Social Responsibility Report reviews various approaches to the incorporation of social responsibility interests in practice by corporations.[149] CAMAC's 'business' approach – which argues that satisfying 'environmental' and 'social' interests is in the interests of the company's long-term value – bears some similarity to Jensen's solution which is to propose a new 'enlightened stakeholder theory' which provides the traditional stakeholder model with:

> the simple specification that the objective function—the overriding goal—of the firm is to maximize total long-term firm market value.[150]

This specification provides a means for managers to assess and compromise competing stakeholder interests.[151]

This may well be, the relational approach submits, the effect of the current *combination* of provisions in Australia. In other words, the effects

---

[143] Bainbridge, 'In Defense of the Shareholder Wealth Maximization Norm', above n 8, 1438–9 and 1440–1. See also Bainbridge, 'Director Primacy: The Means and Ends of Corporate Governance', above n 67, 44.

[144] *Corporations Act* 2001 (Cth), s 180(2). See http://www.austlii.edu.au/au/legis/cth/consol_act/ca2001172/s180.html (accessed 3 March 2015).

[145] CAMAC Social Responsibility, above n 104, Para [3.11.4], pp 109–10.

[146] Ibid, Para [3.11.4], p 109 (emphasis in original). See discussion in section 4.4.1.1 above.

[147] Ibid, Para [3.12], p 111.

[148] Ibid, Para [3.12], pp 111–12.

[149] Ibid, Para [2.3], pp 34–54.

[150] Jensen, 'Value Maximization, Stakeholder Theory, and the Corporate Objective Function', above n 102, 16–17.

[151] Ibid, 17.

of Principle 3 of the ASX 2014 Principles and Recommendations[152] and Corporations Act s 181(1)(a) which provides that a director's powers and duties must be exercised 'in good faith in the best interests of the *corporation*'[153] (that is, under *Walker v Wimborne*, for the benefit of its shareholders[154]) might approximate the 'enlightened stakeholder theory' position. As noted above, the ASX 2014 Principles and Recommendations make reference to 'value over the longer term' and 'building long-term value for its investors' but with no further guidance.[155]

Another way discussed by Turnbull is for stakeholder interests to receive formal recognition through 'stakeholder panels'.[156] In addition, Turnbull describes that a 'stakeholder council' would then be elected from the panels to perform a monitoring role in the organisation[157] and other structures are also contemplated.[158] Capasso also notes (with controversy) the possibility of giving principal stakeholders a seat on the board.[159]

How, then, is the problem of the constituency and priority of shareholder and rival stakeholder interests reflected in the relational approach? This is described in the next section.

4.4.2.3 The constituency and priority of shareholder vis-à-vis stakeholder interests and the purpose of the relational approach

The relational approach – through the three relational axes of good governance, governance factors and interrelationship schemes – is designed to determine the appropriate constituency or priority of stakeholder interests under the stakeholder model which may enhance the long-term efficiency and survival/sustainability of the corporation.

The relational approach minimises agency costs to prioritise stakeholder-shareholder interests Accepting that it is necessary (as described in section 4.4.1.1) to maximise 'other' stakeholder interests in a shareholder-primacy environment, this chapter shows that the relational approach can

---

152 See discussion in section 4.4.1.3 above.

153 Corporations Act 2001 (Cth), s 181(1)(a).

154 *Walker v Wimborne* [1976] HCA 7; (1976) 137 CLR 1 (3 March 1976). See discussion in section 4.4.1.2 above.

155 ASX 2014 Principles and Recommendations, above n 125, p 19.

156 Shann Turnbull, 'A New Way to Govern: Organisations and Society After Enron', *New Economics Foundation Pocketbook 6*, 2002, accessed 3 March 2015 at SSRN: http://ssrn.com/abstract=319867, 33 and 35.

157 Ibid, 36.

158 Ibid, 37–8.

159 Capasso, above n 112, 15.

determine or assess the priority of such interests (including, of course, the pre-eminence of the shareholder interests and/or interests prescribed in 'non-shareholder constituency' statutes and the like).

The relational approach solves the question of the identity and priority of competing stakeholder-shareholder interests with its own overriding goal for the firm – that the function of the firm is to minimise long-term agency costs.

For example, the relational approach will assist directors of the corporation to identify and prioritise interests by the weighing of the eight governance factors as applied to each proposed alternative course of action. Again, this exemplifies the critical nature of the governance factors to the operation of the relational approach.

Continuing this example, in the relational approach's Shareholder Primacy Interrelationship Scheme in Figure 2.6, Alignment Factor No 3 reflects the shareholder model and the Corporations Act s 181(1)(a). It acts as an 'umbrella' or 'guiding' principle over other governance factors (except Compliance Factor No 2). Stakeholders Factor No 6 reflects the influence of the stakeholder model. It remains a relevant and operative governance factor but does not predominate.

Also in the relational approach's shareholder primacy mode, Positional Conflict Axis No 3 will direct the application of Objectives Axis No 1 and Behaviours Axis No 2. It will treat widely-dispersed shareholder-stakeholders as predominant *vis-à-vis* other stakeholders (but, of course, still outside vis-à-vis directors and management). *All this is subject to the overriding requirement above – that the overriding goal for the firm is to minimise long-term agency costs.*

Support for the relational approach's overriding goal of minimising agency costs can be drawn from Jensen's 'enlightened stakeholder theory'.[160] Jensen's own overriding goal in assessing and prioritising competing stakeholder-shareholder interests is to maximise long-term firm market value.[161] The relational approach is constructed on the basis that reducing long-term agency costs in turn enhances the long-term efficiency and sustainability of the firm. As described in section 1.5, the relational approach assumes in Chapters 2–6 that applying the Weighing Mechanism in a manner to reduce agency costs enhances shareholder-wealth welfare proxies or measures such as the firm's cost of capital, firm value (as Jensen would have) and firm operating performance and reduces

---

[160] See discussion in section 4.4.2.2 above.

[161] Jensen, 'Value Maximization, Stakeholder Theory, and the Corporate Objective Function', above n 102,16–17.

earnings management.[162] In Chapters 7–10, the relational approach examines empirical studies to determine the real-world effects of governance variables in enhancing these proxies or measures and reducing earnings management.

In future stages, the relational approach's agency cost:sustainability relationship can be empirically tested.

4.5 CONCLUDING REMARKS FOR CHAPTER 4

This Chapter 4 has explained the theoretical foundations of the relational approach by reference to Key Field No 1 – the Application of the Principal Theories of the Firm to the Relational Approach. In particular, the chapter has examined the theoretical basis of the relational approach's Weighing Mechanism – the three relational axes of good governance, the eight governance factors and the two interrelationship schemes.

This chapter has emphasised the separation of ownership from management which gives rise to agency costs between insiders and outsiders. Thus, the corporation must apply countervailing governance variables to monitor, limit or punish management misconduct or to align the interests of insiders and outsiders.

The chapter has examined the currently pre-eminent theories of the firm to demonstrate how the relational approach adds explanatory power to the nexus of contracts, agency costs theory, the shareholder primacy model, the stakeholder model and the director primacy model. In particular, the examination of these models has highlighted that the foundations of the Weighing Mechanism rests upon the nexus of contracts and agency costs. Indeed, the Weighing Mechanism of the relational approach is a theoretical representation of the nexus of contracts itself. The relational approach's operational Tables – the Coverage Table (Table 3.1) and the Relational Proximity Table (Table 3.2) – are the operational representation of the nexus.

The relational approach utilises two interrelationship schemes in Figures 2.6 and 2.7. The interrelationship schemes represent either shareholder primacy or stakeholder model 'modes'.[163] Each Scheme is a diagrammatic representation of the hypothesised interrelationships between the governance factors under the relevant mode or model. In the shareholder primacy mode, Alignment Factor No 3 is an 'umbrella' or

---

[162] See discussion in section 1.5 above.

[163] See also the discussion in sections 2.7.1–2.7.2 above.

'guiding' principle over all other governance factors except Compliance Factor No 2.

In stakeholder model mode, Stakeholders Factor No 6 together with Alignment Factor No 3 constitute the 'umbrella' or 'guiding' principles over the other governance factors again with the exception of Compliance Factor 2.

Important in this Chapter 4 has been to highlight arguments that maximising stakeholder interests is critical for the sustainability of the corporation. In this respect, this chapter has shown that one purpose of the governance variables in the relational approach is to balance or weigh the various stakeholder interests *inter se* and against the shareholder value-maximisation principle in order to achieve long term efficiency and sustainability of the corporation. The relational approach solves the question of the identity and priority of competing stakeholder-shareholder interests with its own overriding goal for the firm – *to minimise long-term agency costs*.

The next chapter distils the underlying themes and tensions from Key Field No 2 – Autopsies of the Enron and Hastie Corporate Collapses – to determine the extent of the real-world failures in governance variables which spring from the theory in this chapter. This is undertaken for the purposes of the identification, construction and articulation of the eight governance factors,[164] to identify the intervening factors or variables which reduced the effectiveness of the governance variables examined in the relational approach and to show how the governance variables in Table 2.1 behaved in the multitude of failures of those collapses. Many of these governance variables came to form the international and national governance codes examined in Key Field No 3 (*Comparative Corporate Governance Codes*) in Chapter 6 and whose effectiveness is assessed in the empirical studies of the effectiveness of governance variables in Key Field No 4 in Chapters 7–10.

---

[164] See discussion in sections 2.6.1–2.6.8 above.

5. Key Field No 2: 'Autopsies' of the Enron and Hastie corporate collapses

> The firm collapsed for the most mundane of reasons – its managers suffered the behavioral biases of successful entrepreneurs. They overemphasized the upside and lacked patience. They pursued heroic short term growth numbers that their business plan could not deliver. That pursuit of immediate shareholder value caused them to become risk prone, engaging in levered speculation, earnings manipulation, and concealment of critical information.
>
> They were rogues to be sure, but the self regulatory system nevertheless is deeply implicated in their company's failure. Enron's collapse reminds us that our corporate governance system takes some significant risks in the name of encouraging innovation and entrepreneurship and economizing on enforcement costs.
>
> William W Bratton on Enron's demise[1]

5.1 THE ENRON GOVERNANCE FAILURE ABYSS AND THE HASTIE GROUP COLLAPSE

5.1.1 Purpose, Scope and Methodology of Chapter 5 – Enron and Hastie Case Studies of the Behaviour of Governance Variables and Governance Factors

In this chapter, the relational approach examines Key Field No 2 – the well-known corporate collapse of Enron in the United States[2] and the collapse of the Hastie Group in Australia. Enron's dramatic rise from

---

[1] William W Bratton, 'Enron and the Dark Side of Shareholder Value' (2001–2002) 76 *Tulane Law Review* 1275 (May 2002), accessed 3 March 2015 at SSRN: http://ssrn.com/abstract=301475, 7–8. An earlier version of this chapter won the Governance Institute of Australia Best Paper Prize at the 2014 Corporate Law Teachers' Association Annual Conference, Adelaide, 3–4 February, 2014 and was published as 'Enron and Hastie: What Can We Learn' (2014) 29 *Australian Journal of Corporate Law* 169–211.

[2] See, for example, Nancy B Rapoport, 'Enron, Titanic, and The Perfect Storm' (2003) 71 *Fordham Law Review* 1373, accessed 3 March 2015 at SSRN: http://ssrn.com/abstract=498122.

the largest pipeline owner to the seventh largest US company is documented extensively.[3] But while there is a huge volume of information and analysis in relation to Enron, there is little on Hastie. Hastie was selected for a different reason. As a relatively recent example of governance variable failures in a post-GFC climate, Hastie is illuminating on account of the detail provided by the Administrators' Report in relation to the collapse,[4] the facts of which were summarised in Chapter 1.[5] Thus, the analysis will be drawn in this US:Australian comparison to highlight recurring themes and tensions in the two collapses and to demonstrate the purchase of the relational approach in both the US and Australian contexts and in the present post-GFC time.

The three aims of Chapter 5

With these two collapses under the microscope, the approach of this chapter is threefold. First, the chapter extracts the themes and tensions underlying the Enron corporate collapse to support the identification, structure and articulation of the eight governance factors examined in Chapters 1 and 2.[6] For a comparison of the pre- and post-GFC economic and governance climate, the examination of the Enron collapse is juxtaposed with that of the Hastie Group. The second aim is to identify the intervening variables of these organisations and their governance structures which reduced the effectiveness of the governance variables examined in the relational approach. Third, as Bratton's comments suggest in the case of Enron, these collapses involved a multitude of governance failures. These variables continue to be central to the examination of the GFC.[7] In other words, how did the 39 governance variables behave during the Enron and Hastie Group collapses?

---

[3] Douglas G Baird and Robert K Rasmussen, 'Four (or Five) Easy Lessons From Enron' (2002) 55 *Vanderbilt Law Review* 102, available at SSRN: http://ssrn.com/abstract=358442, 108 (footnotes omitted).

[4] PPB Advisory, *Hastie Group Limited and Specific Subsidiaries, Report by Joint and Several Administrators Pursuant to Section 439A of the Corporations Act 2001*, 21 January 2013, accessed 3 March 2015 at http://www.ppbadvisory.com/creditor-information/v/281/hastie-group/2nd-creditor-meeting ('Administrators Report').

[5] See discussion in section 1.3.1 above.

[6] See discussion in sections 2.6.1–2.6.8 above.

[7] See, for example, Julia Black, 'Paradoxes and Failures: "New Governance" Techniques and the Financial Crises' (2012) 75(6) MLR 1037. See also Jennifer G Hill, 'Why Did Australia Fare So Well in the Global Financial Crisis?' in *The Regulatory Aftermath Of The Global Financial Crisis*, E Ferran, N Moloney, J G Hill and J C Coffee, Jr, Cambridge University Press, 2012, pp 203–300; Sydney

5.2 FAILURES IN 'CENTRAL' OR 'PROXIMATE' GOVERNANCE VARIABLES

In a nutshell, Gordon observes that:

> [t]he Enron case has seemed particularly disturbing because the case represents a failed stress test for many institutions of US shareholder capitalism, circa 1990s. As with most catastrophes, many separate systems simultaneously failed: *auditing and accounting, executive compensation, internal monitoring by the board, and external monitoring by securities analysts*.[8]

This chapter focuses on these perceived problems including those relating to board and director-related variables, factors affecting earnings manipulation (including CEO, executive and director compensation structures), the external audit function and other financial intermediaries.

5.2.1 Agency Theory and the Shareholder Model

5.2.1.1 Market for corporate control and efficient market hypothesis undermined in the Enron collapse

Gordon highlights, as a particular aspect of the Enron collapse, failings in the operation of the efficient market hypothesis.[9] For Gordon, the variance between Enron's share price, at one time US$ 90,[10] and its 'intrinsic value' was striking despite the scrutiny of investors and securities analysts for this widely held stock.[11] The answer, for Gordon, had two strands. First, the complexity of the company's structure and off balance-sheet transactions *should* have led (but did not) to a markdown in share price

---

Law School Research Paper No. 12/35, (May 20, 2012), accessed 23 April 2015 at SSRN: http://ssrn.com/abstract=2063267 and P M Vasudev and Susan Watson, "Corporate Governance after the Financial Crisis" in P M Vasudev and Susan Watson, eds, *Corporate Governance After The Financial Crisis*, Edward Elgar Ltd, 2012, accessed 23 April 2015 at SSRN: http://ssrn.com/abstract=209076.

[8] Jeffrey N Gordon, 'Governance Failures of the Enron Board and the New Information Order of Sarbanes-Oxley', Columbia Law and Economics Working Paper No 216; Harvard Law and Economics Discussion Paper No 416 (March 2003), accessed 3 March 2015 at SSRN: http://ssrn.com/abstract=391363, 3 (emphasis added).

[9] Jeffrey N Gordon, 'What Enron Means for the Management and Control of the Modern Business Corporation: Some Initial Reflections' (2002) 69 *University of Chicago Law Review* 1233 (Summer 2002), accessed 3 March 2015 at SSRN: http://ssrn.com/abstract=305343, 5–10.

[10] Ibid, 3.

[11] Ibid, 5.

on account of the information asymmetry problems.[12] Second, the lack of integrity of the auditor's certification (supported by supposed reputational constraints on the auditor) of the financial accounts as 'fairly' presenting Enron's financial position was a 'foreseeable failure' – and, again, *should* have been reflected in a markdown of share price. This was on account of its lack of independence due to non-audit (particularly tax) services and failures of its own internal controls, both of which were known to 'sophisticated' investors.[13] In short, Gordon appears to treat the Enron collapse as an example (at least in part) of two of the problems identified in Chapter 4[14] – information asymmetry and time lag – and without satisfactory explanation for the failure of the market price mechanism to correct for these.[15]

Hastie Group danger signs were prominent By contrast, the Hastie Group collapse had some prominent danger signs truer to the efficient market model. As noted in the introduction in Chapter 1, these included a 'standstill' agreement with its major banking syndicate, the breach, revision and removal of its banking covenants, an equity raising of $158 million to improve its balance sheet position and five Earnings Before Interest and Tax (EBIT) downgrades.[16] The Group suffered large write-downs in each of the financial years 2010, 2011 and 2012 to goodwill, trade and other receivables and work-in-progress (WIP). Resignations of several key management positions took place. Charges against EBIT for Middle East operations were announced of $55 million, then increased to $88 million.[17] And trading in Hastie Group shares were suspended on two occasions. The half-year 2012 financial accounts noted material uncertainty in relation to the 'going concern' of the Group.[18]

However, there were time lag issues with significant effects in relation

12 Ibid, 6.

13 Ibid, 6–9.

14 See discussion in section 4.2.2 above.

15 See also Michael C Jensen, 'Agency Costs of Overvalued Equity', ECGI – Finance Working Paper No 39/2004; Harvard Business School NOM Working Paper No 04-26; (2005) 34(1) *Financial Management* 5–19 (March 2005), accessed 3 March 2015 at SSRN: http://ssrn.com/abstract=480421, 7–9 and Michael C Jensen, "The Agency Cost of Overvalued Equity and the Current State of Corporate Finance" (2004) 10(4) *European Financial Management* 549–565 accessed 23 April 2015 at SSRN: http://ssrn.com/abstract=560961.

16 Administrators' Report, above n 4, section 2.5.2, p 13 of 99 and Timeline of Key Events, p 17 of 99.

17 Ibid, Timeline of Key Events, p 17 of 99.

18 Ibid.

to the asset write-downs.[19] As a result of the overstatement of goodwill, the Administrators considered that the relevant 'financial statements may be materially misstated and misleading to users of that information, particularly the investors who relied on the financial statements and forecasts included in the Prospectus'.[20] Similar comments were made in relation to the late timing of write-offs for trade and other receivables[21] and the construction WIP element of inventories.[22]

Baird and Rasmussen point to a failure to understand (at least part of) the Enron business model as the first of their lessons from the Enron collapse. Translating this in terms of the efficient market hypothesis is that the market cannot correct for what it fails to understand.[23] Indeed, the authors indicate that Enron's complicated trading structure – where each trader was a 'stand-alone profit center' – enhanced the appearance (but obscured the nature) of trading profits.[24] In addition, Baird and Rasmussen tell us that the sheer complexity of the structure of interrelated entities – for example, the Special Purpose Entities described below[25] – made both valuation of Enron as a whole and assessment of the solvency of those entities extremely difficult.[26]

5.2.2 Board and Director Variables

5.2.2.1 Enron director independence undermined by equity holdings and share options

As discussed later in this chapter,[27] director independence is a core governance variable and is considered as critical to the board's function of the monitoring of management. Looking forward, the relational approach's examination of the relationship between firm operating performance and/or value and the level of equity holdings of the CEO, management and both inside and outside directors had inconclusive results.[28] Instead, a balancing exercise is required to 'optimise' the 'incentive alignment' and 'entrenchment' effects of these holdings as identified by Fuerst and

19 Ibid, section 2.5.2, p 13 of 99.
20 Ibid, section 6.2.1, p 39 of 99.
21 Ibid, section 6.2.2, p 41 of 99.
22 Ibid, section 6.2.3, p 43 of 99.
23 Baird and Rasmussen, above n 3, 117.
24 Ibid, 118.
25 See discussion in section 5.2.3.1 below.
26 Baird and Rasmussen, above n 3, 120–122.
27 See also discussion in section 6.8.1 and section 7.3.2.1 below.
28 See discussion in sections 7.3.2.1.4–7.3.2.1.5 below.

Kang.[29] In the Enron collapse, two principal reasons are highlighted. While authors such as Branson point to 'outrageously high' directors' fees and consulting contracts for directors,[30] a more prominent reason given for this lack of independence is the equity holdings and share options of supposedly outside directors. The Hastie Administrator's Report also noted a number of director personal share holdings in the listed HST company[31] but with no questions or conclusions drawn in the Report of the effects, if any, of these holdings.

5.2.2.1.1 Enron share and option holdings may affect monitoring Gillan and Martin's views[32] point squarely to problems in the quality of monitoring as a result of Enron director share and option holdings and conflicts of interest on the audit, finance and nominating and corporate governance committees.[33] The authors are also critical of Enron's director compensation policy for undermining independence.[34] For the authors, these arrangements and the share and option holdings of directors affected the management function as they 'may have attenuated any inclination to aggressively monitor management's practices'.[35]

For Gordon,[36] the director independence variable as a mechanism to enhance the monitoring of management was undermined by similar factors – substantial share ownership, the receipt of share options and excessive director compensation – 'since a director's sharp questioning of senior management may led (sic) to subtle pressures against his/her renomination'.[37] In the case of share options, Gordon explains that,

---

[29] O Fuerst and S Kang, 'Corporate Governance, Expected Operating Performance, and Pricing', available at SSRN: http://ssrn.com/abstract=141357. See sections 7.3.2 and 7.3.2.1.5 and section 10.2.1 below.

[30] Douglas M Branson, 'Enron – When All Systems Fail: Creative Destruction or Roadmap to Corporate Governance Reform?' (2003) 48 *Villanova Law Review* 989; Villanova Law/Public Policy Research Paper No 2003–13, accessed 3 March 2015 at SSRN: http://ssrn.com/abstract=473205, 1003.

[31] Administrators' Report, above n 4, p 83 of 99.

[32] See section 2.6.4 above for a discussion of the Compensation Factor No 4 – *Board, CEO and Management Compensation and Incentives*.

[33] Stuart L Gillan and John D Martin, 'Financial Engineering, Corporate Governance, and the Collapse of Enron', U of Delaware Coll. of Bus. and Econ. Ctr. for Corp. Governance Working Paper No 2002-001 (November 2002), accessed 3 March 2015 at SSRN: http://ssrn.com/abstract=354040, 23–24 (footnotes omitted).

[34] Ibid, 24.

[35] Ibid, 24.

[36] See also the views of Gillan and Martin in section 2.6.4 above.

[37] Gordon, above n 9, 12.

while such options may enhance the 'alignment' of managerial and outside shareholder interests, they may also inhibit directors in their monitoring function of making necessary enquiries of management due to 'ambivalence about uncovering embarrassing facts that will reduce the share price'.[38] The author observes that the problem in relation to stock options is 'that they provide perverse managerial incentives' so 'that managers will be strongly tempted to produce the financial results the market "expects" through manipulation of financial results'.[39] Gordon observes that the Enron options had a significant accelerated vesting feature.[40] Thus the structure of the options themselves exacerbated governance problems related to earnings manipulation which will be further discussed below.[41]

5.2.2.1.2 Enron option holdings and risk management Risk management issues at Enron are discussed below. But for Blanchard and Dionne, risk management also poses conflict of interest issues between inside directors and outside shareholders when stock options are paid to those directors.[42] The authors suggest that directors on the company's risk management committee therefore hold no stock options.[43]

5.2.2.2 Enron board member 'familiarity', 'deference' and the independence of committees

The operation of a number of committees is contemplated by the governance variables listed in Table 2.1 – the audit committee (which, in the case of the Hastie Group, included risk management), nominating committee and the compensation committee. In Enron, problems were raised by independent directors (who were themselves CEOs or former CEOs of other companies) 'deferring' to 'inside' directors, a matter exacerbated by the length of the CEO's tenure.[44] In Enron, Gordon observed 'bonds of long service and familiarity' in the boardroom.[45]

---

[38] Ibid.

[39] Gordon, above n 8, 5.

[40] Ibid (footnote omitted).

[41] See discussion in section 5.2.3 below.

[42] Danielle Blanchard and Georges Dionne, 'Risk Management and Corporate Governance', HEC Montreal Risk Management Chair Working Paper No 03-04, (September 2003), accessed 3 March 2015 at SSRN: http://ssrn.com/abstract=441482, 7.

[43] Ibid.

[44] See discussion in sections 7.3.2.1.1 and 7.3.2.1.3 below. Bratton examines the monitoring failings of the Enron outside directors in Bratton, above n 1, 55.

[45] Gordon, above n 9, 11.

'Dysfunctional deference' of the Enron Board For Sharfman and Toll, the failures in monitoring, questioning and supervision on the Enron board were due to what they call 'dysfunctional deference'[46] so 'that there was little or no deliberation preceding some of the board's most important decisions'.[47] For the authors, the reasons lay in part in 'informational signals' – that directors believed public perceptions of the company and so, with little contact with management, relied on inside directors and executives.[48] This was compounded by the fact that many independent directors had been former CEOs of the company and/or had been long-serving during a long period of perceived success.[49] In addition, they suggest that directors may have been influenced by 'informational cascades' created by 'management-generated' briefing papers and recommendations or followed the 'domino effect' of the decisions and signals of others such as Kenneth Lay, Enron's founding CEO.[50]

The familiarity and deference factors may have affected some critical areas of director interaction in the Enron collapse. Gillan and Martin suggest that the board's monitoring function may have been undermined by the regular attendance of the Chairman and (separate) CEO at various committees – particularly, 'executive', 'finance' and 'audit'.[51] To enhance independence consequent on Enron, Branson urges that independent directors and board committees – including audit, finance and nomination – exclude senior management from meetings.[52] In addition, independent audit firm partners should meet with the audit committee again in absence of senior management.[53]

The Hastie collapse appears also to involve a form of dysfunctional deference, although not named as such by the Administrators. The Hastie Board's dysfunction may be seen as a product of the culture at the company – a culture of failure to enquire into or challenge financial information and of ignoring bad news.[54] But the result is the same as in

---

46 Bernard S Sharfman and Steven J Toll, 'Dysfunctional Deference and Board Composition: Lessons from Enron' (2008) 103 *Northwestern University Law Review Colloquy* 153–62, 2008, accessed 3 March 2015 at SSRN: http://ssrn.com/abstract=1160302.

47 Ibid, 155.

48 Ibid, 157–8.

49 Ibid, 158.

50 Ibid, 156 and 159 and Bratton, above n 1, 3.

51 Gillan and Martin, above n 33, 25.

52 Branson, above n 30, 1016–7.

53 Ibid.

54 Administrators' Report, above n 4, section 2.5.3, p 14 of 99.

Enron – little or no deliberation involved in the Board's decision-making processes in relation to financial reporting.

5.2.2.3 Risk management – 'innovation' vs 'control'

5.2.2.3.1 Enron risk management complexity and the adequacy of reports, monitoring and control Rosen discusses in detail risk management failures within Enron, particularly in the case of various 'off-balance sheet' transactions discussed below.[55] In particular, the author highlights the complexity of the transactions questioning the capacity of finance committee and board members to fully understand risk management reports in relation to the transactions.[56] In addition, Rosen questions the quality of the risk management reports themselves.[57] Finally, Rosen identifies the limited role played by Enron's risk management group in the approval of transactions.[58] The author concludes that the content-standard of risk management reports did not explain risks adequately for monitoring purposes leading to poor decision-making.[59]

---

[55] Robert Eli Rosen, 'Risk Management and Corporate Governance: The Case of Enron' (2003) 35 *Connecticut Law Review* 1157, available at SSRN: http://ssrn.com/abstract=468168. See discussion in section 5.2.3 below.

[56] Ibid, 1175–6.

[57] Ibid, 1176. 'SPEs' or 'Special Purpose Entities' are described in section 5.2.3.1 below. Internal control failures in relation to the SPEs are also examined in Stuart L Gillan and John D Martin, 'Corporate Governance Post-Enron: Effective Reforms, or Closing the Stable Door?' (21 March 2007), accessed 3 March 2015 at SSRN: http://ssrn.com/abstract=977585, 12–15.

[58] Rosen, above n 55, 1178–9.

[59] Ibid, 1179. For a discussion of corporate governance enhancing innovation, creating value and maintaining competitiveness, see Joseph A McCahery and Erik P M Vermeulen, "Six Components of Corporate Governance That Cannot Be Ignored", Lex Research Topics in Corporate Law & Economics Working Paper No. 2014-2; European Corporate Governance Institute (ECGI) – Law Working Paper No. 248/2014; Tilburg Law School Research Paper No. 08/2014, (March 9, 2014), accessed 23 April 2015 at SSRN: http://ssrn.com/abstract=2406565.

For a case study of errors in risk management, see David F Larcker, Sarah M Larcker and Brian Tayan, "Lululemon: A Sheer Debacle in Risk Management", Rock Center for Corporate Governance at Stanford University Closer Look Series: Topics, Issues and Controversies in Corporate Governance and Leadership No. CGRP-41; Stanford University Graduate School of Business Research Paper No. 14-21, (June 17, 2014), accessed 23 April 2015 at SSRN: http://ssrn.com/abstract=2455983.

For further articles on risk management, see also Christoph Van der Elst, "The Risks of Corporate Legal Principles of Risk Management", ECGI – Law Working Paper No. 160/2010; Tilburg Law School Research Paper No. 013/2010, (June 10, 2010), accessed 24 April 2015 at SSRN: http://ssrn.com/abstract=1623526; Christoph Van

INADEQUACIES IN HASTIE AUDIT AND RISK COMMITTEE, MONITORING AND CONTROL The Administrators of the Hastie Group listed as one reason for the group's failure that 'the Audit and Risk Committee (ARC) was largely inactive'.[60] They considered the failure was also caused by inadequate management, reporting, interrogation of reports and control.[61] Further problems included inadequate internal controls and due diligence.[62]

POOR MANAGEMENT AND MONITORING OF HASTIE ACQUISITIONS The introduction to this chapter noted a significant acquisition programme on the part of Hastie with eight businesses acquired in the financial years 2008 to 2010 totalling $278 million.[63] The Administrators concluded that there were 'profitable companies subsidising the loss-making Middle East businesses'.[64] The acquisition strategy resulted in large debt and inadequate reporting which affected the quality of decision-making.[65]

INADEQUATE RISK ASSESSMENT AND CONTROL OF HASTIE MIDDLE EAST PROJECTS Relevant risks in the Middle East not assessed properly included 'project management, the recovery of receivables and options for dispute resolution'.[66] Post-acquisition failures included 'a lack of integration, performance management and appropriate oversight from the Board'.[67]

SIGNIFICANT FAILURES IN RELATION TO CONSTRUCTION WORK-IN-PROGRESS Perhaps most scathing are the Administrators' comments in relation to construction WIP. There a relevant report to the Board had noted inadequate project management, dishonest reporting and hiding losses.[68]

---

der Elst, "The Risk Management Duties of the Board of Directors", Financial Law Institute Working Paper Series 2013-02, (April 22, 2013), accessed 24 April 2015 at SSRN: http://ssrn.com/abstract=2267502 and Georges Dionne, Olfa Maalaoui Chun and Thouraya Triki, "Risk Management and Corporate Governance: The Importance of Independence and Financial Knowledge", (February 2013), accessed 24 April 2015 at SSRN: http://ssrn.com/abstract=2020987.

60 Administrators' Report, above n 4, section 2.5.3, p 14 of 99.

61 Ibid. See also, section 7.9, p 61 of 99 and section 7.9.5, p 65 of 99.

62 Ibid.

63 Ibid, section 2.5.1, p 12 of 99.

64 Ibid, section 7.9, p 61 of 99.

65 Ibid, section 7.9.2, p 62 of 99.

66 Ibid.

67 Ibid, section 7.9.2, p 63 of 99.

68 Ibid, section 6.2.3, pp 43–4 of 99.

5.2.2.3.2 Risk management and company culture The very culture at Enron has been argued to have contributed to the subversion of management control practices.[69] Free and Macintosh describe an ultra-competitive culture where dissent was stifled, misconduct was overlooked and tolerated in the pursuit of risk and gain and where incentives distorted moral and ethical norms to achieve short-term figures.[70]

Culture issues at Hastie were presented in the preceding section in relation to the monitoring and valuation of construction WIP. Further cultural problems reported at Hastie were presented in relation to 'dysfunctional deference' issues.[71]

The Administrators also noted a report to the Board with adverse 'internal cultural issues concerning inflated reported results and optimistic forecasting'.[72] In the latter respect, they observed that 'the 2011 prospectus was not adequately reviewed and challenged with regard to the financial forecasts'.[73] Indeed, the preparation of financial forecasts was highly criticised, the Administrators having found 'no evidence that the Board

---

[69] Clinton Wallace Free and Norman B Macintosh, 'Management Control Practice and Culture at Enron: The Untold Story' (8 August 2006), accessed 3 March 2015 at SSRN: http://ssrn.com/abstract=873636.

[70] Ibid, 28 (footnote omitted). For a system of corporate governance based on increasing powers to an 'ethical' CEO, see David F Larcker and Brian Tayan, "Corporate Governance According to Charles T. Munger", Rock Center for Corporate Governance at Stanford University Closer Look Series: Topics, Issues and Controversies in Corporate Governance and Leadership No. CGRP-38, (March 3, 2014), accessed 23 April 2015 at SSRN: http://ssrn.com/abstract=2404077. For a discussion of the corporate culture of Warren Buffett's Berkshire Hathaway subsidiaries, see Lawrence A Cunningham, "Berkshire Beyond Buffett: The Enduring Value of Values (Chapter 8)", GWU Law School Public Law Research Paper No. 2014-45; GWU Legal Studies Research Paper No. 2014-45, (2014), accessed 23 April 2015 at SSRN: http://ssrn.com/abstract=2488476.

For a discussion of the consequences of culture on corporate governance including CSR, shareholder and stakeholder relations, disclosure, dividends, executive compensation and board factors, see Amir N Licht, "Culture and Law in Corporate Governance", European Corporate Governance Institute (ECGI) – Law Working Paper No. 247/2014, (March 6, 2014), accessed 23 April 2015 at SSRN: http://ssrn.com/abstract=2405538.

For a discussion of how corporate culture affects shareholder governance and may reduce firm value, see Jillian A Popadak, "A Corporate Culture Channel: How Increased Shareholder Governance Reduces Firm Value", (October 25, 2013), accessed 24 April 2015 at SSRN: http://ssrn.com/abstract=2345384.

[71] See discussion in section 5.2.2.2 above.

[72] Administrators' Report, above n 4, section 2.5.2, p 13 of 99 and section 6.1.1, p 33 of 99.

[73] Ibid, section 7.3, p 58 of 99.

reviewed the annual forecasts and compared them with actual results on a regular ongoing basis'.[74]

5.2.3 Earnings Manipulation

Coffee contrasts corporate scandals in the US and Europe to explain that the nature of the scandal is driven by the differences in the structure of share ownership.[75] Thus, for the author, dispersed ownership is the driver of earnings manipulation.[76] If dispersed ownership is *a* factor in earnings manipulation – which is not contested – what structural factors in dispersed-ownership companies *were exacerbated in the Enron and Hastie Group cases* to contribute to the critical paths to collapse?

In the case of Enron, Catanach and Rhoades describe three factors identified by the US Treadway Commission in 1987 relating to the risk of fraudulent financial reporting – performance pressures, oversight issues, and changing structural conditions.[77] In addressing the criteria, the authors highlight a fatal confluence of 'significant contractual incentives' including the substantial debt and stock options of executives, the complex ownership and financial structures which reduced the efficacy of analyst, auditor and regulator monitoring and oversight and changes in the company's innovativeness and business environment all contributing to the risk of earnings manipulation.[78] Yet the authors do not blame the often-argued inadequacy of the then current accounting standards and rules, instead identifying *non-compliance* as the issue at the heart of the accounting fraud and earnings manipulation.[79]

The opportunity for manipulation of financial reports was also a factor in the Hastie collapse through lack of uniformity. There, the Administrators concluded that 'financial reporting from subsidiary level up to HST [Hastie Group Limited] was not uniform and open to manipulation'.[80]

---

[74] Ibid, section 7.13.4, p 77 of 99.

[75] John C Coffee, 'A Theory of Corporate Scandals: Why the U.S. and Europe Differ', Columbia Law and Economics Working Paper No 274 (March 2005), accessed 3 March 2015 at SSRN: http://ssrn.com/abstract=694581, 2.

[76] Ibid.

[77] Anthony H Catanach and Shelley C Rhoades, 'Enron: A Financial Reporting Failure?' (2003) 48(4) *Villanova Law Review* 1057, 2003, accessed 3 March 2015 at SSRN: http://ssrn.com/abstract=418920, 5. The authors cite Treadway Commission, *Report of the National Commission on Fraudulent Financial Reporting*, National Commission on Financial Reporting, 1987, Annexure F.

[78] Ibid.

[79] Ibid, 18.

[80] Administrators' Report, above n 4, section 2.5.3, p 14 of 99. See also section 7.9.2, p 63 of 99.

Additionally, some structural blame for the Enron collapse was attributed to a significant fall in profit margins caused by competitive pressures from new entrants into the energy trading market.[81] In the Hastie case, too, operating performance and margin difficulties arose. This time, some blame was laid at the feet of the GFC.[82] Somewhat akin to Enron, Hastie also experienced an 'increase in competition caused by the lower volume of new tenders' which impacted margins.[83]

5.2.3.1 Enron earnings management and 'off-balance sheet' transactions

In discussing the Enron collapse many commentators including Bratton, and, separately, Gillan and Martin, describe in detail various transactions involving Enron which allegedly involved 'aggressive' accounting treatments, disguised liabilities and concealment – and therefore, inflated revenue figures over several years.[84] The Administrators considered that Hastie, too, may have involved a failure to comply with accounting standards, this time relating to provisioning for asset impairment.[85]

In the case of accounting treatments, Gillan and Martin explain how Enron used 'mark-to-market' (or 'fair value') valuations for certain investments – such as power plants and pipelines – which 'lacked observable market values'[86] and consequently brought into question some of the large 'gains' recorded in the company's profit figures over several periods.[87] In the Hastie case, the failure to recognise asset write-downs in earlier periods resulted in material overstatement.[88] Thus, the Administrators observed that 'compliance with accounting standards appears to be lacking, particularly with reference to provisioning for asset impairment'.[89]

Commentators also describe how Enron established 'Special Purpose Entities' or 'SPEs' – ordinarily permissible – which had the effect of disguising contingent liabilities and other debt which was properly required to be disclosed in the consolidated balance sheet.[90] In one case, an SPE was managed by an Enron employee who reported to Enron's CFO[91] in

---

81 Bratton, above n 1, 23 (footnotes omitted).
82 Administrators' Report, above n 4, section 6.1, p 31 of 99.
83 Ibid, section 6.1, p 32 of 99.
84 Bratton, above n 1, 28–40 and Gillan and Martin, above n 33, 9–20. See also Rosen, above n 55, 1169–81 and Branson, above n 30, 999–1002.
85 Administrators' Report, above n 4, section 2.5.3, p 14 of 99.
86 Gillan and Martin, above n 33, 10.
87 Ibid, 10–11.
88 Administrators' Report, above n 4, section 6.2, p 37 of 99.
89 Ibid, section 7.3, p 58 of 99.
90 Bratton, above n 1, 30–1. See also Gillan and Martin, above n 33, 12–14.
91 Gillan and Martin, above n 33, 12–13.

breach of Enron's own code of conduct for conflicts.[92] The SPE funded a buyout of a joint venture partner by a loan guaranteed by Enron and an 'outside' equity requirement in the capital of the SPE was allegedly funded by a 'disguised' loan taken out by Enron.[93] The result enabled Enron to recognise over US$400 million of income for the years 1997–2001 – which was subsequently restated downwards with over US$600 million of debt additionally recognised.[94] For Fleischer, some of these transactions sought to manipulate earnings but minimise tax.[95]

In another case, the outside equity requirements of two other SPEs established by Enron were allegedly supplied by limited partnerships of which an officer of Enron – the CFO – was allegedly in control and received substantial payment totalling some US$30 million.[96] Yet more SPE-related transactions involved these two SPEs. Through a complicated series of transactions, hedging arrangements were entered into between Enron and the SPEs. Gillan and Martin explain that the arrangements relied, in effect, on the market value of Enron stock held by the SPEs to meet the SPE's commitments and became unravelled once Enron's share price began falling[97] – the resultant 'correction' removed over US$1 billion from the 'net shareholders equity' of Enron.[98] Discussing some of the hedge arrangements entered into by Enron and the relevant SPEs, Gillan and Martin concluded that 'Enron effectively entered into hedges with itself'.[99] Gordon, too, is critical of the conflicts of interest involved in these entities.[100]

Why were these and other transactions entered into by Enron? The answer for some commentators lies – in part – in the form of executive compensation to which this chapter now turns.

5.2.3.2 Enron earnings manipulation and CEO, executive and director compensation

A detailed investigation into the role of executive remuneration in corporate scandals, strategies to address this issue and the on-going

---

92 Ibid, 14.

93 Bratton, above n 1, 31.

94 Ibid, 30–1.

95 Victor Fleischer, 'Enron's Dirty Little Secret: Waiting for the Other Shoe to Drop' (2002) 94(8) *Tax Notes*, accessed 3 March 2015 at SSRN: http://ssrn.com/abstract=301911, 2.

96 Bratton, above n 1, 32–33.

97 Gillan and Martin, above n 33, 16–17.

98 Bratton, above n 1, 37–8. See also Gillan and Martin, above n 33, 17.

99 Gillan and Martin, above n 33, 18.

100 Gordon, above n 8, 4.

evolution of regulation in the area has been undertaken by Professor Hill and will not be repeated in this work.[101] In Chapter 10, the relational approach examines issues relating to 'good' corporate governance and director, CEO and management compensation. Here, this chapter highlights aspects that *recur* in commentator examinations of the Enron collapse, in particular, the short-term structure of compensation schemes.

5.2.3.2.1 Enron short-term share options and earnings manipulation Bratton suggests that the form of executive compensation – the granting of share options – contributed to the behaviour which resulted in earnings manipulation:

> [o]ption holding dulls the actor's sensitivity to degrees of distress on the downside, and at the same time gives the actor an incentive to generate chances for upside gains of high magnitude. Thus directed, a group of managers certainly would be more disposed to high risk strategies.[102]

The Enron story involved a truly huge volume of options which were converted into stock and then sold by Enron executives and management.[103] Certainly Armour and McCahery also identify 'aggressive accounting manipulations' to boost stock option values.[104] Gordon, too, identifies the issue of substantial amounts of share options as a feature of the Enron collapse.[105] In particular, for Gordon – and a tension in executive compensation examined in Chapter 10[106] – the granting of options *exercisable in the short-term* may have increased fraudulent practices and risk-taking by executives to increase the share price.[107] In addition, for Bratton, Enron's

---

[101] See, for example, Jennifer G Hill, 'Regulating Executive Remuneration: International Developments in the Post-Scandal Era' (2006) 3 *European Company Law* 64; Vanderbilt Law and Economics Research Paper No 06-06, accessed 3 March 2015 at SSRN: http://ssrn.com/abstract=887944.

[102] Bratton, above n 1, 49.

[103] Ibid, 17.

[104] John Armour and Joseph A McCahery, 'After Enron: Improving Corporate Law and Modernising Securities Regulation in Europe and the US', Amsterdam Center for Law & Economics Working Paper No 2006–07 (June 2006), accessed 3 March 2015 at SSRN: http://ssrn.com/abstract=910205, 2. See also, Ray Ball, 'Market and Political/Regulatory Perspectives on the Recent Accounting Scandals' (2008) 47(2) *Journal of Accounting Research* 277–323 (May 2009), accessed 3 March at SSRN: http://ssrn.com/abstract=1272804, 11.

[105] Gordon, above n 9, 14–16.

[106] See discussion in section 10.2.5 below.

[107] Gordon, above n 9, 15–16.

bonus payment scheme – linked to share price performance – exacerbated the problem[108] and Gillan and Martin similarly highlight the short-term focus of this issue.[109]

Gordon sums up this area as a four-part failure relating to stock-based compensation combined with the corresponding risk of financial manipulation by management both exacerbated by a lack of financial transparency and failure of sufficient board monitoring which should instead have been heightened by these factors.[110]

5.2.4 External or Independent Audit

5.2.4.1 External/independent audit is a core governance variable

The relational approach will identify external or independent audit – supported by reputational constraints on the auditor – as one of the central planks of corporate governance variable schemes, codes and directives comprising Key Field No 3 – Comparative Corporate Governance Codes.[111] Indeed, this variable will be identified in terms of both continuity and centrality as one of the core variables in global and national corporate governance codes.[112] How, then, did this variable operate in the case of the Enron and Hastie Group corporate collapses?

Following this, the rate of restatements of financial results is treated as an important indicator of the performance and governance of accounting firms in the conduct of audits.[113] In this respect, Professors Eisenberg and Macey tell us that, in the case of the rate of restatements of financial results, Enron's auditor Arthur Andersen did not perform objectively differently to the other major firms for the period 1997–2001.[114] Kroger is of a different view and tells us that Andersen's

---

[108] Bratton, above n 1, 49.

[109] Gillan and Martin, above n 33, 29–31. See also Gillan and Martin, above n 57, 9–11.

[110] Gordon, above n 8, 3–4.

[111] See, for example, Navajyoti Samanta and Tirthankar Das, 'Role of Auditors in Corporate Governance' (11 October 2009), accessed 3 March 2015 at SSRN: http://ssrn.com/abstract=1487050.

[112] See discussion in section 6.8.1 below.

[113] Theodore Eisenberg and Jonathon R Macey, 'Was Arthur Andersen Different? An Empirical Examination of Major Accounting Firms' Audits of Large Clients', Cornell Legal Studies Research Paper No 04-03; Yale Law & Economics Research Paper No 287 (12 November 2003), accessed 3 March 2015 at SSRN: http://ssrn.com/abstract=468761, 2.

[114] Ibid.

failure to protect investors is not isolated to the Enron case.[115] Thus, important for this chapter's analysis of the Enron collapse – and its lessons for the balancing of the eight governance factors identified herein – is to analyse the features of the Arthur Andersen audit function that contributed to gatekeeper failure. In the Enron context, both the independence of the external auditor and the role of non-audit services – tensions identified in Chapter 9[116] – were critically questioned as significant causes of this failure.

In the case of the Hastie collapse, the Administrators have queried the auditor's compliance with a number of Australian Auditing Standards.[117] The Administrators have suggested that, had the true financial position been known, funders and investors may not have supported the 2011 capital raising and remedial action may have been taken sooner.[118] In relation to the December 2010 financial statements, the Administrators noted that the recognition of certain 'significant write-downs' indicated 'internal accounting control deficiencies' yet the auditor's report to the Audit and Risk Management Committee did 'not identify any significant issues with . . . accounting records or internal controls'.[119]

For the June 2011 financial statements, the auditor 'challenged the goodwill assumptions'. Yet, certain of the auditor's calculations and growth rates 'still indicated that no goodwill impairment was required'.[120] Additionally, there were no signs that 'the auditor challenged the valuation of receivables or WIP' which were significantly overstated.[121] Finally, for the December 2011 financial statements, a report to the Audit and Risk Management Committee maintained that the auditor 'did not note any significant issues with . . . corporate accounting records that warranted reporting' and 'had not identified any significant deficiencies in internal controls . . .'.[122] In the report, the auditor had drawn 'attention to the material uncertainty . . . to continue as a going concern' but had stated that

---

115 John R Kroger, 'Enron, Fraud and Securities Reform: An Enron Prosecutor's Perspective' (2005) 76(1) *University of Colorado Law Review* 57–138, (December 2004), accessed 3 March 2015 at SSRN: http://ssrn.com/abstract=537542, 28. See also Kathleen F Brickey, 'Andersen's Fall from Grace' (2004) 81 *Washington University Law Quarterly* 917, accessed 3 March 2015 at SSRN: http://ssrn.com/abstract=508462.

116 See discussion in sections 9.2.3.1–9.2.3.2 below.

117 Administrators' Report, above n 4, section 7.11, p 67 of 99.

118 Ibid.

119 Ibid, section 7.11.2, p 67 of 99.

120 Ibid, section 7.11.3, p 68 of 99.

121 Ibid.

122 Ibid, section 7.11.4, p 68 of 99.

it was not aware of any matter not in accordance with the Corporations Act including the true and fair view requirement.[123]

In summary, the Hastie Audit issues are significant and centre on a number of alleged failures – to comply with Australian Auditing Standards, to identify significant issues with accounting records and internal controls and to challenge the value in assets such as goodwill, receivables and WIP.

5.2.4.2 Independent auditors and reputational constraints

If reputational constraints are an important ingredient of the independence of the auditor – and therefore the attraction of the auditor to the client – audit failures should have significant negative effects on the business and prospects of the auditor itself. This appears to be the case. The reputational fallout on Andersen is attested to by Barton who finds support for the strength of this constraint.[124] The author concludes that 'highly visible clients are more sensitive to auditor reputation'.[125]

Along this line, Chang, Chi and Liu investigated whether Andersen clients – to reduce damage to the perceived integrity of their own reputations and financial information – were likely to switch auditor in the post-Enron fallout.[126] The results supported this view but with the authors finding that the fraction of clients switching to a (then) 'Big 5' accounting firm declined over time.[127]

This, then, is the theory. Callen and Morel used the Andersen reputational damage from Enron to test whether auditor reputation enhances equity prices.[128] The authors found some loss in firm value on the Andersen fallout but less than expected.[129]

Gillan and Martin point out that the Arthur Andersen firm undertook both the internal and external audit function for some two years and

---

[123] Ibid.

[124] Jan Barton, 'Who Cares about Auditor Reputation?', accessed 3 March 2015 at SSRN: http://ssrn.com/abstract=436967, 22.

[125] Ibid.

[126] Chingfu Chang, Wuchun Chi and Chiawen Liu, 'Client Characteristics and Auditor Switch in an Audit Failure' (20 April 2003), accessed 3 March 2015 at SSRN: http://ssrn.com/abstract=403700.

[127] Ibid, 23.

[128] Jeffery L Callen and Mindy Morel, 'The Enron-Andersen Debacle: Do Equity Markets React to Auditor Reputation?', EFMA 2003 Helsinki Meetings (December 2002), accessed 3 March 2015 at SSRN: http://ssrn.com/abstract=341440.

[129] Ibid, 11.

so '[e]ssentially . . . was reviewing its own work'.[130] For Barrett, conflicts of interest are only the surrounding circumstances of the Enron audit failure. For the author, the Arthur Andersen failure is predominantly due to 'unconscious bias' although culture problems are not ignored.[131]

Yet, if the SOX reforms were intended to increase auditor independence, then – on Vakkur *et al's* 2009 empirical study of 149 CEOs and 57 directors – there may be unintended consequences and costs as auditors are perceived to have gained more influence on management.[132]

Bratton[133] suggests, as a 'broadbrush explanation' for Andersen's actions in Enron, a three-pronged failure as undermining auditor independence – the significant size of consulting services revenue, that Enron was Andersen's second-largest client and Enron's practice of hiring former Andersen employees as senior accounting officers.[134]

Yet Ball does not immediately leap to the non-audit services scapegoat, pointing to the 'unusual' relationship between auditor and client:

> they are engaged and compensated by client firm managers, who are interested parties (i.e., prefer a clean audit certificate). The argument here is not that non-audit revenues create a potential conflict of interest, but that audit fees themselves do.[135]

Barrett gets to the heart of the matter which he calls 'attachment':

> [t]he auditor's business interests in fostering a long-term relationship with a client's management encourage auditors to render 'clean' audit opinions in an effort to retain any existing engagements and to secure future business. Auditors that issue anything but an unqualified opinion frequently get replaced.[136]

For Barrett, this 'attachment' was then strengthened – thus undermining the independence of Andersen – by the 'integrated audit' where Andersen

---

130 Gillan and Martin, above n 33, 27.

131 Matthew J Barrett, 'Enron and Andersen – What Went Wrong and Why Similar Audit Failures Could Happen Again', accessed 3 March 2015 at SSRN: http://ssrn.com/abstract=794831, 158.

132 Nicholas V Vakkur, R Preston McAfee and Fred Kipperman, 'The Unintended Effects of the Sarbanes Oxley Act of 2002' (2009) 22(1) *Research in Accounting Regulation* 18–28 (17 February 2009) accessed 3 March 2015 at SSRN: http://ssrn.com/abstract=1345475, 15.

133 Bratton, above n 1.

134 Ibid, 68.

135 Ball, above n 104, 9.

136 Barrett, above n 131, 159

undertook both the internal and external audit function.[137] The integrated audit model, the 'revolving door' practice – that Enron hired many former Andersen employees – together with some personal relationships between Andersen and Enron personnel leads Barrett to conclude that 'familiarity' between auditor and client was a serious flaw leading to a far too uncritical acceptance of management assertions.[138]

In Chapter 9,[139] the relational approach will examine suggestions that the provision of non-audit services[140] by auditors increases the likelihood of earnings manipulation. Yet, Chapter 9 will present conflicting studies in relation to whether such a relation exists.

Gillan and Martin highlight consulting fees as an independence question in Enron.[141] In this respect, Rosen explains the problem for the auditor when reviewing work of its own (tax) partners in terms both of reduced independence and the transformation of 'compliance' functions into a 'risk management' function where 'noncompliance becomes an option'.[142]

As noted above, Coffee suggests the Enron collapse is a case of 'gatekeeper failure'.[143] One theme investigated by Coffee is that 'reputational constraints' on auditors are eroded or overborne by the company's (non-overt) threat of removal or reduction in non-audit services. For Coffee, difficulties for the client to fire the auditor over non-acquiescence with 'aggressive' accounting treatments – which may cause the client public embarrassment and invite investigation by authorities – are replaced by a 'low visibility' sanction of terminating or reducing consulting services.[144] Coffee also points to a movement during the 1990s to 'equity based' executive compensation – particularly short-term share options – as increasing pressure on auditors to 'acquiesce in earnings management'.[145] Related

---

137 Ibid, 160 (footnotes omitted).

138 Ibid, 161–2.

139 See discussion in sections 9.2.3–9.2.3.3 below.

140 For a discussion of different approaches to the regulation of non-audit services, see, International Organization of Securities Commissions (IOSCO), Technical Committee And Emerging Markets Committee Of The International Organization Of Securities Commissions, *Survey On The Regulation Of Non-Audit Services Provided By Auditors To Audited Companies*, March 2007, available at http://www.iosco.org/library/pubdocs/pdf/IOSCOPD241.pdf (accessed 3 March 2015).

141 Gillan and Martin, above n 33, 28.

142 Rosen, above n 55, 1180.

143 John C Coffee, 'Understanding Enron: It's About the Gatekeepers, Stupid', Columbia Law & Economics Working Paper No 207 (30 July 2002), accessed 3 March 2015 at SSRN: http://ssrn.com/abstract=325240, 5.

144 Ibid, 15–16.

145 Ibid, 18–19.

to the consulting services issue, Coffee also suggests that an audit firm's own internal control/monitoring function may fail in the face of sizeable consulting fees.[146]

5.2.4.3 Other gatekeepers

While auditors are perceived as the primary gatekeepers in Anglo-American corporate governance, they are not the only ones. The Enron scandal enveloped the role of other gatekeepers, in particular securities analysts, investment banks, brokers and lawyers. But their roles should be seen in light of the market and (decentralised) regulatory climate of the time to which the chapter now turns.

5.2.4.3.1 'Decentralisation' of US corporate regulation On a structural level, for Roe, the 'porous' and decentralised structure of American corporate regulation is a principal cause of 'instability' in corporate governance and therefore major firm collapse.

> [w]e have multiple regulators, each with strengths and weaknesses. Moreover, the regulated often affect how they're regulated. Some of the breakdowns in the gatekeepers, and in the efforts to shore them up, emanated from the actions of the core group to be controlled—often American managers themselves, sometimes accountants, sometimes promoters of Silicon Valley start-ups. The regulated often sought to weaken the regulation that would have reduced their—the managers'—discretion.[147]

Thus, for Roe, the decentralised regulatory climate of the time reduced the external checks and balances on firm managers. It is in this reduced monitoring environment – for Roe 'porous' – that the relational approach now examines the role of a number of gatekeepers important to the Enron story.

5.2.4.3.2 Securities analysts, investment banks, brokers and credit rating agencies Armour and McCahery, too, note that external auditors were not the only potential gatekeepers nullified by conflicts, securities analysts also having played a role in the failure:

> [m]oreover, analysts at several investment banks, supposedly offering independent advice, were tainted by conflicts of interest arising out of their

[146] Ibid, 21–2.

[147] Mark J Roe, 'The Inevitable Instability of American Corporate Governance', Harvard Law and Economics Discussion Paper No 493 (September 2004), accessed 3 March 2015 at SSRN: http://ssrn.com/abstract=615561, 16.

> firms' involvement in Enron's financing. As a result, Enron's share price was artificially inflated for a considerable period of time.[148]

Indeed, Felton and Kim criticise these investment banks as acting as both 'brokers and bankers' as 'analysts had mostly "buy" and "strong buy" recommendations for Enron at the same time that their firms sought banking relationships with Enron'.[149]

For Julia Black, failure of the financial markets in the Enron case rested with the credit rating agencies which had been 'enrolled' as a strategy of regulation:

> As the corporate accounting scandals of Enron, World-com, Parmalat and their ilk demonstrated, those relied upon to act as gatekeepers can be less than reliable, and need not necessarily perform the role that regulators assume they will play. In the corporate sector, the failings arose from lawyers and accountants. In financial markets, the most significant failure was that of the credit rating agencies (CRAs). The experience of enrolling CRAs illustrated that although gatekeeper regulation is a potentially useful regulatory strategy, whether the strategy is successful depends on the motivation, regulatory capacity, and most importantly, the broader market context, culture and incentives of those being relied upon to act as gatekeepers.[150]

Thus, for Black, alignment of other gatekeepers with the regulatory regime is vital.[151]

5.2.4.3.3 The role of lawyers For Bainbridge, the ethical standards of lawyers acting for Enron (and WorldCom) contributed to those debacles – both in terms of negligence as well as 'facilitators and enablers of management impropriety' – particularly in the area of company disclosures.[152]

---

148 Armour and McCahery, above n 104, 2.

149 James Felton and Jongchai Kim, 'Warnings from the Enron Message Board' (2002) 11(3) *Journal of Investing* 29–52, accessed 3 March 2015 at SSRN: http://ssrn.com/abstract=918519, 2. Kroger gives a detailed account of these and other conflicts of interest in the context of the role of Wall Street analysts in Kroger, above n 115. See also Gillan and Martin, above n 57, 19–21.

150 Black, above n 7, 1049 (footnote omitted). The strategy of using other social actors in the function of 'decentred regulation' is further discussed by Black in section 6.1.3.1 below.

151 Ibid.

152 Stephen M Bainbridge, 'The Tournament at the Intersection of Business and Legal Ethics' (2003–2004) 1(2) *University of St. Thomas Law Journal* 909–24, accessed 3 March 2015 at SSRN: http://ssrn.com/abstract=429304, 2–3 (footnotes omitted). See also Stephen M Bainbridge, 'Corporate Lawyers as Gatekeepers' in

Certainly Cunningham identifies business lawyers at the heart of – and allowing – many accounting frauds such as that at Enron.[153] The author squarely lays the blame for formation, structuring and reporting of Enron's off-balance sheet entities at the feet of lawyers and argues that these gatekeepers should enhance their accounting skills and knowledge.[154]

5.2.5 Inadequate Disclosure Affects the Transparency and Timing of Financial Reporting and Monitoring

5.2.5.1 Non-disclosure and reduced board monitoring

In the Enron case, Gordon identifies enhanced financial disclosure as promoting heightened board monitoring through market monitoring of the board.[155] Indeed, in the relational approach, the Shareholder Primacy Interrelationship Scheme depicts a reflexive relationship between Reporting Factor No 1 and Monitoring & Audit Factor No 5.[156] Gordon criticises the extensive use of the SPEs to conduct transactions which contributed significantly to Enron's earnings as severely hampering the market's ability to monitor the Enron managers[157] concluding that:

> [s]o the Board blinded the external monitors in circumstances where managers would face strong temptations to cheat and where the blinding would make cheating easier.[158]

Thus, not only was the US regulation system 'porous' for authors such as Roe,[159] simultaneous monitoring by the market and board was dulled by non-transparent transaction methods such as off-balance sheet SPEs.

In the Administrators' Report, the Board of the Hastie Group received a very critical assessment of its governance and financial reporting including inadequate review of reports and an inadequate level of control.[160] The

---

Stephen M Bainbridge, *Corporate Governance After The Financial Crisis*, Oxford: Oxford University Press, 2012; UCLA School of Law, Law-Econ Research Paper No 12-03, (January 6, 2012), accessed 3 March 2015 at SSRN: http://ssrn.com/abstract=1980975.

[153] Lawrence A Cunningham, 'Sharing Accounting's Burden: Business Lawyers in Enron's Dark Shadows' (2002) 57(4) *Business Lawyer (ABA)* 1421–62, accessed 3 March 2015 at SSRN: http://ssrn.com/abstract=307978, 18.

[154] Cunningham, ibid, 18–19.

[155] Gordon, above n 8, 7.

[156] See Shareholder Primacy Interrelationship Scheme in Figure 2.6.

[157] Gordon, above n 8, 7.

[158] Ibid, 8.

[159] See discussion in section 5.2.4.3.1 above.

[160] Administrators' Report, above n 4, section 7.9.5, p 65 of 99.

lack of adequate information was extensive, covering areas such as key performance indicators, reporting and details of profit and loss and the balance sheet.[161] The Administrators thus suggest that the Prospectus for the capital raising and the 2011 financial year financial statements 'were possibly materially misstated' leading the banking syndicate and investors to possibly be misled.[162]

The Administrators were highly critical of Hastie's books and records considering that they were inadequate.[163] The Administrators found 'indications of liquidity and cashflow issues' and suspected that the 'financial reports may have been materially misstated'.[164] Additionally, if there was material overstatement of particular key asset values, the Hastie Group 'may have been balance sheet insolvent in the period prior to our [the Administrators'] appointment'.[165]

5.2.5.2 Enron's (non) disclosure – ignored or too complex?

But Armour and McCahery have a different slant on the non-disclosure issue. After citing studies supporting the workings of the efficient market hypothesis,[166] the authors consider that many 'irregularities' and relevant disclosures were not concealed but merely 'ignored'.[167]

But the picture seems less clear at least in relation to Enron's more complex transactions. Indeed, Schwarcz points to the limitations on the effectiveness of disclosure in complex transactions such as the securitisation transactions of the Enron SPEs.[168] The author argues that only one additional measure is required in such cases, that management 'be free of material conflicts of interest stemming from disclosure-impaired transactions'.[169]

---

[161] Ibid.

[162] Ibid.

[163] Ibid, section 7.10, p 66 of 99. See also section 7.13, p 70 of 99.

[164] Ibid, section 7.13.2, p 71 of 99.

[165] Ibid, section 7.13.3, p 75 of 99.

[166] Armour and McCahery, above n 104, 4–5.

[167] Ibid, 5. See also Bala G Dharan and William R Bufkins, 'Red Flags in Enron's Reporting of Revenues & Key Financial Measures' (23 July 2008), accessed 3 March 2015 at SSRN: http://ssrn.com/abstract=1172222.

[168] Steven L Schwarcz, 'Rethinking the Disclosure Paradigm in a World of Complexity' (2004) *University of Illinois Law Review* 1; Duke Law School, Public Law Research Paper No 34, accessed 3 March 2015 at SSRN: http://ssrn.com/abstract=336685, 34.

[169] Ibid, 35 (footnote omitted).

5.3 SUMMARY – SOME RECURRING THEMES IN THE ENRON AND HASTIE GROUP CORPORATE COLLAPSES

In this chapter's presentation of Key Field No 2, the relational approach has reviewed the complex – and often competing – evaluations of the Enron corporate collapse and the detailed Administrators' Report into the Hastie Group collapse to identify common themes. A multitude of theories and suggestions – again competing – permeate this Key Field. Of course, much more than the other Key Fields, this Field – comprised largely of commentator evaluation – represents a much greater degree of individual opinion, conjecture and hypothesis than do the others. With that caveat, the following presents a summary of the principal perceived failures in corporate governance variables in the Enron and Hastie corporate collapses. The aim of this concluding section of the chapter will be to emphasise why the relevant failures are important in the relational approach and how the failures compare to the relative importance (relational proximity) ratings[170] of the governance variables examined in the book.

5.3.1 The Nexus of Contracts and Agency Theory in the Enron and Hastie Failure Scenarios

The market for corporate control – incorporating the efficient market hypothesis – acts in conjunction with nexus theory to punish managerial structures or behaviours which reduce firm value and the relational approach is aligned with this mechanism.[171] In addition, the governance factors and the interrelationship schemes of the relational approach are based on agency cost theory.[172] In short, the relational approach seeks to explain the behaviour and relative importance of governance variables in reducing agency costs – including monitoring costs, bonding costs and residual losses – between inside management and outside dispersed shareholders.[173] In the relational approach, managerial structures or behaviours which increase agency costs will reduce the long-term efficiency and sustainability of the firm.[174] This includes structures or

---

170 For a full list of relational proximity ratings for the governance variables, see the Relational Proximity Table (Table 3.2).

171 See discussion in section 4.2.2 above.

172 See discussion in section 4.2.3.1 above.

173 Ibid.

174 See discussion in section 1.5 above.

behaviours which increase the information asymmetry between insiders and outsiders.[175]

The Enron failure was characterised by significant asymmetric information problems. In particular, the complexity of its company structure and business plan – such as the use of off-balance sheet transactions and SPEs – increased the information asymmetry of investors and the time for market corrections. This undermined the operation of the efficient market hypothesis that the share price will reflect all publicly-available information relating to the company.[176] It is also consistent with the 'bounded rationality' of investors – that there was only so much the market could understand – and time-lag problems both identified by Dent.[177] For Gordon, the problems extended to more sophisticated securities analysts – Enron's high share price failed to reflect its 'intrinsic value' even with the attention of a barrage of such analysts.[178] But complexity in the Enron entities and business plan had further effects which led to problems for the market in determining the ownership of assets and the solvency of group entities.[179]

Lack of disclosure in the Enron case was also significant in harming the quality of monitoring – of both the market and the board. For Gordon, increases in the level and quality of company disclosures increase the level of monitoring by the market which, in turn, increases monitoring by the board.[180] Indeed, this is represented in the relational approach by the **[TransTimeMon] (+)** variable[181] (Transparency and Timing of Reporting – Monitoring Effect) which has the highest coverage/rating of +8/100.00 *rprox*. Further, the reputational constraints on outside directors – emphasised by Fama and Jensen[182] – are represented by the individual

---

175 See discussion in sections 4.2.2 and 4.2.3.1 above.

176 George W Dent, 'Academics in Wonderland: The Team Production and Director Primacy Models of Corporate Governance', Case Legal Studies Research Paper No 07-21 (June 2007), accessed 3 March 2015 at SSRN: http://ssrn.com/abstract=995186, 18–19 of 72. See discussion in section in 4.2.2 above.

177 Ibid.

178 Gordon, above n 9, 3 and 5–10. See discussion in section 5.2.1.1 above.

179 See discussion in section 5.2.1.1 above.

180 Gordon, above n 8, 7. See discussion in section 5.2.5.1 above.

181 Transparency and Timing of Reporting – Monitoring Effect – see discussion in section 9.1.2.1 below.

182 Eugene F Fama and Michael C Jensen, 'Separation of Ownership and Control' in Michael C Jensen, *Foundations Of Organizational Strategy*, Cambridge, MA: Harvard University Press, 1998 and (1983) 26 *Journal of Law and Economics* 301, accessed 3 March 2015 at SSRN: http://ssrn.com/abstract=94034, 19. See discussion in section 4.2.2 above.

governance variables of **[ReputDiscl] (+)**[183] (Reputational Constraints – 'Disclosure Standards', +8/100.00 *rprox*) and **[ReputRep] (+)**[184] (Reputational Constraints – 'Transparent Reporting', +8/100.00 *rprox*). Yet the use of off-balance sheet entities by Enron – in conjunction with significant managerial incentives – increased the sensitivity of management to the share price which consequently reduced the likelihood of adverse disclosures by management. As a consequence, this reduced the quality of monitoring by the market which in turn reduced the quality of board monitoring.[185]

Poor financial reporting also plagued the Hastie Group.[186] The Administrators were highly critical considering that Hastie's books were deficient in representing the Group's financial position[187] and suspected that the 'financial reports may have been materially misstated'.[188] Significantly in the case of the Hastie Group – but hidden from view – profitable businesses within the Group were used to subsidise losses in the Middle East operations[189] thus masking liquidity problems. Yet, unlike Enron, the many danger signs announced to the market[190] should have raised problems much earlier. Why didn't they? The problem for market monitoring was the significant time-lag issues in relation to asset write-downs such as goodwill, trade and other receivables and construction WIP.[191] For the Administrators, earlier disclosure of these deficiencies may have led to 'administrators being appointed earlier [and] changes to investors' and financiers' decisions regarding investing in or supporting the Hastie Group'.[192]

What do these failures tell us about pre- and post-GFC collapses? The answer is that the 'disclosure – market monitoring – board monitoring' cycle is a significant relationship in both eras. Indeed, the efficient market hypothesis is dependent on the quality/transparency and timing of management disclosure – the **[TransTimeMon] (+)**[193] variable. Management

---

183 See discussion in section 10.4.1 below.

184 Ibid.

185 See the views of Gordon in sections 5.2.2.1.1 and 5.2.5.1 above.

186 See discussion in section 5.2.5.1 above.

187 Administrators' Report, above n 4, section 7.10, p 66 of 99. See also section 7.13, p 70 of 99.

188 Ibid, section 7.13.2, p 71 of 99.

189 See discussion in section 5.2.2.3.1 above.

190 See discussion in section 5.2.1.1 above.

191 Ibid.

192 Ibid. See Administrators' Report, above n 4, section 2.5.2, p 13 of 99.

193 Transparency and Timing of Reporting – Monitoring Effect – see discussion in section 9.1.2.1 below.

structures or behaviours which increase information asymmetry – and therefore agency costs – between inside management and outside shareholders will increase the likelihood of a 'lagged' corporate failure. This is a failure whose occurrence is delayed on account of non-disclosing behaviour by management and thus is eventually much greater than otherwise would be the case in effects on wealth-measures of outside shareholders such as operating profit and share price.

5.3.2 Director Independence, Monitoring and Risk Management

In theory, a significant proportion of the integrity of the Anglo-American shareholder protection regime rests on the independence of outside directors. It is considered one of the most important variables for enhancing the monitoring of management in the dispersed-shareholding public company. Such independence is argued to improve the quality of acquisitions and the likelihood of replacement of a CEO in times of falling profitability.[194] The principal variable in this respect is board and director independence and the proportion of non-executive/independent directors – **[BrdIndMon] (+)**.[195] It has a high coverage/rating of +7/87.50 *rprox* reflecting this theoretical importance.[196] Other governance variables with a positive direction related to independence are **[AudIndMon] (+)**,[197] **[AudIndFreq] (+)**[198] and **[NomInd] (+)**,[199] each with the same coverage/rating as **[BrdIndMon] (+)**. The importance of the independence variable is also reflected in Key Field No 3 – Comparative Corporate Governance Codes. There, the key features of global and national listed governance codes include:[200]

- 'board functions and independence – compliance with statutory and legal duties on organisation/directors';
- 'independence from management – non-executive/independent directors'; and

---

194 See discussion in sections 7.3.2.1.1–7.3.2.1.3 below.

195 Board Independent Director: Executive Director Proportion – Monitoring Effect – see discussion in sections 7.3.2.1.1–7.3.2.1.2 below.

196 See the Relational Proximity Table (Table 3.2).

197 Audit Committee – Independence – Monitoring Effect – see discussion in section 8.4.3 below.

198 Audit Committee – Independence in Combination with Frequency of Meeting – Reduction in Earnings Manipulation Effect – see discussion in section 9.2.1 below.

199 Nominating Committee – Independence Proportion – see discussion in section 7.3.1.2.2 below.

200 See discussion in section 6.8.1 below.

- 'independence from management – responsibilities of board sub-committees delineated and disclosed'.

The Enron collapse suggests that 'abnormally' high directors' consulting fees and related-party transactions for outside directors may reduce outside director independence and the quality of monitoring.[201] But commentators place greater reliance for the independence failure on equity and option holdings undermining independence and the quality of monitoring.[202] In an important study in Key Field No 4,[203] Fuerst and Kang identify two opposing effects of inside equity ownership – the 'incentive alignment' effect and the 'entrenchment' effect. This suggests that equity ownership helps to align the interests of insiders and outsiders, but that excessive equity ownership promotes insider self-interest (thus increasing agency costs) to the detriment of outside shareholders.[204] Given the sheer volume of equity and option holdings in Enron,[205] it is not surprising that the entrenchment effect dominated.

The competing 'incentive alignment' and 'entrenchment' effects are reflected in the Enron case and are consistent with the governance variables of the relational approach. These governance variables predict that increases in equity holdings and options for outside directors will:

- improve the 'alignment' of the interests of inside management and outside shareholders consistent with the **[EqOptIncent] (+)**[206] variable; and
- reduce outside director independence and quality of monitoring consistent with the **[EqOptEntrch] (−)**[207] variable.

---

[201] See the views of Branson in section 5.2.2.1 above.

[202] See discussion in section 5.2.2.1.1 above.

[203] *Empirical Studies of the Effectiveness of Governance Variables* – see discussion in section 10.2.1 below.

[204] Fuerst and Kang, above n 29, 6–7. The authors cite R Morck, A Shleifer and R W Vishny, 'Management Ownership and Corporate Performance: An Empirical Analysis' (1988) 20 *Journal of Financial Economics* 293–316.

[205] See discussion in section 5.2.3.2.1 above.

[206] Equity/Option Plans and Holdings of Directors/Executives – Incentive/'Alignment' Effect (excludes short-term options). See also section 10.2.4 below.

[207] Equity/Option Plans and Holdings of Directors/Executives – 'Entrenchment' Effect (excludes short-term options). See also section 10.2.4 below.

The significance of these effects – testified to by the Enron collapse – is consistent with the coverage/ratings of these governance variables of 7/87.50 *rprox* but in opposite directions.[208] Similar effects on the quality of monitoring are predicted by the relational approach for the granting of short-term options to outside audit committee members (**[AudShortOpts] (−)**[209]) and to directors generally (**[ShortTOpts] (−)**[210]). Both these governance variables have the second-highest negative coverage/rating of −7/87.50 *rprox*.

Enron also suggests that equity holdings and options for outside directors increase agency costs for outside shareholders by:

- increasing the potential for earnings manipulation or management[211] to meet market expectations; and
- increasing conflict of interest issues for outside directors on the audit or risk management committees.[212]

Again, this is consistent with the 'incentive alignment' and 'entrenchment' effects identified by Fuerst and Kang and the coverage/ratings of the above governance variables of the relational approach.

The monitoring effects of director independence can also be undermined by familiarity and deference among board members. Both Enron and Hastie tell us that such behaviour can be a product of corporate culture issues. A study in Key Field No 4[213] suggests that CEO turnover after poor performance is more likely with increases in the independence of the board but that 'board independence declines over the course of a CEO's tenure' on account of the CEO's control over the director nomination and appointment process.[214] For Dent, the appointment of former CEOs as outside directors reduces monitoring, questioning and deliberation of outside directors due to the reciprocal practice of CEOs

---

208 See Relational Proximity Table (Table 3.2).

209 Audit Committee – Short Term Options Granted to Outside Directors – Reduction in Monitoring Effect – see discussion in section 10.2.5.1 below.

210 Short-Term Option Holdings/Plans of Directors and Executives – see discussion in section 10.2.5.1 below.

211 See discussion in sections 5.2.2.1.1 and 5.2.3.2.1 above.

212 See discussion in section 5.2.2.1.2 above.

213 *Empirical Studies of the Effectiveness of Governance Variables.*

214 M S Weisbach and B E Hermalin, 'Boards of Directors as an Endogenously Determined Institution: A Survey of the Economic Literature' (15 June 2000), accessed 3 March 2015 at SSRN: http://ssrn.com/abstract=233111, 9–10. See discussion in section 7.3.2.1.1 below.

deferring to one another and loyalty by outside directors to the person who nominated them.[215]

In Key Field No 4, the relational approach hypothesises that the **[NomCom] (+/−)**[216] variable has a dual direction marker as it can affect the board's skill mix in a positive or negative direction. Its relational effect path thus follows that of the **[BrdSkills] (+)** variable but in both directions with a coverage/rating of +/−7/87.50 *rprox*.[217] By analogy to board skills, the quality of board monitoring and decision-making is also dependent in part on the independence and qualities of those selected to be directors by the nominating committee. In other words, the relational approach hypothesises that increases in the independence proportion of the nominating committee (**[NomInd] (+)**[218]) will similarly have a positive effect on the monitoring and decision-making – and therefore board skills – attributes of directors nominated by that committee.[219] Again, its relational effect path follows that of the **[BrdSkills] (+)** variable this time in the positive direction with a coverage/rating of +7/87.50 *rprox*.[220]

Enron displayed a significant level of familiarity in the boardroom.[221] But the level of 'dysfunctional deference' – particularly to the CEO Ken Lay – was alarming and even extended to important decisions.[222] Should this be surprising? Certainly not for Dent whose warning from Key Field No 1[223] could be applied to the Enron case:

> most boards are passive, dominated by CEOs who exert their power in their own interests.[224]

This is consistent, too, with other studies in Key Field No 4. For example, Cremers, Bebchuk and Peyer measure the 'relative importance' of the CEO in the firm and find that CEO 'centrality' is negatively associated

---

[215] Dent, above n 176, 14 of 72. See discussion in section 7.3.2.1.3 below. See also discussion in section 5.2.2.2 above.

[216] Nominating Committee – Presence, Operation and Frequency – see discussion in section 7.3.1.2.2 below.

[217] Ibid.

[218] Nominating Committee – Independence Proportion – see discussion in section 7.3.1.2.2 below.

[219] Ibid.

[220] Ibid.

[221] See the views of Gordon in section 5.2.2.2 above.

[222] See the views of Sharfman and Toll in section 5.2.2.2 above.

[223] Key Field No 1: Application of the Principal Theories of the Firm to the Relational Approach. See discussion in Chapter 4.

[224] Dent, above n 176, 14 of 72.

with firm value[225] and results in 'lower CEO turnover'[226] which 'might reflect governance problems':[227]

> [t]he probability of CEO turnover is lower if CEO centrality is higher controlling for the CEO's length of service and performance.[228]

The Enron experience tells us that the complexity of transactions – again including any off-balance sheet aspects – reduce outside director understanding of risk management reports. In turn, this reduces the quality of monitoring and risk management functions of the board.[229] Again, this undermines the operation of the efficient market hypothesis consistent with the 'bounded rationality' of investors and time-lag problems identified by Dent.[230] The Enron discussion also suggests that inadequacies in risk management reports – including failure to establish adequate procedures for approving projects and ensuring that all projects enter the approval process – result in:

- failure to describe risks adequately for board members;
- reduction in the quality of the monitoring and risk management functions of the board; and
- a reduction in the quality of board decision-making.[231]

5.3.3 Earnings Manipulation

Earnings manipulation or management – through 'aggressive' accounting treatments, misstatement, non-compliance[232] with accounting standards, disguise or concealment[233] – is clearly an anathema to the efficient market

---

225 Martijn Cremers, Lucian Bebchuk and Urs Peyer, 'CEO Centrality', Harvard Law and Economics Discussion Paper No 601 (December 2007, Revised May 2008), accessed 3 March 2015 at SSRN: http://ssrn.com/abstract=1030107, 1. The authors define this as the relative importance of the CEO in the corporation's upper management as measured by the 'CEO's pay slice' or 'CPS' being the percentage of the total compensation of the top five executives paid to the CEO. See discussion in section 7.3.2.1.1 and section 10.2.3 below.

226 Ibid.

227 Ibid, 3.

228 Ibid, 3.

229 See discussion in section 5.2.2.3.1 above.

230 See the views of Dent in section 4.2.2 above.

231 See discussion in section 5.2.2.3.1 above.

232 See discussion in section 5.2.3 above.

233 See the views of Bratton and, separately, Gillan and Martin in section 5.2.3.1 above.

hypothesis on account of an increase in asymmetric information between insiders and outsiders.

Again, this is represented in the relational approach by governance variables which all have the maximum coverage/rating – the **[TransTimeMon] (+)** variable[234] (Transparency and Timing of Reporting – Monitoring Effect, +8/100.00 *rprox*) and the individual governance variables of **[ReputDiscl] (+)**[235] (Reputational Constraints – 'Disclosure Standards', +8/100.00 *rprox*) and **[ReputRep] (+)**[236] (Reputational Constraints – 'Transparent Reporting', +8/100.00 *rprox*). Thus, management structures or behaviours which reduce the effectiveness of these governance variables have a significant effect on agency costs and, in turn, the long-term efficiency and sustainability of the firm.

Structural factors such as performance pressures, oversight issues and changing structural conditions appear to increase the risk of fraudulent financial reporting.[237] More particularly from the case studies, Enron-specific structural factors such as:

- performance incentives including equity options;
- complexity in the structure and financing of inter-related entities which reduced the efficacy of analyst, auditor and regulator monitoring and oversight;
- innovation in technology and financing methods; and
- decline in sector in which Enron operated,[238]

resulted in increases in the risk of earnings manipulation.

Lack of uniformity in financial reporting method also causes a problem. In Hastie, 'financial reporting from subsidiary level up to HST [Hastie Group Limited] was not uniform and open to manipulation'.[239] It was thus not surprising to see the Administrators found that the financial statements may have been materially misstated and misleading.[240]

In the Enron case-study, CEO, executive and director compensa-

---

[234] Transparency and Timing of Reporting – Monitoring Effect – see discussion in section 9.1.2.1 below.

[235] See discussion in section 10.4.1 below.

[236] Ibid.

[237] Catanach and Rhoades, above n 77, 5. See discussion in section 5.2.3 above.

[238] Ibid.

[239] Administrators' Report, above n 4, section 2.5.3, p 14 of 99. See also section 7.9.2, p 63 of 99.

[240] See discussion in section 5.2.1.1 above.

tion factors such as share options, the short-term structure of those options and bonus payments linked to share-price performance appear to have:

- increased the likelihood of the adoption of high risk-taking/strategies by management;[241]
- increased the risk of 'aggressive accounting manipulations' to boost stock option values;[242] and
- increased the likelihood of fraud and risk-taking.[243]

Again these results are consistent with the following predicted outcomes for relational approach governance variables:

- improvement in the 'alignment' of the interests of inside management and outside shareholders consistent with the **[EqOptIncent] (+)**[244] variable;
- reduction in outside director independence and quality of monitoring consistent with the **[EqOptEntrch] (−)**[245] variable;
- the behaviour of the **[DirCEO$] (+/−)**[246] variable, the **[AudShortOpts] (−)**[247] variable and the **[ShortTOpts] (−)**[248] variable; and
- the behaviour of the **[NomCom] (+/−)**[249] and the **[CompCom] (+/−)**[250] variables.

---

241 See discussion in section 5.2.3.2.1 above.

242 Armour and McCahery, above n 104, 2. See discussion in section 5.2.3.2.1 above.

243 See discussion in section 5.2.3.2.1 above.

244 Equity/Option Plans and Holdings of Directors/Executives – Incentive/'Alignment' Effect (excludes short-term options), +7/87.50 *rprox* – see discussion in section 10.2.4 below.

245 Equity/Option Plans and Holdings of Directors/Executives – 'Entrenchment' Effect (excludes short-term options), −7/87.50 *rprox* – see discussion in section 10.2.4 below.

246 Director/CEO Compensation Levels, +/−7/87.50 *rprox* – see discussion in section 10.2.4 below.

247 Audit Committee – Short Term Options Granted to Outside Directors – Reduction in Monitoring Effect, −7/87.50 *rprox* – see discussion in section 10.2.5.1 below.

248 Short-Term Option Holdings/Plans of Directors and Executives, −7/87.50 *rprox* – see discussion in section 10.2.5.1 below.

249 Nominating Committee – Presence, Operation and Frequency, +/−7/87.50 *rprox* – see discussion in section 7.3.1.2.2 below.

250 Compensation Committee – Presence, Operation and Frequency, +/−7/87.50 *rprox* – see discussion in section 10.2.4.1 below.

These are some of the most significant governance variables in the relational approach in their effect on long-term efficiency and sustainability. All these governance variables have the second-highest coverage/rating of 7/87.50 *rprox* (in various directions).

5.3.4 External/Independent Audit

Chapter 6's examination of Key Field No 3 – Comparative Corporate Governance Codes – identifies external/independent audit as a 'core' feature of both global and national corporate governance codes.[251]

Thus, management – and particularly auditor – structures or behaviours which reduce the effectiveness of the independent audit will significantly affect the long-term sustainability of the firm. For example, the **[ExtAudEarn] (+)**[252] variable representing the external/independent audit function has a coverage/rating of +7/87.50 *rprox* which predicts a reduction in earnings management as a result of the external audit function. On account of the 'externality' and consequent independence of the auditor, it is a 'strong form' independence variable. In other words, the relational approach predicts **[ExtAudEarn] (+)** to have a stronger monitoring 'improvement' or 'enhancement' effect on Monitoring & Audit Factor No 5 than any of **[BrdIndMon] (+)**,[253] **[AudIndMon] (+)**[254] or **[AudExpAcc] (+)**[255] which are outside-director-based.

As part of this, structures or behaviours that affect the quality of the independent audit will have a flow-on effect to Reporting Factor No 1 – Transparency, Timing and Integrity of Financial and Other Reports. The Shareholder Primacy Interrelationship Scheme[256] depicts a reflexive relationship between Monitoring & Audit Factor No 5 and Reporting Factor No 1. From Monitoring & Audit Factor No 5, the reflexive relationship with Decision-making Factor No 7 is also harmed and, from this, there is a single-direction flow-on to Reporting Factor No 1 again. Thus, the Enron

---

[251] See discussion in section 6.8.1 below.

[252] External/Independent Audit Function – see discussion in section 9.2.3.3 below.

[253] Board Independent Director: Executive Director Proportion – Monitoring Effect – see discussion in sections 7.3.2.1.1–7.3.2.1.2 below.

[254] Audit Committee – Independence – Monitoring Effect – see discussion in section 8.4.3 below.

[255] Audit Committee – Financial Expertise (Accounting) – see discussion in section 8.4.4 below.

[256] See Figure 2.6.

case study shows us that if the external audit fails significantly, the whole house of cards comes crashing down.

Non-audit services of the auditing firm

The audit firm 'self-review' of tax or consulting services advice provided by partners of the same firm increases conflicts of interest for the audit firm and in turn reduces the independence of the auditor.[257] It is also argued that it results in the transformation of 'compliance' functions into a 'risk management' function with, again, consequent reduction in independence of the auditor.[258]

Factors around the performance of non-audit services such as:

- the client's (non-overt) threat of removal or reduction in non-audit services;
- equity-based compensation including short-term options for management; and
- increases in the size of consulting and non-audit fees for the auditor,

together are predicted to result in:

- the erosion or overbearing of 'reputational constraints' on the auditor with consequent reduction in auditor independence;[259]
- increases in the likelihood that management will use consulting contracts/fees to encourage the auditor to 'acquiesce in earnings management';[260] and
- increases in the likelihood of a failure in an audit firm's own internal controls/monitoring.[261]

Thus, the **[NonAuditS] (−)**[262] variable – representing the non-audit services of the external auditor – is a significant governance variable in the relational approach with a coverage/rating of −7/87.50 *rprox*. This represents a negative effect on all the governance factors with the exception of the overriding nature of Compliance Factor No 2.[263] Thus, increases in

---

257 See the views of Gillan and Martin in section 5.2.4.2 above.

258 See the views of Rosen in section 5.2.4.2 above.

259 See the views of Coffee in section 5.2.4.2 above.

260 Ibid.

261 Ibid.

262 Non-Audit Services of External Auditor – see the discussion in sections 9.2.3.2–9.2.3.3 below.

263 See the discussion in section 9.2.3.3 below.

non-audit services by the external auditor are predicted to significantly reduce the firm's long-term efficiency and sustainability.

5.4 CONCLUDING REMARKS

This chapter has extracted the themes and tensions underlying the Enron and Hastie corporate collapses to support the identification, structure and articulation of the eight governance factors.[264] Importantly, the chapter has identified the factors which reduced the effectiveness of some of the governance variables in Table 2.1 in deterring or punishing management misconduct or which led to a misalignment between inside managers and outside dispersed shareholders.

The relational approach now turns in Chapter 6 to examine the Comparative Corporate Governance Codes Key Field No 3. This Key Field is comprised of international and national (US, UK and Australian) governance codes. Many of these codes emerged out of the collapse of Enron and other companies. Hence, the Chapter 6 analysis takes place in the context of the Enron collapse that came before and the Hastie collapse which took place post-GFC. Chapter 6 will assess the position and relative importance of many of the governance variables in Table 2.1 and this Chapter 5. Again, a critical goal will be to identify the underlying themes and tensions in these governance codes for the construction of the governance factors.

---

[264] These are examined in sections 2.6.1–2.6.8 above.

6. Key Field No 3: Comparative corporate governance codes

6.1 THE PURPOSE, SCOPE AND FUNCTION OF CHAPTER 6

6.1.1 Exploring Relative Importance

This chapter has three principal purposes. First is to identify underlying themes of the Comparative Codes Key Field No 3 (Comparative Corporate Governance Codes) for the identification, construction and articulation of the three relational axes of good governance[1] and the eight governance factors[2] in Chapter 2. As a continuing theme, the governance factors are the eight most significant and recurrent themes underlying the four Key Fields as drawn from the SSRN platform. In other words, the chapter assesses the *continuity* and *commonality* of particular aspects of governance in global and national governance codes.

Continuity is measured by identifying governance variables which recur over time throughout the evolution (including reform) of governance codes in a sector. Relative importance is measured by 'commonality' of

---

1 See discussion in sections 2.3.1–2.3.3 of Chapter 2. An expanded version of this chapter was presented at the 2015 Corporate Law Teachers' Association Annual Conference, Melbourne, Australia, February, 2015 and will be published as Francesco de Zwart, 'Global and National Comparative Corporate Governance Codes' in (2015) 30 *Australian Journal of Corporate Law*, forthcoming. For an earlier working paper version of this chapter by de Zwart, see Francesco de Zwart (90% author) and George Gilligan, 'Comparative Corporate Governance Schemes and their Relevance for the Sporting Sector', Monash University Department of Business Law and Taxation, Working Paper No 16 (November 2008), accessed 3 March 2015 at http://ssrn.com.abstract=1295682. See also Francesco de Zwart (95% author) and George Gilligan, 'Sustainable Governance in Sporting Organisations' in Placido Rodriguez, Stefan Kesenne and Helmut Dietl (eds), *Social Responsibility and Sustainability in Sports*, Oviedo: Ediciones de la Universidad de Oviedo, 2009, pp 165–227.

2 See the construction of the eight governance factors in sections 2.6.1–2.6.8 above.

governance variables in the codes of a particular sector and across all sectors. The list of recurring variables is known as a 'commonality table'.

Second, flowing from this, the chapter assesses the relative importance of governance variables in the context in which they primarily operate – the various global and national governance codes – in order to identify:

- a comparative scheme in table-form for comparing governance codes; and
- a 'core' set of governance variables for each sector.

Finally, what is the significance of these outputs for the relational approach? The analysis in Chapter 1 identified governance codes as one of the four Key Fields that together represent a simulation of the 'real world' of corporate governance discourse.[3] Critically, the 'core' set of governance variables identified at the end of this chapter have already been used to construct the three relational axes of good governance and the governance factors in Chapter 2. Here in Chapter 6, the relational approach justifies the selection of that core set.

6.1.2 The Function of Commonality – How to Use Chapter 6

This chapter is not intended to present in detail the content of the various governance codes presented. The detailed content, nature and operation of the relevant governance variables will be examined in Chapters 7–10. Instead, Chapter 6 is intended to demonstrate the underlying foundation for the relational approach by demonstrating the significant structural aspects of these codes. Commonality is the methodology chosen for highlighting these structures.

6.1.3 Justification for Selection of Global and National Corporate Governance Codes

The examination in this chapter will involve a selection of the major well-established codes in the world today – both global/cross-border and national Anglo-American (US, UK and Australian) – in relation to publicly-traded for-profit companies. While the four Key Fields are determined largely by the size of the literature base,[4] it is not sufficient to include governance codes among those Fields merely by the number of

---

3 See discussion in sections 1.3.2 and 1.3.2.3 above.

4 See discussion in section 1.3.2 above.

articles. Instead, justification is required on a number of levels. First, what is the justification for focusing on governance codes? In other words, what explains the prevalence of the so-called 'soft law'? Then, why does the chapter first examine international codes and then move onto the national codes? Lastly, what is the reason for selecting particular international and national codes?

6.1.3.1 The 'soft law' – the prevalence of governance codes

Black's seminal 'decentred' regulation In her seminal work, Julia Black examined the phenomenon of 'decentred' regulation – that regulation does not flow solely from governments (nor should it) but extends to other social actors.[5] This is based on various aspects.[6] First, 'complexity' in which:

> social problems are the result of various interacting factors, not all of which may be known, the nature and relevance of which changes over time, and the interaction between which will be only imperfectly understood.[7]

Second, for Black, is the 'fragmentation' of knowledge or:

> information asymmetry between regulator and regulated: that government cannot know as much about industry as industry does about itself.[8]

Third, for Black – again on avoiding a monopoly for governments – is the 'fragmentation of the exercise of power and control . . . between social actors and between actors and the state'.[9] This fragmentation leads to a fourth element to the nature of Black's decentred regulation – 'a recognition of the autonomy of social actors . . . [who] will continue to develop or act in their own way in the absence of intervention'.[10] The final aspect of decentred regulation for Black is:

> the existence and complexity of interactions and interdependencies between social actors, and between social actors and government in the process of regulation.[11]

---

5 Julia Black, 'Decentring Regulation: Understanding the Role of Regulation and Self-Regulation in a "Post-Regulatory" World' (2001) 54 *Current Legal Problems* 103, 103 and 106–7.

6 Ibid, 106–10.

7 Ibid, 106–7.

8 Ibid, 107.

9 Ibid, 108 (footnote omitted).

10 Ibid, 108.

11 Ibid, 109.

The relational approach seeks to contribute to the understanding of the interrelationships and interactions between the 'factors' of Black's first aspect and between 'social actors' in her final aspect. Of course narrower than Black, for the relational approach, the factors and actors are limited to economic ones in and about the corporation. Similar to Black, for Colin Scott, the 'post-regulatory state' is typified by a shift away from sole governmental control to 'other bases for control' and this underpins much of (corporate) governance regulation.[12]

Putting aside questions of categorisation, the chapter will now examine the development of governance codes to understand their prevalence in modern corporate governance regulation.

6.1.3.2 The influence of structural issues from pre-millennium corporate collapses

In general terms, impetus for the development of many governance codes came from the loss of investor and public confidence occasioned by pre-millennium corporate disasters which received global attention. Many commentators identify the governance codes as emerging from the significant corporate collapses of the 1990's including America's Enron and WorldCom and, in Australia, HIH Insurance and One.Tel.[13] In the UK, the collapse of BCCI Bank and depletion of pension funds connected with Robert Maxwell companies were the 'smoking guns' for the establishment of the Cadbury Committee and its now seminal report.[14]

What does this mean for the foundations of the relational approach in this book? The answer is that an examination of these codes is in part justified on account of the detailed analysis of the Enron and Hastie collapses in Chapter 5. Commentator evaluations of those collapses form Key Field No 2 of the four Key Fields of the relational approach. Having examined the collapses in detail, this chapter demonstrates that Key Field No 3 of

---

[12] Colin Scott, 'Regulation in the Age of Governance: the Rise of the Post-Regulatory State', Chapter 7 in Jacint Jordana and David Levi-Faur (eds), *The Politics of Regulation: Institutions and Regulatory Reforms for the Age of Governance*, Cheltenham, UK and Northampton, MA, USA: Edward Elgar, 2005, 163–4 (footnotes omitted).

[13] Ibid, p 159 and Jennifer G Hill, 'Regulatory Responses to Global Corporate Scandals' (2005) 32 *Wisconsin International Law Journal* 367; Sydney Law School Research Paper No 06/35, accessed 3 March 2015 at SSRN: http://ssrn.com/abstract=886104, 369.

[14] *The UK Approach to Corporate Governance*, November 2006, London ('FRC UK Governance Approach 2006'), pp 3–4 (copy on file with author). This was revised in *The UK Approach to Corporate Governance*, October 2010, London ('FRC UK Governance Approach 2010') accessed 3 March 2015 at http://www.frc.org.uk/.

the relational approach is similarly founded on the structural changes which regulatory responses to those collapses sought to achieve and which continue to this day.

Flowing from this, the governance codes reflect particular emphasis on the following key features identified by Ross Grantham and which resound with many of the failures identified by Chapter 5:

- that the board should have independent directors; . . .
- that the board should be composed of individuals having a mix of skills and knowledge; . . .
- that there should be subcommittees of the board to deal with matters such as audit and remuneration; . . .
- to put in place robust procedures for reporting financial and governance information. . .[and] to adopt procedures and policies to ensure the integrity and accuracy of that information; . . .
- that the remuneration of the board should be fair and reasonable and should be the result of transparent procedures . . . [and] . . . should be linked to the performance of the company; . . .[and]
- the board is enjoined to observe the highest standards of ethical behaviour and to adopt a code of ethics against which the behaviour of directors might be measured.[15]

Indeed, Grantham identifies as common to the Australian and US codes that they are based on 'the agency cost problem as the central obstacle to good governance'.[16] Again, this is consistent with Key Field No 1 of the relational approach which is based on the concept of agency costs.[17]

6.1.3.3 The development of norms of behaviour

Professor Hill shows that changes to the role and structure of the board 'have been driven, not by legislative intervention and direct regulation, but by the development of commercial practices and norms'.[18] Hill identifies at least two influences deriving from these norms on the prevalence of governance codes. First is the wide range of sources from which so-called 'voluntary' codes spring:

> [n]orms have become increasingly important in corporate governance. They have generally emanated from voluntary adoption of guidelines from a range of

---

[15] Ross Grantham, 'Corporate Governance Codes in Australia and New Zealand: Propriety and Prosperity' (2004) 23 *The University of Queensland Law Journal* 218, 219–20 (footnotes omitted, formatting altered and bullet-points added).

[16] Ibid, 221.

[17] See discussion in sections 4.2.2–4.2.3.1 above.

[18] Hill, above n 13, 376 (footnote omitted).

> sources. A comparative study of corporate governance codes in Europe identified such sources as including governmental or quasi-governmental entities; committees organized by governments or by stock exchanges; business, industry and academic associations; directors' associations and investor-related groups.[19]

Indeed, Hill identified in the mid-nineties a trend of greater involvement in corporate governance regulation by stock exchanges.[20] Second, the codes have also performed a 'gap-filling' function where 'hard law' was inadequate or to stave it off:

> [t]here is, nonetheless, a relationship between governmental regulation and voluntary corporate governance codes of this kind. The development of self-regulatory codes of conduct has tended to be either a response to the lack of specific governmental regulation in particular areas or, in some cases, a justification for the absence of such regulation.[21]

For the relational approach, this raises a theoretical justification for these codes. That governance codes should perform a gap-filling function resounds with the nexus of contracts theory. On this view, 'voluntary' governance codes are an additional set of 'contractual relationships' between the inputs to the firm (for example, shareholders and management) envisaged by Bainbridge.[22] This does not mean, however, that 'enrolling' other social actors – such as stock exchanges – in the regulation function is without its own difficulties. Julia Black, in an article in the 2012 *Modern Law Review*, tells us that this regulation technique had its own difficulties in the GFC.[23] Thus, for Black, additional social actors in the regulation function caused their own brand of problems related to the vulnerabilities of each actor.

6.1.3.4 The harmonisation[24] or convergence of global and national corporate governance codes

The inclusion of governance codes within the Key Fields is also justified by an examination of the reasons promoting or inhibiting convergence

---

[19] Ibid, 376 (footnote omitted).

[20] Ibid, 377.

[21] Ibid 376 (footnote omitted).

[22] See discussion in section 1.2.2 above and Stephen M Bainbridge, 'In Defense of the Shareholder Wealth Maximization Norm: A Reply to Professor Green' (1993) 50 *Washington & Lee Law Review* 1423, accessed 3 March 2015 at SSRN: http://ssrn.com/abstract=303780, 1426–7 (footnote omitted).

[23] Julia Black, 'Paradoxes and Failures: "New Governance" Techniques and the Financial Crisis' (2012) 75(6) *Modern Law Review* 1037–63, 1062.

[24] This term is taken from Lawrence A Cunningham, 'Commonalities and Prescriptions in the Vertical Dimension of Global Corporate Governance' (1999)

in global and national corporate governance structures, mechanisms and processes. For example, convergence or divergence may take place between dispersed-shareholding and concentrated-shareholding countries and continues to be examined by many commentators.[25] The relational

---

84 *Cornell Law Review* 1133, accessed 3 March 2015 at SSRN: http://ssrn.com/abstract=244665, 12.

[25] See, for example, Theodor Baums and Kenneth E Scott, 'Taking Shareholder Protection Seriously? Corporate Governance in the United States and Germany' (2005) 53 *American Journal of Comparative Law* 31, accessed 3 March 2015 at SSRN: http://ssrn.com/abstract=473185; Markus Berndt, 'Global Differences in Corporate Governance Systems – Theory and Implications for Reforms' (November 2000), Harvard Law and Economics Discussion Paper No 303, accessed 3 March 2015 at SSRN: http://ssrn.com/abstract=255886; Margaret M Blair, 'Post-Enron Reflections on Comparative Corporate Governance' (6 June 2002), Georgetown Law and Economics Research Paper No 316663, accessed 3 March 2015 at SSRN: http://ssrn.com/abstract=316663; Udo C Braendle and Juergen Noll, 'On the Convergence of National Corporate Governance Systems' (August 2005), accessed 3 March 2015 at SSRN: http://ssrn.com/abstract=506522; Douglas Branson, 'The Very Uncertain Prospect of "Global" Convergence in Corporate Governance' (2001) 34 *Cornell International Law Journal* 321, accessed 3 March 2015 at SSRN: http://ssrn.com/abstract=244742; Henry Hansmann and Reinier Kraakman, 'Reflections on the End of History for Corporate Law' in *Convergence of Corporate Governance: Promise and Prospects*, Abdul Rasheed and Toru Yoshikawa (eds), Basingstoke: Palgrave-Macmillan, 2012; Yale Law & Economics Research Paper No 449 (August 15, 2011), accessed 3 March 2015 at SSRN: http://ssrn.com/abstract=2095419; Paul L Davies and Klaus J Hopt, 'Boards in Europe – Accountability and Convergence' (2013) 61 *American Journal of Comparative Law* 301–75; ECGI – Law Working Paper No 205/2013; Oxford Legal Studies Research Paper No 40/2013 (1 April 2013), accessed 3 March 2015 at SSRN: http://ssrn.com/abstract=2212272.

Coffee discusses the effect on corporate governance of competition – including regulatory competition – between securities markets and cross-listing of companies on securities exchanges in John C Coffee, 'Racing Towards the Top?: The Impact of Cross-Listings and Stock Market Competition on International Corporate Governance' (30 May 2002), Columbia Law and Economics Working Paper No 205, accessed 3 March 2015 at SSRN: http://ssrn.com/abstract=315840. See also John C Coffee, 'The Future as History: The Prospects for Global Convergence in Corporate Governance and Its Implications' (February 1999), Columbia Law School Center for Law and Economic Studies Working Paper No 144, accessed 3 March 2015 at SSRN: http://ssrn.com/abstract=142833; John C Coffee, 'A Theory of Corporate Scandals: Why the U.S. and Europe Differ' (March 2005), Columbia Law and Economics Working Paper No 274, accessed 3 March 2015 at SSRN: http://ssrn.com/abstract=694581; Jeffrey N Gordon, 'An International Relations Perspective on the Convergence of Corporate Governance: German Shareholder Capitalism and the European Union, 1990–2000' (February 2003), ECGI – Finance Research Paper Series, accessed 3 March 2015 at SSRN: http://ssrn.com/abstract=374620 and Jennifer G Hill, 'Evolving "Rules of the Game" in

approach in this chapter contributes to the debate in this area by using commonality as a measure of convergence.

With similar themes or objectives, it is not surprising that convergence is a readily observable phenomenon between governance codes. Cunningham, for one, describes that many national jurisdictions have enhanced their governance regimes by the adoption of structures and mechanisms from other countries.[26] For Cunningham, an important driver of this convergence in governance structures and mechanisms is the growing competition between capital markets.[27]

Based on an underlying harmonisation theme, the function of the Governance Code Tables is to suggest a comparative scheme in table-form for comparing governance codes. Thus, Table 6.8[28] is comprised of features that have been identified over time and across schemes as prominent in the construction of global and national US, UK and Australian codes. The question to be answered here is with which code to commence the comparison? The answer the relational approach explains below is the OECD Principles.[29] But before that, the wide range of codes will be identified.

6.1.4 The Governance Codes Examined in Chapter 6

Accordingly, the review in this chapter will concentrate on the governance codes listed in Table 6.1.

Corporate Governance Reform' (July 2007), Sydney Law School Research Paper No 07/47, accessed 3 March 2015 at SSRN: http://ssrn.com/abstract=1000085.

For a discussion of how to improve the effectiveness of corporate governance codes in relation to (at 2) 'the level of adoption of the codes' recommendations themselves (substantive effectiveness) or only to the comply-explain mechanism (disclosure effectiveness)', see Peter Böckli, Paul L Davies, Eilis Ferranan, Guido A Ferrarini, José M Garrido Garcia, Klaus J Hopt, Alain Pietrancosta, Katharina Pistor, Markus Roth, Rolf Skog, Stanislaw Soltysinski, Jaap W Winter and Eddy Wymeersch, 'Making Corporate Governance Codes More Effective: A Response to the European Commission's Action Plan of December 2012' (11 December 2013), accessed 3 March 2015 at SSRN: http://ssrn.com/abstract=2366273.

For the determinants of corporate governance reform and how these flow through to national governance codes including their convergence, see Carsten Gerner-Beuerle, 'Determinants of Corporate Governance Codes', LSE Legal Studies Working Paper No 5/2014 (10 February 2014), accessed 3 March 2015 at SSRN: http://ssrn.com/abstract=2346673.

[26] Cunningham, above n 24, 12.

[27] Ibid.

[28] Table 6.8: Australian Corporate Governance Codes.

[29] See discussion in section 6.2.1 below.

Table 6.1 Global and National Governance Codes

International/Cross-Border	OECD Principles[1] ICGN Statement[2] CACG Guidelines[3]
United States	Final NYSE Corporate Governance Rules[4] Business Roundtable *Principles of Corporate Governance 2012*[5] The Conference Board *Commission on Public Trust and Private Enterprise*[6] California Public Employees' Retirement System (CalPERS) *Global Principles of Accountable Corporate Governance*[7]
United Kingdom	The Cadbury Report[8] FRC Combined Code on Corporate Governance[9] FRC UK Corporate Governance Code 2010–12[10] FRC UK Corporate Governance Code 2014[11]
Australia	ASX 2003 Best Practice Recommendations[12] ASX 2007–10 Revised Principles[13] IFSA Blue Book[14] ASX 2014 Principles and Recommendations[15]

Notes:

1. Organisation for Economic Co-Operation and Development, *OECD Principles of Corporate Governance 2004*, 2004, OECD Publications Service, Paris ('OECD Principles'). See http://www.oecd.org/document/49/0,3343,en_2649_34813_31530865_1_1_1_37439,00.html (accessed 3 March 2015).
2. International Corporate Governance Network, *ICGN Statement on Global Corporate Governance Principles*, 8 July 2005, ICGN Annual Conference, London ('ICGN Statement'). The *Principles* in the ICGN Statement were updated in 2009 and appear as Part C *International Principles of Accountable Corporate Governance* of the CalPERS Global Governance Principles 2014, n 7 of this Table 6.1 below available at http://www.calpers-governance.org/docs-sof/principles/2014-05-calpers-global-principles-accountable-corp-gov.pdf. (accessed 13 March 2015).
3. Commonwealth Association for Corporate Governance, *Principles for Corporate Governance in the Commonwealth, Towards Global Competitiveness and Economic Accountability*, Final Version, November 1999 ('CACG Guidelines'), accessed 5 February 2015 at http://www.ecseonline.com/PDF/CACG%20Guidelines%20-%20Principles%20for%20Corporate%20Governance%20in%20the%20Commonwealth.pdf.
4. New York Stock Exchange, *Final NYSE Corporate Governance Rules* ('NYSE Final Rules'), approved by SEC 4 November 2003 (except s 303A.08) and 30 June 2003 (s 303A.08). The Rules (as amended from time to time) comprise section 303A.00 of the NYSE Listed Company Manual. See section 303A.00 Corporate Governance Standards (approved 25 November 2009), accessed 3 March 2015 at http://nysemanual.nyse.com/lcm/. Subsequent amendments have been made to:

   - Section 303A.00 – Corporate Governance Standards (approved 22 August 2013)
   - Section 303A.02 – Corporate Governance Standards (approved 11 January 2013)

Table 6.1 (continued)

- Section 303A.05 – Corporate Governance Standards (approved 11 January 2013)
- Section 303A.07 – Audit Committee Additional Requirements (approved 22 August 2013).

These Rule amendments are available at http://nysemanual.nyse.com/lcm/ (accessed 3 March 2015).

5. Business Roundtable, *Principles of Corporate Governance 2005, A White Paper by Business Roundtable*, November 2005, Washington, DC ('Business Roundtable Principles 2005'). The 2005 Principles were updated in April 2010 and June 2012. For the current Principles, see Business Roundtable, *Principles of Corporate Governance 2012*, June 2012, Washington, DC ('Business Roundtable Principles 2012') available at http://businessroundtable.org/resources/business-roundtable-principles-of-corporate-governance-2012.
6. The Conference Board, Inc., *Commission on Public Trust and Private Enterprise*, 9 January 2003, accessed 3 March 2015 at http://www.conference-board.org/publications. The Conference Board Commission's corporate governance scheme is contained in Part 2: 'Corporate Governance: Principles, Recommendations and Specific Best Practice Suggestions', pp 2–28 ('Conference Board Principles').
7. California Public Employees' Retirement Scheme (CalPERS), *Global Principles of Accountable Corporate Governance*, Sacramento, California, were updated on 14 November 2011. For the current *Global Principles*, see California Public Employees' Retirement Scheme (CalPERS), *Global Principles of Accountable Corporate Governance*, 19 May 2014, Sacramento, California, available at http://www.calpers-governance.org/docs-sof/principles/2014-05-calpers-global-principles-accountable-corp-gov.pdf (accessed 13 March 2015), ('CalPERS Global Governance Principles 2014').
8. The Committee on the Financial Aspects of Corporate Governance *Report of the Committee on the Financial Aspects of Corporate Governance*, 1 December 1992, London: Gee & Co Ltd ('Cadbury Report').
9. Financial Reporting Council (FRC), *The Combined Code on Corporate Governance*, June 2006, London ('UK Combined Code').
10. Financial Reporting Council (FRC), *The UK Corporate Governance Code*, June 2010, as amended in September 2012, London, accessed 3 March 2015 at http://www.frc.org.uk/ ('UK Corporate Governance Code 2010–12'). For a discussion of the development of Governance Codes in the UK, see Andrew R Keay, 'Accountability and the Corporate Governance Framework: From Cadbury to the UK Corporate Governance Code' (August 31, 2012), accessed 3 March 2015 at SSRN: http://ssrn.com/abstract=2143171.
11. Financial Reporting Council (FRC), *The UK Corporate Governance Code*, September 2014, London, accessed 3 March 2015 at http://www.frc.org.uk/ (accessed 23 October 2014) ('UK Corporate Governance Code 2014'). For the 2014 amendments to the UK Corporate Governance Code 2010–12, above n 10 of this Table 6.1, see Financial Reporting Council (FRC), *Feedback Statement – Revisions to the UK Corporate Governance Code*, September 2014, London, also available at http://www.frc.org.uk/ (accessed 3 March 2015).
12. The original ASX best practice recommendations were contained in the ASX Corporate Governance Council, *Principles of Good Corporate Governance and Best Practice Recommendations*, Australian Securities Exchange, March 2003 ('ASX 2003 Best Practice Recommendations'). Proposed changes to the ASX 2003 Best Practice Recommendations were the subject of public comment. See ASX Corporate Governance Council, *Principles of Good Corporate Governance and Best Practice Recommendations, Exposure Draft of Changes*, Australian Securities Exchange, 2 November 2006 ('ASX Draft Recommendations').

13. The ASX 2003 Best Practice Recommendations were revised on 2 August 2007. See ASX Corporate Governance Council, *Corporate Governance Principles and Recommendations, Second Edition*, Australian Securities Exchange, 2 August 2007. These Principles and Recommendations were further amended in June 2010. See ASX Corporate Governance Council:

    - *Corporate Governance Principles and Recommendations with 2010 Amendments*, June 2010 ('ASX 2007–10 Revised Principles');
    - *Revised Corporate Governance Principles and Recommendations* (Second Edition, August 2007);
    - *Marked-Up Amendments dated 30 June 2010 to the Second Edition of the Corporate Governance Principles and Recommendations* ('ASX 2010 Marked-Up Amendments'); and
    - *Summary Table of the 30 June Changes to the Second Edition of the Corporate Governance Principles and Recommendations* ('ASX 2010 Summary Table').

    These documents are available at http://www.asxgroup.com.au/corporate-governance-council.htm (accessed 3 March 2015).
14. See Investment & Financial Services Association Limited (IFSA), *Blue Book, IFSA Guidance Note No 2.00, Corporate Governance: A Guide for Fund Managers and Corporations*, 6th edn, June 2009, accessed 3 March 2015 at http://www.fsc.org.au/downloads/file/IFSAGuidanceNotes/2GN_2_Corporate_Governance_2009.pdf ('IFSA Blue Book').
15. The ASX 2007–10 Revised Principles were revised and replaced by the Third Edition of the Principles and Recommendations which were released on 27 March 2014 and (at p 7) took effect for a company's financial year commencing on or after 1 July 2014 ('ASX 2014 Principles and Recommendations'). For a comparison of the ASX 2007–10 Revised Principles and the ASX 2014 Principles and Recommendations, see *Translation Table, Corporate Governance Council Recommendations (New to Old) and (Old to New)* ('CGC Recommendations Translation Tables'). These documents are available at http://www.asx.com.au/regulation/corporate-governance-council.htm (accessed 3 March 2015).

6.2 GLOBAL/CROSS-BORDER CORPORATE GOVERNANCE CODES

6.2.1 Selection of the Global Sector and OECD Principles

Why have the global sector and, representing that sector, the OECD Principles been selected as the foundation of the convergence exercise in this chapter? For du Plessis *et al*, the OECD Principles provide a criterion to measure the effectiveness of a corporate governance code:

> [t]hus, according to the OECD Principles, whether or not a corporate governance regulatory framework is effective depends on whether the following three criteria are satisfied:
> - promotion of transparent and efficient markets;
> - consistency with rule-of-law principles (namely accountability, accessibility and clarity; [and]

- clear articulation of the division of responsibilities among the different supervisory, regulatory and enforcement authorities.[30]

This has compelling explanatory power for the relational approach. But the selection of the OECD Principles is justified for three additional reasons particular to the relational approach. First, the OECD Principles have been used as a model in the development of many other 'global' codes (including the ICGN Statement[31] and the CACG Guidelines[32]). Second, the OECD Principles were retained in the construction of the 'national' Governance Code Tables as the Principles themselves state – following a harmonisation theme – that they are intended to be a model for OECD and non-OECD countries alike in the development of corporate governance frameworks.[33] In other words, the OECD Principles are not intended to regulate companies directly but to encourage countries to adopt principles which will enhance their national codes. Finally, in this way, a consistent measure for comparison, commonality (continuity across codes and over time) and relative importance is retained throughout all the Tables. The result is that the nature and extent of the harmonisation of governance variables between global, US, UK and Australian corporate governance codes can be identified and discussed.

---

[30] Jean Jacques du Plessis, Anil Hargovan and Mirko Bagaric, *Principles of Contemporary Corporate Governance*, 2nd edn, Cambridge: Cambridge University Press, 2011, p 175.

[31] International Corporate Governance Network, *ICGN Statement on Global Corporate Governance Principles*, 8 July 2005, ICGN Annual Conference, London ('ICGN Statement'). The *Principles* in the ICGN Statement were updated in 2009 and appear as Part C *International Principles of Accountable Corporate Governance* of the CalPERS Global Governance Principles 2014, n 7 of Table 6.1 above available at http://www.calpers-governance.org/docs-sof/principles/2014-05-calpers-global-principles-accountable-corp-gov.pdf. (accessed 13 March 2015).

[32] Commonwealth Association for Corporate Governance, *Principles for Corporate Governance in the Commonwealth, Towards Global Competitiveness and Economic Accountability*, Final Version, November 1999 ('CACG Guidelines'), accessed 5 February 2015 at http://www.ecseonline.com/PDF/CACG%20Guidelines%20-%20Principles%20for%20Corporate%20Governance%20in%20the%20Commonwealth.pdf, Preface, pp [2–3].

[33] Organisation for Economic Co-Operation and Development, *OECD Principles of Corporate Governance 2004*, 2004, OECD Publications Service, Paris ('OECD Principles'). See http://www.oecd.org/document/49/0,3343,en_2649_34813_31530865_1_1_1_37439,00.html (accessed 3 March 2015), Preamble, p 11.

6.2.2 Principal Governance Variables in Global Corporate Governance

Table 6.2 below demonstrates the 'sphere of operation' of the three global governance codes to be examined in the relational approach. In other words, the chapter demonstrates in a comparative table form the place that the governance variables examined in Chapters 7–10 have in an overall governance scheme for publicly-traded for-profit organisations.

A comparison of the three global codes will then be undertaken in section 6.2.3. This will again be in table form – this time using a Commonality Table. This will identify the core features of those global governance codes to distil the main themes and variables derived from those codes. Table 6.2 represents the principal governance themes and governance variables that underpin the global governance codes listed in Table 6.1.

6.2.3 Global 'Core' Variables – Comparison and Commonality of Global/ Cross-Border Corporate Governance Codes

6.2.3.1 Global 'core' variables as a product of commonality

The CACG Guidelines reproduce more of the OECD Principles than the ICGN Statement, but a number of issues have been directly transplanted from the OECD Principles to both the ICGN Statement and CACG Guidelines. Table 6.3 represents the core corporate Governance Variables common to all three global governance codes.

Which governance variables represent these themes and how are they analysed in the relational approach? Taken from this Table, the following areas have ongoing prominence in corporate governance discourse and are included in the governance variables listed in Table 2.1:

- Appropriate legal structures/agencies **(1.i)**, shareholder voting and meetings **(2.iv)**, disclosure of disproportionate control structures or arrangements **(2.v)**, equality within share classes **(3.ii)** and interested or conflicted director disclosure **(3.v and 6.iv.e)** – these raise the strength of the national governance regime;
- **Items 3.v, 6.iv.e and 6.v.a**: director independence;
- **Items 2.iii, 5.i and 5.iii**: timely/regular disclosure of material information and the quality and integrity of information – these raise the transparency and timeliness of reporting;
- **Items 4.iv and 5.i.b**: incentive-based performance and participation schemes for directors and executives and disclosure of remuneration policies;
- **Item 5.ii**: independent/external audit; and

Table 6.2 Global/Cross-border Governance Codes

No	Governance Variable (Based on OECD Principles)	OECD Principles	ICGN Statement	CACG Guidelines
1.	**External Governmental Legal and Governance Structure/Compliance:**[1]	IA–D		
i	Appropriate legal structures/agencies		7.2	5, 7
ii	Governance structures and practices consistent with law and transparent/ enforceable			
iii	Demarcation and transparency for governmental and regulatory agencies			
2.	**Owner Shareholding and Participation Rights:**[2]	IIA–G	4.1–4.16	
i	Ownership and transfer structures		2.2	
ii	Participation in profits		2.1	
iii	Timely/regular disclosure of information		2.1–2.2	6, 7
iv	Questions and voting in meetings		4.4, 4.6	
	including re:		4.7, 4.8–4.10	
	a. Appointment/removal of directors		4.5	2
	b. Key/extraordinary changes		4.5, 4.9	2, 9
	c. Corporate governance		4.5, 4.9	
	d. External audit		3.1–3.5	
	e. Remuneration policy re board/execs			
v	Disclosure of disproportionate control structures/arrangements		2.2, 4.3	9
vi	Protection for market for corporate control		4.5, 8.2	
vii	Disclosure of institutional shareholder governance/voting policies and conflicts		2.2, 4.11–4.12	
3.	**Fairness:**[3]	IIIA-C		7
i	Ability to bring action for breach of shareholder rights		4.16	
ii	Equality within share classes		4.2	7
iii	Safeguards for minority		4.2	
iv	Prohibition re inside/self dealings			6, 7
v	Interested or conflicted director disclosure		5.5, 5.14–5.15	7, 9
4.	**Stakeholder Participation:**[4]	IVA-F	7	8
i	Identification, consultation and participation		7.3	3, 6, 8
ii	Ability to bring action for breach of enforceable stakeholder rights			
iii	Timely disclosure of information			6
iv	Employee/management/director incentive and participation schemes		5.1(4), 5.18 7.4	3, 7

No	Governance Variable (Based on OECD Principles)	OECD Principles	ICGN Statement	CACG Guidelines
5.	**Access/Transparency of Information:**[5]	VA-F		8
i	Timely disclosure of material information including:		2.1–2.2	6, 7
	a. results			
	b. remuneration policies		6.1, 5.18	7
	c. director qualifications/independence			
	d. risk factors			
	e. governance codes/policies		7.3, 8.1	
ii	Independent/external audit		3.1–3.5	10, 15
iii	Quality and integrity of information		5.1(7), 3.1, 3.5	6, 10
6.	**Board Functions and Independence:**[6]	VIA-F	5	
i	Compliance with statutory and legal duties on organisation/directors		5.3, 7.2	1, 5, 7
ii	Fair and ethical decision making and corporate social responsibility[7]		7.5–7.6	5, 8
iii	Recognition of stakeholder interests			8
iv	Principal Responsibilities:		5.1(1)–(8)	1,3
	a. Strategic/long-term planning; budget; performance review		(1)	2, 3, 4, 7, 14
	b. Corporate governance compliance		(2)	3, 4
	c. Selection and monitoring of key management		(3)	3, 4, 7, 11, 12
	d. Fair and open election of directors		(5), 5.10	2
	e. Interested director or management conflicts or transactions		(5), 5.5, 5.14–15	7, 9
	f. Reporting, audit, financial/ operational control, risk management and internal audit		(7)	4, 6, 10, 14
	g. Disclosure of information		(8)	6
v	Independence from management:			3, 9
	a. Non-executive/independent directors		5.4–5.8, 5.11	1, 2, 9
	b. Responsibilities of Board sub-committees delineated and disclosed		5.12–5.13	10
vi	Board access to accurate/timely info			3
vii	Competency/experience and skills of directors	**No**	5.2, 5.9	2, 9
viii	Disclosure of director contribution/ independence	**No**	5.9	
ix	Board/director performance review	**No**	5.16	11
x	Maintenance/review of internal controls/ procedures	**No**	3.5	4, 10
xi	Use of Technology	**No**	4.4	13
xii	Evaluation of Solvency	**No**		15
xiii	Director term of office	**No**	5.10	
7.	**Maximising Profits/Value**	**No**	1.1–1.2	1, 14

Table 6.2 (continued)

Notes:
1. Organisation for Economic Co-Operation and Development, *OECD Principles of Corporate Governance 2004*, 2004, OECD Publications Service, Paris ('OECD Principles'). See http://www.oecd.org/document/49/0,3343,en_2649_34813_31530865_1_1_1_37439,00.html (accessed 3 March 2015), p 17.
2. Ibid, pp 18–19.
3. Ibid, p 20.
4. Ibid, p 21.
5. Ibid, pp 22–23.
6. Ibid, pp 24–25.
7. International Corporate Governance Network, *ICGN Statement on Global Corporate Governance Principles*, 8 July 2005, ICGN Annual Conference, London ('ICGN Statement'). The *Principles* in the ICGN Statement were updated in 2009 and appear as Part C *International Principles of Accountable Corporate Governance* of the CalPERS Global Governance Principles 2014, n 7 of Table 6.1 above available at http://www.calpers-governance.org/docs-sof/principles/2014-05-calpers-global-principles-accountable-corp-gov.pdf. (accessed 13 March 2015), p. 9.

- **Item 6.v.b**: responsibilities of board subcommittees delineated and disclosed.

6.2.3.1.1 The national regime and 'overall' governance level Chapter 7 identifies the strength of the national governance/shareholder protection regime as a significant contributor to firm performance:

- **[NationGov] (+)**: National Governance/Shareholder Protection Regime, +100.00 *rprox* (section 7.3.1.3.2).

The selection of this variable is supported by the presence of the core variables displayed in Table 6.3, particularly **Items 1.i, 2.iv, 2.v, 3.ii, 3.v and 6.iv.e**. That this should be the case in the global code sphere is not surprising as these codes seek to be models for national adoption.[34] But the national company governance regime is also comprised of additional aspects examined individually in the relational approach.

6.2.3.1.2 Director independence The director independence theme is a feature of a significant number of governance variables found in Chapters 7–10 of the relational approach, both in relation to directors individually and in committee:

[34] See discussion in section 6.1.3.2 above.

Table 6.3 Global Commonality: 'Core' Global Governance Variables

No	Table 6.2 Reference	'Core' Global Governance Variable
1	1.i	Appropriate legal structures/agencies
2	2.iii, 5.i	Timely/regular disclosure of material information
3	2.iv	Questions and voting in meetings re:
	a. b.	a. Appointment/removal of directors b. key/extraordinary changes
4	2.v	Disclosure of disproportionate control structures or arrangements
5	3.ii	Equality within share classes
6	3.v, 6.iv.e	Interested or conflicted director disclosure
7	4.i	Stakeholder identification, consultation and participation
8	4.iv	Employee/management/director incentive and participation schemes
9	5.i.b	Disclosure of remuneration policies
10	5.ii	Independent/external audit
11	5.iii	Quality and integrity of information
12	6.i	Compliance with statutory and legal duties on organisation/directors
13	6.ii	Fair and ethical decision-making
14	6.iv	Principal board responsibilities:
	a. b. c. d. e. f. g.	a. Strategic/long-term planning; budget; performance review b. Corporate governance compliance c. Selection and monitoring of key management d. Fair and open election of directors e. Interested director or management conflicts or transactions f. Reporting, audit, financial/operational control, risk management and internal audit g. Disclosure of information
15	6.v.a	Independent/non-executive directors
16	6.v.b	Responsibilities of board subcommittees delineated and disclosed

- **[AudIndFreq] (+)**: Audit Committee – Independence in Combination with Frequency of Meeting – Reduction in Earnings Manipulation Effect, +7/87.50 *rprox* (section 9.2.1);
- **[AudIndInfo] (−)**: Audit Committee – Independence – Information Flow and Decision Quality 'Trade-off', −4/50.00 *rprox* (section 8.4.3);
- **[AudIndMon] (+)**: Audit Committee – Independence – Monitoring Effect, +7/87.50 *rprox* (section 8.4.3);
- **[BrdIndInfo] (−)**: Board Independent: Executive Director Proportion – Information Flow and Decision Quality 'Trade-off', −4/50.00 *rprox* (section 7.3.2.1.3);
- **[BrdIndMon] (+)**: Board Independent: Executive Director Proportion – Monitoring Effect, +7/87.50 *rprox* (sections 7.3.2.1.1–7.3.2.1.2);
- **[CompCom] (+/−)**: Compensation Committee – Presence, Operation and Frequency, +/−7/87.50 *rprox* (section 10.2.4.1);
- **[NomInd] (+)**: Nominating Committee – Independence Proportion, +7/87.50 *rprox* (section 7.3.1.2.2); and
- **[OutBrdPos] (−)**: Outside Board Positions of Independent Directors, −6/75.00 *rprox* (section 8.2.3.1)

Thus the aspect of director independence receives substantial focus in Chapter 7 as it figures prominently in Table 6.3 – **items 3.v, 6.iv.e and 6.v.a**.

6.2.3.1.3 Transparency and timeliness of information and quality of monitoring of management Also prominent are items relating to transparency and timeliness of information – **items 2.iii, 5.i, 5.iii, 6.iv.f and 6.iv.g**. Examples of relevant governance variables from the relational approach in this respect are:

- **[TransTimeMon] (+)**: Transparency and Timing of Reporting – Monitoring Effect, +8/100.00 *rprox* (section 9.1.2.1); and
- **[TransTimeRedn] (−)**: Transparency and Timing of Reporting – Information Flow Reduction Effect, −4/50.00 *rprox* (section 9.1.2.1).

In Chapter 9, the relational approach will examine whether the transparency and timing of information is effective in the reduction of agency costs and, flowing from this, a consequent reduction in the cost of equity capital.[35] In addition, improvement in the quality of monitoring of management is one of the prominent perceived benefits of many of the governance

---

[35] See discussion in sections 9.1.1–9.1.2.1 below.

variables examined in Chapters 7–10 and all three global governance codes recognise this as a principal responsibility of the board (**item 6.iv.c**).

6.2.3.1.4 Compensation, incentive schemes and the quality of monitoring Chapter 10 examines whether there is a causative relation between increases in the level of director or CEO compensation and improvements in the quality of monitoring of management. The relevant governance variable is:

- **[DirCEO$] (+/−)**: Director/CEO Compensation Levels, +/−7/87.50 *rprox* (section 10.2.4)

The relational approach examines whether improvements in monitoring require intervening factors. For example, that the directors are independent and the compensation incentive-based and/or that those directors have 'substantial' equity holdings.[36] The following variables are examples of intervening factors examined for their effect on the quality of monitoring:

- **[AudIndMon] (+)**: Audit Committee – Independence – Monitoring Effect, +7/87.50 *rprox* (section 8.4.3);
- **[AudShortOpts] (−)**: Audit Committee – Short Term Options Granted to Outside Directors – Reduction in Monitoring Effect, −7/87.50 *rprox* (section 10.2.5.1);
- **[BrdIndMon] (+)**: Board Independent: Executive Director Proportion – Monitoring Effect, +7/87.50 *rprox* (section 7.3.2.1.1–7.3.2.1.2);
- **[EqOptIncent] (+)**: Equity/Option Plans and Holdings of Directors/Executives – Incentive/'Alignment' Effect (excludes short-term options), +7/87.50 *rprox* (section 10.2.4);
- **[EqOptEntrch] (−)**: Equity/Option Plans and Holdings of Directors/Executives – 'Entrenchment' Effect (excludes short-term options), −7/87.50 *rprox* (section 10.2.4); and
- **[ShortTOpts] (−)**: Short-Term Option Holdings/Plans of Directors and Executives, −7/87.50 *rprox* (section 10.2.5.1).

Using these variables, Chapter 10 also examines the relationship between director/CEO pay levels and firm performance and/or firm value.

As can be seen from the Global Commonality Table, the presence of employee/management/director incentive and participation schemes (**item 4.iv**) and the disclosure of remuneration policies (**item 5.i.b**) are

---

[36] See discussion in sections 10.2–10.2.6 below.

prescribed by all three global governance codes. 'Disclosure standards' and 'transparent reporting' are also highlighted in Singh's study in Chapter 10[37] as being necessary for reputational constraints to operate (downwardly) on the level of executive remuneration and this end is also served by item **5.i.b**. The relevant governance variables reflecting this are:

- **[ReputDiscl] (+)**: Reputational Constraints – 'Disclosure Standards', +8/100.00 *rprox* (section 10.4.1); and
- **[ReputRep] (+)**: Reputational Constraints – 'Transparent Reporting', +8/100.00 *rprox* (section 10.4.1).

6.2.3.1.5 Independent/external audit Independent/external audit has already been identified as significant in the corporate collapses of Enron and the Hastie Group.[38] Not surprisingly then, it is identified in Table 6.3 as a core variable of international/cross-border governance codes **(item 5.ii)**. The following variables are relevant to this area. The latter is an intervening factor examined for its effect on the quality of the independent audit:

- **[ExtAudEarn] (+)**: External/Independent Audit Function, +7/87.50 *rprox* (section 9.2.3.3); and
- **[NonAuditS] (−)**: Non-Audit Services of External Auditor, −7/87.50 *rprox* (section 9.2.3.2–3).

6.2.3.1.6 Board subcommittees Table 6.3 identifies as significant that the responsibilities of board subcommittees be delineated and disclosed **(item 6.v.b)**. In Chapter 5, the relational approach noted that the monitoring function of several Enron committees may have been undermined by the regular attendance of the Chairman and separate CEO.[39] With Audit Committee variables as a particular focus, the relational approach therefore includes the following committee features as governance variables in Table 2.1:

- **[AudAccEarn] (+)**: Audit Committee – Accounting Expertise – Earnings Manipulation Reduction Effect, +6/75.00 *rprox* (section 9.2.1.1.2);
- **[AudCom] (+)**: Audit Committee – Presence, Operation and Frequency, +6/75.00 *rprox* (section 8.4.2);

---

37 See discussion in section 10.4.1 below.
38 See discussion in section 5.2.4 above.
39 See discussion in section 5.2.2.2 above.

- **[AudExpAcc] (+)**: Audit Committee – Financial Expertise (Accounting), +6/75.00 *rprox* (section 8.4.4);
- **[AudFree] (−)**: Audit Committee – Non-Accounting Expertise – 'Free Rider' Effect, −6/75.00 *rprox* (section 9.2.1.1.2);
- **[AudIndFreq] (+)**: Audit Committee – Independence in Combination with Frequency of Meeting – Reduction in Earnings Manipulation Effect, +7/87.50 *rprox* (section 9.2.1);
- **[AudIndInfo] (−)**: Audit Committee – Independence – Information Flow and Decision Quality 'Trade-off', −4/50.00 *rprox* (section 8.4.3);
- **[AudIndMon] (+)**: Audit Committee – Independence – Monitoring Effect, +7/87.50 *rprox* (section 8.4.3);
- **[AudShortOpts] (−)**: Audit Committee – Short Term Options Granted to Outside Directors – Reduction in Monitoring Effect, −7/87.50 *rprox* (section 10.2.5.1);
- **[CompCom] (+/−)**: Compensation Committee – Presence, Operation and Frequency, +/− 7/87.50 *rprox* (section 10.2.4.1);
- **[NomCom] (+/−)**: Nominating Committee – Presence, Operation and Frequency, +/−7/87.50 *rprox* (section 7.3.1.2.2); and
- **[NomInd] (+)**: Nominating Committee – Independence Proportion, +7/87.50 *rprox* (section 7.3.1.2.2).

6.3 NATIONAL CORPORATE GOVERNANCE CODES

6.3.1 Focus on US, UK and Australian National Codes

Of all the national corporate governance codes, the relational approach focuses on the principal codes of the United States, United Kingdom and Australia for four reasons.

First, these national governance regimes govern 'dense' markets comprised of companies with widely-dispersed shareholdings, being the type of shareholdings envisaged by the agency theory component of the shareholder primacy and stakeholder models examined in Chapter 4.[40] Second, again aligned with such agency theory, the relevant governance regimes contemplate a single-tier board model.[41] Third, these jurisdictions are all common-law based or, at the least, English in origin which

[40] See discussion in section 2.1 above.
[41] Ibid.

the relational approach identifies in Chapter 7 as being considered (as a relative measure) 'high' or 'strong' shareholder protection countries.[42] Finally, these three jurisdictions have experienced continual, and at times substantial, change and development to their corporate governance codes in the past 20 years, reflecting, and as the chapter will demonstrate, often spearheading good corporate governance practice. In this way, core variables or other harmonisation/underlying themes and tensions for each of these national sectors have temporal (as a measure of continuity over time) and, related to this, developmental comparative integrity.

6.4 UNITED STATES CORPORATE GOVERNANCE CODES

6.4.1 SOX Effects on Securities Exchange Act and NYSE Final Rules

SOX[43] is still one of the most important[44] reforms to US corporate governance, in particular for its consequential effects on the Securities Exchange Act of 1934 ('SEA'),[45] exchange rules issued by the Securities Exchange Commission ('SEC') and listing requirements such as the NYSE Final Rules.

While the SOX reforms are significant, they are not displayed *in themselves* in the following Table because SOX is clearly a 'hard law' instrument unlike the 'soft law' governance codes examined in this chapter.[46] Instead, for 'soft law' comparability, the significance of SOX is its 'downstream' consequences. These comprise the detailed governance variables and requirements introduced by the NYSE Final Rules consequent on the passing of SOX and are presented in Table 6.4.

---

[42] See discussion in sections 7.3.1.3–7.3.1.3.2 below.

[43] PL 107-204, 2002 HR 3763, July 30, 2002, 116 Stat 745, available at http://www.sec.gov/about/laws/soa2002.pdf ('SOX').

[44] Robert C Clark, 'Corporate Governance Changes in the Wake of the Sarbanes-Oxley Act: A Morality Tale for Policymakers Too' (5 December 2005), Harvard Law and Economics Discussion Paper No 525, accessed 3 March 2015 at SSRN: http://ssrn.com/abstract=808244, 6.

[45] *Securities Exchange Act* of 1934 (United States), June 6, 1934, Chapter 404, Title I, Sec. 1, 48 Stat. 881 (as Amended Through P.L. 111-72, Approved Oct. 13, 2009), accessed 3 March 2015 at http://www.sec.gov/about/laws/sea34.pdf ('SEA').

[46] See discussion in section 6.1.3.1 above.

Table 6.4 US National Corporate Governance Codes

No	Governance Variable (Based on OECD Principles)	NYSE Final Rules Listed Company Manual s 303A.00	Business Roundtable Principles 2005–12	Conference Board (Part 2 unless specified)	CalPERS Global Governance Principles 2014 (Parts B, C and D)
1.	External Governmental Legal and Governance Structure/Compliance:				
i	Appropriate legal structures/agencies			IX	
ii	Governance structures and practices consistent with law and transparent/ enforceable				
iii	Demarcation and transparency for governmental and regulatory agencies				
2.	Owner Shareholding and Participation Rights:		I		B7, C8.1–7, C9.1–7
i	Ownership and transfer structures				
ii	Participation in profits				
iii	Timely/regular disclosure of information	.07	I, IV		B4, B4.1–16, C2.3b, j, C7.1–6
iv	Questions and voting in meetings including re:	.08	I, IV	VIII	B7, B7.1–11, C8.3–4, C9.5
	a. Appointment/removal of directors		I	VIII1	B7.2
	b. Key/extraordinary changes			VIII1	C8.3.3
	c. Corporate governance				C8.2
	d. External audit				
	e. Remuneration policy re board/execs	.08			B3, B3.1–7, C5.1–8
v	Disclosure of disproportionate control structures/arrangements				
vi	Protection for market for corporate control				

Table 6.4 (continued)

No	Governance Variable (Based on OECD Principles)	NYSE Final Rules Listed Company Manual s 303A.00	Business Roundtable Principles 2005–12	Conference Board (Part 2 unless specified)	CalPERS Global Governance Principles 2014 (Parts B, C and D)
vii	Disclosure of institutional shareholder governance/voting policies and conflicts				
viii	Participation of institutional shareholders				C8, C9
3.	<u>Fairness</u>:	.10			
i	Ability to bring action for breach of shareholder rights				C8.5
ii	Equality within share classes		II		
iii	Safeguards for minority		II		
iv	Prohibition re inside/self dealings	.10	II		C2.3g, C2.11
v	Interested or conflicted director disclosure	.01, .02a–b, .10	II	II4	
4.	<u>Stakeholder Participation</u>:		III, IV		
i	Identification, consultation and participation		IV		B6
ii	Ability to bring action for breach of enforceable stakeholder rights				
iii	Timely disclosure of information	.07	II, III, IV		B4, B4.1–16, C2.3b, j, C7.1–6
iv	Employee/management/director incentive and participation schemes	.05, .08, .09	II, III, IV		B3, B3.1–7, C2.3e, C5.1–8

5.	Access/Transparency of Information:		IV		B4
i	Timely disclosure of material information including:	.07	II, IV		B4.1–16, C2.3j, C5.4,C7.1–6
	a. results		II, IV		B4.1
	b. remuneration policies	.05, .08, .09	II, III		B3,B3.1–7,B5d,C2.3e,C5.1–8
	c. director qualifications/independence	.01–.02, .04, .07, .09	III	II4	B1.1–12, C2.4.3, C2.6
	d. risk factors	.07	III		B5, C4
	e. governance codes/policies	.09, .10, .11, .12	III, IV	IV, VI	B2.1, B6, C3.1–7, C8.2, D2
ii	Independent/external audit	.06–.07	III	Pt3 IV–VII	B4, B4.1–16, C6.1–7
iii	Quality and integrity of information	.07	II, IV		B4, B4.1–16, C2.3j
6.	Board Functions and Independence:		I, II, III	I	
i	Compliance with statutory and legal duties on organisation/directors	.09–.10	I, II, III, IV	IV, VI	C2, C3.1–7, D1–2
ii	Fair and ethical decision making and corporate social responsibility	.09–.10	I, II, III, IV	IV, VI	B2.1, B6, C3.1–7, D1–2
iii	Recognition of stakeholder interests		IV		B6
iv	Principal Responsibilities:			II	C2.3
	a. Strategic/long-term planning; budget; performance review		I, II	II	C2.3a
	b. Corporate governance compliance	.09, .10, .11, .12	I, II, III, IV	IV, VI	B2.1, B6, C2.3h, C3.1–7, C8.2, D1–2
	c. Selection and monitoring of key management	.04, .05	I, II, III	I, II, IV, V, VI1, 3	B2.7, C2.3d
	d. Fair and open election of directors	.04	III, IV	IV	B7.2,C2.3c,C2.9.1
	e. Interested director or management conflicts or transactions	.01,.02a–b,.09, .10	II, III	II4	C2.3g C2.11
	f. Reporting, audit, financial/ operational control, risk management and internal audit	.06, .07a–c	I, II, III, IV	II	B4, B4.1–16, B5, C2.3b, f, C4, C6.1–7, C7.1–6

Table 6.4 (continued)

No	Governance Variable (Based on OECD Principles)	NYSE Final Rules Listed Company Manual s 303A.00	Business Roundtable Principles 2005–12	Conference Board (Part 2 unless specified)	CalPERS Global Governance Principles 2014 (Parts B, C and D)
	g. Disclosure of information	.07a–c	II		B5, B6, C2.3j, C7.1–6
v	Independence from management:	.01, .02, .03, .04	I, II, III	I, II	B1.1–12, C2.4.3, C2.6
	a. Non-executive/independent directors	.01–.04, .09–.10	II, III	I1–8, III1–2, V3	B1.1–12, C2.4.3, C2.6, C5.3
	b. Responsibilities of Board sub-committees delineated and disclosed	.04, .05, .06, .07	II, III	II5, IV, V, VI, VIII Pt3 I–II, V	B1.12, B2.3, B4.11, B4.15–16, B5 C2.4.4, C2.5, C6.7
vi	Board access to accurate/timely info	.07, .09	I, II, III		B1.7, B1.11, C2.8
vii	Competency/experience and skills of directors	.04, .05, .07, .09	II, III	III	B2.1–9, B2.2, C2.4
viii	Disclosure of director contribution/ independence	.01, .02, .04–.05, .09	III	II4	B1.3, C2.4.3, C2.6
ix	Board/director performance review	.04, .05. .07, .09	II, III	I5, V	B2, B2.1–9, B5, C2.3i, C2.10
x	Maintenance/review of internal controls/ procedures	.06, .07	II, III	Pt3 III	B5, C2.3b, C4
xi	Use of Technology		IV		
xii	Evaluation of Solvency				
xiii	Director term of office	.04, .09	III		B1.5
xiv	Board size		III		B2.6
xv	Independent investigation of management			VII	
xvi	Company Secretary				C2.7
xvii	Board Diversity				B2.2
7.	<u>Maximising Profits/value</u>		I, II, III	IX	C1.1, C5.2, D1
8.	<u>Enforcement/disclosure of non-compliance with best practice</u>	.12, .13	III		

6.4.2 US National Corporate Governance Codes

Table 6.4 above presents the US governance codes listed in Table 6.1 of this Chapter 6. As can be seen from the Table, the governance variables are based on those in global codes so as to further build up the landscape of variables to create a comparative scheme in table-form for comparing governance codes. Significantly, the Table represents in table form how the SOX reform requirements have been incorporated into the NYSE Final Rules.[47]

6.4.2.1 US 'core' variables as a product of commonality

The core governance variables as shown in Table 6.5 are revealed as relatively important in all four columns of the US national governance codes depicted in Table 6.4. The chapter thus submits that these represent the major themes in US corporate governance regulation.

6.4.2.2 Competency/experience and skills of directors

Example governance variables which represent these areas were presented above in relation to the global sphere.[48] In addition, the examination of the above US governance codes highlights the emergence of:

- **[BrdSkills] (+)**: Board – Director Skills 'Mix', +7/87.50 *rprox* (section 7.3.1.2.1).

The review in this chapter demonstrates that this US governance variable is also significant (through commonality) to the national governance codes of the UK,[49] Australia[50] and the listed governance codes of these three countries.[51]

This governance variable is demonstrated in Chapter 7 to be part of the important groupings or combinations which emerge from the relational approach's examination of multi-variable studies in section 7.3.1.2. But its significance goes beyond this. In the relational approach, the **[BrdSkills]**

---

47 See above n 4 to Table 6.1.

48 See discussion in sections 6.2.3.1.1–6.2.3.1.6 above. Again, these core US governance variables will be considered in more detail in Chapters 7–10 in Key Field No 4 – Empirical Studies of the Effectiveness of Governance Variables.

49 See Table 6.7.

50 See Table 6.8.

51 See Table 6.9.

Table 6.5 US Commonality: 'Core' US National Governance Variables

No	Table 6.4 Reference	'Core' US National Governance Variable
1	2.iv	Questions and voting in meetings
2	5.i	Timely disclosure of material information including:
	c.	c. director qualifications/independence
	e.	e. governance codes/policies
3	5.ii	Independent/external audit
4	6	Board Functions and Independence:
	i	i. Compliance with statutory and legal duties on organisation/directors
	ii	ii. Fair and ethical decision making and corporate social responsibility
5	6.iv	Principal board responsibilities:
	b	b. Corporate governance compliance
	c	c. Selection and monitoring of key management
	d	d. Fair and open election of directors
	e	e. Interested director or management conflicts or transactions
	f	f. Reporting, audit, financial/operational control, risk management and internal audit
6	6.v	Independence from management:
	a.	a. Non-executive/independent directors
	b.	b. Responsibilities of board sub-committees delineated and disclosed
7	6.vii	Competency/experience and skills of directors
8	6.viii	Disclosure of director contribution/independence
9	6.ix	Board/director performance review
10	6.x	Maintenance/review of internal controls/procedures

(+) variable is demonstrated to be the 'spine' or model for the relational effect paths of many governance variables.[52]

6.4.2.3 Board/director performance review

Also emerging from the US sector is the prominence of the Board and director performance review:

[52] See discussion in section 7.3.1.2.1 below.

- **[BrdReview] (+)**: Board – Annual Review, +7/87.50 *rprox* (section 7.3.2.1.2).

Again, the review in this chapter demonstrates that this governance variable is also significant to the national governance codes of the UK,[53] Australia[54] and the listed governance codes of these three countries.[55]

In the next section, the chapter examines the governance variables that underpin the UK governance codes listed in Table 6.1. As part of this, the analysis identifies a core set of UK public company corporate governance variables for the purpose of identification and articulation of the three relational axes of good governance[56] and the eight governance factors.[57]

6.5 UNITED KINGDOM CORPORATE GOVERNANCE CODES

6.5.1 UK National Corporate Governance Codes

Table 6.6 represents the principal governance codes and variables that underpin the UK governance codes listed in Table 6.1. Again, the governance variables are based on those in the global sphere to create a comparative scheme in table-form for comparing governance codes.

6.5.1.1 UK 'core' variables as a product of commonality

In Table 6.7, the core governance variables from UK governance codes are drawn from the Cadbury Report, the UK Combined Code, the UK Corporate Governance Code 2010–12 and the UK Corporate Governance Code 2014.

That the list of variables in UK Commonality (Table 6.7) covers so many areas is not, of course, surprising as the UK Combined Code, the UK Corporate Governance Code 2010–12 and the UK Corporate Governance Code 2014 are, in effect, direct descendants of the Cadbury Report.[58] Because the latter Codes have developed from the former, there is much commonality. But that commonality still displays an important feature – that these codes have remained consistent during periods of reform.

---

53 See Table 6.7.
54 See Table 6.8.
55 See Table 6.9.
56 See discussion in sections 2.3.1–2.3.3 above.
57 See the construction of the governance factors in sections 2.6.1–2.6.8 above.
58 FRC UK Governance Approach 2006, above n 14, p 4.

Table 6.6 UK National Corporate Governance Codes

No	Governance Variable (Based on OECD Principles)	Cadbury Report (1992)	UK Combined Code (2006)	UK Corporate Governance Code 2010-12	UK Corporate Governance Code 2014
1.	External Governmental Legal and Governance Structure/Compliance:				
i	Appropriate legal structures/agencies				
ii	Governance structures and practices consistent with law and transparent/enforceable				
iii	Demarcation and transparency for governmental and regulatory agencies				
2.	Owner Shareholding and Participation Rights:		D1–2		
i	Ownership and transfer structures				
ii	Participation in profits				
iii	Timely/regular disclosure of information	4.40, 6.13–15	D1, E1–2	C1, C1.1–3, C2.1 E1, E1.1–2	C1, C1.1–3, C2.1–3 E1, E1.1–2
iv	Questions and voting in meetings including re:	6.5–8	E3	E2, E2.1–4	E2, E2.1–4
	a. Appointment/removal of directors	6.1, 6.6	A7.1-2	B7, B7.1–2	B7, B7.1–2
	b. Key/extraordinary changes				
	c. Corporate governance				
	d. External audit	6.1	D2.3		
	e. Remuneration policy re board/execs	4.40, 4.43–5			
v	Disclosure of disproportionate control structures/arrangements				
vi	Protection for market for corporate control				
vii	Disclosure of institutional shareholder governance/voting policies and conflicts				
viii	Participation of institutional shareholders	6.9–12, 6.15–16	D, D1.1–2, E1–3		

3.	Fairness:				
i	Ability to bring action for breach of shareholder rights				
ii	Equality within share classes				
iii	Safeguards for minority				
iv	Prohibition re inside/self dealings	6.14			
v	Interested or conflicted director disclosure	4.6	A3.1	B1.1	B1.1
4.	Stakeholder Participation:				
i	Identification, consultation and participation				
ii	Ability to bring action for breach of enforceable stakeholder rights				
iii	Timely disclosure of information			C1, C1.1–3, C2.1 E1, E1.1–2	C1, C1.1–3, C2.1–3 E1, E1.1–2
iv	Employee/management/director incentive and participation schemes	4.40	B1–2	D1, D1.1–5, D2, D2.1–4, Sch A	D1, D1.1–5, D2, D2.1–4, Sch A
5.	Access/Transparency of Information:				
i	Timely disclosure of material information including:		C1, D1–2, E1–2	C1, C1.1–3, C2.1 E1, E1.1–2	C1, C1.1–3, C2.1–3 E1, E1.1–2
	a. results				
	b. remuneration policies		A1, B1–2, Sch A	A4, D1, D1.1–5 D2, D2.1–4,Sch A	A4, D1, D1.1–5 D2, D2.1–4, Sch A
	c. director qualifications/independence			B1.1	B1.1
	d. risk factors			C2.1	C2.1–3
	e. governance codes/policies	4.11, 4.29	E2, Sch C	Sch B	Sch B
ii	Independent/external audit	4.35, 5.1–37	A1, C3	C3, C3.1–8	C3, C3.1–8
iii	Quality and integrity of information	4.31, 4.47–9	A5	C1, C1.1–3	C1, C1.1–3

Table 6.6 (continued)

No	Governance Variable (Based on OECD Principles)	Cadbury Report (1992)	UK Combined Code (2006)	UK Corporate Governance Code 2010-12	UK Corporate Governance Code 2014
6.	Board Functions and Independence:				
i	Compliance with statutory and legal duties on organisation/directors		A1	A1	A1
ii	Fair and ethical decision making; corporate social responsibility and codes of conduct	4.11 4.29			
iii	Recognition of stakeholder interests				
iv	Principal Responsibilities:		A1	A1, B3, B3.1–3	A1, B3, B3.1–3
	a. Strategic/long-term planning; budget; performance review	4.11		A4	A4
	b. Corporate governance compliance		Sch C	Sch B	Sch B
	c. Selection and monitoring of key management	4.5, 4.11		A4.1–3	A4.1–3
	d. Fair and open election of directors		A4, A7	B2, B2.1–4, B7, B7.1–2	B2, B2.1–2 B7.1–2
	e. Interested director or management conflicts or transactions	4.6	A3.1	B1.1–2	B1.1–2
	f. Reporting, audit, financial/operational control, risk management and internal audit	4.28, 4.35 4.50–8, 5.1–37		C1, C1.1–3, C2.1 C3, C1.1–8	C1, C1.1–3, C2.1–3 C3, C3.1–8
	g. Disclosure of information	4.50			
v	Independence from management:	4.7, 4.9, 4.23			
	a. Non-executive/independent directors	4.1, 4.10–17	A1.3, A3.1–3 A7, Sch B	A3.1, A4, A4.1–2, B1.1–2, B1.1–2 B2.1–4, B3.2–3, B4.1–2, B5.1–2	A3.1, A4, A4.1–2 B1.1–2 B2.1–4, B3.2–3 B4.1–2, B5.1–2

	b. Responsibilities of Board sub-committees delineated and disclosed	4.21, 4.30, 4.33–7, 4.42, 4.44	A1.2, A3, A4.1–3, C3	A1.2, B2.1–4, C3, C3.1–8, D1.1–5, D2, D2.1–4	A1.2, B2.1–4, C3 C3.1–8, D1.1–5 D2, D2.1–4
	c. Distinguish and specify the board and management roles		A1.1, A2	A1.1, A2, A3, A4, A4.1–2	A1.1, A2, A3, A4 A4.1–2
vi	Board access to accurate/timely info	4.8, 4.14		B5, B5.1–2	B5, B5.1–2
vii	Competency/experience and skills of directors	4.19, 4.5	A3, A4	B1, B1.1, B2, B2.1–4, B4, B4.1–2, B6.1–3	B1, B1.1, B2, B2.1–4, B4, B4.1–2, B6.1–3
viii	Disclosure of director contribution/ independence	4.12		B1.1	B1.1
ix	Board/director performance review	4	A6, A7	B6, B6.1–3	B6, B6.1–3
x	Maintenance/review of internal controls/procedures	4.31–2, 4.39, 5.16	C2	A4, C2, C2.1, C3, C3.1–8	A4, C2, C2.1–3, C3, C3.1–8
xi	Use of Technology				
xii	Evaluation of Solvency	5.18–22	C1.2	C1, C1–3	C1, C1–3
xiii	Director term of office	4.16, 4.41	A7.1	B7, B7.1–2	B7, B7.1–2
xiv	Board size				
xv	Independent investigation of management				
xvi	Company Secretary	4.25–27			
xvii	Board Diversity				
7.	<u>Maximising Profits/value</u>				
8.	<u>Enforcement/Disclosure of non-compliance with best practice</u>	ss 1.10, 3.7–3.10 and 3.13–3.16	Preamble ss 2–4	Comply or Explain ss 1–6 pp 4–5	Comply or Explain ss 1–6 p 4

Table 6.7 UK Commonality: 'Core' UK National Governance Variables

No	Table 6.6 Reference	'Core' UK National Governance Variable
1	2.iii	Timely/regular disclosure of information
2	2.iv a.	Questions and voting in meetings including re: a. Appointment/removal of directors
3	3.v	Interested or conflicted director disclosure
4	4.iv	Employee/management/director incentive and participation schemes
5	5.i e.	Timely disclosure of material information including: e. governance codes/policies
6	5.ii	Independent/external audit
7	5.iii	Quality and integrity of information
8	6.iv e.	Principal board responsibilities: e. Interested director or management conflicts or transactions
9	6.v a. b.	Independence from management: a. Non-executive/independent directors b. Responsibilities of board sub-committees delineated and disclosed
10	6.vii	Competency/experience and skills of directors
11	6.ix	Board/director performance review
12	6.x	Maintenance/review of internal controls/procedures
13	6.xii	Evaluation of solvency
14	6.xiii	Director term of office
15	8	Enforcement/disclosure of non-compliance with best practice

6.6 AUSTRALIAN CORPORATE GOVERNANCE CODES

6.6.1 ASX 2003 Best Practice Recommendations, ASX 2007–10 Revised Principles, IFSA Blue Book and ASX 2014 Principles and Recommendations

Table 6.8 represents the principal governance themes and variables which underpin the Australian national governance codes listed in Table 6.1. Here, *no* commonality table will follow as the ASX Codes are virtually identical, the ASX 2007–10 Revised Principles containing some re-arrangement of their predecessor but with some important additions in

Table 6.8 Australian Corporate Governance Codes

No	Governance Variable (Based on OECD Principles)	ASX 2003 Best Practice Recommendations	ASX 2007–10 Revised Principles	IFSA Blue Book Guidelines 2009	ASX 2014 Principles and Recommendations
1.	<u>External Governmental Legal and Governance Structure/Compliance</u>:				
i	Appropriate legal structures/agencies				
ii	Governance structures and practices consistent with law and transparent/enforceable				
iii	Demarcation and transparency for governmental and regulatory agencies				
2.	<u>Owner Shareholding and Participation Rights</u>:	6, 6.1	6, 6.1		6, 6.1–4
i	Ownership and transfer structures				
ii	Participation in profits				
iii	Timely/regular disclosure of information	6, Attach A	6	8.1.3, 8.2.15, 11.16, 11.16.1–6	1.6, 2.3, 3.1, 5.1 6, 6.1–4, 7.1–4, 8.1–3
iv	Questions and voting in meetings including re:	6, Attach A	6	8.2.15, 10.2, 10.4, 10.4.1, 11.16, 11.16.1–6	4.3, 6.3
	a. Appointment/removal of directors	2.4	2.4		2.1
	b. Key/extraordinary changes			8.2.17, 11.18	
	c. Corporate governance				
	d. External audit	6.2			4.3
	e. Remuneration policy re board/execs	9.1	5.1–2, 8, 8.1–4		8.1–3

Table 6.8 (continued)

No	Governance Variable (Based on OECD Principles)	ASX 2003 Best Practice Recommendations	ASX 2007–10 Revised Principles	IFSA Blue Book Guidelines 2009	ASX 2014 Principles and Recommendations
v	Disclosure of disproportionate control structures/arrangements			10.4.1	
vi	Protection for market for corporate control				
vii	Disclosure of institutional shareholder governance/voting policies and conflicts				
viii	Participation of institutional shareholders				
ix	Disclosure of beneficial shareholder information			8.2.16, 11.17	
x	Development of policies and procedures to ensure lawful securities lending activity			10.4.1	
3.	<u>Fairness</u>:				
i	Ability to bring action for breach of shareholder rights				
ii	Equality within share classes				
iii	Safeguards for minority				
iv	Prohibition re inside/self dealings	3, 3.2	3, 3.2	8.2.12, 10.3.5, 11.13	
v	Interested or conflicted director disclosure	2.1, 3.1–3	2.1, 3.1–3	8.2.12, 11.13	1.2, 2.3, 3.1, 8.1–3
4.	<u>Stakeholder Participation</u>:	10	3		
i	Identification, consultation and participation	10.1	3.1–2, 7.1	8.1.5, 10.6	3.1,6.2–4,7.1–4

ii	Ability to bring action for breach of enforceable stakeholder rights				
iii	Timely disclosure of information	5, 5.1–2	5, 5.1–2, 7.1		5, 5.1, 6, 6.1–4, 7.1–4, 8.1–3
iv	Employee/management/director incentive and participation schemes	9.1–5	8, 8.1–4	8.2.11, 8.2.14, 11.12, 11.15, 11.15.1	8.1–3
5.	<u>Access/Transparency of Information</u>:				
i	Timely disclosure of material information including:	5, 5.1–2, 6	3.1–3, 5, 5.1–2	9.4.1, 11.1	1.6, 3.1, 5, 5.1, 6, 6.1–4, 7.1–4
	a. results			10.3.1	6.1–4
	b. remuneration policies	9.1–5	5.1–2, 8.1–4	8.2.14, 11.1, 11.15, 11.15.1	8.1–3
	c. director qualifications/independence			8.2.2, 8.2.3, 11.3–4	1.2, 2.3–6,8.1–3
	d. risk factors	7.1–3	7.1–5		7.1–4
	e. governance codes/policies		3.1	8.1.1, 8.2.1, 8.2.18, 10.2, 11.2	3.1
	f. diversity		3.2–5		1.5, 2.1, 8.1–3
	g. gender diversity		3.2–5		1.5, 2.1, 8.1–3
	h. material exposure to economic, environmental and social sustainability risks				7.1–4
ii	Independent/external audit	4, 4.1–5, 6.2	4, 4.1–4	11.1	1.1, 4, 4.1–3
iii	Quality and integrity of information	4, 4.1–5	3.1–5, 4, 4.1–4	11.1	1.1, 3.1, 4,4.1–3, 5.1, 6, 6.1–4, 7.1–4
iv	Electronic communications	6.1	6.1	8.2.15	6.1–4
v	Website	6.1	6.1	10.2	6.1–4
vi	Briefings		6.1	10.3, 10.3.1–5	5.1, 6.1–2
vii	Direct contact with company's senior management and board members			8.1.2, 10.3, 10.3.2–4	
viii	Reporting to client of voting and other corporate governance activities			8.1.4, 10.5	

Table 6.8 (continued)

No	Governance Variable (Based on OECD Principles)	ASX 2003 Best Practice Recommendations	ASX 2007–10 Revised Principles	IFSA Blue Book Guidelines 2009	ASX 2014 Principles and Recommendations
6.	Board Functions and Independence:				
i	Compliance with statutory and legal duties on organisation/directors	1.1, 3.1	1.1, 3.1–5	10.3.5	1.1
ii	Fair and ethical decision making; corporate social responsibility and codes of conduct	3, 3.1, 10.1	3, 3.1–5, 7.1	8.1.5, 8.2.18, 10.6, 11.19	3.1, 7.1–4
iii	Recognition of stakeholder interests	10.1	3, 3.1–5	8.1.5, 8.2.18, 10.6, 11.19	3.1, 6.2–4, 7.1–4
iv	Principal Responsibilities:	1.1	1.1, 1.2	11.1	1.1
	a. Strategic/long-term planning; budget; performance review	1.1	1.1	11.1	1.1
	b. Corporate governance compliance	1.1	1.1	8.2.1, 10.2, 11.2	1.1, 1.4
	c. Selection and monitoring of key management	1.1, 8.1	1.1, 1.2–3	11.1	1.1, 1.7
	d. Fair and open election of directors			8.2.8, 11.9	1.2
	e. Interested director or management conflicts or transactions	2.1, 3.1–3	2.1, 3.1	8.2.12, 11.13	1.2, 2.3–5, 3.1, 8.1–3
	f. Reporting, audit, financial/ operational control, risk management and internal audit	1.1, 7	1.1, 7	8.2.1, 10.3.1, 11.1–2	1.1, 4.2–3, 5.1 7.1–4
	g. Disclosure of information	1.1	1.1, 3.1–5	8.2.1, 10.3.1, 10.3.5, 11.2	1.1, 2.1–3, 3.1 4.3, 5.1, 6.1–4 7.1–4
	h. Provision of resources for management		1.1		1.1
	i. Approving the entity's remuneration framework				1.1, 8.1–3

v	Independence from management:				
	a. Non-executive/independent directors	2.1–3, 4.3, 9.3	2.1–3, 4.2	8.2.3, 8.2.5, 8.2.6, 8.2.9, 8.2.11, 11.3, 11.6–7, 11.10, 11.12	1.2, 2.1, 2.3–5, 4.1, 7.1–4, 8.1–3
	b. Responsibilities of Board sub-committees delineated and disclosed	2.4, 4.2–5, 7, 9.1–5	2.4–6, 4.1–4, 7.1, 8.1–4.	8.2.6–7, 11.1, 11.7, 11.8, 11.8.1–3	1.1, 1.5, 2.1, 4.1–2, 7.1–4, 8.1–3
	c. Distinguish/specify board and management roles	1.1	1.1, 1.3	8.2.13, 11.4	1.1
vi	Board access to accurate/timely info	4.1, 8.1	2.5	8.2.6, 11.7	1.1, 1.4, 4.1–2
vii	Competency/experience and skills of directors	2.4–5	1.2, 2.4–6, 3.1–5	8.2.2, 11.3	2.1–2, 2.6, 3.1
viii	Disclosure of director contribution/ independence	2.1, 2.5		8.2.9, 11.10	1.2, 2.3–5
ix	Board/director performance review	2.4, 8.1	1.2–3, 2.4–6	8.2.2, 8.2.10, 11.3, 11.5, 11.11	1.1, 1.6–7, 2.1–2
x	Maintenance/review of internal controls/procedures	1.1, 4.4, 7.1–3	1.1, 7.1–5	11.1	1.1, 4.2, 7.1–4
xi	Use of Technology			8.2.15, 11.6	6.1–4
xii	Evaluation of Solvency				
xiii	Director term of office	2.1	2.1, 2.4, 2.6		2.3
xiv	Board size	2.4	2.4		2
xv	Independent investigation of management				
xvi	Company Secretary	8.1	2.5		1.4
xvii	Board Diversity		2.4, 2.6, 3.2–5		1.5, 2.1–2
xviii	Limiting number of outside board positions			8.2.4, 11.5	1.2, 2.1, 2.5
xix	Written contracts of appointment for directors and senior executives				1.3
7.	Maximising Profits/value				
8.	Enforcement/disclosure of non-compliance with best practice	Guides To Reporting (various)	Guides To Reporting (various)	5.2, 11.1–2	'if not, why not' approach (p 3) and Principles and Recommendations (various)

2007 and 2010.[59] The ASX 2014 Principles and Recommendations continue a similar structure for the ASX Codes this time taking into account corporate governance practices before and after the GFC.[60] Among other things, enhancements are made to the Principles and Recommendations relating to[61]:

- the risk committee;
- annual risk review;
- internal audit; and
- sustainability risks.

The IFSA Blue Book, too, is complementary to the ASX Codes, its Guidelines explaining in relation to the 'Disclosure Standard' that:

> [o]ver time, a number of the Guidelines have been incorporated into the law, and they are reflected in the ASX Corporate Governance Principles and Recommendations.[62]

In relation to the 'Guidelines for Corporations', again the IFSA Blue Book states it is complementary to the ASX Codes.[63] As a result, the Australian governance codes in Table 6.8 display significant overlap. Thus, a commonality table is not required to demonstrate their extensive consistency and convergence aspects.

6.7 'CORE' NATIONAL LISTED GOVERNANCE VARIABLES

6.7.1 Comparison of US, UK and Australian National Listed Corporate Governance Codes

In this section, the relational approach will display continuity (across codes, over time and developmentally) and centrality in US, UK and Australian national governance codes.

---

[59] ASX 2010 Marked-Up Amendments, above n 13 of Table 6.1 and ASX 2010 Summary Table, above n 13 of Table 6.1.

[60] ASX 2014 Principles and Recommendations, above n 15 of Table 6.1, Foreword, p 2.

[61] CGC Recommendations Translation Tables, above n 15 of Table 6.1, New to Old, p 2 of 4.

[62] IFSA Blue Book, above n 14 of Table 6.1, Guideline 9.4.1, p 11.

[63] Ibid, Guideline 11.1, p 15.

Again, the relational approach adopts the measure of the commonality of governance variables across the various Governance Code Tables. However, the relevant Commonality Table will compare only one code from the relevant national Governance Code Tables – the national codes that are:

- currently in force/operation; and
- backed with an enforcement or disclosure regime stemming from the Listing Rules of the relevant stock or securities exchanges.

This approach has been adopted in order to ensure that the chapter is drawing out governance variables that have similar currency and national standing. Therefore, Table 6.9 represents the principal governance variables common to all three of the national corporate governance codes which are currently in operation and which are underpinned by Listing Rule enforcement or disclosure regimes – the NYSE Final Rules,[64] the UK Corporate Governance Code 2014[65] and the ASX 2014 Principles and Recommendations.[66]

6.8 CONCLUSION – CORE FEATURES AND ASPECTS OF CORPORATE GOVERNANCE CODES

In this final section, the relational approach's examination of the relative importance of underpinning themes in corporate governance codes culminates with the comparison in section 6.8.1. This is a comparison of the core national listed governance variables derived from the US, UK and Australia in National Listed Commonality Table 6.9 above with their counterpart core variables from the global/cross-border sector.

6.8.1 Core Features – Global and National Listed Governance Codes Combined

All of the governance variables listed in Table 6.9 are important recurring themes in the policy and practice of corporate governance. Of the governance variables appearing in the Tables 6.3 (global core variables) and 6.9

---

[64] See above n 4 of Table 6.1.
[65] See above n 11 of Table 6.1.
[66] See above n 15 of Table 6.1.

Table 6.9 National Listed Commonality: 'Core' National Listed Governance Variables

No	Table 6.8 Reference	'Core' National Listed Governance Variable
1	2.iii	Timely/regular disclosure of information
2	2.iv	Questions and voting in meetings
3	3.v	Interested or conflicted director disclosure
4	4.iii	Timely disclosure of information
5	4.iv	Employee/management/director incentive and participation schemes
6	5.i	Timely disclosure of material information including:
	b.	b. remuneration policies
	c.	c. director qualifications/independence
	d.	d. risk factors
	e.	e. governance codes/policies
7	5.ii	Independent/external audit
8	5.iii	Quality and integrity of information
9	6	Board Functions and Independence:
	6.i	i. Compliance with statutory and legal duties on organisation/directors
10	6.iv	Principal board responsibilities:
	b.	b. Corporate governance compliance
	c.	c. Selection and monitoring of key management
	d.	d. Fair and open election of directors
	e.	e. Interested director or management conflicts or transactions
	f.	f. Reporting, audit, financial/operational control, risk management and internal audit
11	6.v	Independence from management:
	a.	a. Non-executive/independent directors
	b.	b. Responsibilities of board subcommittees delineated and disclosed
12	6.vi	Board access to accurate/timely information
13	6.vii	Competency/experience and skills of directors
14	6.viii	Disclosure of director contribution/independence
15	6.ix	Board/director performance review
16	6.x	Maintenance/review of internal controls/procedures
17	6.xiii	Director term of office
18	8	Enforcement/disclosure of non-compliance with best practice

(core national listed variables), the governance variables that have been prominent in *all* columns of those Tables are:

- Timely/regular disclosure of information (item 2.iii);
- Questions and voting in meetings (item 2.iv);
- Interested or conflicted director disclosure (items 3.v and 6.iv.e);
- Employee/management/director incentive and participation schemes (item 4.iv);
- Timely disclosure of material information including remuneration policies (item 5.i.b);
- Independent/external audit (item 5.ii);
- Quality and integrity of information (item 5.iii);
- Board functions and independence – compliance with statutory and legal duties on organisation/directors (item 6.i);
- Principal board responsibilities – corporate governance compliance (item 6.iv.b);
- Principal board responsibilities – Selection and monitoring of key management (item 6.iv.c);
- Principal board responsibilities – fair and open election of directors (item 6.iv.d);
- Principal board responsibilities – interested director or management conflicts or transactions (item 6.iv.e);
- Principal board responsibilities – Reporting, audit, financial/operational control, risk management and internal audit (item 6.iv.f);
- Independence from management – non-executive/independent directors (item 6.v.a); and
- Independence from management – responsibilities of board sub-committees delineated and disclosed (item 6.v.b).

On the basis of this commonality, the relational approach hypothesises that these could be the most important governance variables in corporate or for-profit governance code discourse. They have already been used in Chapter 2 for the identification, design and articulation of the three relational axes of good governance[67] and the governance factors.[68]

In the following Chapters 7–10, the relational approach begins its analysis of the nature, content and behaviour of individual governance variables. This is achieved through the examination of Key Field No 4 – Empirical Studies of the Effectiveness of Governance Variables. Most

---

67 See discussion in sections 2.3.1–2.3.3 above.

68 See discussion in sections 2.6.1–2.6.8 above.

important in Chapters 7–10 is to hypothesise the 'relational effect path' of each governance variable. This is the evaluation of the number of governance factors affected by each governance variable and the direction of that effect. This relational effect path was summarised in the Coverage Table (Table 3.1) and ultimately translated into a relational proximity rating (*rprox*) in the Relational Proximity Table (Table 3.2). This rating depicts the relative importance of the governance variables in affecting agency costs and the long-term efficiency and sustainability of the for-profit firm.

7. Empirical studies Key Field No 4 (Part 1): National shareholder protection regime and Board factors I

7.1 AIMS AND PURPOSE OF CHAPTER 7

In this chapter, the relational approach begins the process of examining the governance variables taken from the governance codes in Chapter 6. Chapter 7 reviews in detail law, economic and econometric literature from the US, UK, Europe and Australia that comprises empirical studies outlined in Key Field No 4. In Chapter 2, the relational approach introduced the perceived general effects said to flow from the adoption of governance variables in the for-profit sphere.[1] This was not challenged at that time. Beginning in this Chapter 7, Key Field No 4 examines the *firm-specific* benefits or, on the contrary, costs or disadvantages argued to flow from these variables. This will be done by reference to empirical studies of the effectiveness of governance variables in reducing agency costs and enhancing the long-term survival of the firm. Such efficiency and survival – an over-arching purpose of the relational approach – is assessed in these studies principally by measures of firm operating performance/profit and firm value. Other firm-specific outcomes such as 'shareholder payout',[2] the cost of equity capital and the probability of earnings manipulation are also examined.

There are three types of empirical studies examined in this chapter. First, Chapter 7 examines questions relating to whether a particular *group* of governance variables together improve firm operating performance, firm value and shareholder payout.[3] The studies suggest that these measures may be improved by *groupings* of governance variables.

---

[1] See discussion in section 2.2 above.

[2] L D Brown and M L Caylor, 'Corporate Governance and Firm Performance' (December 7, 2004), accessed 3 March 2015 at SSRN: http://ssrn.com/abstract=586423.

[3] See discussion in section 7.3.1.2 below.

The second group of studies in this chapter examine the strength of the national shareholder protection regime.[4] The studies examine first whether increases in the level of national shareholder protection improve firm performance and firm value. The second issue is whether common law origin shareholder protection regimes provide a higher level of protection than civil code origin regimes.

The final group of studies examines the effects on firm operating performance and firm value of a number of *individual* governance variables – the board skills 'mix',[5] the independence of directors,[6] the proportion of non-executive/independent directors, annual review of the board, a high attendance level at board meetings and external advisors to the board.[7]

Of course, a large number of factors – economic and otherwise – combine to affect firm performance and firm value. It is, accordingly, sometimes difficult to separate the effect of individual governance variables on these measures. Thus, the examination in this chapter will often highlight conflicting results relating to how those governance variables affect the economic actors inside and outside the corporation. But the chapter does not contrast the methodology of opposing studies in the text or footnotes. The relational approach does not rely on the empirical studies for their results *per se*. Instead, the empirical studies are used as a springboard to construct the 'relational effect path' of each governance variable. The relational effect path for each individual governance variable is constructed from the empirical studies examined in Chapters 7–10 in combination with the interrelationship scheme representing the shareholder primacy model.[8]

The relational effect path presented is not the only operational zone of effect for a governance variable. Instead, it is a pathway suggested by the empirical studies presented in Chapters 7–10 and the analysis of significant interrelationships employed in the selection and design of the governance factors.[9] These interrelationships are summarised in the Shareholder Primacy Interrelationship Scheme in Figure 2.6. In other words, the starting point of the relational effect path will be provided by the empirical studies presented here and the shareholder model of corporate governance. And the relevant relational effect

---

[4] See discussion in section 7.3.1.3 below.
[5] See discussion in sections 7.3.1.2.1–7.3.1.2.2 below.
[6] See discussion in section 7.3.2.1 below.
[7] See discussion in section 7.3.2.1.2 below.
[8] See Figure 2.6 in section 2.7.2 above.
[9] See discussion in sections 2.6.1–2.6.8 above.

path will seek to be the most 'direct' route between the governance factors it represents. Over time, for future research, it will be possible to amass a wide range of different relational effect paths for the same governance variable for a complete profile of its zone of effect and behaviour.

Given its expanse, Empirical Studies Key Field No 4 has four parts. Part 1, in this chapter, comprises studies of 'overall' governance (or groupings of governance variables), board skills, the strength of the relevant national shareholder protection regime and 'Board Factors I' – independence or the proportion of non-executive/independent directors.

7.2 STRUCTURE AND APPROACH OF CHAPTER 7

Chapter 7 will now undertake the examination of the perceived firm-specific effects (whether positive or negative) of 'good' governance variables as follows in Table 7.1.

7.3 FIRM-SPECIFIC EFFECTS OF 'GOOD' CORPORATE GOVERNANCE – FIRM VALUE AND OPERATING PERFORMANCE

While the comparison of many of the studies may reveal contradictory results or explanations or lack of causative effect, the present purpose of the examination of these studies is to build-up a *normative* landscape of governance variables which commentators have investigated or emphasised for the purposes of maintaining or improving the economic value or operating performance of general for-profit organisations. As part of this,

Table 7.1 Empirical Studies Key Field No 4 (Part 1): National Shareholder Protection Regime and Board Factors I

No	Section	Firm-Specific Governance Variable
1	7.3	Firm-Specific Effects of 'Good' Corporate Governance – Firm Value and Operating Performance
2	7.3.1	'Overall' Governance Structure and Level and Strength of the National Shareholder Protection Regime
3	7.3.2	Board Factors I – 'Independence', the Proportion of Non-Executive/Independent Directors and Equity Ownership

commentator explanations, sometimes contradictory, for the operation of the relevant variables will be discussed.

7.3.1 'Overall' Governance Structure and the Level and Strength of the National Shareholder Protection Regime

The [NationGov] (+) variable: National governance/shareholder protection regime

The first two governance variables to be examined will be the 'overall' governance structure of the firm (measured by sets or groupings of governance variables) and the level of shareholder protection or otherwise provided by the national regulatory regime.

The following studies measure firm operating performance and value as a product of the existence and interaction of a group or 'slate' of governance variables. In other words, which governance variables operating in conjunction with other variables affect operating performance and/or firm value? And what are the perceived beneficial combinations or groupings of variables?

7.3.1.1 'Overall' governance structure and level

In the case of 'multi-variable' governance studies, the observations relating to those variables are limited to the case of the particular combinations or groupings of variables in which they are found. In other words, as these studies examine multiple variables *at the same time*, the more tentative are the conclusions relating to those variables than in the case of individual variable studies.

7.3.1.2 Detailed 'overall' governance studies

In an influential study in 2004, Brown and Caylor undertook a detailed examination of the relationship between 51 corporate governance variables and 'operating performance', 'valuation' and 'shareholder payout'.[10] The authors conclude that 'better-governed firms are relatively more profitable, more valuable, and pay out more cash to their shareholders'.[11] Among these conclusions, the authors noted that:

> the 13 factors associated most often with good performance are all directors attended at least 75% of board meetings or had a valid excuse for non-attendance, board is controlled by more than 50% independent outside directors, nominating committee is independent, governance committee meets

---

[10] Brown and Caylor, above n 2.

[11] Ibid, Abstract, 1 and Section VIII, Summary and Implications, 28–32.

once a year, board guidelines are in each proxy statement, option re-pricing did not occur in the last three years, option burn rate is not excessive, option re-pricing is prohibited, executives are subject to stock ownership guidelines, directors are subject to stock ownership guidelines, mandatory retirement age for directors exists, performance of the board is reviewed regularly, and board has outside advisors.[12]

Governance Variables representing a high attendance level at board meetings (**[BrdAttend] (+)**[13]), the annual review of the board (**[BrdReview] (+)**[14]) and outside board advisors (**[OutBrdAdv] (+)**[15]) are presented below.

Later, in 2005, Brown and Caylor identified seven variables positively linked to firm value[16] and, in 2006, several variables linked to operating performance.[17] On a similar multi-variable theme, Larcker, Richardson and Tuna identified 14 'constructs' (that is, groups) from 39 variables that affect future operating performance.[18]

---

[12] Ibid, 29.

[13] Board – Attendance Level (High) – see discussion in section 7.3.2.1.2 below.

[14] Board – Annual Review – see discussion in section 7.3.2.1.2 below.

[15] Outside/External Board Advisors – see discussion in section 7.3.2.1.2 below.

[16] L D Brown and M L Caylor, 'Corporate Governance and Firm Valuation' (20 December 2005), accessed 3 March 2015 at SSRN: http://ssrn.com/abstract=754484, 3. The seven variables positively linked to firm value include (at 3):

(1) annual election of directors (rather than staggered board elections);
(2) absence of a 'poison pill';
(3) no option repricing in the last 3 years;
(4) the company did not grant options exceeding 3% of all shares in the prior 3 years;
(5) 75% board attendance for all directors;
(6) board governance guidelines contained in the proxy statement; and
(7) share ownership guidelines for directors.

[17] L D Brown and M L Caylor, 'Corporate Governance and Firm Operating Performance' (7 December 2006), accessed 3 March 2015 at SSRN: http://ssrn.com/abstract=814205, 3 and 11, 14, 16 and 18. Variables linked to firm operating performance include (at 3):

(1) only independent directors sit on the nominating committee;
(2) director participation in an education programme; and
(3) the company did not grant options exceeding 3% of all shares in the prior 3 years.

[18] D F Larcker, S A Richardson and A I Tuna, 'How Important is Corporate Governance?' (May 2005), available at SSRN: http://ssrn.com/abstract=595821, 3 and 48 and Tables 2 and 3 thereto. The authors consider that the following 14

Not surprisingly, given the implications of agency theory,[19] a review of the variables identified by Brown and Caylor, as well as Larcker, Richardson and Tuna, highlights the prominent presence and operation of board and director-related governance mechanisms.

Important groupings or combinations in multi-variable studies Here, the studies by Brown and Caylor and, separately, Larcker *et al*, highlight the importance of groupings or combinations that include (some or all) variables taken from the following (noted here with the name of the relevant governance variable and section of discussion in the relational approach):

- Board and committee size – **[BrdCmSize] (+/−)**;[20]
- A high level of attendance at board meetings – **[BrdAttend] (+)**;[21]
- Director independence and the proportion of independent: executive

---

'constructs' derived from the 39 variables affect future operating performance (at 3 and 48 and Tables 2 and 3 thereto):

(1) 'activist variables';
(2) 'blockholding';
(3) 'affiliation' of the directors;
(4) directors appointed by 'inside' directors;
(5) 'compensation mix' of the CEO;
(6) board, audit committee and compensation committee meetings;
(7) whether there is a 'lead' director or executive/'insider' chairperson;
(8) anti-takeover provisions and mechanisms (e.g. 'poison pill', staggered board elections rather than whole board);
(9) age of directors exceeding 70;
(10) debt ratios;
(11) proportion of executive/'insider' directors on the board;
(12) the size of the board, compensation and audit committees;
(13) further anti-takeover mechanisms including 'supermajority' for voting on takeovers; and
(14) the number of outside board positions directors hold.

For a 2014 study refuting that there is any link between a firm's corporate governance arrangements and financial performance, see Roberto E Wessels and Tom Wansbeek, 'What is the Relation (If Any) between a Firm's Corporate Governance Arrangements and its Financial Performance?', CESifo Working Paper Series No. 4599, (January 31, 2014), accessed 23 April 2015 at SSRN: http://ssrn.com/abstract=2393995.

[19] See discussion in sections 4.2.3–4.2.4.1 above.

[20] Board and Committee Size – see discussion in sections 8.2–8.2.2.2 below.

[21] Board – Attendance Level (High) – see discussion in section 7.3.2.1.2 below.

directors – **[BrdIndMon] (+)**,[22] **[BrdIndInfo] (−)**,[23] **[AudIndMon] (+)**,[24] **[AudIndInfo] (−)**[25] and **[AudIndFreq] (+)**;[26]

- The presence and operation (including frequency of meeting) of board committees – in particular, the:
  - o audit committee (**[AudCom] (+)**[27]),
  - o nominating committee (**[NomCom] (+/−)**[28] and **[NomInd] (+)**[29]); and
  - o compensation committee (**[CompCom] (+/−)**[30]);
- The equity (including option) compensation and/or holdings of directors and executives – **[DirCEO$] (+/−)**,[31] **[EqOptIncent] (+)**,[32] **[EqOptEntrch] (−)**[33] and **[ShortTOpts] (−)**;[34]
- Board skills 'mix' – **[BrdSkills] (+)**;[35]
- External audit function – **[ExtAudEarn] (+)**;[36]

---

22 Board Independent Director: Executive Director Proportion – Monitoring Effect – see discussion in sections 7.3.2.1.1–7.3.2.1.2 below.

23 Board Independent Director: Executive Director Proportion – Information Flow and Decision Quality 'Trade-Off' – see discussion in section 7.3.2.1.3 below.

24 Audit Committee – Independence – Monitoring Effect – see discussion in section 8.4.3 below.

25 Audit Committee – Independence – Information Flow and Decision Quality 'Trade-off' – see discussion in section 8.4.3 below.

26 Audit Committee – Independence in Combination with Frequency of Meeting – Reduction in Earnings Manipulation Effect – see discussion in section 9.2.1 below.

27 Audit Committee – Presence, Operation and Frequency – see discussion in section 8.4.2 below.

28 Nominating Committee – Presence, Operation and Frequency – see discussion in section 7.3.1.2.2 below.

29 Nominating Committee – Independence Proportion – see discussion in section 7.3.1.2.2 below.

30 Compensation Committee – Presence, Operation and Frequency – see discussion in section 10.2.4.1 below.

31 Director/CEO Compensation Levels – see discussion in section 10.2.4 below.

32 Equity/Option Plans and Holdings of Directors/Executives – Incentive/'Alignment' Effect (excludes short-term options) – see discussion in section 10.2.4 below.

33 Equity/Option Plans and Holdings of Directors/Executives – 'Entrenchment' Effect (excludes short-term options) – see discussion in section 10.2.4 below.

34 Short-Term Option Holdings/Plans of Directors and Executives – see discussion in section 10.2.5.1 below.

35 Board – Director Skills 'Mix' – see discussion in section 7.3.1.2.1 below.

36 External/Independent Audit Function – see discussion in section 9.2.3.3 below.

- The annual review of the board – **[BrdReview] (+)**;[37]
- The board has 'outside' board advisors – **[OutBrdAdv] (+)**;[38]
- Annual election of directors instead of staggered board elections – Staggered Board Elections – **[StagBrdElect] (−)**;[39]
- Absence of other anti-takeover mechanisms – Other Anti-Takeover Mechanisms (excludes staggered board elections) – **[OtherATMs] (−)**;[40]
- Blockholding and activism variables – **[BlockMon] (+)**[41] and **[BlockCosts] (−)**;[42] and
- Outside board positions held by independent directors – **[OutBrdPos] (−)**.[43]

As an additional indicator of the relative importance of board and director-related governance variables to firm sustainability, the governance variables in these bullet points represent over one-half (24 out of 39) of the variables examined in the relational approach. Their individual relative importance is examined below.

Continuing the review of multi-variable studies, in a well-known study, Gompers, Ishii and Metrick examine the relationship between an index of 24 governance variables comprised in the Investor Responsibility Research Center ('IRRC') index[44] and various measures of firm value and performance.[45] The authors found that returns for 'strong' governance

---

[37] Board – Annual Review – see discussion in section 7.3.2.1.2 below.

[38] Outside/External Board Advisors – see discussion in section 7.3.2.1.2 below.

[39] Staggered Board Elections – see discussion in section 8.3.1.1 below.

[40] Other Anti-Takeover Mechanisms (excludes staggered board elections) – see discussion in section 8.3.1.1 below.

[41] Block Shareholding – Monitoring Effect – see discussion in sections 8.5.1–2 below.

[42] Block Shareholding – Other Shareholder Agency Costs – see discussion in sections 8.5.1–2 below.

[43] Outside Board Positions of Independent Directors – see discussion in section 8.2.3.1 below.

[44] For a review of the problems associated with the use of corporate governance indices, see Sanjai Bhagat, Brian J Bolton and Roberta Romano, 'The Promise and Peril of Corporate Governance Indices', ECGI – Law Working Paper No 89/2007 (7 October 2007), accessed 3 March 2015 at SSRN: http://ssrn.com/abstract=1019921 and Philip H Dybvig and Mitch Warachka, 'Tobin's q Does Not Measure Firm Performance: Theory, Empirics, and Alternative Measures' (10 September 2012), accessed 3 March 2015 at SSRN: http://ssrn.com/abstract=1562444.

[45] P A Gompers, J L Ishii and A Metrick, 'Corporate Governance and Equity Prices' (2003) 118(1) *Quarterly Journal of Economics* 107–55, February 2003,

firms exceeded returns for 'weak' governance firms by more than 9 per cent.[46] They also found that strong governance firms had better performance than weak governance firms during the 1990s[47] and 'some significant evidence' of stronger governance firms having higher performance.[48]

On a similar theme, Goldman Sachs JBWere ('GSJBW') produced a Research Report in 2006 entitled *Good Corporate Governance = Good Investment Returns*.[49] In the Research Report, GSJBW concluded in relation to the Australian market that there was 'a good relationship between corporate governance ratings and share price performance for [financial year 2006]'.[50] There was a significant advantage to investors in purchasing the shares of companies which scored high ratings in the Overall Governance, Board Skills, Overall Board and Remuneration categories and, as a corollary, selling the shares of companies with low scores in these categories.[51] Flowing from this, board skills, board-specific variables, audit and remuneration variables are examined individually in the relational approach.

Again, as with the studies undertaken by Brown and Caylor and, separately, Larcker *et al*, the GSJBW study lends significant weight to the prominence of board and director variables. Here, however, a further refinement is present in the case of the board and highlighted by GSJBW – the board skills 'mix'. The board skills variable, **[BrdSkills] (+)**,[52] and its relational effect path are examined in the next section.[53]

In addition, but outside the board and director-related category, the position of external audit, **[ExtAudEarn] (+)**,[54] as an important plank of governance is emphasised by the findings of this study and its individual operation will also be examined below.[55] The individual director and CEO compensation and remuneration variables, including **[DirCEO$]**

---

accessed 3 March 2015 at SSRN: http://ssrn.com/abstract=278920, Appendix A, 36–42.

46 Ibid, 13.

47 Ibid, 20.

48 Ibid, 21.

49 Goldman Sachs JBWere (A Gray, analyst), Research Report, *Good Corporate Governance = Good Investment Returns, A strong result from governance investment strategies again for FY06*, June 2006, available at www.gsjbw.com. Source: Corporate Governance International, subscriber letter, 16 June 2006 and attachments ('GSJBW Research Report') (copy on file with author).

50 Ibid, GSJBW Research Report, 6.

51 Ibid, Key Points, 4.

52 Board – Director Skills 'Mix'.

53 See discussion in section 7.3.1.2.1 below.

54 External/Independent Audit Function.

55 See discussion in section 9.2.3.3 below.

(+/−),[56] **[EqOptIncent] (+)**,[57] **[EqOptEntrch] (−)**[58] and **[ShortTOpts] (−)**[59] are examined in Chapter 10.

In the case of profit results, GSJBW also reviewed 'earnings surprise', which it defined as 'results above or below market expectations'.[60] Their observations in relation to the financial year 2005 imply that 'overall' or multi-variable good governance in firms – particularly in the case of board and director-related variables – seems to be good for ratios of return on investment capital.[61]

In 2007, the indices used by Gompers, Ishii and Metrick ('GIM'), as well as those used by Brown and Caylor (and others), were considered in a study by Bhagat and Bolton who conclude:

> [w]e find that better governance as measured by the GIM and [other] indices, stock ownership of board members, and CEO-Chair separation is significantly positively correlated with better contemporaneous and subsequent *operating* performance.[62]

Yet, Bhagat and Bolton disagree with the conclusions reached by Caylor and Brown in their studies:

> [a]dditionally, better governance as measured by Brown and Caylor, and [other] is *not significantly correlated* with better contemporaneous or subsequent operating performance.[63]

Recent studies support link between good governance and firm value and performance but precise groupings uncertain In 2010, Ammann, Oesch and Schmid examined 64 governance attributes classified into six categories being:

---

[56] Director/CEO Compensation Levels – see discussion in sections 10.1.1 and 10.2.2–10.2.4 below.

[57] Equity/Option Plans and Holdings of Directors/Executives – Incentive/'Alignment' Effect (excludes short-term options) – see discussion in section 10.2.4 below.

[58] Equity/Option Plans and Holdings of Directors/Executives – 'Entrenchment' Effect (excludes short-term options) – see discussion in section 10.2.4 below.

[59] Short-Term Option Holdings/Plans of Directors and Executives – see discussion in section 10.2.5.1 below.

[60] GSJBW Research Report, above n 49, 4.

[61] Ibid.

[62] Sanjai Bhagat and Brian J Bolton, 'Corporate Governance and Firm Performance' (June 2007), accessed 3 March 2015 at SSRN: http://ssrn.com/abstract=1017342, 5 (emphasis in original).

[63] Ibid, 5–6 (emphasis added).

- board accountability;
- financial disclosure and internal control;
- shareholder rights;
- remuneration;
- market for control; and
- corporate behaviour.[64]

The authors conclude that good corporate governance enhances firm value, increases cash flow and lowers the cost of capital.[65]

Cuñat, Gine and Guadalupe[66] in 2010 (revised in February 2012) investigated the market effects of the passing of governance-related proposals at meetings, finding a positive relationship with firm value.[67]

Thus, a cautionary note for the relational approach's adoption and description of governance variables as enhancing firm survival, is that while governance indexes may be of use in the determination of 'overall' good governance (and, the argument follows, positive operating performance[68]), the precise make-up or constitution of those indexes remains a matter for contention.

Today – Bebchuk, Cohen and Wang's caveat on the use of multi-variable studies In a study more recently published on SSRN in 2011 and in the *Journal of Financial Economics* in 2013, Bebchuk, Cohen and Wang[69]

---

64 Manuel Ammann, David Oesch and Markus M Schmid, 'Corporate Governance and Firm Value: International Evidence' (3 November 2010), at SSRN: http://ssrn.com/abstract=1692222, 4 (formatting altered and bullet-points added).

65 Ibid, 30–1.

66 Vicente Cuñat, Mireia Gine and Maria Guadalupe, 'The Vote is Cast: The Effect of Corporate Governance on Shareholder Value' (17 February 2010), at SSRN: http://ssrn.com/abstract=1555961.

67 Ibid, 30.

68 The *direction* of the causality is, however, disputed by Hermalin who states:

> [p]rofits and strength of governance will, therefore, be positively correlated. But note carefully the direction of causality: firms are not more profitable because they have better governance; rather, they have better governance because they will be more profitable.

See Benjamin E Hermalin, 'Firm Value and Corporate Governance: Does the Former Determine the Latter?' (2 January 2008), accessed 3 March 2015 at SSRN: http://ssrn.com/abstract=1080090, 1.

69 Lucian A Bebchuk, Alma Cohen and Charles C Y Wang, 'Learning and the Disappearing Association Between Governance and Returns' (2013) 108(2) *Journal of Financial Economics* 323–48; Harvard Law and Economics Discussion

concluded that the association that existed between 'good' governance indexes and abnormal returns in the 1990s had disappeared during the 2000s due to:

> market participants' learning during the 1990s to appreciate the difference between firms scoring well and poorly on the governance indices.[70]

Thus, the explanatory power of multi-variable governance indices studies would appear – for these authors – to be problematic[71] at this time in pursuing a trading strategy based on abnormal returns. Yet the authors confirm that such indices are still of value in determining links with firm performance.[72] Thus studies on the use of such indices and how public information on companies is interpreted and used to determine them and the relationship with firm performance remain relevant in determining the relational effect path of governance variables in the relational approach.

7.3.1.2.1 The 'spine' of relational effect paths and the comparator variable: [BrdSkills] (+) With that caveat, the studies in the previous section highlight the importance within the 'grouped' variables of the skills 'mix' of the board. Looking ahead, the analysis in the relational approach indicates that the interrelationships depicted in the relational effect path for this governance variable are used as the model or spine for many governance variables.

The studies in the previous section seek to link, most directly, this skills mix with both enhancement of the monitoring function (Monitoring & Audit Factor No 5[73]) and the quality of decision-making (Decision-making Factor No 7).[74] As the relational approach has demonstrated[75] the interrelationship between these governance factors is a close one in which

---

Paper No 667 (1 June 2011), accessed 3 March 2015 at SSRN: http://ssrn.com/abstract=1589731.

[70] Ibid, 35.

[71] Ibid.

[72] Ibid, 5. For a useful review of selected literature on the relationship between corporate governance and firm performance, see Anup Agrawal and Charles R Knoeber, 'Corporate Governance and Firm Performance' in Christopher R Thomas, William F Shughart II (eds), *Oxford Handbook In Managerial Economics*, Oxford: Oxford University Press, 2012 (15 March 2012), accessed 3 March 2015 at SSRN: http://ssrn.com/abstract=2024764.

[73] See discussion in section 2.6.5 above.

[74] See discussion in section 2.6.7 above.

[75] See Figure 2.6 and the discussion in section 2.7.2 above.

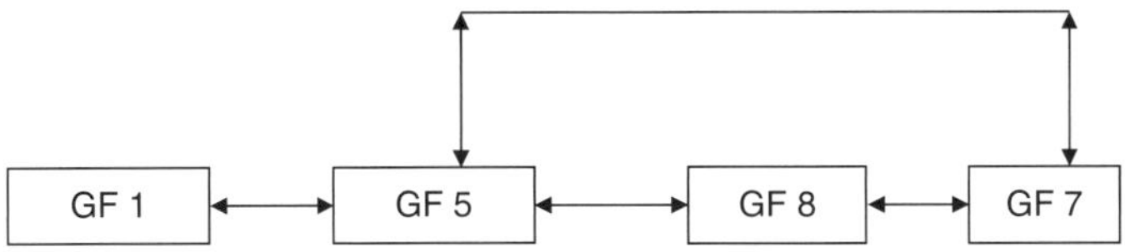

Figure 7.1 Relational effect path spine

the two themes inform and shape each other in a continuous cycle. Indeed, Monitoring & Audit Factor No 5 and Decision-making Factor No 7 are part of the configuration of governance factors which forms the 'spine' of the relational effect paths of a large number of governance variables (see Figure 7.1).

This spine of the relational effect paths is, like all relational effect paths, derived from the shareholder primacy interrelationship scheme in Figure 2.6 (albeit depicted in a simplified manner for explanatory purposes). Now, from that interrelationship scheme, Reporting Factor No 1[76] and Responsibility Factor No 8[77] are the additional factors in the spine.

As demonstrated earlier, the maintenance and enhancement of Reporting Factor No 1 is dependent on the effectiveness of all the components of Monitoring & Audit Factor No 5. Again demonstrated earlier, Responsibility Factor No 8 is critical to the operation of many other governance factors, in particular Decision-making Factor No 7 and Monitoring & Audit Factor No 5.[78] As the relational approach shows in the following section, this spinal configuration of interrelationships between governance factors Nos 1, 5, 8 and 7 is the foundation of the **[BrdSkills] (+)** variable. Thus, this governance variable will be used as a foundation-block in the construction and analysis of many other governance variables.

BOARD SKILLS MIX VARIABLE: [BRDSKILLS] *(+)*[79] VARIABLE RELATIONAL EFFECT PATH Thus, the **[BrdSkills] (+)** variable's relational effect path is positive (+) and begins with Monitoring & Audit Factor No 5 and the Decision-making Factor No 7. As noted above, each of these governance factors has a reflexive relationship with the other as described in section

76 See discussion in section 2.6.1 above.
77 See discussion in section 2.6.8 above.
78 Ibid.
79 Board – Director Skills 'Mix' – see discussion in this section 7.3.1.2.1 above.

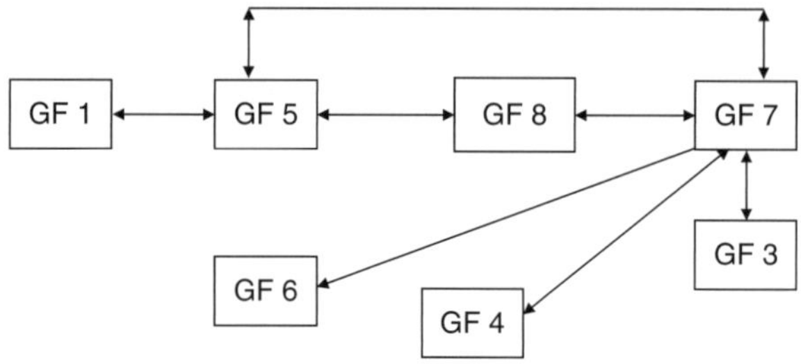

Figure 7.2 [BrdSkills] (+) variable relational effect path

2.6.7 above and the shareholder primacy interrelationship scheme in Figure 2.6. The factors are depicted in Figure 7.2.

In the shareholder primacy interrelationship scheme in Figure 2.6, there is a reflexive relationship between Monitoring & Audit Factor No 5 and Reporting Factor No 1 as described in section 2.6.5 above. The effect of Decision-making Factor No 7 is hypothesised to be both significant and extensive. It extends to all other governance factors *except* the overriding nature of Compliance Factor No 2[80] (as shown in Compliance Factor No 2 Interrelationships in Figure 2.4 and section 2.6.2 above). Compliance with corporate governance and legal requirements on the company – an obligation which remains constant by force of 'hard', 'soft' or 'hybrid' laws – is hypothesised not to be affected by the skills mix of the board. Compliance Factor No 2 remains constant and cannot be modified by the decision-making or actions of the directors. Decision-making Factor No 7's zone of effect reflexively affects Alignment Factor No 3, Compensation Factor No 4 and Responsibility Factor No 8. Decision-making Factor No 7 also directly affects in a single direction Stakeholders Factor No 6.

What is the effect of this within the company? An example would be a company which has devoted resources to the internal monitoring, internal audit and external audit functions (Monitoring & Audit Factor No 5). The diagram shows that such a company is more likely to have more timely reports with higher information quality, transparency and integrity (Reporting Factor No 1). Such reporting will thus increase the quality of external or market monitoring of the company with consequential improvement in internal monitoring and, again, improvement in the transparency and timing of financial and other reports. Thus, the diagram shows that Monitoring & Audit Factor No 5 affects Reporting

80 See discussion in section 2.6.2 above.

Factor No 1 in a reflexive manner, that is, these factors affect each other. But how are the monitoring, internal audit and external audit functions improved in the first place? The diagram shows that skills of the board affect these functions in a positive direction beginning with Monitoring & Audit Factor No 5. Thus, increases in board skills (the **[BrdSkills] (+)** variable) will positively affect both monitoring and audit within and outside the company and the transparency, quality and timing of reporting.

Therefore, the **[BrdSkills] (+)** variable is hypothesised to affect all governance factors except the overriding Compliance Factor No 2 (Corporate Governance and Legal Compliance). This equates to a coverage/rating of +7/87.50 *rprox* in the Coverage Table (Table 3.1) and the Relational Proximity Table (Table 3.2).

7.3.1.2.2 Board skills mix dependent on existence and independence of nominating committee

NOMINATING COMMITTEE – PRESENCE, OPERATION AND FREQUENCY: [NOMCOM] (+/−) RELATIONAL EFFECT PATH The discussion of the 'overall' or grouped-variable governance level above highlighted, among other governance variables, the presence and operation (including frequency of meeting) of board committees – in particular, the audit committee (**[AudCom] (+)**[81]), the nominating committee (**[NomCom] (+/−)**[82] and **[NomInd] (+)**[83]) and the compensation committee (**[CompCom] (+/−)**[84]).

The structure and operation of the **[BrdSkills] (+)** variable is itself dependent on the operation and structure of the **[NomCom] (+/−)** variable as the composition – and therefore skills mix – of the board flows from the nominating committee. For example, in a study further examined below, Weisbach and Hermalin suggest that 'board independence declines over the course of a CEO's tenure'[85] on account of studies which explain that

---

[81] Audit Committee – Presence, Operation and Frequency – see discussion in section 8.4.2 below.

[82] Nominating Committee – Presence, Operation and Frequency – see discussion in this section 7.3.1.2.2.

[83] Nominating Committee – Independence Proportion – see discussion in this section 7.3.1.2.2.

[84] Compensation Committee – Presence, Operation and Frequency – see discussion in section 10.2.4.1 below.

[85] M S Weisbach and B E Hermalin, 'Boards of Directors as an Endogenously Determined Institution: A Survey of the Economic Literature' (15 June 2000), accessed 3 March 2015 at SSRN: http://ssrn.com/abstract=233111, 9–10.

the decrease of independence over time is due to the CEO's participation in or control over the director nomination and appointment process.[86]

Therefore, the **[NomCom] (+/−)** variable has a dual direction marker (+/−) as the board's skill mix will be affected positively or negatively by the operation of this governance variable. Further, as the operation of the **[NomCom] (+/−)** variable directly precipitates the operation of the **[BrdSkills] (+)** variable, **[NomCom] (+/−)** has an identical relational effect path to **[BrdSkills] (+)** but in both directions. Therefore, the **[NomCom] (+/−)** variable affects all governance factors with the exception of the overriding Compliance Factor No 2 which remains constant and is not affected. This equates to a coverage/rating of +/−7/87.50 *rprox* in the Coverage Table (Table 3.1) and the Relational Proximity Table (Table 3.2).

NOMINATING COMMITTEE – INDEPENDENCE PROPORTION: [NOMIND] (+) RELATIONAL EFFECT PATH As will be demonstrated from studies below,[87] the **[BrdIndMon] (+)**[88] variable has a positive effect on the quality of monitoring of management (Monitoring & Audit Factor No 5) and the quality of decision-making (Decision-making Factor No 7). Here, by analogy to the studies considered by Weisbach and Hermalin in relation to the **[NomCom] (+/−)** variable, increases in the independence proportion of the nominating committee (**[NomInd] (+)**) will similarly have a positive effect on the monitoring and decision-making – and therefore board skills – attributes of directors nominated by that committee. Thus, like **[NomCom] (+/−)**, as the operation of the **[NomInd] (+)** variable directly precipitates the operation of the **[BrdSkills] (+)** variable, **[NomInd] (+)** has an identical relational effect path but only in the positive direction. This equates to a coverage/rating of +7/87.50 *rprox* in the Coverage Table (Table 3.1) and the Relational Proximity Table (Table 3.2).

7.3.1.3 The strength of the national shareholder protection regime

The implication of studies relating to the strength or otherwise of shareholder protection provided by the national regulatory regime in which the firm operates suggest that increases in the level of national regime governance/protection (at least, to a certain point) improve firm performance and that common law regimes appear to provide the highest level

---

86 Ibid, 27–8.

87 See discussion in section 7.3.2.1.2 below.

88 Board Independent Director: Executive Director Proportion – Monitoring Effect – see discussion in sections 7.3.2.1.1–7.3.2.1.2 below.

of protection. In addition, firm-specific governance variables appear to be able to perform a 'gap filling' function in relation to omissions from, or weaknesses in, the national regulatory regime.

7.3.1.3.1 Detailed national regime studies Indicative of this conclusion, for Bruno and Claessens, there is a positive relationship between firm performance and the level of shareholder protection provided by the national governance regime.[89] This is supported by a 2007 study by Ng, Gul and Mensah where the authors observe the effects of the US' Sarbanes-Oxley Act (SOX)[90] reforms and the relative value of firms.[91] For the authors, increases in the level of shareholder protection flowing from the national governance regime during the relevant period enhance firm value.

Bruno and Claessens further find that, for a positive effect on firm value, improvements in company-specific governance variables can compensate ('substitution effect') for deficiencies in the national regime.[92] In this respect, the authors considered that:

> excessive regulation can harm valuation, consistent with the hypothesis that excessive regulation can harm managerial initiative and generate lower returns.[93]

Klapper and Love also found a positive relationship between firm-specific and national regime governance and investor protection.[94]

---

[89] V Bruno and Stijn Claessens, 'Corporate Governance and Regulation: Can There Be Too Much of a Good Thing?' (1 March 2007), World Bank Policy Research Working Paper No 4140, accessed 3 March 2015 at SSRN: http://ssrn.com/abstract=964802, 4. For an index to measure or quantify the investor protection of various national corporate laws, see Brian R Cheffins, Steven A Bank and Harwell Wells, "Law and History by Numbers: Use, But with Care", ECGI – Law Working Paper No. 230/2013; University of Cambridge Faculty of Law Research Paper No. 50/2013; UCLA School of Law, Law-Econ Research Paper 13-21; Temple University Legal Studies Research Paper No. 2013-47, (October 28, 2013), accessed 23 April 2015 at SSRN: http://ssrn.com/abstract=2348654.

[90] PL 107-204, 2002 HR 3763, July 30, 2002, 116 Stat 745, available at http://www.sec.gov/about/laws/soa2002.pdf ('SOX').

[91] Anthony Ng, Ferdinand Gul and Yaw Mensah, 'Managerial Entrenchment and Value-Relevance of Earnings During the Pre- and Post-Sarbanes Oxley Periods' (September 2007), accessed 3 March 2015 at SSRN: http://ssrn.com/abstract=1012746, 7.

[92] Bruno and Claessens, above n 89, 4–5.

[93] Ibid (footnote omitted).

[94] L F Klapper and I Love, 'Corporate Governance, Investor Protection and Performance in Emerging Markets' (March 2002), World Bank Policy Research

Similarly to Bruno and Claessens, they find that 'better corporate governance is associated with higher operating performance'.[95] They conclude that companies in weak-protection countries should adopt governance variables from strong-protection countries to improve their operating performance and firm value.[96] This helps to explain the harmonisation or convergence effect relating to corporate governance variables demonstrated in Chapter 6.[97] Which, then, are the strong-governance countries?

LA PORTA, ET AL – COMMON LAW ORIGIN OF 'STRONG' GOVERNANCE COUNTRIES In Bratton and McCahery's comparison of 'market' and 'blockholder' share-ownership and governance systems, the authors discuss the well-known and seminal investor protection study by La Porta, Lopez-de-Silanes, Shleifer and Vishny[98] concluding in relation to that study:

> (*a*) common law countries provide the strongest protection for investors; (*b*) France and similar civil law countries provide the weakest level of protection; and (*c*) Germany and similar civil law countries provide an intermediate level of protection.[99]

Similarly, Gugler, Mueller and Yurtoglu examine as a governance variable

---

Working Paper No 2818, available at SSRN: http://ssrn.com/abstract=303979, 3–4.

[95] Ibid, 5.

[96] Ibid.

[97] See discussion in section 6.1.3.4 above.

[98] William W Bratton and John A McCahery, 'Comparative Corporate Governance and the Theory of the Firm: The Case Against Global Cross Reference' (1999) 38(2) *Columbia Journal of Transnational Law* 213, accessed 3 March 2015 at SSRN: http://ssrn.com/abstract=205455, 10. The authors cite R La Porta, F Lopez-de-Silanes, A Shleifer, and R Vishny, *Law and Finance*, NBER Working Paper No 5661 (July 1996). See also Rafael La Porta, Florencio Lopez-de-Silanes, Andrei Shleifer and R W Vishny, 'Investor Protection and Corporate Governance' (June 1999), accessed 3 March 2015 at SSRN: http://ssrn.com/abstract=183908, 29. For a more recent discussion by the authors, see Rafael La Porta, Florencio Lopez-de-Silanes and Andrei Shleifer, 'The Economic Consequences of Legal Origins' (2008) 46(2) *Journal of Economic Literature* 285–332, accessed 3 March 2015 at SSRN: http://ssrn.com/abstract=1028081. See also John Armour, Simon Deakin, Prabirjit Sarkar, Mathias Siems and Ajit Singh, "Shareholder Protection and Stock Market Development: An Empirical Test of the Legal Origins Hypothesis", University of Cambridge, CBR Working Paper, (February 2008), accessed 23 April 2015 at SSRN: http://ssrn.com/abstract=1094355.

[99] Bratton and McCahery, ibid, 10 (footnote omitted).

the origin of the national corporate governance regime.[100] In a 2003 study of 61 countries, the authors conclude that '. . . English-origin legal systems produce corporate governance systems that better protect shareholders against managers than other systems'.[101] Consistent with Alignment Factor No 3, the authors conclude that:

> [s]trong corporate governance institutions help to align managerial and shareholder interests, and prevent dominant individual or family shareholders from exploiting minority shareholders.[102]

This result accords with the study by Bris and Cabolis who found firm value was increased in the case of 'acquisitions of firms in weaker shareholder protection countries by firms in stronger protective regimes'.[103]

7.3.1.3.2 The [NationGov] (+)[104] *variable relational effect path* The review of the perceived effects of the strength of the national shareholder protection regime adds support to the proposition that firm performance and the national level of shareholder protection/governance may well turn out to be positively related.

SUMMARY – STUDIES INDICATE POSITIVE DIRECTION FOR [NATIONGOV] (+) VARIABLE The above examination thus signifies a positive (+) effect for the direction of the **[NationGov] (+)** variable. In other words, improvements in this governance variable normatively *should* enhance the profitability and, thus survival, of the firm. Compliance Factor No 2 (Corporate Governance and Legal Compliance) is an overriding requirement of *all* governance factors as explained in Chapter 2.[105] These overriding legal provisions provide the content of the national shareholder protection regime. In the case of the **[BrdSkills] (+)** variable, it was hypothesised

---

[100] K P Gugler, D C Mueller and B B Yurtoglu, 'Corporate Governance and the Returns on Investment', EFA 2002 Berlin Meetings Presented Paper; ECGI – Finance Working Paper No 06/2003 (January 2003), accessed 3 March 2015 at SSRN: http://ssrn.com/abstract=299520.

[101] Ibid, 26.

[102] Ibid, 27.

[103] A Bris and C Cabolis, 'Corporate Governance Convergence by Contract: Evidence from Cross-Border Mergers', Yale ICF Working Paper No 02-32 (September 2002), accessed 3 March 2015 at SSRN: http://ssrn.com/abstract=321101, 30–1.

[104] National Governance/Shareholder Protection Regime.

[105] See discussion in section 2.6.2 above.

that, through Decision-making Factor No 7, all governance factors were affected with the exception of the overriding nature of Compliance Factor No 2 which is not itself affected by the skills mix of the board. Compliance Factor No 2 was there said to be constant. However, in the case of **[NationGov] (+)**, changes in the content of this governance variable will actually change the requirements of the law, whether 'hard', 'soft' or 'hybrid'.

Thus, the relational effect path for the **[NationGov] (+)** variable affects all governance factors in a manner identical to Figure 2.4 (Compliance Factor No 2 Interrelationships).

This gives rise to a coverage/rating of +8/100.00 *rprox* for the **[NationGov] (+)** variable in the Coverage Table (Table 3.1) and Relational Proximity Table (Table 3.2).

Having now concluded the examination of 'overall' or multi-variable governance studies, the relational approach now turns to consider studies on the nature and operation of *individual* board and director governance variables.

7.3.2 Board[106] Factors I – 'Independence', the Proportion of Non-Executive/Independent Directors and Equity Ownership

In attempting to measure firm operating performance and/or firm value as a product of individual board and director-related governance variables, the principal governance variables to be examined are:

- board and director independence and the proportion of non-executive/independent directors – **[BrdIndMon] (+)**[107] and **[BrdIndInfo] (−)**;[108]
- the annual board review **[BrdReview] (+)**;[109] and

[106] The discussion of board factors in this chapter is centred on 'unitary' boards. Turnbull tells us that such a board structure exists for most listed companies in the US, UK, Canada and Australia. See Shann Turnbull, 'Why Unitary Boards Are Not Best Practice: A Case for Compound Boards' (November 2000), accessed 3 March 2015 at SSRN: http://ssrn.com/abstract=253803, 2.

[107] Board Independent Director: Executive Director Proportion – Monitoring Effect – see discussion in sections 7.3.2.1.1–7.3.2.1.2 below.

[108] Board Independent Director: Executive Director Proportion – Information Flow and Decision-Quality 'Trade-off' – see discussion in section 7.3.2.1.3 below.

[109] Board – Annual Review – see discussion in section 7.3.2.1.2 below.

- director equity ownership – **[EqOptIncent] (+)**[110] and **[EqOptEntrch] (−)**.[111]

Summary of director independence studies

It is often argued that enhancing board and director independence improves the quality of monitoring of management and thus reduces agency costs. However, this result is by no means certain. In particular, the negative effect of such an independent monitoring structure may be to curtail the information flow (particularly that which is firm-specific or manager-specific) to the board in turn reducing the quality of board decision-making.

In the case of the perceived relationship between board or director independence and firm operating performance and/or firm value, there are conflicting results. In the case of both firm performance and value, many studies find no link with the degree of independence. Though fewer studies suggest a positive relationship, these are often affected by intervening or complicating variables such as the degree of director equity ownership and firm size.

Similarly, in the case of the proportion of equity held by inside directors and/or management, little can be predicted on account of two counterbalancing effects of this governance variable. An important study[112] suggests that, on the one hand, parallel interests between directors and outside shareholders result from such equity holdings. However, after a certain point, increasing the size of management ownership may well harm outsider interests.

7.3.2.1 Director independence

The studies examined below indicate that a wide range of results have been obtained for this governance variable. Consequently, only tentative conclusions can be drawn from the studies overall.

---

110 Equity/Option Plans and Holdings of Directors/Executives – Incentive/'Alignment Effect' (excludes short-term options) – see discussion in section 10.2.4 below.

111 Equity/Option Plans and Holdings of Directors/Executives – 'Entrenchment Effect' (excludes short-term options) – see discussion in section 10.2.4 below.

112 O Fuerst and S Kang, 'Corporate Governance, Expected Operating Performance, and Pricing', accessed 3 March 2015 at SSRN: http://ssrn.com/abstract=141357, 6–7. The authors cite R Morck, A Shleifer and R W Vishny, 'Management Ownership and Corporate Performance: An Empirical Analysis' (1988) 20 *Journal of Financial Economics* 293–316.

7.3.2.1.1 Improvements in the quality of monitoring are not certain The forthcoming studies show that the result of increasing board or director independence on the board's supervisory function is uncertain. While some studies suggest a beneficial or positive (+) effect of greater independence among board members on the quality of board monitoring (the **[BrdIndMon] (+)**[113] variable), this is difficult to ensure due to a perceived negative effect in terms of information flow to the board with consequent negative (−) effects on the quality of board decision-making (the **[BrdIndInfo] (−)**[114] variable).

In the positive direction, board or director independence is often cited as one of the most important governance variables for enhancing the monitoring of management (Monitoring & Audit Factor No 5) in the dispersed-shareholding public company.[115] As Black and Kim explain, the probability of firing the CEO after poor performance is an important indicator of the quality of board monitoring.[116] This suggests that a company with improved monitoring is more likely to improve the quality of its decision-making in relation to acquisitions but also the quality of decision-making in relation to the make-up of its monitoring structures.

---

113 Board Independent Director: Executive Director Proportion – Monitoring Effect – see discussion in sections 7.3.2.1.1–7.3.2.1.2 below.

114 Board Independent Director: Executive Director Proportion – Information Flow and Decision-Quality 'Trade-off' – see discussion in section 7.3.2.1.3 below.

115 See, for example, R Morck, 'Behavioral Finance in Corporate Governance – Independent Directors and Non-Executive Chairs', Harvard Institute of Economic Research Discussion Paper No 2037 (May 2004), accessed 3 March 2015 at SSRN: http://ssrn.com/abstract=527723; Jeffrey N Gordon, "Independent Directors and Stock Market Prices: The New Corporate Governance Paradigm", ECGI – Law Working Paper No 74/2006, (August 2006), accessed 23 April 2015 at SSRN: http://ssrn.com/abstract=928100; Jeffrey N Gordon, "The Rise of Independent Directors in the United States, 1950–2005: Of Shareholder Value and Stock Market Prices" (2007) 59 *Stanford Law Review* 1465, accessed 23 April 2015 at SSRN: http://ssrn.com/abstract=1086397 and Brian R Cheffins, Bernard S Black and Michael D Klausner, "Outside Directors, Liability Risk and Corporate Governance: A Comparative Analysis (English Version)", ECGI – Law Working Paper No 48, accessed 23 April 2015 at SSRN: http://ssrn.com/abstract=800584.

116 Bernard S Black and Woochan Kim, 'The Effect of Board Structure on Firm Value in an Emerging Market: IV, DiD, and Time Series Evidence from Korea', Finance Working Paper No 179/2007 (June 2007), accessed 3 March 2015 at: http://ssrn.com/abstract=968287, 5. For a discussion of the effects of 'powerful' independent directors including higher firm value, see Kathy Fogel, Liping Ma and Randall Morck, "Powerful Independent Directors", European Corporate Governance Institute (ECGI) – Finance Working Paper No. 404/2014, (January 9, 2014), accessed 23 April 2015 at SSRN: http://ssrn.com/abstract=2377106.

Thus, in a 2007 study by Bhagat and Bolton, a positive relationship was found between 'disciplinary management turnover' and both board independence and director shareholdings in times of poor performance.[117] Similarly, under a model proposed by Weisbach and Hermalin referred to above, 'CEO turnover is more sensitive to performance when the board is *more independent*' and '[t]he probability of independent directors being added to the board rises following poor firm performance'.[118] The authors noted empirical support for both propositions[119] and for the proposition that:

> board independence declines over the course of a CEO's tenure.[120]

In the case of the third proposition, the authors point to studies which explain that the decrease of independence over time is due to the CEO's participation in or control over the director nomination and appointment process.[121]

Despite the argued monitoring improvements, in a 2012 paper, Erkens, Hung and Matos found that, in the Global Financial Crisis (GFC), stock returns were worse for companies with more independent boards and higher institutional ownership.[122] Asking whether this was because 'independent directors and institutional shareholders encouraged managers to increase shareholder returns through greater risk-taking prior to the crisis',[123] the authors confirmed the conclusion in relation to institutional ownership but not independent directors.[124] For the authors, the equity raisings during the GFC increased the likelihood that the firms with independent directors would survive the crisis.[125] One implication for the authors is that independent boards made better financing decisions in relation to debt/equity ratios in times of poor performance.[126] The second is that the effect of the structure of the board is more significant during crises

---

117 Bhagat and Bolton, above n 62, 6.

118 Weisbach and Hermalin, above n 85, 9 (emphasis added).

119 Ibid, 9–10.

120 Ibid.

121 Ibid, 27–8.

122 David H Erkens, Mingyi Hung, and Pedro P Matos, 'Corporate Governance in the 2007–2008 Financial Crisis: Evidence from Financial Institutions Worldwide' (2012) 18(2) *Journal of Corporate Finance* 389–411 (15 January 2012), accessed 3 March 2015 at SSRN: http://ssrn.com/abstract=1397685, 32.

123 Ibid, 2.

124 Ibid, 3.

125 Ibid, 4.

126 Ibid, 6.

events than in day-to-day management of the firm's business as suggested by an earlier study by Hermalin and Weisbach.[127]

A complicating governance factor in the CEO turnover measure is likely to be the 'relative importance' of the CEO in the organisation. In a 2007 study discussed further in Chapter 10,[128] Cremers, Bebchuk and Peyer find a negative relationship between 'CEO centrality' and firm value.[129] The authors also find that CEO centrality results in 'lower CEO turnover'[130] which 'might reflect governance problems'.[131]

Weir, Laing and McKnight emphasize the necessary characteristics of non-executive directors which, *it is argued*, safeguard the interests of shareholders in separation of ownership and/or agency theory – independence and (relying on the work of Fama and Jensen) reputational constraints.[132]

Fuerst and Kang, however, cite the well-known work of Jensen to identify the problems which may flow from the pivotal role of the board in such separation theories:

> Jensen (1993). . .attributes the BOD's governance failures to factors such as CEO's agenda-setting power, low equity ownership of the board members, overcrowding of the board, and a board culture that encourages consent rather than dissent.[133]

This would suggest that 'independence' and 'reputational constraints' as suggested by Weir, Laing and McKnight are themselves open to erosion from a wide collection of factors.

---

127 Ibid. The authors cite B Hermalin and M Weisbach, 'Boards of Directors as an Endogenously Determined Institution: A Survey of the Economic Literature' (2003) 9(1) *FRBNY Economic Policy Review* 7–26, 17.

128 See discussion in section 10.2.3 of chapter 10.

129 Martijn Cremers, Lucian Bebchuk and Urs Peyer, 'CEO Centrality', Harvard Law and Economics Discussion Paper No 601 (December 2007, Revised May 2008), available at SSRN: http://ssrn.com/abstract=1030107, 1.

130 Ibid.

131 Ibid, 3.

132 C Weir, D Laing and P J McKnight, 'An Empirical Analysis of the Impact of Corporate Governance Mechanisms on the Performance of UK Firms', accessed 3 March 2015 at SSRN: http://ssrn.com/abstract=286440, 6. The authors cite Eugene Fama, 'Agency Problems and the Theory of the Firm' (1980) 88 *Journal of Political Economy* 134–45; Cadbury Committee, *Report of the Committee on the Financial Aspects of Corporate Governance* London: Gee & Co, 1992 and Eugene F Fama and Michael C Jensen, 'Separation of Ownership and Control' (1983) 26 *Journal of Law and Economics* 301–49.

133 Fuerst and Kang, above n 112, 8. The authors cite Michael C Jensen, 'The Modern Industrial Revolution, Exit, and The Failure of Internal Control Systems' (1993) 48 *Journal of Finance* 831–80.

7.3.2.1.2 [BrdIndMon] (+), [BrdReview] (+) [BrdAttend] (+) and [OutBrdAdv] (+) variables relational effect paths

[BRDINDMON] (+): BOARD INDEPENDENT: EXECUTIVE DIRECTOR PROPORTION – MONITORING EFFECT The behaviour of the **[BrdIndMon] (+)** variable is identical to the **[BrdSkills] (+)**[134] variable. In this case, however, the effect of this governance variable is predicted to be significant on Reporting Factor No 1, Monitoring & Audit Factor No 5, Decision-making Factor No 7 and Responsibility Factor No 8 on account of the substantial guidance in governance codes in Chapter 6 relating to director independence. Director independence was found in that chapter to be a core variable/feature of global/cross-border and national governance codes.[135]

Thus, like the **[BrdSkills] (+)** variable, the **[BrdIndMon] (+)** variable affects all governance factors except the overriding effect of Compliance Factor No 2 (as described in section 2.6.2 above). Similarly to the **[BrdSkills] (+)** variable, compliance with corporate governance and legal requirements on the company – an obligation which remains constant by force of law – is not affected by the independence element of the board. Compliance Factor No 2 thus remains constant for this variable. This equates to a coverage/rating of +7/87.50 *rprox* in the Coverage Table (Table 3.1) and the Relational Proximity Table (Table 3.2).

[BRDREVIEW] (+): BOARD – ANNUAL REVIEW The **[BrdReview] (+)** variable acts as a 'strong-form' version of the **[BrdIndMon] (+)**. The term 'strong-form' here means that the monitoring effect of the variable is greater or more escalated than in the case of the **[BrdIndMon] (+)** variable. This is because **[BrdReview] (+)** concentrates on the monitoring or supervision (Monitoring & Audit Factor No 5) of the *board itself* while the monitoring function of **[BrdIndMon] (+)** is applied to all levels of the company which is an expansive area. Having a stronger or more concentrated monitoring effect than **[BrdIndMon] (+)**, it therefore has a positive directional marker identical to that for **[BrdIndMon] (+)** and with an identical relational effect path. This equates to a coverage/rating of +7/87.50 *rprox* for **[BrdReview] (+)** in the Coverage Table (Table 3.1) and the Relational Proximity Table (Table 3.2).

---

134 See discussion in section 7.3.1.2.1 above.

135 See discussion in section 6.8.1 above.

[BRDATTEND] (+): BOARD – ATTENDANCE LEVEL (HIGH) The **[BrdAttend] (+)** variable – denoting a high attendance level at board meetings – also acts as a 'strong-form' version of the **[BrdIndMon] (+)** variable as it (again) concentrates on the monitoring function of directors on the board (Monitoring & Audit Factor No 5). As the time spent in review improves both the quality of monitoring (Monitoring & Audit Factor No 5) and the quality of decision-making (Decision-making Factor No 7), **[BrdAttend] (+)** has a positive directional marker and is hypothesised to have an identical relational effect path to that for **[BrdIndMon] (+)**. This equates to a coverage/rating of +7/87.50 *rprox* for **[BrdAttend] (+)** in the Coverage Table (Table 3.1) and the Relational Proximity Table (Table 3.2).

[OUTBRDADV] (+): OUTSIDE/EXTERNAL BOARD ADVISORS Like **[BrdReview] (+)** and **[BrdAttend] (+)**, the outside or independent advisors to the board variable is a 'strong-form' version of the **[BrdIndMon] (+)** variable. Again, the use of such advisors – drawing on their independent and expert natures – is hypothesised to improve both the quality of monitoring (Monitoring & Audit Factor No 5) and the quality of decision-making by the board (Decision-making Factor No 7). Thus, **[OutBrdAdv] (+)** has a positive directional marker and – again drawing on the independence aspect – is hypothesised to have an identical relational effect path to that for **[BrdIndMon] (+)**. This equates to a coverage/rating of +7/87.50 *rprox* for the **[OutBrdAdv] (+)** variable in the Coverage Table (Table 3.1) and the Relational Proximity Table (Table 3.2).

7.3.2.1.3 [BrdIndInfo] (−)[136] *variable relational effect path*

NEGATIVE EFFECT OF INDEPENDENCE ON INFORMATION-FLOW TO THE BOARD Contrary to the above studies as to the beneficial effects of greater independence among board members on the quality of board monitoring, there may well be drawbacks for the firm in terms of information flow. This comes from two sources. First, as Adams explains, while the board can improve the quality of its advice to management if it receives more detailed and transparent information, this may consequently enable the board to revise downward its opinion of particular managers leading,

[136] Board Independent Director: Executive Director Proportion – Information Flow and Decision Quality 'Trade-off'.

eventually, to a reduction in 'firm specific' information flow to the board.[137] The degree of independence of the board is also a factor in the 'trade-off' for Adams and Ferreira. The authors consider that 'independent boards monitor more intensively' with the result that 'the CEO will not communicate firm specific information to a board which is too independent'.[138]

Second, for Professor Hill, independent directors may lack the depth of understanding of the company's business or operations that inside directors bring.[139] This is explained below by Duchin, Matsusaka and Ozbas as a form of 'inferior information' or information asymmetry of independent directors compared to inside directors.[140]

What are the consequences for the **[BrdIndInfo] (−)** variable in light of the trade-off on information-flow to the board and Hill's risk of deficiency in knowledge? The implication is that the relational effect path for the **[BrdIndInfo] (−)** variable is *not* predicted to be merely the same as the preceding path for **[BrdIndMon] (+)** but with a negative direction. The negative zone of effect of this governance variable is much narrower than its positive counterpart. Primarily and significantly, the reviewed studies show that the important Decision-making Factor No 7 is negatively affected. But this negative effect is likely to extend to a significant degree only to the board component of the three-level decision-making hierarchy of the board, CEO and management contemplated by Decision-making Factor No 7. In other words, the decision-making quality of the CEO and management are not affected by limitations on the information supplied to the board and deficiencies in the knowledge of independent directors. Thus, the relational effect path for **[BrdIndInfo] (−)** is as shown in Figure 7.3.

Thus, in terms of Figure 7.2 (the **[BrdSkills] (+)** variable relational effect path), it is difficult to conceive of any significant negative 'flow-on' effects (on account of withholding 'manager-specific' and 'firm-specific' information) from Decision-making Factor No 7 to Alignment Factor No 3,

---

137 Renee B Adams, 'The Dual Role of Corporate Boards as Advisors and Monitors of Management: Theory and Evidence', previously titled 'The Dual Role of Corporate Boards as Advisors and Monitors of Management', accessed 3 March 2015 at SSRN: http://ssrn.com/abstract=241581, 2.

138 Renee B Adams and Daniel Ferreira, 'A Theory of Friendly Boards' (2007) 62(1) *Journal of Finance* 217–50, available at SSRN: http://ssrn.com/abstract=866625, 2.

139 J G Hill, 'Regulatory Responses to Global Corporate Scandals' (2005) 23 *Wisconsin International Law Journal* 367, accessed 3 March 2015 at SSRN: http://ssrn.com/abstract=886104, 389.

140 Ran Duchin, John G Matsusaka and Oguzhan Ozbas, 'When Are Outside Directors Effective?', USC CLEO Research Paper No C07-13 (February 2008), accessed 3 March 2015 at SSRN: http://ssrn.com/abstract=1026488, 1.

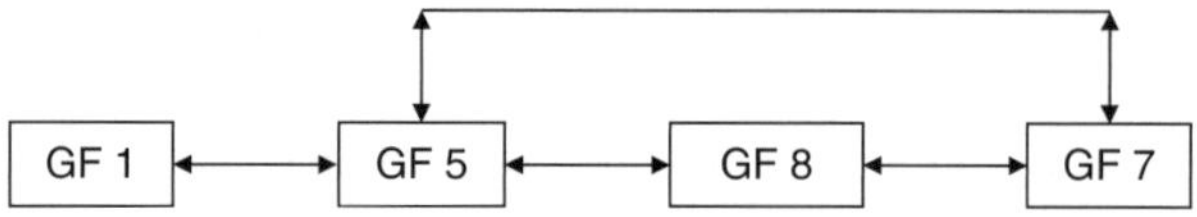

Figure 7.3 [BrdIndInfo] (−) variable relational effect path

Compensation Factor No 4 and Stakeholders Factor No 6. This is because the themes contained in these governance factors are submitted to be outside the nature of the 'manager-specific' and 'firm-specific' information contemplated by the negative effect identified in the relevant studies. Thus, these governance factors are omitted from the **[BrdIndInfo] (−)** relational effect path. The overriding nature of the legal and corporate governance requirements contemplated by Compliance Factor No 2 is again unaffected by the board's decision-making actions and so is omitted. Thus the zone of effect of the **[BrdIndInfo] (−)** variable is hypothesised to extend to only four governance factors giving a coverage/rating of −4/50.00 *rprox*.

ENHANCING THE QUALITY OF MONITORING BY LESS INDEPENDENCE? Commentators have also noted some further negative effects of the **[BrdIndInfo] (−)** variable, this time in relation to the independence of the board itself. In terms of effective governance, and considering a single-tier board model, Adams and Ferreira observe that:

> [s]pecifically, to encourage the manager to share information, shareholders may optimally elect a less independent or friendlier board which does not monitor the CEO too intensively.[141]

For Dent, too, the monitoring ability (or even desire) of the board is questionable. The author, in stating that the 'reality' of corporate governance lies in 'CEO domination' rather than any other model, considers that the 'overwhelming' evidence is that:

> most boards are passive, dominated by CEOs who exert their power in their own interests.[142]

Dent gives reasons including the CEO's role in recommending directors for board vacancies, the view that (purported) outside directors who

---

[141] Adams and Ferreira, above n 138, 2.

[142] G W Dent, 'Academics in Wonderland: The Team Production and Director Primacy Models of Corporate Governance' (June 2007), Case Legal Studies Research Paper No 07-21, accessed 3 March 2015 at SSRN: http://ssrn.com/abstract=995186, 14 of 72 (footnote omitted).

are themselves CEOs 'defer' to one another as a reciprocal practice and loyalty by outside directors to the person who nominated them.[143]

7.3.2.1.4 Conflicting results for independence, firm value and operating performance Important for the firm-specific benefits or effects of good governance in enhancing the long-term efficiency and sustainability of the for-profit corporation, is whether an increase in the proportion of independent directors increases firm value and/or operating performance? An overview of the following studies delivers particularly conflicting results[144] for this independence variable.

STUDIES SHOWING NO LINK BETWEEN INDEPENDENCE AND FIRM PERFORMANCE/VALUE For Adams and Mehran (who examine banking industry firms), the independence proportion does not affect firm performance[145] and, in relation to firms generally, the same is the case for the first large-sample study by Bhagat and Black who found no evidentiary link between independence and firm performance.[146] Indeed, in the 2007 study by Bhagat and (this time) Bolton already discussed in section 7.3.1.2 above, the independence factor was found to have a negative effect on firm operating performance.[147]

Weir, Laing and McKnight[148] examine UK companies where they note that, unlike the US, the majority of directors are executive directors rather than independent.[149] They find that company performance is not linked to the proportion of non-executive directors or their independence[150] and this is also noted in the literature review undertaken by Weisbach and Hermalin.[151]

In the case of firm value, Brick, Palia and Wang similarly find no link

---

[143] Ibid.

[144] Indeed, Bainbridge similarly finds 'decidedly mixed' results for the link between director independence and profitability, concluding that '. . . the bulk of the evidence suggests that board composition has no effect on profitability'. See Stephen M Bainbridge, 'The Creeping Federalization of Corporate Law' (2003) 26(1) *Regulation* 32–9, Spring 2003, accessed 3 March 2015 at SSRN: http://ssrn.com/abstract=389403, 29.

[145] R B Adams and H Mehran, 'Corporate Performance, Board Structure and its Determinants in the Banking Industry', EFA 2005 Moscow Meetings (8 August 2005), accessed 3 March 2015 at SSRN: http://ssrn.com/abstract=302593, 3.

[146] S Bhagat and B S Black, 'The Non-Correlation Between Board Independence and Long-Term Firm Performance' (2002) 27 *Journal of Corporation Law* 231–73, accessed 3 March 2015 at SSRN: http://ssrn.com/abstract=133808, 233.

[147] Bhagat and Bolton, above n 62, 6.

[148] Weir, Laing and McKnight, above n 132, 5–11, 18–21, 27–8.

[149] Ibid, 18.

[150] Ibid, 19.

[151] Weisbach and Hermalin, above n 85, 2.

with board independence[152] and this is supported by the findings of Lasfer and Faccio who found no link between management shareholdings and the value of the company.[153] The relational approach's overarching purpose of enhancing the long-term sustainability of the firm is, on one view, partly a natural consequence of continual firm operating performance and/or value. Yet Buckland found 'no evidence' of any substantial link between compliance with the Cadbury Report requirements (including director independence) and company 'survival'.[154]

STUDIES SHOWING POSITIVE LINK BETWEEN INDEPENDENCE AND FIRM PERFORMANCE/VALUE ARE FEWER Despite the above findings, several (though, it is conceded, fewer) studies identify a positive relationship between firm performance and/or value and the independence proportion. For Bruno and Claessens, a positive relationship exists between firm performance and several factors including board independence.[155] Hutchinson found, too, that increases in the proportion of independent directors improve monitoring quality (and therefore performance) in relation to investment opportunities.[156] Similarly, for studies including Aggarwal, Erel, Stulz and Williamson, an increase in board independence is a factor increasing firm *value*.[157]

More recently in 2009, Bebchuk and Weisbach review the literature to explain that while initial studies found no link between independence and higher firm value:

---

152 Ivan E Brick, Darius Palia and Chia-Jane Wang, "Simultaneous Estimation of CEO Compensation, Leverage, and Board Characteristics on Firm Value", unpublished working paper, AFA 2006 Boston Meetings Paper (March 2005).

153 M Lasfer and M Faccio, 'Managerial Ownership, Board Structure and Firm Value: The UK Evidence', Cass Business School Research Paper (August 30, 1999), accessed 3 March 2015 at SSRN: http://ssrn.com/abstract=179008, 3–4.

154 R Buckland, 'UK Company Board Structures and Corporate Performance: A Cohort Study of 1990s IPOs in the UK', EFMA 2001 Lugano Meetings; Aberdeen Accountancy, Finance & Mgmt Working Paper 01-01 (2001), accessed 3 March 2015 at SSRN: http://ssrn.com/abstract=269807, 19.

155 Bruno and Claessens, above n 89, 4.

156 M R Hutchinson, 'An Analysis of the Association Between Firms' Investment Opportunities, Board Composition, and Firm Performance', accessed 3 March 2015 at SSRN: http://ssrn.com/abstract=295483, 24.

157 R Aggarwal, I Erel, R M Stulz and R G Williamson, 'Do U.S. Firms Have the Best Corporate Governance? A Cross-Country Examination of the Relation Between Corporate Governance and Shareholder Wealth', Fisher College of Business Working Paper No 2006-03-006 (2006), accessed 3 March 2015 at SSRN: http://ssrn.com/abstract=954169, 4–5.

> there is a growing body of empirical research indicating that director independence is associated with improved decisions with respect to some specific types of decisions . . . In particular, it has been shown that director independence has an impact on CEO turnover . . . executive compensation decisions . . . the incidence of fraud . . . and on the incidence of opportunistic timing of stock option grants.[158]

Of course, these decision areas include two of the most controversial in governance discourse. Both executive compensation and the granting of stock options are examined in Chapter 10.

INCREASES IN INSIDE DIRECTORS MAY INCREASE LIKELIHOOD OF FIRM FAILURE In terms of the incidence of corporate failures, Hsu and Wu distinguish between inside, outside and 'grey' directors – that is, non-independent non-executive directors.[159] The authors conclude that increases in the number of outside directors on the board and audit committee do not reduce the likelihood of corporate failure but that increases in inside directors do increase that likelihood of failure.[160]

7.3.2.1.5 Intervening or confounding factors for director independence

EQUITY OWNERSHIP MAY BE AN INTERVENING FACTOR ON THE EFFECTS OF DIRECTOR INDEPENDENCE The study by Fuerst and Kang introduces a complicating (or intervening) factor to the independence variable and is therefore best considered on its own. For Fuerst and Kang, the number or proportion of independent directors alone is *not* sufficiently explanatory. Questions of equity ownership (to be discussed in more detail in Chapter 10[161]) must also be considered.

FUERST AND KANG: EQUITY OWNERSHIP OF INDEPENDENT DIRECTORS ENHANCES FIRM PERFORMANCE AND VALUE The authors concluded that firm performance and value is generally increased by (1) shareholdings by

---

158 Lucian A Bebchuk and Michael S Weisbach, 'The State of Corporate Governance Research', Fisher College of Business Working Paper No 2009-03-20; (2010) 23(3) *Review of Financial Studies* 939–61; Fisher College of Business Working Paper No 2009-03-20; Charles A. Dice WP 2009-21; Harvard Law and Economics Discussion Paper No 652 (November 17, 2009), accessed 3 March 2015 at SSRN: http://ssrn.com/abstract=1508146, 7–8 (references omitted).

159 Hwa-Hsien Hsu and Yu-Hsuan Wu, 'Board Composition, Audit Committee Structure, "Grey Directors" and the Incidences of Corporate Failure in the UK' Finance and Corporate Governance Conference 2010 Paper (10 December 2009), accessed 3 March 2015 at SSRN: http://ssrn.com/abstract=1532997, 3.

160 Ibid, 21–2.

161 See discussion in section 10.2.1 below.

the CEO, executives and 'inside' directors and (2) greater shareholdings by independent directors.[162] By contrast, firm performance is reduced by (1) a rise in the number of independent directors (unless accompanied by a rise in equity holdings by those directors)[163]; (2) a rise in number of total directors[164]; (3) large (>5%) shareholdings by independent/non-management shareholders[165] and (4) increases in the CEO's term of office.[166]

THE SIZE OF THE FIRM IS AN INTERVENING FACTOR ON THE EFFECTS OF DIRECTOR INDEPENDENCE Another complicating or intervening factor in a consideration of the independence variable is the size of the firm. In this respect, Chhaochharia and Grinstein[167] find that the effect of board independence in turn depends on the size factor.

> small firms with less board independence underperform small firms with more board independence by 12%-18% during the announcement year. In contrast, we do not observe underperformance in large firms. In fact, large firms with less board independence outperform large firms with more board independence by about 18%.[168]

By contrast to Chhaochharia and Grinstein, in the emerging market of Korea, Black and Kim found an opposite result for large companies. The authors found a positive causal connection between governance rules requiring 'large' companies to have at least half the board independent (and an audit committee with an independent chair and two-thirds independent directors) and both market value and later year increased profitability and dividend payments.[169]

7.3.2.1.6 Summary for studies of the director independence variable Given the number of studies, it would be premature to draw any conclusions relating to the seemingly financially negative effect of rising director independence for large firms identified by Chhaochharia and Grinstein.

---

162 Fuerst and Kang, above n 112, 3.
163 Ibid.
164 Ibid.
165 Ibid, 4.
166 Ibid.
167 V Chhaochharia and Y Grinstein, 'Corporate Governance and Firm Value: The Impact of the 2002 Governance Rules' (March 2007), Johnson School Research Paper Series No 23-06, accessed 3 March 2015 at SSRN: http://ssrn.com/abstract=556990.
168 Ibid, 3.
169 Black and Kim, above n 116, 2–3.

However, in the case of the positive effect identified by Black and Kim in an emerging market, the finding is not surprising given the 'substitution' or 'gap-filling' effect previously discussed in relation to firm-specific governance variables and, in this case, possible weaknesses in the shareholder protection regime in comparison to common-law regimes.[170]

Given the conflicting results for the effect of director independence on firm value and performance, Duchin, Matsusaka and Ozbas sought in a 2008 study to explain the results for this effect in terms of the 'inferior information' (that is, asymmetric information) of independent directors when compared to insiders.[171]

This also accords with the views of Hill noted above in relation to the likelihood that independent directors bring less in-depth knowledge of the company's business and operations than in the case of inside directors.[172] Studying a sample of firms which were required to increase the number of independent directors on their boards consequent on recent US corporate governance rules including SOX[173] and the NYSE Final Rules,[174] Duchin *et al* concluded that a positive (or negative) effect on firm performance was dependent on the low (or high) cost of acquiring information relating to the firm.[175] For the authors, this cost is reflected in the number of outsiders on the board with 'high' information cost firms having comparatively less

---

170 See discussion in sections 7.3.1.3–7.3.1.3.2 above.

171 Duchin, Matsusaka and Ozbas, above n 140, 1.

172 Hill, above n 139, 389. See discussion in section 7.3.2.1.3 above.

173 SOX, above n 90.

174 New York Stock Exchange, *Final NYSE Corporate Governance Rules* ('NYSE Final Rules'), approved by SEC 4 November 2003 (except s 303A.08) and 30 June 2003 (s 303A.08). The Rules (as amended from time to time) comprise section 303A.00 of the NYSE Listed Company Manual. See section 303A.00 Corporate Governance Standards (approved 25 November 2009), available at http://nysemanual.nyse.com/lcm/ (accessed 3 March 2015). Subsequent amendments have been made to:

- Section 303A.00 – Corporate Governance Standards (approved 22 August 2013)
- Section 303A.02 – Corporate Governance Standards (approved 11 January 2013)
- Section 303A.05 – Corporate Governance Standards (approved 11 January 2013)
- Section 303A.07 – Audit Committee Additional Requirements (approved 22 August 2013)

These Rule amendments are available at http://nysemanual.nyse.com/lcm/ (accessed 3 March 2015).

175 Duchin, Matsusaka and Ozbas, above n 140, 4.

outsiders.[176] Bebchuk and Weisbach, too, recognise the inferior information problem of independent directors.[177]

Thus, inferior information problems reduce the effectiveness of outside directors in monitoring and evaluating management in a similar manner to the reduction in 'firm-specific' and 'manager-specific' information flow to the board described for the **[BrdIndInfo] (−)** variable.[178]

In summary then, in the case of the perceived relationship between board or director independence and firm operating performance and/or firm value, there are conflicting results. In the case of *both* firm performance and value, many studies find *no* link with the degree of independence. Thus, the importance of director independence as an individual governance variable (rather than as part of a slate of variables) in governance discourse is not, at this time, supported by the empirical results. Though fewer studies suggest a positive relationship, these are often affected by intervening or complicating variables, in particular:

- the degree of equity ownership – for the CEO, executives and both 'inside' and independent directors; and
- firm size.

Additionally, the direction (positive or negative) of the effect of director ownership on firm performance is suggested, in one study, to be dependent on the costs of acquiring information for outside directors to remedy asymmetric information problems. The first of the intervening variables – the degree of equity ownership – is examined in Chapter 10 relating to 'good' governance and director, CEO and management compensation.[179] The second, firm size, is discussed in Chapter 8 below as part of the discussion of board size.[180]

7.3.2.1.7 Conclusion for Board Factors I – 'Independence' and the proportion of non-executive/independent directors This section concludes its examination of the first slate of individual board factors with little conclusive support for the perceived benefits that were suggested by the earlier examination of the 'overall' or multi-variable governance level.

In the case of the director independence variable, an elegant case is

---

176 Ibid, 5.

177 Bebchuk and Weisbach, above n 158, 8.

178 Board Independent Director: Executive Director Proportion – Information Flow and Decision Quality 'Trade-off'. See discussion in section 7.3.2.1.3 above.

179 See discussion in section 10.2.1 below.

180 See discussion in sections 8.2–8.2.2.2 below.

argued that one of the perceived benefits may include enhanced monitoring. However, other studies suggest that possible resultant problems in the quality of the information flow to board level may well arise with detrimental effects on the quality of board decision-making. This does not mean, of course, that the independence variable should be abandoned altogether. The relational approach's methodology does not consider the governance review of any organisation to be a 'box-ticking' exercise. For the relational approach, the overarching purpose of governance variables is to seek to balance a number of competing interests across various relational axes in order to achieve long-term efficiency and sustainability of the for-profit corporation. While the independence of directors may well, all things being equal, enhance the quality of monitoring, it is equally important to recognise the beneficial effects in terms of the quality of information and decision-making which is brought to the table by the more in-depth operational knowledge of executive directors.

Thus, in terms of the balancing of competing interests across the various relational axes which the relational approach calls for, the circumstances of each individual firm, the executive or independent nature of its directors and the dynamics of the interaction between board, CEO and management will require close examination in order to determine the optimal board structure to maximise the monitoring: board information flow 'trade-off' and the information asymmetry of independent directors.

In the case of the perceived positive link between the independence variable and firm operating performance and/or firm value, results are conflicting with many of the studies examined finding no such relation. An insufficient number of studies with positive findings have been identified to draw any confident conclusions. However, the size of the board would appear to be an intervening factor with, at this time, inconclusive results. Another intervening factor is the level of equity holdings – for the CEO, management and both inside and independent directors. This is examined in Chapter 10.[181]

In the next Chapter 8, the relational approach examines Part 2 of the Empirical Studies Key Field No 4. Again, a wide range of governance variables are presented and their relational effect paths tracked. This includes studies on board size and 'outside' board positions and studies relating to anti-takeover mechanisms, the audit subcommittee, 'block' and institutional shareholdings and division in the CEO/chairperson role. Again, the long-term efficiency and sustainability of the firm will be measured principally by firm value and/or operating performance.

---

[181] See discussion in section 10.2.1 below.

8. Empirical studies Key Field No 4 (Part 2): Board factors II and other firm-specific variables

8.1 AIMS AND APPROACH OF CHAPTER 8

The aims and approach of this Chapter 8 mirror those of Chapter 7 which considered the effectiveness of governance variables drawn from Part 1 of Key Field No 4 – National Shareholder Protection Regime and Board Factors I. In Chapter 8, the effectiveness of firm-specific governance variables will again be assessed principally by studies with measures of firm operating performance and firm value as proxies for the long-term efficiency and sustainability of the firm. Chapter 8 continues with the process of examining empirical studies as follows:

- Board Factors II – Board Size and Outside Board Positions;
- Anti-Takeover Mechanisms and the Market for Corporate Control – 'Whole' Board and 'Staggered' Board Elections;
- Audit Sub-Committee – Presence, Independence and Expertise;
- 'Block' and Institutional Shareholdings; and
- Division in the CEO/Chairperson Roles.

Again, a relational effect path for each variable will be constructed from relevant empirical studies and the Shareholder Primacy Interrelationship Scheme in Figure 2.6. This means that the greater the number of governance factors[1] affected by a governance variable in either direction, then the greater is its 'relational proximity rating' and its effect on agency costs and the sustainability of the firm.

[1] See the construction of the eight governance factors in sections 2.6.1–2.6.8 above.

8.2 BOARD FACTORS II – BOARD SIZE AND OUTSIDE BOARD POSITIONS

The relational approach now examines a selection of studies that attempt to measure the firm-specific effects of a second group of individual board and director-related governance variables. The first variables to be examined are board size (**[BrdCmSize] (+/−)**[2]) and outside board positions of independent directors (**[OutBrdPos] (−)**).[3]

A review of studies below reveals that a significant number of factors would appear to affect the size of the board. Some of these factors are exogenous (imposed from outside the firm) such as the national/statutory governance code or regime requirements and the practicability of 'external verification' or monitoring. Other factors are endogenous depending on the individual characteristics of the firm such as the compatibility of insider and outside shareholder interests, the size of the firm and the level of firm 'diversification'/complexity and debt.

8.2.1 Determinants of Optimum Board Size

Raheja has proposed a model to determine optimal board size and composition (proportion of insiders *vs* outsiders).[4] The author seeks to combine considerations relating to the alignment of insider interests with those of shareholders and the ease or otherwise of external verification of the firm's activities. The first consideration is straightforward. Better alignment between outsiders and the incentives of insiders (such as performance-based compensation, equity holdings and option grants for inside directors) means that the shareholders require fewer insiders than otherwise would be the case to effectively align their interests – for example, in relation to firm operating performance and firm value.

The second consideration can be explained in terms of the phenomenon explained in Chapter 7 – that increases in the number of outside/independent directors on the board can lead to a reduction in the 'firm-specific' and 'manager-specific' information-flow to the board.[5] Additionally, for commentators like Hill and Duchin *et al*, there may be 'inferior

---

[2] Board and Committee Size – see discussion in section 8.2.2.2 below.

[3] Outside Board Positions of Independent Directors – see discussion in section 8.2.3.1 below.

[4] Charu G Raheja, 'Determinants of Board Size and Composition: A Theory of Corporate Boards' (2005) 40(2) *Journal of Financial and Quantitative Analysis* 283–306, accessed 4 March 2015 at SSRN: http://ssrn.com/abstract=522542, 4.

[5] See discussion in section 7.3.2.1.3 above.

information' or information asymmetry on the part of outside directors compared to inside directors.[6] Thus, a company in which financial and operational matters are easier for an outside director to verify – that is, matters which require no or little insider information – will sustain more outside directors. For example, the company's share price at any time is a matter of public information and so can be verified by outside directors. Similarly, material customer contracts may be inspected and examined. But it is otherwise in relation to the company's suppliers. The reliability, suitability and viability of those suppliers is likely to be insider information. The more specialised and complex the company's financial (including debt) and operational profile, the more reliant that outside directors are on CEO and management information and thus the lower the proportion of outside directors.

Board size has also been shown to be dependent on the size of the firm and governance regime requirements. Lehn, Patro and Zhao find that the major determinant of board size and the proportion of insiders is the size of the firm.[7] Linck, Netter and Yang found that as firm size increases, board size and the proportion of independent directors both increase.[8] In addition, as inside ownership increases, board size and the proportion of independent directors reduces. The authors also found that the requirements of SOX[9] and consequent mandatory NYSE Final Rule changes[10]

---

6 Ibid.

7 K Lehn, S Patro and M Zhao, 'Determinants of the Size and Structure of Corporate Boards: 1935–2000' (November 2003), accessed 4 March 2015 at SSRN: http://ssrn.com/abstract=470675, 2.

8 J S Linck, J M Netter and T Yang, 'The Determinants of Board Structure' (23 March 2007), accessed 4 March 2015 at SSRN: http://ssrn.com/abstract=729935, 1.

9 PL 107-204, 2002 HR 3763, July 30, 2002, 116 Stat 745, available at http://www.sec.gov/about/laws/soa2002.pdf ('SOX').

10 New York Stock Exchange, *Final NYSE Corporate Governance Rules* ('NYSE Final Rules'), approved by SEC 4 November 2003 (except s 303A.08) and 30 June 2003 (s 303A.08). The Rules (as amended from time to time) comprise section 303A.00 of the NYSE Listed Company Manual. See section 303A.00 Corporate Governance Standards (approved 25 November 2009), accessed 4 March 2015 at http://nysemanual.nyse.com/lcm/. Subsequent amendments have been made to:

- Section 303A.00 – Corporate Governance Standards (approved 22 August 2013)
- Section 303A.02 – Corporate Governance Standards (approved 11 January 2013)
- Section 303A.05 – Corporate Governance Standards (approved 11 January 2013)

have caused both board size and the proportion of independent directors to increase.[11]

Coles, Daniel and Naveen found, too, that board size increases with the size of the firm and, in addition, with the 'level of diversification' and 'leverage' concluding that:

> firms that are diversified, large, and have high debt have 2 more board members, who are outsiders.[12]

Thus, the board size factor appears to be itself affected by a wide range of other factors. Accordingly, optimal board size cannot be determined in isolation of individual firm, industry and regulatory characteristics. The results would appear to coincide with intuitive arguments in relation to factors which affect the quality and difficulty of the monitoring, advisory and strategic decision-making functions of the board – that the wider the gap between insider and outsider interests, the more difficult the practicability of external monitoring, the larger the firm's operations, their diversity and/or complexity and debt level, the larger the size of the board.

8.2.2 The Relationship between Board Size and Firm Operating Performance/Value is Inconclusive

What is the effect on firm operating performance and/or value of changes in the size of the board? A review of the studies below displays conflicting results. Accordingly, no consistent or conclusive result can be confidently predicted in relation to the relationship between board size and firm operating performance and/or firm value.

8.2.2.1 Conflicting results for board size and firm performance/value

Adams and Mehran found that (banking) firm *performance* was positively influenced by an increase in the size of the board.[13] For Fuerst and Kang,

---

- Section 303A.07 – Audit Committee Additional Requirements (approved 22 August 2013)

These Rule amendments are available at http://nysemanual.nyse.com/lcm/ (accessed 4 March 2015).

[11] Linck, Netter and Yang, above n 8, 2.

[12] L J Coles, N D Daniel and L Naveen, 'Boards: Does One Size Fit All?' (February 2005), accessed 4 March 2015 at SSRN: http://ssrn.com/abstract=665746, 3.

[13] R B Adams and H Mehran, 'Corporate Performance, Board Structure and its Determinants in the Banking Industry', EFA 2005 Moscow Meetings (August 8, 2005), accessed 4 March 2015 at SSRN: http://ssrn.com/abstract=302593, 3.

however, firm performance is reduced by a number of factors including a rise in the number of total directors.[14] Bhagat and Black, however, found 'no consistent correlation' between firm performance and the size of the board.[15]

Mak and Kusnadi investigate the link between firm *value* and the size of the board in Singapore and Malaysia.[16] After noting that the corporate governance codes in those countries are based on the UK Combined Code,[17] the authors refer to a 1993 study by Jensen in relation to an argued negative relationship between board size and consequent board effectiveness:

> Jensen (1993) argues that boards with more than about 7 to 8 members are unlikely to be effective. According to him, large boards result in less effective coordination, communication and decision-making, and are more likely to be controlled by the CEO.[18]

Of course, the size of the company is relevant. For Mak and Kusnadi, also relevant is leverage and the total fixed asset ratio. Thus, what might be an effective size of board for a small company may be too few given the size, complexity and leverage of a large company. In the case of these Singapore and Malaysian companies, the authors found that increases in board size after five directors reduced firm value.[19] Important for this section of the relational approach is the *effects* of increases in board size on the effectiveness of the board as a governance structure. The authors suggest that, not only is the effectiveness of decision-making reduced by increases in the size of the board, but so too is the board's likelihood of replacing a director with a more suitable candidate.[20]

---

[14] O Fuerst, and S Kang, 'Corporate Governance, Expected Operating Performance, and Pricing', accessed 4 March 2015 at SSRN: http://ssrn.com/abstract=141357, 3.

[15] S Bhagat and B S Black, 'The Non-Correlation Between Board Independence and Long-Term Firm Performance' (2002) 27 *Journal of Corporation Law* 231–73, accessed 4 March 2015 at SSRN: http://ssrn.com/abstract=133808, 233.

[16] Y T Mak and Y Kusnadi, 'Size Really Matters: Further Evidence on the Negative Relationship Between Board Size and Firm Value', NUS Business School Working Paper (March 2002), accessed 4 March 2015 at SSRN: http://ssrn.com/abstract=303505.

[17] Ibid, 3.

[18] Ibid. The authors cite Michael C Jensen, 'The Modern Industrial Revolution, Exit and the Failure of Internal Control Systems' (1993) 48 *Journal of Finance* 831–80.

[19] Mak and Kusnadi, above n 16, 4.

[20] Ibid, 21. The authors cite Jensen, above n 18 and J R Hackman (ed.), *Groups That Work*, San Francisco, CA: Jossey-Bass, 1990.

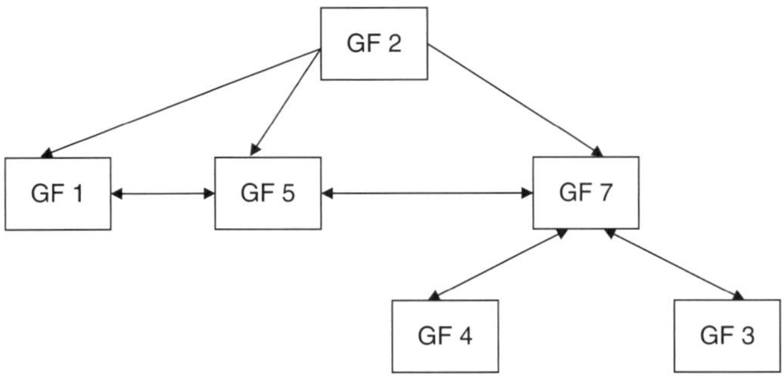

Figure 8.1 [BrdCmSize] (+/−) variable relational effect path

8.2.2.2 [BrdCmSize] (+/−)[21] variable relational effect path

Perceived negative relationship between board size above 'optimal' level and board effectiveness Intuitively, arguments concerning a perceived negative relationship between board size above a particular point and board effectiveness appeal. The difficulty given the wide range of firms which exist would appear to be determining that 'optimal' point. This would appear to be dependent, at the very least, on the following factors:[22]

- compatibility of insider and outside shareholder interests;
- practicability of 'external verification' or monitoring;
- size of the firm;
- national/statutory governance code or regime requirements; and
- level of firm 'diversification'/complexity and debt.

The analysis therefore suggests that the **[BrdCmSize] (+/−)** direction of effect may be either positive or negative (+/−) depending upon the point for the 'optimal' number of directors for that particular firm. Taking Jensen's 1993 view as the starting point, notions of the effectiveness of coordination, communication and decision-making raise squarely Decision-making Factor No 7 as shown in Figure 8.1.

The analysis and relational effect path for **[BrdCmSize] (+/−)** is in part similar to that for the **[BrdIndMon] (+)**[23] variable (which is itself based on

[21] Board and Committee Size.

[22] These factors are also described in section 8.2.1 above.

[23] Board Independent Director: Executive Director Proportion – Monitoring Effect – see discussion in sections 7.3.2.1.1–7.3.2.1.2 above.

the relational effect path for the **[BrdSkills] (+)**[24] variable). Additionally, the size of the board, which Linck, Netter and Yang find is affected by mandatory statutory and exchange rules,[25] is thus affected by Compliance Factor No 2 (Corporate Governance and Legal Compliance).

The reflexive relationship between Decision-making Factor No 7 and Responsibility Factor No 8 is employed in relation to the **[BrdIndMon] (+)** variable. Conceivably, this reflexive relationship could operate here. But it is difficult to make a sufficiently compelling hypothesis (even on intuitive grounds) that matters of board size should have a similar effect on Responsibility Factor No 8[26] as opposed to director independence. It will be recalled that, in the case of the **[BrdIndMon] (+)** variable, director independence is hypothesised to affect Responsibility Factor No 8 on account of the significance afforded to director independence in governance codes in Chapter 6.[27] In other words, director independence cuts across the delineation of different monitoring and responsibility organs, whether the board or committee. By contrast, while board size affects the efficacy of decision-making (Decision-making Factor No 7), it is unlikely to affect the delineation and disclosure of powers, duties and lines of responsibility of those organs.

Similar considerations apply for the relational approach to exclude any significant hypothetical effect of board size on Stakeholders Factor No 6 (Identification, Participation and Protection of Stakeholder Interests). In other words, increases in board size should not normatively affect the ability of the board to identify, facilitate participation and to protect stakeholder interests. This is unless one hypothesises that there is some sort of 'crowding-out' effect on (non-shareholder) stakeholder interests by increases in board size. This seems very unlikely given the assumption of a constant independent/non-executive director proportion. If this proportion remains constant, then there is no greater or lesser consideration of non-shareholder stakeholder interests by the board or committees.

This is by contrast to the effect of increases in the size of the board on the alignment of management and shareholder interests (Alignment Factor No 3). Again taking the relational effect path of the **[BrdIndMon] (+)** variable,[28] the reflexive relationship between Decision-making Factor

---

24 Board – Director Skills 'Mix' – see discussion in section 7.3.1.2.1 above.

25 Linck, Netter and Yang, above n 8, 2.

26 Delineation and Disclosure of Powers, Duties and Lines of Responsibility – see discussion in section 2.6.8 above.

27 See discussion in sections 6.8.1 and 7.3.2.1.2 above.

28 Board Independent Director: Executive Director Proportion – Monitoring Effect – see discussion in sections 7.3.2.1.1–7.3.2.1.2 above.

No 7 and the Alignment Factor No 3 remains in place and operative. This is because of Raheja's identification of the compatibility (or alignment) of insider and outside shareholder interests as one of the determinants of board size.[29]

Taking these considerations together, the relational effect path for **[BrdCmSize] (+/−)** affects all governance factors except Responsibility Factor No 8 and Stakeholders Factor No 6. This results in a coverage/rating of +/− 6/75.00 *rprox* for the **[BrdCmSize] (+/−)** variable in the Coverage Table (Table 3.1) and the Relational Proximity Table (Table 3.2).

8.2.3 Do Board Positions of Outside Directors Reduce Monitoring Quality?

This section highlights four studies. The first in 2002 suggests that multiple directorships do not cause directors to monitor less effectively nor to avoid time commitments such as serving on board committees. The second study in 2004 suggests that increases in the number of outside positions held by outside directors may reduce the effectiveness of the board's monitoring function. The third study in 2008 suggests that 'busy' directors have more absences from board meetings which may reduce firm performance while the final study suggests some benefit from outside directorships – that networking through outside board positions may increase firm performance.

The relationship between the time commitment of multiple directorships and the quality of board monitoring and service on committees was examined by Pritchard, Ferris and Jagannathan in 2002.[30] The authors find that '[d]irectors who serve larger firms and sit on larger boards are more likely to attract additional directorships'.[31] Indeed, the authors suggest that there is a 'reputational effect' – that favourable financial results at a firm increase the likelihood of further directorships.[32]

Not surprisingly given this finding, Pritchard *et al* further find that multiple directorships do not reduce future firm performance nor do such

---

29 Raheja, above n 4.

30 Adam C Pritchard, Stephen P Ferris and Murali Jagannathan, 'Too Busy to Mind the Business? Monitoring by Directors with Multiple Board Appointments', University of Michigan Law School, Working Paper No 99-013; CORI Working Paper No 2001-02 (June 2002), accessed 4 March 2015 at SSRN: http://ssrn.com/abstract=167288, 2.

31 Ibid, 20.

32 Ibid. The authors cite Eugene Fama and Michael Jensen, 'Separation of Ownership and Control' (1983) 26 *Journal of Law and Economics* 301–26.

directors 'shirk' (in an agency cost sense[33]) committee responsibilities or increase the likelihood of securities fraud litigation against the company.[34]

A 2004 study by Fich and Shivdasani examines the relationship between the number of board positions held by outside directors and the level of firm governance.[35] The implication from the study is that an excessive number of outside board positions held by outside directors may reduce the quality of board monitoring. This monitoring has previously been argued to be enhanced by increases in the proportion of outside directors.[36] The authors find that 'busy' outside directors are associated with weaker firm governance.[37] More particularly, the authors find that their governance measure is reduced 'where a majority of outside directors hold three or more board seats'.[38] The authors also find that more independent boards increase the probability of removal of the CEO after poor performance.[39] But this probability may well fall with increases in the number of outside board positions of those directors.

The more recent 2008 study by Jiraporn, Davidson, Ning and DaDalt[40] examines whether busy directors have more absences from board meetings.[41] The authors find that the likelihood of board absences increases with the number of outside board positions.[42] However, for the authors, this relationship disappeared after the passing of the SOX reforms[43] on account of the additional focus on directors.[44]

Despite the two negative studies above, there may be benefits of outside board positions. In this respect, Larcker, So and Wang consider the advantages of the 'boardroom network formed by shared board directorates'.[45] The authors suggest that the advantages of these connections include

---

[33] See discussion in section 4.2.3 above.

[34] Pritchard, Ferris and Jagannathan, above n 30, 20.

[35] E M Fich and A Shivdasani, 'Are Busy Boards Effective Monitors?', ECGI – Finance Working Paper No 55/2004; AFA 2005 Philadelphia Meetings (October 2004), accessed 4 March 2015 at SSRN: http://ssrn.com/abstract=607364.

[36] See discussion in sections 7.3.2.1.1–7.3.2.1.2 above.

[37] Fich and Shivdasani, above n 35, 2–3.

[38] Ibid, 2.

[39] Ibid, 3.

[40] Pornsit Jiraporn, Wallace N Davidson III, Yixi Ning and Peter J DaDalt, 'Too Busy to Show Up? An Analysis of Directors' Absences' (21 January 2008), accessed 4 March 2015 at SSRN: http://ssrn.com/abstract=1254642.

[41] Ibid, 4 (footnote omitted).

[42] Ibid, 4–5 and 21.

[43] Ibid, 22.

[44] Ibid, 5.

[45] David F Larcker, Eric C So and Charles C Y Wang, 'Boardroom Centrality and Firm Performance', Rock Center for Corporate Governance at Stanford

that they foster communication of information that enhances strategic decision-making, reduce information asymmetry in designing contracts, provide useful contacts for business relationships and other economic benefits and facilitate value-enhancing innovation in areas such as corporate governance, technology and compensation contracts.[46] The authors thus conclude that 'well-connectedness' enhances firm performance.[47]

Thus, in the design of the board, the counterbalancing effects of outside board positions must be weighed. Reductions in the probability of dismissing the CEO after poor performance must be matched against the improvements that 'well-connectedness' brings to the firm.

8.2.3.1 [OutBrdPos] (−)[48] variable relational effect path

Thus, while Fich and Shivdasani's 2004 study[49] would support the relational approach's earlier discussion that independent boards increase the likelihood of replacement of a CEO in times of falling profitability,[50] it also contains a cautionary finding that increases in the number of outside positions held by outside directors may reduce the effectiveness of the board's monitoring function. The 2008 study by Jiraporn, Davidson, Ning and DaDalt[51] suggests that busy directors have more absences from board meetings, a factor which may reduce firm performance. In the positive direction, the 2002 study by Pritchard, Ferris and Jagannathan[52] suggests that multiple directorships do not affect the quality of monitoring nor cause directors to shirk.

Based on the 2004 and 2008 studies, the relational effect path for the **[OutBrdPos] (−)** variable is hypothesised to be negative (−). Clearly, the negative studies outweigh the positive studies by only one. Putting that aside, the zone of effect for **[OutBrdPos] (−)** begins at Monitoring & Audit Factor No 5. The relational effect path then follows the pathway for **[BrdSkills] (+)**[53] and **[BrdIndMon] (+)**[54] with one exception. The number of outside positions of independent directors is unlikely to affect to a

---

University Working Paper No 84 (17 August 2012), accessed 4 March 2015 at SSRN: http://ssrn.com/abstract=1651407, 3.

46 Ibid.

47 Ibid, 29.

48 Outside Board Positions of Independent Directors.

49 Fich and Shivdasani, above n 35.

50 See discussion in section 7.3.2.1.1 above.

51 Jiraporn, Davidson III, Ning and DaDalt, above n 40.

52 Pritchard, Ferris and Jagannathan, above n 30.

53 Board – Director Skills 'Mix' – see discussion in section 7.3.1.2.1 above.

54 Board Independent Director: Executive Director Proportion – Monitoring Effect – see discussion in sections 7.3.2.1.1–7.3.2.1.2 above.

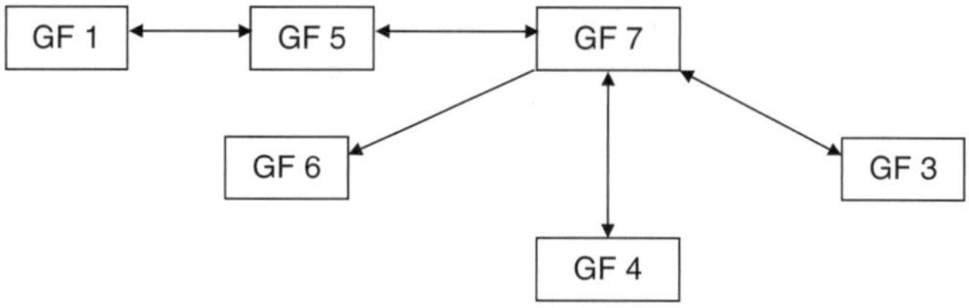

Figure 8.2 [OutBrdPos] (−) variable relational effect path

significant degree Responsibility Factor No 8 (Delineation and Disclosure of Powers, Duties and Lines of Responsibility) and so it is omitted (see Figure 8.2).

Again, Compliance Factor No 2 (Corporate Governance and Legal Compliance) is omitted as the legal obligations and requirements contemplated by this governance factor – whether 'hard', 'soft' or 'hybrid' laws – remain constant and are not affected by the outside board positions of independent directors. Thus, Compliance Factor No 2 remains constant for this variable.[55] Accordingly, **[OutBrdPos] (−)** is hypothesised not to affect Compliance Factor No 2 and Responsibility Factor No 8 and so has a coverage/rating of −6/75.00 *rprox* in the Coverage Table (Table 3.1) and the Relational Proximity Table (Table 3.2).[56]

8.3 ANTI-TAKEOVER MECHANISMS AND MARKET FOR CORPORATE CONTROL – 'WHOLE' BOARD AND 'STAGGERED' BOARD ELECTIONS

This section begins with a discussion of the argued effects of a number of anti-takeover mechanisms, particularly on the market for corporate control. The examination will then focus on a selection of studies which attempt to measure the firm-specific effects of a particular anti-takeover mechanism related to the election of directors – the holding of a 'staggered' board election. This is where a proportion only of the directors in office face a re-election vote as opposed to the whole board. As less than the entire board (perhaps only one-third) is due for re-election at any

---

[55] See discussion for **[BrdSkills] (+)** in section 7.3.1.2.1 and **[BrdIndMon] (+)** in 7.3.2.1.2 above.

[56] See the Coverage Table (Table 3.1) and the Relational Proximity Table (Table 3.2).

general meeting, this means that shareholders cannot remove all the directors at once even in times of poor performance. Thus, the staggered board election is an entrenching mechanism against removal as shareholders cannot vote-in an entire set of new directors.

8.3.1 Overview – Anti-Takeover Mechanisms May Reduce the Effectiveness of the Market for Corporate Control and May Reduce Firm Value

Anti-takeover mechanisms may reduce the effectiveness of the market for corporate control by interfering with its disciplinary 'management replacement' function, thus reducing firm value. More specifically, in terms of the elements of the nexus of contracts theory described in Chapter 4,[57] anti-takeover provisions thus constitute, for shareholders, 'welfare-reducing' terms of the voluntary 'contract' between inside managers and those shareholders. This causes a reduction in market price and, therefore, return on investment causing investors to seek more profitable investments.

The relevance of the market for corporate control as a governance variable where there is a separation of ownership and control of a company has also been discussed in detail in Chapter 4.[58] For Cremers and Nair, the market for corporate control is an important 'external governance mechanism', the authors observing that '[t]he importance of internal governance crucially depends on the extent of external governance and vice versa'.[59]

Importantly, Masulis, Wang and Xie, observe that anti-takeover mechanisms *reduce* shareholder value by shielding management who acquire investments at an over-value[60] from the market for corporate control.[61] This shielding effect is significant in terms of the perceived governance

---

57 See discussion in section 4.2.2 above.

58 Ibid.

59 K J M Cremers and V B Nair, 'Governance Mechanisms and Equity Prices', Yale ICF Working Paper No 03-15; NYU, Center for Law and Business Research Paper No 03-09; AFA 2004 San Diego Meetings (August 2003), accessed 4 March 2015 at SSRN: http://ssrn.com/abstract=412140, 38–39.

60 The acquisition of an asset at an over-value means that the company has paid out more than the asset's true value (putting aside how that value is calculated). Consequently, there is a reduction of the net asset value of the company. Thus, such behaviour amounts to a 'residual' cost in Jensen and Meckling's theory of agency costs. See discussion in section 4.2.3.1 above.

61 Ronald W Masulis, Cong Wang and Fei Xie. 'Corporate Governance and Acquirer Returns' (2007) 62(4) *The Journal of Finance* 1851–1889, 1852–3.

effect which the market for corporate control brings in the public for-profit sphere. Weir, Laing and McKnight, for example, found that the market for corporate control was a stronger mechanism than firm-specific governance variables.[62]

8.3.1.1 Types of anti-takeover mechanisms likely to reduce value

The nature of anti-takeover provisions likely to cause a reduction in firm value is described by Bebchuk, Cohen and Ferrell. The authors examine the staggered board and, in addition, five other 'entrenching provisions' in the period 1990–2003.[63] The relevant anti-takeover variables tested were:

- staggered boards;
- limits to shareholder amendments of the bylaws;
- supermajority requirements for mergers;
- supermajority requirements for charter amendments;
- poison pills; and
- golden parachute arrangements.[64]

The authors concluded that *each* of these variables individually and in aggregate was negatively linked to both firm value and share price returns during that period.[65]

It appears that the anti-takeover provisions identified by Bebchuk, Cohen and Ferrell may have a similarly negative effect on firm value as

---

[62] C Weir, D Laing and P J McKnight, 'An Empirical Analysis of the Impact of Corporate Governance Mechanisms on the Performance of UK Firms', accessed 4 March 2015 at SSRN: http://ssrn.com/abstract=286440, 27–8.

[63] Lucian Bebchuk, Alma Cohen and Allen Ferrell, 'What Matters in Corporate Governance?' (1 September 2004); (2009) 22(2) *Review of Financial Studies* 783–827 (February 2009); Harvard Law School John M. Olin Center Discussion Paper No 491 (2004), accessed 4 March 2015 at SSRN: http://ssrn.com/abstract=593423, 2–3 and 39–40.

[64] Ibid, 2 (format altered). An explanation of the operation of each of these mechanisms is set out at 7–13. See also Lucian Bebchuk, Alma Cohen and Charles C Y Wang, 'Golden Parachutes and the Wealth of Shareholders', Harvard Law and Economics Discussion Paper No 683 (1 December 2010), accessed 4 March 2015 at SSRN: http://ssrn.com/abstract=1718488 and Lucian A Bebchuk and Robert J Jackson, 'Toward a Constitutional Review of the Poison Pill' (2014) 114 *Columbia Law Review* 1549–94, October 2014; Harvard Law School John M. Olin Center Discussion Paper No 772; Columbia Public Law Research Paper No 14-386 (September 2014), accessed 4 March 2015 at SSRN: http://ssrn.com/abstract=2401098.

[65] Bebchuk, Cohen and Ferrell, above n 63, 2–3 and 39–40.

that identified by Masulis, Wang and Xie.[66] An important connecting factor between the studies may be the effect identified by the latter study – that anti-takeover mechanisms may reduce the 'effectiveness' of the market for corporate control by interfering with or reducing its disciplinary 'management replacement' function. Thus, as stated above in terms of the 'nexus of contracts' theory, a reduction in firm value is likely to result through the market price-reducing effects of such shareholder 'welfare-reducing' variables.

As noted above, a common anti-takeover mechanism is the 'staggered' board election.[67] In this respect, Bebchuk and Cohen note that staggered board elections take place for the majority of US public companies.[68] The authors suggest that, while the effects of staggered board elections may be causative in relation to reducing firm value, this is not the only explanation such that 'the association might be produced by the selection of staggered boards by low-value firms that seek to protect themselves from a takeover'.[69] However, the authors conclude that, despite this and other possible explanations, 'we . . . provide some suggestive evidence that staggered boards at least partly bring about, and not merely reflect, a lower firm value'.[70] This also accords with the view of Aggarwal, Erel, Stulz and Williamson. As noted above,[71] Aggarwal *et al* found that firm value increases with independence of the board. As part of the same study, they also found that such value is also enhanced by annual elections for the *whole* board.[72]

Yet, in 2010 and contrary to these findings, Larcker, Ormazabal and Taylor found that regulation of staggered boards (for example, by banning them) caused a:

---

66 See above n 61.

67 See L A Bebchuk, J C Coates IV and G Subramanian, 'The Trouble with Staggered Boards: A Reply to Georgeson's John Wilcox' (2003) 11(2) *Corporate Governance Advisor* 17–19, accessed 4 March 2015 at SSRN: http://ssrn.com/abstract=384980.

68 L A Bebchuk and A Cohen, 'The Costs of Entrenched Boards' (2005) 78 *Journal of Financial Economics* 409–33; Harvard Law and Economics Discussion Paper No 478, accessed 4 March 2015 at SSRN: http://ssrn.com/abstract=556987, 1.

69 Ibid, 2.

70 Ibid.

71 See discussion in section 7.3.2.1.4 above.

72 R Aggarwal, I Erel, R M Stulz and R G Williamson, 'Do U.S. Firms Have the Best Corporate Governance? A Cross-Country Examination of the Relation Between Corporate Governance and Shareholder Wealth', Fisher College of Business Working Paper No 2006-03-006 (2006), accessed 4 March 2015 at SSRN: http://ssrn.com/abstract=954169, 4–5.

> significant *negative* relation between abnormal returns to these events and the presence of a staggered board . . . This is inconsistent with the market viewing the elimination of staggered boards as value increasing.[73]

This result is itself inconsistent with Bebchuk, Cohen and Yang who, in 2010 (revised in July 2011), investigated two Delaware court rulings (the Supreme Court ruling reversing the Chancery Court ruling) and found the results consistent with the hypothesis that staggered boards reduce firm value.[74] For the authors, the effect was more pronounced for firms which had factors which increase their exposure to control contests especially 'underperformance', 'high asset pledgibility', 'small size' and 'high industry takeover intensity'.[75]

In a 2013 article, Bebchuk continues his opposition to measures which – like anti-takeover defences – 'insulate' the board from shareholder activism.[76] In attacking the claims that insulating boards is beneficial in the long-term as a protection for boards and companies against shareholder 'short-termism', Bebchuk challenges four areas of debate – including that of takeover defences – and concludes that board insulation has long-term costs.[77] Thus, for Bebchuk, the fear of agency costs looms close on the horizon of anti-takeover mechanisms.

---

[73] David F Larcker, Gaizka Ormazabal and Daniel J Taylor, 'The Market Reaction to Corporate Governance Regulation', (2011) 101(2) *Journal of Financial Economics* 431–448, 433; Rock Center for Corporate Governance at Stanford University Working Paper Series No 82 (October 14, 2010).

[74] Lucian A Bebchuk, Alma Cohen and Charles C Y Wang, 'Staggered Boards and the Wealth of Shareholders: Evidence from Two Natural Experiments', Harvard Law and Economics Discussion Paper No 697 (1 June 2010 and revised July 2011), accessed 4 March 2015 at SSRN: http://ssrn.com/abstract=1706806, 23.

[75] Ibid, 14.

[76] Lucian A Bebchuk, 'The Myth that Insulating Boards Serves Long-Term Value' (2013) 113 *Columbia Law Review* 1637–94; Harvard Law and Economics Discussion Paper No 755. (1 September 2013), accessed 4 March 2015 at SSRN: http://ssrn.com/abstract=2248111. Cohen and Wang's study of staggered boards (revised 2013) also confirms that staggered boards lead to lower firm value. See Alma Cohen and Charles C Y Wang, "How Do Staggered Boards Affect Shareholder Value? Evidence from a Natural Experiment" (2013) *Journal of Financial Economics*, Forthcoming; Harvard Business School Accounting & Management Unit Working Paper No. 13-068, (July 3, 2013), accessed 23 April 2015 at SSRN: http://ssrn.com/abstract=2141410.

[77] Bebchuk, ibid, 15–16 and 41. For further reasons to reject short-termism as a ground for insulating boards and CEOs, see Mark J Roe, "Corporate Short-Termism – In the Boardroom and in the Courtroom" (2013) 68 *Business Lawyer* 977; ECGI – Law Working Paper No. 210; Harvard Public Law Working Paper No. 13-18, (August 1, 2013) accessed 23 April 2015 at SSRN: http://ssrn.com/abstract=2239132.

Negative effect on firm value for [OtherATMs] (−): other anti-takeover mechanisms (excludes staggered board elections) and [StagBrdElect] (−): staggered board elections The implication from these studies appears to be that staggered board elections have – by virtue of constituting a shareholder welfare-reducing term of the nexus of contracts – a negative effect on firm value by interfering with or reducing the effectiveness of the market for corporate control as a market-efficiency sanction. Thus the relational effect paths for both **[OtherATMs] (−)** and **[StagBrdElect] (−)** are negative reflecting this corresponding diminution in firm value.

Chapter 4 explained the underlying or constituent elements of the market for corporate control. The market for corporate control is itself a component of the efficient market hypothesis which (theoretically at least) disciplines or deters insider-managers that engage in value or performance-reducing behaviour by exposing them to (again, at least the risk) of hostile takeover.[78]

In the design of the relational approach, Compliance Factor No 2[79] provides the content of the national shareholder protection regime including significant provisions in relation to mergers and hostile and other takeovers. Compliance Factor No 2 is an overriding requirement of *all* governance factors.[80] In the case of the **[NationGov] (+)** variable in section 7.3.1.3.2 above, changes in the content of this governance variable actually change the requirements of 'hard', 'soft' and 'hybrid' laws which apply to the company. Thus, Compliance Factor No 2 is itself affected by changes in the content of the national shareholder protection regime contemplated by the **[NationGov] (+)** variable. In the case of **[OtherATMs] (−)** and **[StagBrdElect] (−)**, there is a similar effect. These variables provide the content of the merger, takeover and shareholder activism/intervention laws of the national shareholder protection regime. As the content of those merger, takeover and shareholder activism/intervention laws change, so too will the content of Compliance Factor No 2.

For a discussion of the effects of the shareholder base of 'short-term shareholders' *versus* 'long-term shareholders', see Anne Beyer, David F Larcker and Brian Tayan, "Does the Composition of a Company's Shareholder Base Really Matter?", Rock Center for Corporate Governance at Stanford University Closer Look Series: Topics, Issues and Controversies in Corporate Governance and Leadership No. CGRP-42, (July 31, 2014), accessed 23 April 2015 at SSRN: http://ssrn.com/abstract=2474792.

[78] See discussion in section 4.2.2 above.

[79] Corporate Governance and Legal Compliance – see discussion in section 2.6.2 above.

[80] Ibid.

Thus, the most direct or proximate relational effect path for the **[OtherATMs] (−)** and **[StagBrdElect] (−)** variables is identical to that for **[NationGov] (+)** *but in the negative direction*. The **[OtherATMs] (−)** and **[StagBrdElect] (−)** variables affect all governance factors in a manner identical to Figure 2.4 (Compliance Factor No 2 Interrelationships) but again in the negative direction. This gives rise to a coverage/rating of −8/100.00 *rprox* for each of these variables in the Coverage Table (Table 3.1) and the Relational Proximity Table (Table 3.2).

8.4 AUDIT SUB-COMMITTEE – PRESENCE, INDEPENDENCE AND EXPERTISE

This section focuses on studies which attempt to measure the firm-specific effects of the presence, independence and expertise of the audit sub-committee.

Before discussing matters of firm value and performance, it is apt to note some of the structural determinants of audit committee independence and financial expertise in order to identify underlying factors or variables which may affect the ability of firms to effect changes or modifications to the structure of audit committees.

Statutory and Governance Code Mandated Requirements

First, requirements as to audit committee presence, independence and financial literacy may be mandated by relevant corporate governance legislation or governance codes. In this respect, significant changes to US corporate governance requirements in relation to audit committee composition, independence and financial expertise were introduced through the reforms of SOX[81] and the NYSE Final Rules.[82]

Second, while only a single study, Beasley and Salterio explain that, in Canada, an increase in outside directors on the audit committee in excess of compulsory minimum requirements is positively related to:

(1) an increase in the percentage of outsiders on the board;
(2) division of CEO and Chairperson functions; and
(3) increases in the size of the board.[83]

[81] SOX, above n 9.

[82] NYSE Final Rules, above n 10.

[83] M S Beasley and S E Salterio, 'The Relationship Between Board Characteristics and Voluntary Improvements in Audit Committee Composition

These same three factors are also related to increases in audit committee financial expertise of outsiders.[84] In respect of audit committee financial expertise, some corporate governance codes specify that audit committee members be financially literate – for example, the Commentary to Section 303A.07(a) of the NYSE Final Rules.[85]

As noted in Chapter 6, the NYSE Final Rules are a downstream effect of SOX.[86] Yet for Nosworthy, Symes and Le Mire, the US' Securities Exchange Commission (SEC) watered-down the original financial expertise requirement of the SOX provisions.[87]

Putting this question aside, what then is the effect of audit committee independence and financial expertise on firm value and firm operating performance?

8.4.1 Effect of Audit Committee Independence and Financial Expertise on Firm Value and Operating Performance

The perceived link between audit committee independence and firm value and/or operating performance remains, at this time, a matter for debate.

As noted above, independence of the audit committee (along with board independence) was one of the factors that Black and Kim found in the emerging market of Korea to be positively connected with both market value and later year increased profitability and dividend payments of 'large' companies.[88] However, as suggested earlier, the 'gap-filling' function of internal governance measures such as these may well be compensating for possible weaknesses in the national governance regime thus overstating the value-enhancing and performance-enhancing effect of this variable in comparison to a developed market or a common-law regulatory regime. Still, for Aggarwal, Erel, Stulz and Williamson, too,

---

and Experience' (28 February 2001), accessed 4 March 2015 at SSRN: http://ssrn.com/abstract=272590, 2.

84 Ibid, 2–3.

85 NYSE Final Rules, above n 10, Section 303A.07(a).

86 See discussion in section 6.4.1 above.

87 Beth Nosworthy, Christopher Symes and Suzanne Le Mire, 'Expertise is the New Game? Obligations on Corporate Managers in Solvent and Insolvent Companies', Working Paper for Conference, *Corporate Law – Progressive Possibilities*, Australian National University (ANU), 3–5 February 2013, 19 of 28 (footnotes omitted) (copy on file with author).

88 B S Black and W Kim, 'The Effect of Board Structure on Firm Value in an Emerging Market: IV, DiD, and Time Series Evidence from Korea', Finance Working Paper No 179/2007 (June 2007), accessed 4 March 2015 at SSRN: http://ssrn.com/abstract=968287, 2–3. See discussion in section 7.3.2.1.1 above.

firm value increases with annual ratification of the audit committee and composition of the audit committee of five 'outsiders'.[89]

On a similar theme but different measure, Ashbaugh-Skaife, Collins and LaFond find that agency risk and, consequently, cost of equity capital reduces with greater audit committee and board independence.[90] It is also suggested by Smith that the quality of monitoring of management is enhanced both by independence of the audit committee as well as the number of meetings.[91]

However, not all studies have found a link between company performance and/or value and audit committee independence. In their study of UK firms, Weir, Laing and McKnight found that firm value was not significantly linked to the existence of an audit committee[92] and that firm performance was not significantly linked to the quality or composition (proportion of non-executive/independent directors) of the audit committee.[93]

Clearly, the **[AudCom] (+)**[94] and **[AudIndMon] (+)**[95] variables have intuitive appeal – that increases in the independence of the audit committee and the number of meetings enhances the committee's quality of monitoring. Yet, given the conflicting results, further empirical investigation will be required to confirm a significant causal relationship.

8.4.2 [AudCom] (+)[96] Variable Relational Effect Path

Subject to this important caveat, the **[AudCom] (+)** variable should exert a positive effect on six governance factors with a coverage/rating

---

[89] Aggarwal, Erel, Stulz and Williamson, above n 72, 4–5.

[90] H Ashbaugh-Skaife, D W Collins and R LaFond, 'Corporate Governance and the Cost of Equity Capital' (December 2004), accessed 4 March 2015 at SSRN: http://ssrn.com/abstract=639681, 2–3.

[91] M Smith, 'Audit Committee Effectiveness: Did the Blue Ribbon Committee Recommendations Make a Difference?' (2006) 3(2) *International Journal of Accounting, Auditing and Performance Evaluation* 240–51, accessed 4 March 2015 at SSRN: http://ssrn.com/abstract=1001531, 249–50.

[92] Weir, Laing and McKnight, above n 62, 19.

[93] Ibid, 20–21. In a 2005 study posted in January 2012, Dionne and Triki find independence has *no* effect on risk management activity, this being affected only by the degree of financial knowledge/education (at 24). See Georges Dionne and Thouraya Triki, "Risk Management and Corporate Governance: The Importance of Independence and Financial Knowledge for the Board and the Audit Committee", (March 28, 2005 posted January 14, 2012), accessed 23 April 2015 at SSRN: http://ssrn.com/abstract=686470, 24.

[94] Audit Committee – Presence, Operation and Frequency.

[95] Audit Committee – Independence – Monitoring Effect.

[96] Audit Committee – Presence, Operation and Frequency.

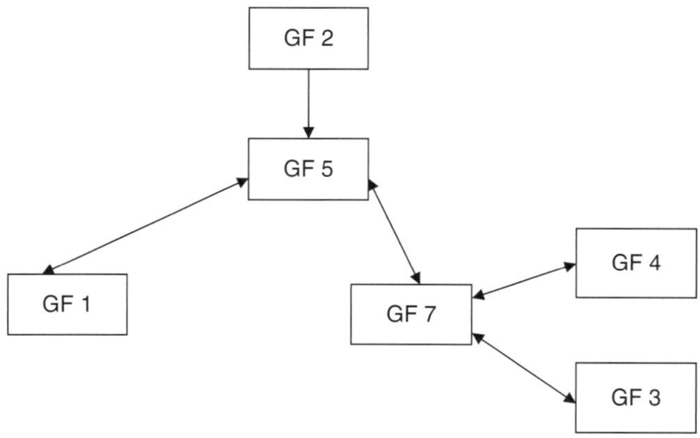

Figure 8.3 [AudCom] (+) variable relational effect path

of +6/75.00 *rprox* in the Coverage Table (Table 3.1) and the Relational Proximity Table (Table 3.2). Corporate governance statutes and governance codes contain – as depicted in the governance code Tables in Chapter 6 – significant input and guidance in relation to audit committee powers and functions. Thus, the themes in Compliance Factor No 2[97] have significant effect on the audit committee. If, following the results of some of the above studies, the presence and frequency of meeting of the audit committee enhances the quality of monitoring, the starting point for this relational effect path is Monitoring & Audit Factor No 5.[98] The most direct or proximate links are two-pronged.

First is the reflexive relationship between Monitoring & Audit Factor No 5 and Decision-making Factor No 7.[99] The second prong is the also reflexive relationship between (again) Monitoring & Audit Factor No 5 and Reporting Factor No 1.[100]

Decision-making Factor No 7 itself has two other reflexive relationships depicted in the Shareholder Primacy Interrelationship Scheme in Figure 2.6. The first is an important reflexive link with Alignment Factor No 3[101]

---

97 Corporate Governance and Legal Compliance – see section 2.6.2 above.

98 Internal and External/Audit Monitoring Quality – see discussion in section 2.6.5 above.

99 Quality of Board, CEO and Management Decision-making – see discussion in section 2.6.7 above.

100 Transparency, Timing and Integrity of Financial and Other Reports – see discussion in section 2.6.1 above.

101 Alignment of Management and Shareholder Interests – see discussion in section 2.6.3 above.

that represents – through the enhancing effect of the **[AudCom] (+)** variable – the 'alignment' between insider and outside interests. The other relevant link of Decision-making Factor No 7 for the purposes of the **[AudCom] (+)** variable is the reflexive relationship with Compensation Factor No 4.[102] This reflects the significance of the audit committee in disclosing – and therefore (theoretically) exposing to market and reputational constraints – the compensation and incentive themes within Compensation Factor No 4.

In the absence of more targeted studies and therefore following an intuitive line, it is difficult to hypothesise that Stakeholders Factor No 6 and Responsibility Factor No 8 will be influenced by the functions undertaken by the audit committee to the same order or magnitude as the other governance factors influenced by the **[AudCom] (+)** variable. Implied in this respect is that audit committee-level decision-making may be more removed or indirect in relation to these two governance factors (but not others) than the effect of board-level decision-making inherent in variables such as the **[BrdIndMon] (+)**[103] variable. More on this point appears in relation to the next two variables.

8.4.3 [AudIndMon] (+): Audit Committee – Independence – Monitoring Effect and [AudIndInfo] (−): Audit Committee – Information Flow and Decision Quality 'Trade-Off'

In the case of the independence of the audit committee, the relational effect path of the **[AudIndMon] (+)** variable is, also for the reasons set out in sections 7.3.2.1.1–7.3.2.1.2, hypothesised to be identical to the **[BrdIndMon] (+)**[104] zone of effect. In other words, a company which has an independent audit committee is likely, through that independence, to have a positive effect on the governance factors in the same manner as **[BrdIndMon] (+)**. This equates to a coverage/rating of +7/87.50 *rprox* for the **[AudIndMon] (+)** variable in the Coverage Table (Table 3.1) and the Relational Proximity Table (Table 3.2).

Similarly, the relational effect path of the **[AudIndInfo] (−)** variable is hypothesised to be identical to the **[BrdIndInfo] (−)**[105] variable. Again, there is a reduction of the information flow to (this time) the audit

---

[102] Board, CEO and Management Compensation and Incentives – see discussion in section 2.6.4 above.

[103] Board Independent Director: Executive Director Proportion – Monitoring Effect. See discussion in sections 7.3.2.1.1–7.3.2.1.2 above.

[104] Ibid.

[105] Board Independent Director: Executive Director Proportion – Information Flow and Decision Quality 'Trade-off'. See discussion in section 7.3.2.1.3 above.

committee in relation to 'firm-specific' and 'manager-specific' information as well as information asymmetry of outside audit committee members. This equates to a coverage/rating of −4/50.00 *rprox* for the **[AudIndInfo] (−)** variable in the Coverage Table (Table 3.1) and the Relational Proximity Table (Table 3.2).

8.4.3.1 The direction and strength of the effect in board and sub-committee counterpart variables

That the zone of effect is hypothesised to be identical in the corresponding board and audit committee independence governance variables merely means that the themes underlying the relevant governance factors are affected in the same direction and direct/proximate path. However, it does not mean that the *strength* of the effect on these governance factors will be identical. In this respect, in discussing the direction of effect in the interrelationship schemes, it was hypothesised that while a particular governance variable may 'impact' a particular governance factor significantly, the flow-on of that governance variable may not be of the same order, magnitude or direction.[106]

Thus, the hypotheses as to the zone of effect of a governance variable identify the number and identity of the governance factors affected and the direction of effect. But the relational approach can also make hypotheses in relation to the causal strength of the effect in two ways. The first way relates to the observations as to the significance (in relation to firm value and/or operating performance) and/or conflicting nature or otherwise of the results for the empirical field studies comprising the Empirical Studies Key Field No 4 in chapters 7–10.

The second way includes intuitive assumptions or judgments as to the 'level' in the company hierarchy in which the decision is made. Thus, as was suggested above in relation to the **[AudCom] (+)** variable, the relational approach hypothesises that committee-level and lower management-level decision-making may have no or only an insignificant effect (in which case it is ignored) on a particular governance factor compared to a board-level decision. Of course, whether this is the case depends on the nature of the committee-level or lower management level decision. For example, an audit committee-level decision in relation to the materiality or otherwise of a reporting issue will have a significant effect on Reporting Factor No 1 (*Transparency, Timing and Integrity of Financial and Other Reports*) as this committee is where the most significant audit issues are discussed. This is even more so than many board-level decisions. This specialisation – and

[106] See discussion in section 2.7.2 above.

complexity – in the audit committee helps to explain the accounting financial expertise requirements of governance codes noted above.

8.4.4 Likely Positive Effect between Accounting Financial Expertise and Firm Value and Operating Performance

The studies presented below in relation to the perceived link between audit committee financial expertise and firm value and/or operating performance all display positive results for this variable. In this respect, to measure the market effects of financial literacy, DeFond, Hann and Hu use positive share market reaction as a measure of the improvement in a company's corporate governance consequent on the appointment of an accounting financial expert to the company's audit committee.[107] DeFond, Hann and Hu also highlight that *independence* of the accounting expert is crucial to improvements in governance.[108]

In terms of the market effects of improvements in audit committee financial literacy, Weil, Coates and Marais found that the returns for firms whose financial literacy improved were considerably greater than those for non-improving firms.[109]

Thus, there is some cause for optimism that a positive link – again confirming intuitive argument – exists between audit committee financial expertise and firm value and/or operating performance on account of perceived improvements in the quality of monitoring. However, following this intuitive line and the confirming study of DeFond, Hann and Hu, it is likely that *accounting* expertise will be most significant again on monitoring quality grounds given the complexity of modern company accounting and reporting requirements.

In light of the above studies, there is a positive directional effect (+) for the **[AudExpAcc] (+)** governance variable. Being a variable that affects the quality of monitoring, the starting point for this relational effect path is again Monitoring & Audit Factor No 5. **[AudExpAcc] (+)**

---

[107] M L DeFond, R N Hann and X Hu, 'Does the Market Value Financial Expertise on Audit Committees of Boards of Directors?', Leventhal School of Accounting, University of Southern California, Los Angeles, California 90089-1421 (January 2004), accessed 4 March 2015 at SSRN: http://ssrn.com/abstract=498822, 3–4 and 6.

[108] Ibid, 6–7.

[109] R L Weil, D J Coates and M L Marais, 'Audit Committee Financial Literacy: A Work in Progress', CRSP Working Paper No 605 (11 March 2005), accessed 4 March 2015 at SSRN: http://ssrn.com/abstract=680281, 13. Dionne and Triki find (at 24) that financial literacy/education improves the ability to manage risk. See Dionne and Triki, above n 93, 24.

is a variable affecting committee-level monitoring and decision-making. Thus – putting aside questions of the strength of the zone of effect – the relational effect path for **[AudExpAcc] (+)** is hypothesised to be identical to that for **[AudCom] (+)**[110] above. On that view, the zone of effect of **[AudExpAcc] (+)** would extend to all governance factors except Stakeholders Factor No 6 (*Identification, Participation and Protection of Stakeholder Interests*) and Responsibility Factor No 8 (Delineation and Disclosure of Powers, Duties and Lines of Responsibility). This equates to a coverage/rating for the **[AudExpAcc] (+)** variable of +6/75.00 *rprox* in the Coverage Table (Table 3.1) and the Relational Proximity Table (Table 3.2).

Comparing relational effect paths, this view considers that there are fewer flow-on effects extending from Decision-making Factor No 7 than in the case of the **[BrdIndMon] (+)**[111] and **[AudIndMon] (+)**[112] variables, each of which has a coverage/rating of +7/87.50 *rprox*. In other words, considering *only* the accounting expertise aspect of **[AudExpAcc] (+)** (and not any accompanying independence ingredient), it is difficult to hypothesise that this committee-level function would affect in a significant way the identification or participation of non-shareholder stakeholder interests (Stakeholders Factor No 6). Thus, Stakeholders Factor No 6 is omitted. By contrast, in the case of the **[BrdIndMon] (+)**[113] and **[AudIndMon] (+)**[114] variables, Stakeholders Factor No 6 is positively affected as a flow-on from the Decision-making Factor No 7.

Of course, the interests of shareholders are hypothesised to be affected and so the reflexive relationship between Decision-making Factor No 7 and Alignment Factor No 3 is hypothesised to remain significantly operative. Also significantly operative is the reflexive relationship between Monitoring & Audit Factor No 5 and Reporting Factor No 1.

---

110 Audit Committee – Presence, Operation and Frequency. See discussion in section 8.4.2 above.

111 Board Independent Director: Executive Director Proportion – Monitoring Effect – see discussion in sections 7.3.2.1.1–7.3.2.1.2 above.

112 Audit Committee – Independence – Monitoring Effect – see discussion in section 8.4.3 above.

113 Board Independent Director: Executive Director Proportion – Monitoring Effect – see discussion in sections 7.3.2.1.1–7.3.2.1.2 above.

114 Audit Committee – Independence – Monitoring Effect – see discussion in section 8.4.3 above.

8.5 'BLOCK' AND INSTITUTIONAL SHAREHOLDINGS

In Chapters 1 and 2, the traditional 'outsiders' to the firm were described to include small/widely-dispersed shareholders. But what is the position of large shareholders also known as 'block-holders'? Do such shareholders display any 'inside' behaviour? And what is the consequence of such action?

The aim of this section is to demonstrate that, at least theoretically, 'block' or large institutional shareholdings may enhance the monitoring of management. However, the literature suggests that the effects may be positive or negative.

8.5.1 Governance Effects Both Positive and Negative

While a detailed examination of institutional shareholder activism is beyond the scope of this book,[115] Fuerst and Kang cite a study by Shleifer and Vishny which explains that the governance effects of the existence of (independent) blockholders can be both positive in terms of enhancing the monitoring of management and negative in terms of the distribution of benefits.[116]

Thus a weighing exercise confronts the relational approach in relation to blockholdings. This is resolved below by designating two variables – one positive and one negative – for the constituent elements of this variable.

---

[115] See, for example, S L Gillan and L T Starks, 'Corporate Governance, Corporate Ownership, and the Role of Institutional Investors: A Global Perspective', Weinberg Center for Corporate Governance Working Paper No 2003-01 (August 2003), accessed 4 March 2015 at SSRN: http://ssrn.com/abstract=439500.

For a discussion of the empirical evidence on the benefits of blockholders for corporate governance and outside shareholders, see Lucian A Bebchuk and Robert J Jackson Jr, "The Law and Economics of Blockholder Disclosure", Harvard Law and Economics Discussion Paper No. 702; (2012) 2(1) *Harvard Business Law Review* 39; Harvard Law and Economics Discussion Paper No. 702; Columbia Law and Economics Research Paper No. 405, (July 12, 2011), accessed 23 April 2015 at SSRN: http://ssrn.com/abstract=1884226, 13–16. Then see Lucian A Bebchuk, Alon Brav, Robert J Jackson and Wei Jiang, "Pre-Disclosure Accumulations by Activist Investors: Evidence and Policy", (2013) 39 *Journal of Corporation Law*, forthcoming; Columbia Business School Research Paper No. 13-33, (April 1, 2013), accessed 23 April 2015 at SSRN: http://ssrn.com/abstract=2258083.

[116] Fuerst and Kang, above n 14, 7. The authors cite A Shleifer and R Vishny, 'A Survey of Corporate Governance' (1997) 52(2) *Journal of Finance* 737–83.

For Fuerst and Kang, firm performance is *reduced* by large (greater than 5 per cent) shareholdings by independent or non-management shareholders.[117] Supporting the second or negative explanation put forward above, for Ashbaugh-Skaife, Collins and LaFond, agency risk and the cost of equity capital were found to increase with the number of large blockholders.[118] This, the authors note, was 'consistent with blockholders increasing agency problems between themselves and dispersed shareholders'.[119]

Short of a takeover, Black explains that institutional shareholders may seek to engage in activism in the form of shareholder proposals or 'jawboning' the board or management into change.[120] Black's study, however, expresses 'doubt' as to whether such activism improves firm performance.[121]

Moving forward to 2009, Armour and Cheffins present a model for hedge-fund activism[122] and identify the 'demand side' factors that the authors consider affect the propensity for 'offensive shareholder activism'. These include 'financing costs',[123] 'transaction costs'[124] and potential hurdles or obstacles within the 'regulation of collective investment vehicles'.[125] For the authors, hedge-fund activism will continue to form part of the landscape of US corporate governance but with the effects of the GFC difficult to predict.[126]

---

117 Fuerst and Kang, above n 14, 4.

118 Ashbaugh-Skaife, Collins and LaFond, above n 90, 2–3.

119 Ibid.

120 B S Black, 'Shareholder Activism and Corporate Governance in the United States', as published in *The New Palgrave Dictionary of Economics and the Law*, Basingstoke: Palgrave Macmillan, 1998, Vol 3, pp 459–65, accessed 4 March 2015 at SSRN: http://ssrn.com/abstract=45100, 3.

121 Ibid, 12.

122 John Armour and Brian R Cheffins, 'The Rise and Fall (?) of Shareholder Activism by Hedge Funds', ECGI – Law Working Paper No 136/2009 (1 September 2009), accessed 4 March 2015 at SSRN: http://ssrn.com/abstract=1489336.

123 Ibid, 13.

124 Ibid, 14.

125 Ibid, 15.

126 Ibid, 36. See also Dionysia Katelouzou, "Worldwide Hedge Fund Activism: Dimensions and Legal Determinants" (2014) *University of Pennsylvania Journal of Business Law*, forthcoming; King's College London Law School Research Paper No. 2014-8, (September 22, 2014), accessed 23 April 2015 at SSRN: http://ssrn.com/abstract=2357547. For a discussion of the implications of a shift in equity ownership distribution in the last 30 years to "sophisticated but reticent institutional shareholders", see Ronald J Gilson and Jeffrey N Gordon, "Agency Capitalism: Further Implications of Equity Intermediation", European Corporate Governance Institute (ECGI) – Law Working Paper No. 239/2014; Stanford Law and Economics Olin Working Paper No. 456; Columbia Law and Economics

Later in 2010, McCahery, Starks and Sautner found a majority of institutional investors in their survey engaged in shareholder activism[127] and that these investors preferred firm-level governance mechanisms such as:

> equity ownership of management, equity-based compensation, board independence, transparency about the holdings of large shareholders, and high free float. The responses to the survey questions suggest that institutional investors focus on issues related to reducing agency conflicts between managers

---

Working Paper No. 461, (February 1, 2014), accessed 23 April 2015 at SSRN: http://ssrn.com/abstract=2359690.

For a discussion of shareholder activism in the context of the director primacy model, see Stephen M Bainbridge, 'Preserving Director Primacy by Managing Shareholder Interventions', *Research Handbook on Shareholder Power and Activism*, forthcoming; UCLA School of Law, Law-Econ. Research Paper No. 13-09 (August 27, 2013), accessed 24 April 2015 at SSRN: http://ssrn.com/abstract=2298415.

For a comparative discussion on the balance of power between shareholders and directors including an analysis of arguments in the shareholder empowerment debate, see Jennifer G Hill, 'The Rising Tension between Shareholder and Director Power in the Common Law World' (2010) 18 *Corporate Governance: An International Review* 344-359; Sydney Law School Research Paper No. 10/34; Vanderbilt Law and Economics Research Paper No. 10-11; ECGI – Law Working Paper No. 152/2010 (March 30, 2010), accessed 24 April 2015 at SSRN: http://ssrn.com/abstract=1582258.

[127] Joseph A McCahery, Laura T Starks and Zacharias Sautner, 'Behind the Scenes: The Corporate Governance Preferences of Institutional Investors' AFA 2011 Denver Meetings Paper; Tilburg Law School Research Paper No 010/2010 (13 December 2010), accessed 4 March 2015 at SSRN: http://ssrn.com/abstract=1571046, 37. For a discussion of the different forms of blockholder activism including "voice" and "exit" strategies, see Alex Edmans, "Blockholders and Corporate Governance", ECGI – Finance Working Paper No. 385, (October 11, 2013), accessed 23 April 2015 at SSRN: http://ssrn.com/abstract=2285781.

For a study on how institutional investors can influence firm-level governance mechanisms and contentious issues through proxy voting, see Reena Aggarwal, Pedro A C Saffi and Jason Sturgess, "The Role of Institutional Investors in Voting: Evidence from the Securities Lending Market", AFA 2013 San Diego Meetings Paper, (July 7, 2012), accessed 23 April 2015 at SSRN: http://ssrn.com/abstract=2023480.

For a recent discussion of the importance of shareholder voting in hedge fund activism, see Paul H Edelman, Randall S Thomas and Robert B Thompson, "Shareholder Voting in an Age of Intermediary Capitalism" (2014) *Southern California Law Review*, forthcoming; European Corporate Governance Institute (ECGI) – Law Working Paper No. 246/2014; Vanderbilt Law and Economics Research Paper No. 14-9, (August 27, 2014), accessed 23 April 2015 at SSRN: http://ssrn.com/abstract=2401746.

and shareholders (e.g., equity-based pay) as well as between large and small shareholders (e.g., transparency about the holdings of large shareholders).[128]

Thus, the aim of the firm-specific measures favoured by blockholders resonates with the over-arching aims of the relational approach – to reduce long-term agency costs.

In a 2012 paper discussed earlier in relation to director independence, Erkens, Hung and Matos found that stock returns during the financial crisis were worse for companies with higher institutional ownership because '. . . firms with higher institutional ownership took more risk prior to the crisis, which resulted in larger shareholder losses during the crisis period . . .'[129]

Thus, the implications of this review are that, while the presence of block or institutional shareholdings presents the opportunity for enhanced monitoring of management and, consequently, improvements in firm value, current evidence suggests the effects may be positive or negative.

8.5.2 [BlockMon] (+)[130] and [BlockCosts] (−)[131] Variables Relational Effect Paths

The relational effect path for **[BlockMon] (+)** is as follows as shown in Figure 8.4.

[BlockMon] (+) is, on the first view of Fuerst and Kang in the previous section, hypothesised to affect the quality of monitoring (Monitoring & Audit Factor No 5) in the positive direction (+). In other words, the presence of a blockholder enhances monitoring quality. How does this take place under the relational approach?

---

[128] McCahery, Starks and Sautner, ibid, 4. For a study refuting that the long-term effects of hedge fund activism are negative on operating performance, see Lucian A Bebchuk, Alon Brav and Wei Jiang, "The Long-Term Effects of Hedge Fund Activism", Columbia Business School Research Paper No. 13-66, (July 9, 2013), accessed 23 April 2015 at SSRN: http://ssrn.com/abstract=2291577. See also Paul Rose and Bernard S Sharfman, "Shareholder Activism as a Corrective Mechanism in Corporate Governance", Ohio State Public Law Working Paper No. 225, (September 11, 2013), accessed 23 April 2015 at SSRN: http://ssrn.com/abstract=2324151.

[129] David H Erkens, Mingyi Hung, and Pedro P Matos, 'Corporate Governance in the 2007–2008 Financial Crisis: Evidence from Financial Institutions Worldwide' (2012) 18(2) *Journal of Corporate Finance* 389–411 (15 January 2012), accessed 4 March 2015 at SSRN: http://ssrn.com/abstract=1397685, 32.

[130] Block Shareholding – Monitoring Effect.

[131] Block Shareholding – Other Shareholder Agency Costs.

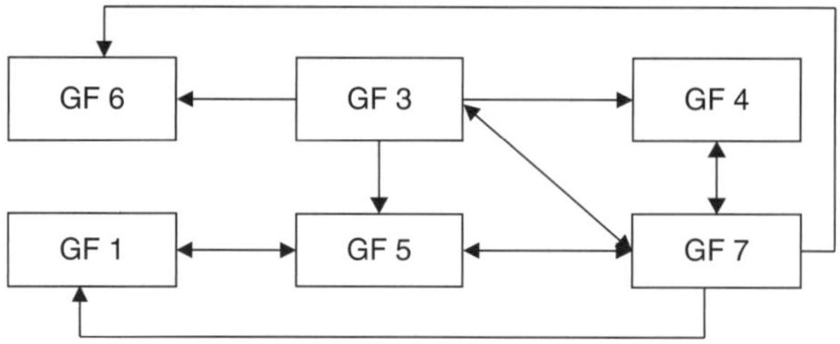

Figure 8.4 [BlockMon] (+) variable relational effect path

As shown in the diagram, there are a number of influences operating simultaneously on Monitoring & Audit Factor No 5. The first influence on Monitoring & Audit Factor No 5 is through Alignment Factor No 3 (Alignment of Management and Shareholder Interests). But this does not depend on blockholder activism. The underlying assumption here is that the threat of hostile takeover – in the absence of actual or positive activism – will deter management from misconduct or value-reducing behaviour or align the interests of management with those of the blockholder. This is akin to the concept of agency costs and the market for corporate control, but narrowed in effect to apply to the blockholder rather than widely-dispersed shareholders generally.[132]

Simultaneously with the effect of Alignment Factor No 3 on Monitoring & Audit Factor No 5 is the reflexive effect of Alignment Factor No 3 on Decision-making Factor No 7 (Quality of Board, CEO and Management Decision-making). This is as depicted in Figure 2.6's Shareholder Primacy Interrelationship Scheme. Thus, governance variables which affect issues relating to the alignment of management and shareholder interests will flow-on and affect the nature, operation and quality of decision-making at board, CEO and management level. In other words, the nature and degree of management-shareholder alignment will be reflected in those decisions. In turn, those decisions flow-back (hence, reflexively) to affect the nature and degree of management-shareholder alignment.

Also depicted in this interrelationship scheme is that Decision-making Factor No 7 has a reflexive relationship with Responsibility Factor No 8 (Delineation and Disclosure of Powers, Duties and Lines of Responsibility). But it is difficult to hypothesise on the literature or intuitively that **[BlockMon] (+)** will significantly affect Responsibility Factor No 8 even through the

[132] See discussion in section 4.2.2 above.

connection with Decision-making Factor No 7. Thus Responsibility Factor No 8 is omitted from the hypothesised relational effect path.

Compliance Factor No 2 (Corporate Governance and Legal Compliance)[133] is also omitted. Clearly, Compliance Factor No 2 has a single-directional effect on Decision-making Factor No 7 in Figure 2.6. Compliance Factor No 2 provides the content for the national shareholder protection regime.[134] Similarly to the **[BrdSkills] (+)**, **[NationGov] (+)** and **[BrdIndMon] (+)** variables, the obligations to comply with corporate governance and legal requirements are not affected by the presence, actions or inactions of blockholders. Again, Compliance Factor No 2 remains constant for this variable. Thus, the zone of effect of **[BlockMon] (+)** extends to six governance factors (that is, omitting Responsibility Factor No 8 and Compliance Factor No 2) giving rise to a coverage/rating of +6/75.00 *rprox*.

For the same reasons, the relational effect path for the **[BlockCosts] (−)** variable is hypothesised to be identical to the **[BlockMon] (+)** variable but in the negative direction. This gives rise to a coverage/rating of −6/75.00 *rprox* in the Coverage Table (Table 3.1) and the Relational Proximity Table (Table 3.2).

8.6 DIVISION IN CEO/CHAIRPERSON ROLES

8.6.1 Enhanced Firm Knowledge and 'Trade-off' with Board Control/ Monitoring

Available studies do not find any *significant* effect on firm value of dividing the roles of the CEO and the chairperson. Indeed, the governance effects of combining these roles appear to be opposing and requiring a balancing of the improvements in the quality of board decision-making which inside/specific knowledge of the firm brings on the one hand with possible deficiencies in the quality of the monitoring of management on the other.

In this respect, Weir, Laing and McKnight explain the opposing arguments in the case of CEO and chairperson 'duality':

> [t]he potential advantage. . .is that they should exhibit a greater understanding and knowledge of the company's operating environment. In contrast, Fama

[133] See discussion in section 2.6.2 above.

[134] See the discussion of **[BrdSkills] (+)** in section 7.3.1.2.1, **[NationGov] (+)** in section 7.3.1.3.2 and **[BrdIndMon] (+)** in section 7.3.2.1.2 above.

> and Jensen (1983) argue that boards dominated by inside directors are more difficult to control, a situation that would clearly apply to duality.[135]

However, the authors found that, in UK companies, company *value* was not significantly linked to a separation or division in the CEO and chairperson roles.[136] Yet, in a 2007 study by Bhagat and Bolton discussed above, separation of the CEO and chair functions was one variable which 'is significantly positively correlated with better contemporaneous and subsequent *operating performance*'.[137]

In a 2010 study also examined above in relation to staggered boards and later in relation to CEO pay, Larcker, Ormazabal and Taylor observed that regulation of CEO-Chair duality (for example, by banning this practice) resulted in '. . . no evidence of a relation between abnormal returns to these events and CEO-chairman duality'.[138] The authors proffered alternative explanations including that the 'market correctly anticipated the portion of the regulation relating to CEO-chairman duality' or, alternatively, 'that CEO-chairman duality does not affect shareholder value incremental to the provisions of the regulation related to CEO pay . . .'.[139]

8.6.2 [DualTrade] (+/−)[140] Variable Relational Effect Path

In light of these results alone, a single directional marker (in either direction) for the **[DualTrade] (+/−)** variable is difficult to ascribe with compelling weight. The UK Corporate Governance Code 2014[141] prescribes that these roles be divided and that the chairperson be an independent director with the Australian ASX 2014 Principles and Recommendations[142] position being similar. That, by itself, however, is not conclusive in terms of

---

135 Weir, Laing and McKnight, above n 62, 7. The authors cite Eugene F Fama and Michael C Jensen, 'Separation of Ownership and Control' (1983) 26 *Journal of Law and Economics* 301–49.

136 Weir, Laing and McKnight, above n 62, 19.

137 Sanjai Bhagat and Brian J Bolton, 'Corporate Governance and Firm Performance' (June 2007), accessed 4 March 2015 at SSRN: http://ssrn.com/abstract=1017342, 5 (emphasis in original). See discussion in section 7.3.1.2 above.

138 Larcker, Ormazabal and Taylor, above n 73, 5.

139 Ibid.

140 Duality of CEO/Chair Positions – Monitoring and Decision-quality 'Trade-off'.

141 Financial Reporting Council (FRC), *The UK Corporate Governance Code*, September 2014, London, accessed 4 March 2015 at http://www.frc.org.uk/ ('UK Corporate Governance Code 2014'), Code Provisions A.2.1 and A.3.1, p 8.

142 ASX Corporate Governance Council, Principles and Recommendations, Third Edition were released on 27 March 2014 and (at p 7) took effect for a com-

the relational approach which requires hypotheses to be based on the number and identity of the governance factors which are affected.

This variable may act (that is, as a net effect) either positively or negatively depending on which of the opposing effects 'outweighs' the other. For example, the advantage to the board in terms of inside/specific knowledge of a dual CEO-chairperson would be readily apparent in a situation already considered in the relational approach. Where the information is highly 'firm-specific' or 'manager-specific', there may be a reduction in information-flow to the board if the board is perceived to be 'too independent'.[143] Yet, if the CEO and chair are the same person, this information deficit may be lessened. In such a case, the decision-making benefits to the Board of reducing that information deficit may outweigh the agency costs of a reduced level of control over inside directors. But the situation may well be otherwise if the nature of the information is such that outside directors have no information asymmetry – for example, where the information lends itself readily to external verification.[144] In that case, the agency costs of reduced control outweigh the information benefits. Thus, a dual-direction marker (+/−) is ascribed to this variable.[145]

The zone of effect of the relational effect path for the **[DualTrade] (+/−)** variable is hypothesised to extend to all of the eight governance factors except Compliance Factor No 2 (Corporate Governance and Legal Compliance).[146] The studies relating to the **[BrdIndMon] (+)**[147] variable seek to link, most directly, the independence proportion of the board with both enhancement of the monitoring function (Monitoring & Audit Factor No 5) and enhancement of the quality of decision-making (Decision-making Factor No 7). Thus, the **[BrdIndMon] (+)** variable's relational effect path is positive (+) beginning with Monitoring & Audit Factor No 5 (Internal and External/Audit Monitoring Quality[148]) and Decision-making Factor No 7 (Quality of Board, CEO and Management Decision-making).[149] And both these Factors are influenced positively.

---

pany's financial year commencing on or after 1 July 2014 ('ASX 2014 Principles and Recommendations'). See Recommendation 2.5, p 18.

[143] See discussion in section 7.3.2.1.3 above.

[144] See ibid and discussion in section 8.2.1 above.

[145] See discussion of 'dual direction' governance variables in section 3.3.1.2 above.

[146] See discussion in section 2.6.2 above.

[147] Board Independent Director: Executive Director Proportion – Monitoring Effect – see discussion in sections 7.3.2.1.1–7.3.2.1.2 above.

[148] See discussion in section 2.6.5 above.

[149] This is explained in sections 7.3.2.1.1–7.3.2.1.2 above.

But this intersection between Monitoring & Audit Factor No 5 and Decision-making Factor No 7 is also the crux of the trade-off represented by the **[DualTrade] (+/−)** variable. For example, in terms of the literature above, where the benefits of insider information of a dual CEO/Chairperson outweigh the agency costs associated with a reduction in control over the board, the **[DualTrade] (+/−)** variable will exert a positive influence over Decision-making Factor No 7 which outweighs the negative effect on Monitoring & Audit Factor No 5. Where, instead, the information is not specialised or is readily verified externally, the agency costs of the reduction in control over the board may be greater than any benefits of insider information. In that case, the negative influence over Monitoring & Audit Factor No 5 will outweigh the positive influence on Decision-making Factor No 7. Again, this explains the dual-direction marker (+/−). Thus, **[DualTrade] (+/−)** has an identical relational effect path to **[BrdIndMon] (+)**[150] but with a dual-direction marker (+/−) which equates to a coverage/rating of +/− 7/87.50 *rprox*.

Of course, the two governance variables depict a different *facet* to the aspect of decision-making quality (Decision-making Factor No 7). **[BrdIndMon] (+)** is concerned with enhancing decision quality by the application of the more impartial judgment that independence is said to bring. The **[DualTrade] (+/−)** variable also concerns enhancing decision-making – but by the application of judgment more familiar with the firm's operations, particularly where those operations are highly specialised or cannot be externally verified.

But, in the case of both variables, the positive effect on the quality of monitoring of the **[BrdIndMon] (+)** variable *and* the negative effect on the quality of monitoring of the **[DualTrade] (+/−)** variable arises from the presence or absence of the independence element. **[BrdIndMon] (+)** retains the independence element and so positively affects Monitoring & Audit Factor No 5. By contrast, **[DualTrade] (+/−)** is without the independence element and so negatively affects that Factor. Thus, the relational effect path of the **[DualTrade] (+/−)** variable will be identical to that for **[BrdIndMon] (+)** variable in section 7.3.2.1.2 above (which is itself identical to **[BrdSkills] (+)**[151] in Figure 7.2) but with a dual-directional marker (+/−).

---

150 Board Independent Director: Executive Director Proportion – Monitoring Effect – see discussion in sections 7.3.2.1.1–7.3.2.1.2 above.

151 Board – Director Skills 'Mix' – see discussion in section 7.3.1.2.1 above.

8.6.3 [DualDismiss] (−)[152] and [DualStrat] (−)[153] Variables Relational Effect Paths

In addition to the above effects, the *likelihood* of dismissal of a dual CEO/chairperson is suggested to be substantially less than where these functions are separated. For Goyal and Park, central to the role of the board is its ability to monitor management measured, in their study, by the sensitivity of CEO turnover to firm performance.[154] The authors found that this sensitivity *significantly reduced* where the CEO and chairperson roles were combined. In other words, the probability of dismissing the CEO was less in the combined-role firm for a given fall in share returns.[155] In an Australian study, Chapple, Ferguson and Kang found that, where there is combination of the CEO and chairperson roles, 'the likelihood of fraud increases'.[156]

Thus, the relational effect path for the **[DualDismiss] (−)** variable is negative (−) beginning with a negative effect on internal monitoring quality and therefore Monitoring & Audit Factor No 5. Again, like **[DualTrade] (+/−)**[157] above, the reduction in monitoring quality is – most directly – due to the lack of independence in the monitoring function. Thus, the relational effect path of the **[DualDismiss] (−)** variable will be identical to that for **[BrdIndMon] (+)**[158] (which, again, is identical to that for **[BrdSkills] (+)**[159]) but with a negative-directional marker (−). This equates to a coverage/rating of −7/87.50 *rprox* for the **[DualDismiss] (−)** variable in the Coverage Table (Table 3.1) and the Relational Proximity Table (Table 3.2).

An important role for the board highlighted by Ruigrok, Peck and

---

152 Duality of CEO/Chair Positions – CEO Dismissal Probability.

153 Duality of CEO/Chair Positions – Effect on Strategic Decision-making.

154 V K Goyal and C W Park, 'Board Leadership Structure and CEO Turnover' (July 2001), accessed 4 March 2015 at SSRN: http://ssrn.com/abstract=224055, 1–2.

155 Ibid, 3.

156 Larelle Chapple, Colin Ferguson and Diana Kang, 'Corporate Governance and Misappropriation' (15 June 2007), accessed 4 March 2015 at SSRN: http://ssrn.com/abstract=1011936, 3.

157 Duality of CEO/Chair Positions – Monitoring and Decision-quality 'Trade-off' – see discussion in section 8.6.2 above.

158 Board Independent Director: Executive Director Proportion – Monitoring Effect – see discussion in sections 7.3.2.1.1–7.3.2.1.2 above.

159 Board – Director Skills 'Mix' – see discussion in section 7.3.1.2.1 and Figure 7.2 above.

Keller is strategic decision-making.[160] The authors found only 'marginal evidence' that the participation of directors in strategic decision-making was reduced by the dual CEO/Chairperson role, perhaps through the meeting agenda-setting function.[161]

With the caveats that this is a single study and the evidence slight, the **[DualStrat] (−)** variable is hypothesised to have a negative (−) directional marker. The relational effect path for **[DualStrat] (−)** is akin – in fact identical – to the zone of effect of the **[BrdIndInfo] (−)**[162] relational effect path. This latter variable sought to map the effect of a reduction of manager-specific and firm-specific information flow – on the part of management – to the board on account of the presence of independent directors.[163] The **[DualStrat] (−)** variable is similarly hypothesised to represent a reduction of information flow – or some type of screening or adjustment to the information flow – again on the part of executive or non-independent action encapsulated in the agenda-setting function. Thus, the **[DualStrat] (−)** variable is hypothesised to affect Reporting Factor No 1, Monitoring & Audit Factor No 5, Decision-making Factor No 7 and Responsibility Factor No 8 in the same manner as the **[BrdIndInfo] (−)** variable set out in Figure 7.3. This gives rise to a coverage/rating of −4/50.00 *rprox* for the **[DualStrat] (−)** variable in the Coverage Table (Table 3.1) and the Relational Proximity Table (Table 3.2).

In summary and like the **[DualTrade] (+/−)** variable in the previous section, the effects of combining the CEO and chairperson roles can cut both ways. While there appears to be no significant effect on firm value by separating these functions, such separation was found in a 2007 study to increase operating performance. In addition, the likelihood of dismissal of a dual CEO/chairperson is suggested to be substantially less than where these functions are separated, a consideration that is particularly significant where firm performance or returns are falling.

---

[160] W Ruigrok, S I Peck and H Keller, 'Board Characteristics and Involvement in Strategic Decision Making: Evidence from Swiss Companies' (2006) 43(5) *Journal of Management Studies* 1201–26, accessed 4 March 2015 at SSRN: http://ssrn.com/abstract=910636.

[161] Ibid, 1218–19.

[162] Board Independent Director: Executive Director Proportion – Information Flow and Decision Quality 'Trade-Off' – see discussion in section 7.3.2.1.3 above.

[163] See Figure 7.3.

8.7 CONTINUATION OF EMPIRICAL STUDIES KEY FIELD NO 4 IN CHAPTER 9

This concludes the examination of Part 2 of the Empirical Studies Key Field No 4. In this chapter, the relational approach has examined the effects on firm operating performance and firm value of another wide variety of governance variables. The chapter has presented a relational effect path for governance variables including board size and 'outside' board positions, studies relating to anti-takeover mechanisms, the audit subcommittee, 'block' and institutional shareholdings and division in the CEO/chairperson role.

In the following Chapter 9, the relational approach will again examine the effectiveness of governance variables in reducing (or increasing) agency costs and enhancing (or reducing) the long-term efficiency and sustainability of the firm. But the measure of efficiency and sustainability is a reduction in the probability of earnings manipulation.

9. Empirical studies Key Field No 4 (Part 3): Board and audit committee factors and earnings manipulation

9.1 EARNINGS MANIPULATION AND PURPOSE AND APPROACH OF CHAPTER 9

This chapter presents Part 3 of the detailed review of law, economic and econometric studies from the US, UK, Europe and Australia that comprises the Empirical Studies Key Field No 4. In this chapter, another measure of, or proxy for, 'good' governance is examined – the probability of earnings manipulation or 'management'. Increases in earnings management represent increases in agency costs of outside shareholders and therefore a fall in firm sustainability. Again drawing upon these empirical studies and the Shareholder Primacy Interrelationship Scheme presented in Figure 2.6, this chapter presents a 'relational effect path' for a range of individual board and audit committee governance variables. This relational effect path describes the number and identity of the governance factors[1] affected by a governance variable and the direction of effect. The nature and operation of many of these variables was encountered in Chapters 7 and 8. But, in this chapter, the relational approach examines the effect of these variables on the earnings management measure.

9.1.1 Principal Aim of Reporting – To Reduce Information Asymmetry and Agency Risk

The principal aim of reporting – and, in particular, enhanced transparency and timeliness of that reporting (Reporting Factor No 1) – is to remedy problems associated with the information asymmetry aspects of agency costs. In other words, inside management possesses much greater knowledge than outside shareholders in relation to the firm's business, value,

[1] For the construction of the eight governance factors, see sections 2.6.1–2.6.8 above.

performance and prospects. In section 4.2.2, the relational approach explained that the efficient market hypothesis assumes that a firm's value is accurately reflected in the stock price.[2] But Dent[3] explains that there are three problems with this hypothesis. First, an 'information problem' which reduces the accuracy of information released to the market. Second, that investors have 'bounded rationality' in their ability to process all that information. Finally, that the market may take time to correct for new information released to it.

But asymmetric information problems also exist in relation to determining the quality of the management. Ashbaugh-Skaife, Collins and LaFond explain that this information asymmetry creates agency risk for shareholders.[4] In this respect, the authors find that agency risk (and, again, the cost of equity capital) reduces with increased transparency and timeliness of financial reporting[5] and Patel and Dallas are of a similar view.[6]

Thus, in this Chapter 9, the relational approach will identify and analyse governance variables and themes relating to 'good' corporate governance and the reduction of the management of reported earnings by firms.

---

2 Lawrence A Cunningham, 'Behavioral Finance and Investor Governance' (2002) 59 *Washington & Lee Law Review* 767, accessed 4 March 2015 at SSRN: http://ssrn.com/abstract=255778, 3. The author cites Donald C Langevoort, 'Theories, Assumptions and Securities Regulation: Market Efficiency Revisited' (1992) 140 *U Pa L Rev* 85. See also, Eugene F Fama, Michael C Jensen, Lawrence Fisher and Richard Roll, 'The Adjustment of Stock Prices to New Information' (1969) 10 *International Economic Review* 1–22, accessed 4 March 2015 at SSRN: http://ssrn.com/abstract=321524.

3 George W Dent, 'Academics in Wonderland: The Team Production and Director Primacy Models of Corporate Governance', Case Legal Studies Research Paper No 07-21 (June 2007), accessed 4 March 2015 at SSRN: http://ssrn.com/abstract=995186, 18–19 of 72. See discussion in section 4.2.2 above.

4 H Ashbaugh-Skaife, D W Collins and R LaFond, 'Corporate Governance and the Cost of Equity Capital' (December 2004), accessed 4 March 2015 at SSRN: http://ssrn.com/abstract=639681, 1.

5 Ibid, 2–3.

6 S A Patel and G S Dallas, 'Transparency and Disclosure: Overview of Methodology and Study Results – United States' (16 October 2002), accessed 4 March 2015 at SSRN: http://ssrn.com/abstract=422800, 4 of 29. For a study examining how a high degree of compliance with a governance code reduces information asymmetry and agency problems, see Ahmed Elbadry, Dimitrios Gounopoulos and Frank S Skinner, 'Governance Quality and Information Asymmetry' *Financial Markets, Institutions and Instruments*, forthcoming, (January 3, 2014), accessed 23 April 2015 at SSRN: http://ssrn.com/abstract=2373902.

9.1.2 Transparency and the 'Trade-Off' Effect on the Quality of Board and Market Monitoring

Hermalin and Weisbach[7] explain the corporate governance effects of increasing transparency in terms of the benefits of a higher quality of board monitoring which must be balanced[8] against the costs of exposing management to greater scrutiny.[9] This means that, first, the greater the firm-specific or manager-specific information[10] which the CEO or management divulges to the board or market, the higher is the risk of an adverse assessment of their performance. The CEO and management will thus seek a premium for this in their compensation.[11]

In relation to the second point – the distortion of information – Hermalin and Weisbach explain that there are three types of distorting actions or efforts the CEO can take in response to increased transparency. The authors call the first two efforts the 'exaggerating effort' and the 'obscuring effort'.[12] The third type of response by the CEO can be 'concealing information' which, for the authors, resounds with corporate collapses.[13] Thus, Hermalin and Weisbach conclude that increases in the level of disclosure above the optimum level reduce firm value:

> [p]rofits decrease both because managers will have to be paid higher salaries to compensate them for the increased career risk they face, and because greater transparency increases managerial incentives to engage in costly and counter-productive efforts to distort information.[14]

The implication of this study is that the effects of transparency are not absolute nor, necessarily, positive. In this respect, this finding would accord with the earlier discussion (in terms of board independence) of

---

7 B E Hermalin and M S Weisbach, 'Transparency and Corporate Governance' (21 January 2007), accessed 4 March 2015 at SSRN: http://ssrn.com/abstract=958628.

8 Ibid, 19.

9 Ibid, 1.

10 See discussion in section 7.3.2.1.3 above.

11 Hermalin and Weisbach, above n 7, 2–3. For a discussion of behavioural and psychological influences on managerial behaviour as a result of 'assessments' of a manager by corporate actors, see Benjamin E Hermalin and Michael S Weisbach, 'Understanding Corporate Governance Through Learning Models of Managerial Competence', Fisher College of Business Working Paper No. 2014-03-04, (March 27, 2014), accessed 23 April 2015 at SSRN: http://ssrn.com/abstract=2417278.

12 Hermalin and Weisbach, above n 7, 12.

13 Ibid, 18

14 Ibid, 19.

the argued 'trade-off' between the quality of board monitoring and possible negative effects on the quality of manager-specific and firm-specific information flow to the board which, in turn, reduces the quality of board decision-making.[15]

Coming shortly after the Asian financial crisis, a detailed examination of the role and benefits of transparency in governance and capital markets has been undertaken by Vishwanath and Kaufmann.[16] Again, the role of asymmetric information and consequent agency costs are highlighted.[17] The authors identify several 'attributes' of transparency necessary for effective governance processes – access,[18] relevance[19] and quality and reliability.[20]

As was demonstrated in Chapter 6, these attributes also form the basis of the access and transparency of information provisions of a large number of international and national for-profit corporate governance codes. For example, the Global Governance Code Table[21] includes the following features originally drawn from the OECD Principles[22] and forming part of the relational approach's model comparative scheme:

- item 1.ii – governance structures and practices consistent with law and transparent/enforceable;
- item 1.iii – demarcation and transparency for governmental and regulatory agencies;
- items 2.iii and 4.iii – timely/regular disclosure of information;
- item 2.v – disclosure of disproportionate control structures/arrangements;
- item 2.vii – disclosure of institutional shareholder governance/voting policies and conflicts;
- item 5.i – timely disclosure of material information including:
  a. results;
  b. remuneration policies;

15 See discussion in section 7.3.2.1.3 above.

16 Tara Vishwanath and Daniel Kaufmann, 'Towards Transparency in Finance and Governance' (September 1999), accessed 4 March 2015 at SSRN: http://ssrn.com/abstract=258978.

17 Ibid, 2 (footnotes omitted).

18 Ibid, 3–4.

19 Ibid, 4.

20 Ibid, 4.

21 See Table 6.2.

22 Organisation for Economic Co-Operation and Development, *OECD Principles of Corporate Governance 2004*, 2004, OECD Publications Service, Paris ('OECD Principles'). See http://www.oecd.org/document/49/0,3343,en_2649_34813_31530865_1_1_1_37439,00.html (accessed 4 March 2015), p 13.

c. director qualifications/independence;
d. risk factors; and
e. governance codes/policies;

- item 5.ii – independent/external audit;
- item 5.iii – quality and integrity of information;
- item 6.iv – principal responsibilities:
  f. reporting, audit, financial/operational control, risk management and internal audit; and
  g. disclosure of information; and
- item 6.viii – disclosure of director contribution/independence.

9.1.2.1 [TransTimeMon] (+)[23] and [TransTimeRedn] (−)[24] variables relational effect paths

The preceding two sections adopt two governance variables to represent, on the one hand, the enhanced (+) monitoring effect of transparency and timing of reporting and, on the other, the negative (−) effects on the quality of 'manager-specific' and 'firm-specific' information flow from management to the board with consequential reductions in the quality of decision-making and monitoring of management.

The studies described in section 9.1.2 above seek to link, most directly, the transparency and timing of reporting with both enhancement of the monitoring function (Monitoring & Audit Factor No 5[25]) and the quality of decision-making (Decision-making Factor No 7[26]). Given its focus on monitoring and decision-making, the **[TransTimeMon] (+)** variable's relational effect path is positive (+) and the zone of effect of that relational effect path is hypothesised to be similar to that of the **[BrdSkills] (+)**[27] and **[BrdIndMon] (+)**[28] variables but with an additional overriding requirement of Compliance Factor No 2 (Corporate Governance and Legal Compliance[29]). Compliance Factor No 2 is present because of the substantial guidance in governance codes relating to the access, timeliness, quality and reliability of information. The features listed in the previous section from Table 6.2 are examples of the width of this requirement.

---

23 Transparency and Timing of Reporting – Monitoring Effect.

24 Transparency and Timing of Reporting – Information Flow Reduction Effect.

25 See discussion in section 2.6.5 above.

26 See discussion in section 2.6.7 above.

27 Board – Director Skills 'Mix' – see Figure 7.2 and discussion in section 7.3.1.2.1 above.

28 Board Independent Director: Executive Director Proportion – Monitoring Effect – see discussion in sections 7.3.2.1.1–7.3.2.1.2 above.

29 See discussion in section 2.6.2 above.

Compliance Factor No 2 is also significant in the **[TransTimeMon] (+)** variable because of its (very) direct influence on Reporting Factor No 1 (Transparency, Timing and Integrity of Financial and Other Reports). In this respect, Compliance Factor No 2 provides much of the (mandated and other) content for the financial and other reports contemplated by Reporting Factor No 1. For example, the overriding themes of Compliance Factor No 2 include the requirements of the international/cross-border and national (US, UK and Australian) corporate governance codes (Comparative Corporate Governance Codes Key Field No 3) again presented in Chapter 6. Similarly direct (and strong) is the influence of Compliance Factor No 2 on Monitoring & Audit Factor No 5 as described in Figure 2.4 (Compliance Factor No 2 Interrelationships[30]). In that diagram, Compliance Factor No 2 affects all other governance factors.

An alternative way to consider the presence of Compliance Factor No 2 is to liken the effect of the **[TransTimeMon] (+)** variable to the operation of the **[NationGov] (+)** variable.[31] In the case of the **[NationGov] (+)** variable, Compliance Factor No 2 is hypothesised to be affected. This is because changes in the content of this variable will actually change the requirements of 'hard', 'soft' or 'hybrid' laws[32] which apply to the company. Similarly, the nature and operation of the transparency and timing of reporting contemplated by the **[TransTimeMon] (+)** variable can also change with changes in the law. In other words, the **[TransTimeMon] (+)** variable is like the **[NationGov] (+)** variable but only insofar as the provisions which govern the transparency/quality, content and timing of financial and other reports.

Thus, the relational effect path for the **[TransTimeMon] (+)** variable is hypothesised to be as follows (see Figure 9.1).

What does this reveal about this variable? First, that the relational effect path of **[TransTimeMon] (+)** is similar (but with an additional Compliance Factor No 2) to the relational effect paths for **[BrdSkills] (+)**[33] and **[BrdIndMon] (+)**.[34] But this is not to engage in 'double-counting'. This is because both the **[BrdSkills] (+)** and **[BrdIndMon] (+)** variables are hypothesised to *begin* with Monitoring & Audit Factor No 5 and

---

30 See discussion in section 2.6.2 above.

31 See discussion in section 7.3.1.3.2 above.

32 See discussion in section 6.1.3.1 above.

33 Board – Director Skills 'Mix' – see Figure 7.2 and discussion in section 7.3.1.2.1 above.

34 Board Independent Director: Executive Director Proportion – Monitoring Effect – see discussion in sections 7.3.2.1.1–7.3.2.1.2 above.

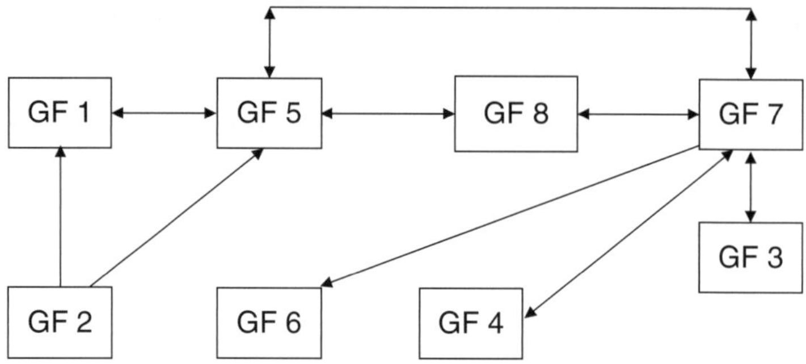

Figure 9.1 [TransTimeMon] (+) variable relational effect path

Decision-making Factor No 7. Each of these governance factors has a reflexive relationship with the other as described in section 2.6.7 of Chapter 2.

So how is the **[TransTimeMon] (+)** variable different from this? Instead and significant in the case of the **[TransTimeMon] (+)** variable is that the relational effect path is hypothesised to *begin* with Reporting Factor No 1 and Compliance Factor No 2 as the 'drivers' of this zone of effect. For example, as noted above, the effect of Compliance Factor No 2 on Reporting Factor No 1 is significant on account of the requirements of governance codes. Thus the access, relevance and quality and reliability measures of Vishwanath and Kaufmann are translated into the relational approach and flow in part from Compliance Factor No 2.

There is also a reflexive relationship between Reporting Factor No 1 and Monitoring & Audit Factor No 5 as described in section 2.6.5 above. Thus, these two governance factors inform each other. For example, if the company applies additional resources to the board, CEO and management monitoring functions – including internal and external audit – then the relational approach predicts an improvement in the quality and reliability of information which flows to the board and, therefore, the market. This, in turn, enhances the quality of external or market monitoring of the board with, it is predicted, improvements in internal monitoring. Thus, it is Compliance Factor No 2 and the reflexive relationship between Reporting Factor No 1 and Monitoring & Audit Factor No 5 which are hypothesised to be the 'sources' of the positive influence represented in Figure 9.1 above for **[TransTimeMon] (+)**.

Therefore, the **[TransTimeMon] (+)** variable is hypothesised to affect all governance factors including Compliance Factor No 2's overriding effect

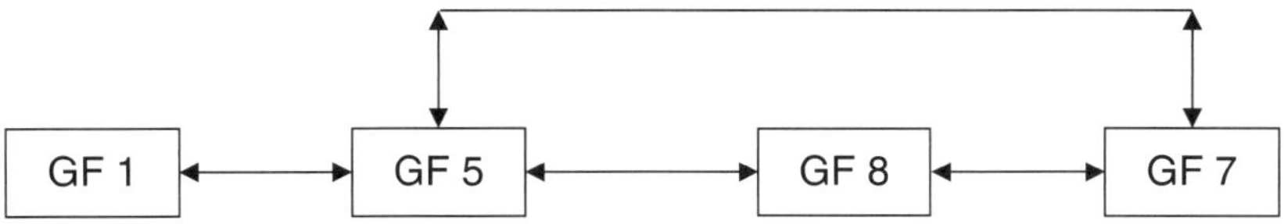

Figure 9.2 [TransTimeRedn] (−) variable relational effect path

on Reporting Factor No 1 and Monitoring & Audit Factor No 5. This equates to a coverage/rating of +8/100.00 *rprox* in the Coverage Table (Table 3.1) and the Relational Proximity Table (Table 3.2).

In the case of the **[TransTimeRedn] (−)** variable, the relational effect path of this variable is identical to the corresponding **[BrdIndInfo] (−)**[35] variable (see Figure 9.2).

The starting point for this relational effect path is hypothesised to be Reporting Factor No 1 as the 'driver' of this zone of effect. Again, as discussed above in relation to the **[TransTimeMon] (+)** variable, there is a reflexive relationship between Reporting Factor No 1 and Monitoring & Audit Factor No 5 as described in section 2.6.5 above.

But the relational effect path for **[TransTimeRedn] (−)** is negative for two reasons. First, as described in relation to **[BrdIndInfo] (−)**,[36] the relational approach predicts a reduction in 'firm-specific' and 'manager-specific' information flow to the board. Here, as there, more detailed and transparent information may allow the board to monitor more intensively and revise downwards its opinion of particular managers such as the CEO. Thus, the flow of such information is reduced over time. For consistency with the **[BrdIndInfo] (−)** variable, this negative effect is likely to extend to a significant degree only to the board component of the three-level decision-making hierarchy of the board, CEO and management contemplated by Decision-making Factor No 7. Again for consistency, the single-direction overriding effect of Compliance Factor No 2 is omitted. This is for the reasons set out in relation to **[BrdIndInfo] (−)**. There, Compliance Factor No 2 was omitted because the themes contained in this governance factor are outside the type of information contemplated by the studies in that section which relate only to 'manager-specific' and 'firm-specific' information.

The second reason for a negative direction for **[TransTimeRedn] (−)**

---

[35] Board – Independent Director: Executive Director Proportion – Information Flow and Decision Quality 'Trade-off' – see discussion in section 7.3.2.1.3 above.

[36] Ibid.

is based on the observations of Hermalin and Weisbach above.[37] The authors there noted that the effects of enhanced timing and transparency of information are, again, to intensify board monitoring of the CEO and management. This gives rise to demands for higher compensation on the part of executives to reflect the added risk to their careers and may cause the CEO and management to engage in costly efforts to exaggerate, obscure or conceal information.

Thus the zone of effect of the **[TransTimeRedn] (−)** variable is hypothesised to extend to four governance factors giving rise to a coverage/rating of −4/50.00 *rprox* in the Coverage Table (Table 3.1) and the Relational Proximity Table (Table 3.2).

9.2 EARNINGS MANIPULATION AND BOARD AND COMMITTEE STRUCTURES

In section 9.1.1 above, the examination highlighted that the principal aim of reporting – and, in particular, enhanced transparency and timeliness of that reporting – is to remedy problems associated with the information asymmetry aspects of agency costs in the agency theory component of the shareholder and stakeholder models examined in Chapter 4. As is readily apparent, factors which detract from the transparency and timeliness of reporting – in other words, the integrity of reports and financial information – increase those agency costs. Thus, one purpose of 'good' corporate governance variables, structures and mechanisms is to enhance this integrity consideration.

In this respect, Klein defines earnings manipulation as 'the practice of distorting the true financial performance of the company'.[38] At first blush, of course, such a practice would appear undesirable, particularly

---

37 See discussion in section 9.1.2 above.

38 A Klein, 'Audit, Committee, Board of Director Characteristics, and Earnings Management', New York University School Of Law, NYU Center for Law and Economics, Law & Economics Research Paper Series, Working Paper No 06-42, October 2006, accessed 4 March 2015 at SSRN: http://papers.ssrn.com/paper.taf?abstract_id=246674, 1.

For a discussion of practices of 'overvaluing' equity including earnings management, see Michael C Jensen, 'The Agency Cost of Overvalued Equity and the Current State of Corporate Finance', Harvard NOM Working Paper No 04-26, accessed 4 March 2015 at SSRN: http://ssrn.com/abstract=560961, especially 556–62. See also Michael C Jensen, 'Agency Costs of Overvalued Equity', Harvard NOM Working Paper No 04-26; ECGI – Finance Working Paper No 39/2004 (March 2005), accessed 4 March 2015 at SSRN: http://ssrn.com/abstract=480421.

if it increases agency costs for outside shareholders. Peasnell, Pope and Young, however, explain that earnings manipulation may, at different times, benefit or disadvantage such shareholders.[39] But earnings management is generally seen as undesirable on account of the increase in agency costs to outside shareholders. For further effects, Dallas found extensive 'short-termism' to have contributed to the Global Financial Crisis.[40]

Thus, many studies have now been undertaken with respect to understanding the relationship, if any, between good governance and minimising earnings manipulation or management by a company. In this respect, and taking as the focus the risk of agency costs identified by Peasnell, Pope and Young above, the purpose of the following subsections of this section 9.2 is to identify and examine the governance variables which seek to eliminate or reduce the potential for management to engage in earnings manipulation.

9.2.1 Board and Audit Committee Independence, Time, Financial Expertise and Duality of CEO/Chairperson

As in the case of firm value and operating performance, audit committee independence and board independence are again often cited as important variables that can reduce earnings manipulation. Independence requirements for company boards and audit committees are contained in the international/cross-border and national (US, UK and Australian) corporate governance codes (Comparative Corporate Governance Codes Key Field No 3) in Chapter 6. Here, instead, the relational approach reviews empirical studies in relation to the effects of these variables on earnings manipulation and results remain inconclusive.

For a discussion of internal and external factors affecting earnings misrepresentation, see Ilia D Dichev, John R Graham, Campbell R Harvey and Shivaram Rajgopal, "The Misrepresentation of Earnings", (September 12, 2014), accessed 23 April 2015 at SSRN: http://ssrn.com/abstract=2376408. See also Ilia D Dichev, John R Graham, Campbell R Harvey and Shivaram Rajgopal, "A Guide to Earnings Quality", (October 30, 2013), accessed 23 April 2015 at SSRN: http://ssrn.com/abstract=2347428.

[39] Ken V Peasnell, Peter F Pope and Steven Young, 'Board Monitoring and Earnings Management: Do Outside Directors Influence Abnormal Accruals?' (October 2000), accessed 4 March 2015 at SSRN: http://ssrn.com/abstract=249557, 2.

[40] Lynne Dallas, 'Short-Termism, the Financial Crisis, and Corporate Governance' (2011) 37 *Journal of Corporation Law* 264; San Diego Legal Studies Paper No 12-078 (16 February 2012), accessed 4 March 2015 at SSRN: http://ssrn.com/abstract=2006556, 267 (footnotes omitted).

A review of the studies below provides some (but inconclusive) support for a positive relationship between independence *alone* of the board or audit committee and the quality or integrity of a company's financial information (Reporting Factor No 1).

However, some factors or trends which recur *in combination with* the independence factor appear to affect the likelihood of earnings manipulation, in particular:

- time spent in review or number of audit committee meetings – **[AudIndFreq] (+)**;[41]
- financial expertise of the relevant directors and/or committee – **[AudAccEarn] (+)**;[42] and
- combination or separation (as the case may be) of the CEO/chairperson roles – **[DualEarn] (−)**.[43]

Turning to the studies in detail, for Klein, there is a positive relationship between independence and a reduction in earnings manipulation on account of enhanced monitoring (Monitoring & Audit Factor No 5[44]). Klein's study concludes that independent boards and audit committees result in better monitoring and 'more unbiased financial statements'.[45] Klein ascribes as reasons for this 'the ability to withstand pressure from the firm to manipulate earnings' and reputational constraints.[46]

Peasnell, Pope and Young also find support for the enhanced monitoring of independent directors in relation to upward earnings manipulation.[47] However, in a study further examined below, for Agrawal and Chadha, independence of the board and audit committee is *not* related to the probability of earnings manipulation.[48]

Klein undertakes a study of whether independent directors on the

---

[41] Audit Committee – Independence in Combination with Frequency of Meeting – Reduction in Earnings Manipulation Effect – see discussion in this section 9.2.1 below.

[42] Audit Committee – Accounting Expertise – Earnings Manipulation Reduction Effect – see discussion in section 9.2.1.1.2 below.

[43] Duality of CEO/Chair Positions – Probability of Earnings Manipulation – see discussion in section 9.2.1.1.3 below.

[44] See discussion in section 2.6.5 above.

[45] Klein, above n 38, 3.

[46] Ibid, 7 (footnotes omitted).

[47] Peasnell, Pope and Young, above n 39, 3–4.

[48] A Agrawal and S Chadha, 'Corporate Governance and Accounting Scandals', AFA 2004 San Diego Meetings (September 2004), available at SSRN: http://ssrn.com/abstract=595138, 4.

audit committee reduce earnings manipulation.[49] While Klein finds that a reduction in earnings manipulation is associated with whether there is a majority of independent directors, there is no relation between earnings manipulation and 100 per cent independence on the audit committee.[50]

Thus, of note here for the relational approach is that Klein considers that her results do *not* support the current US requirement under NYSE Final Rules section 303A.07(a)[51] that independence from management exist for *all* audit committee members.[52] The relational approach can contribute some explanation of this result – that this may be due to the effect of the **[AudIndInfo] (−)**[53] variable discussed in section 8.4.3 above. There it was hypothesised that, on account of a high degree of independence, there is a reduction in the information flow to the audit committee in relation to 'firm-specific' and 'manager-specific' information as well as information asymmetry of outside committee members.[54]

Contrary to Klein, Marrakchi Chtourou, Bédard and Courteau, find that earnings misstatement reduces with 100 per cent audit committee independence[55] – but only when other factors are present.[56] Studies like

---

49 Klein, above n 38, 22.

50 Ibid, 22.

51 New York Stock Exchange, *Final NYSE Corporate Governance Rules* ('NYSE Final Rules'), approved by SEC 4 November 2003 (except s 303A.08) and 30 June 2003 (s 303A.08). The Rules (as amended from time to time) comprise section 303A.00 of the NYSE Listed Company Manual. See section 303A.00 Corporate Governance Standards (approved 25 November 2009), available at http://nysemanual.nyse.com/lcm/ (accessed 4 March 2015). Subsequent amendments have been made to:

- Section 303A.00 – Corporate Governance Standards (approved 22 August 2013)
- Section 303A.02 – Corporate Governance Standards (approved 11 January 2013)
- Section 303A.05 – Corporate Governance Standards (approved 11 January 2013)
- Section 303A.07 – Audit Committee Additional Requirements (approved 22 August 2013)

These Rule amendments are available at http://nysemanual.nyse.com/lcm/ (accessed 4 March 2015). See section 303A.07, Audit Committee Additional Requirements, Rule (a), p 14 of 40.

52 Klein, above n 38, 22.

53 Audit Committee – Independence – Information Flow and Decision Quality 'Trade-off'. See discussion in section 8.4.3 above.

54 Ibid.

55 Marrakchi Chtourou, Bédard and Courteau, 'Corporate Governance and Earnings Management' (21 April 2001), accessed 4 March 2015 at SSRN: http://ssrn.com/abstract=275053, 4.

56 Ibid, 4.

Marrakchi Chtourou *et al* introduce, as intervening factors on the effects of independence, a combination of additional factors as affecting the probability of earnings manipulation. These include the time in review or number of audit committee meetings, the financial expertise of audit committee members and separation of the CEO/chairperson roles. It is to these factors that the relational approach now turns.

Agrawal and Chadha introduce an intervening factor that, for the authors, has much greater explanatory power than independence – the time factor or number of audit committee meetings. As noted above, for Agrawal and Chadha, independence of the board and audit committee is *not* related to the probability of earnings manipulation.[57] The authors explain that, contrary to the notion that independence of the audit committee improves monitoring,[58] the *time* dedicated to identifying relevant problems is more critical and that the relatively few meetings of an audit committee make it difficult '. . . for a small group of outsiders to detect fraud or accounting irregularities in a large, complex corporation in such a short time'.[59]

Thus, for Agrawal and Chadha, the time factor or number of meetings reduces both accounting irregularities and fraud. In relation to the latter, Farber investigates the relationship between financial reporting fraud and governance variables.[60] The author finds that governance variables linked to financial reporting fraud include:

(1) a low number or proportion of independent directors;
(2) a reduction in the number of meetings of the audit committee;
(3) lesser number of audit committee financial experts; and
(4) a greater proportion of CEO board chairpersons.[61]

Returning to earnings manipulation, these findings are supported by those of Xie, Davidson and DaDalt who find a correlation (though not necessarily causation) between a reduction in earnings manipulation and:

(1) increases in the number of independent directors;
(2) increases in the proportion of audit committee members with financial expertise; and

---

57 Agrawal and Chadha, above n 48, 4.

58 Ibid, 5.

59 Ibid.

60 D B Farber, 'Restoring Trust After Fraud: Does Corporate Governance Matter?' (4 October 2004), accessed 4 March 2015 at SSRN: http://ssrn.com/abstract=485403.

61 Ibid, 27.

(3) increases in the number of board and audit committee meetings.[62]

Abbott, Parker and Peters are of a similar view though they place the frequency of audit committee meetings at a minimum of four per year to achieve a reduction in earnings misstatement[63] while finding no relationship between financial misstatement and a failure to comply with stipulations as to minimum size.[64] Similarly, for Anderson, Deli and Gillan, increases in the independence of the board and audit committee and in the frequency of board and audit committee meetings increase the degree of information relating to the reports as does division of the CEO and chairperson functions.[65]

The elements of independence, financial expertise and regularity of meetings would also accord with the findings of Bryan, Liu and Tiras.[66] Similarly, for the study by Marrakchi Chtourou *et al* noted above in relation to independence, earnings misstatement similarly reduces with increases in the number of outside directors and financial experts on the committee.[67] Again, in relation to the time spent in review, the authors find that earnings misstatement also reduces where a company has a '*completely* independent audit committee' holding more than two audit committee meetings per year.[68]

Thus, it would appear that there is some support that the independence factor alone is of some explanatory power in minimising earnings manipulation but this is inconclusive. However, an increase in the independence factor appears from the studies to be *critical* in reducing earnings manipulation when combined with:

---

62 B Xie, W N Davidson III and P J DaDalt, 'Earnings Management and Corporate Governance: The Roles of the Board and the Audit Committee' (5 July 2001), accessed 4 March 2015 at SSRN: http://ssrn.com/abstract=304195, 20.

63 L J Abbott, S Parker and G F Peters, 'Audit Committee Characteristics and Financial Misstatement: A Study of the Efficacy of Certain Blue Ribbon Committee Recommendations' (March 2002), accessed 4 March 2015 at SSRN: http://ssrn.com/abstract=319125, 3.

64 Ibid, 31.

65 K L Anderson, D N Deli and S L Gillan, 'Boards of Directors, Audit Committees, and the Information Content of Earnings', Weinberg Center for Corporate Governance Working Paper No 2003-04 (September 2003), available at SSRN: http://ssrn.com/abstract=444241, 24.

66 Daniel M Bryan, Carol Liu and Samuel L Tiras, "The Influence of Independent and Effective Audit Committees on Earnings Quality" (January 2004), available at http://www.researchgate.net/publication/228306548_The_Influence_of_Independent_and_Effective_Audit_Committees_on_Earnings_Quality.

67 Marrakchi Chtourou, Bédard and Courteau, above n 55, 4.

68 Ibid (emphasis added).

- increases in the time spent in review (or the number of audit committee meetings) – **[AudIndFreq] (+)**;[69] and/or
- increases in the financial expertise of the relevant directors or committee – **[AudAccEarn] (+)**.[70]

This is in contrast with the combination of the CEO/chairperson roles which, for the studies noted above by Farber and, separately, Anderson, Deli and Gillan, appears to increase the likelihood that earnings management will occur. This is represented by the **[DualEarn] (−)**[71] variable below.

[AudIndFreq][72] ***(+) variable relational effect path***

Thus, the relational approach assigns to the **[AudIndFreq] (+)** variable a positive (+) directional marker to describe a reduction in the probability of earnings manipulation. The zone of effect of the **[AudIndFreq] (+)** variable is hypothesised to be identical to the **[AudIndMon] (+)**[73] and, in turn, the **[BrdIndMon] (+)**[74] variables. Again, there is a similarity in the starting point for the relational effect paths. In the case of **[AudIndMon] (+)** and **[BrdIndMon] (+)** variables – and reflecting the argued independence effect on monitoring and the quality of decision-making – the relational effect path is hypothesised to start at the reflexive relationship between Monitoring & Audit Factor No 5 and Decision-making Factor No 7.

This starting point for **[AudIndMon] (+)** and **[BrdIndMon] (+)** also applies to **[AudIndFreq] (+)** as the frequency of meeting is hypothesised to affect the themes encapsulated in both Monitoring & Audit Factor No 5 and Decision-making Factor No 7. As explained earlier in the relational approach:

> the Decision-Making Factor No. 7 is closely aligned (or interrelated) to the Monitoring & Audit Factor No. 5. In other words, these themes should

---

[69] Audit Committee – Independence in Combination with Frequency of Meeting – Reduction in Earnings Manipulation Effect – see discussion in this section 9.2.1 below.

[70] Audit Committee – Accounting Expertise – Earnings Manipulation Reduction Effect – see discussion in section 9.2.1.1.2 below.

[71] Duality of CEO/Chair Positions – Probability of Earnings Manipulation – see discussion in section 9.2.1.1.3 below.

[72] Audit Committee – Independence in Combination with Frequency of Meeting – Reduction in Earnings Manipulation Effect.

[73] Audit Committee – Independence – Monitoring Effect – see discussion in section 8.4.3 above.

[74] Board Independent Director: Executive Director Proportion – Monitoring Effect – see discussion in sections 7.3.2.1.1–7.3.2.1.2 above.

> normatively inform and shape each other. Thus, in real world terms, as the monitoring process within the corporation identifies that some action is required, so then is the decision-making process engaged. In turn, decision-making action should again normatively engage the monitoring and evaluation/assessment functions in a continuous cycle.[75]

So a company which holds more regular audit committee meetings is predicted to enhance its internal and external monitoring and audit quality. As a result, it is predicted to be more likely to detect and reduce earnings manipulation. In addition, like the case of **[TransTimeMon] (+)**, the relational approach predicts an improvement in the quality and reliability of information which flows to the board and, therefore, the market. This, in turn, enhances the quality of external or market monitoring of the board with, it is predicted, improvements in internal monitoring. From this should flow enhanced quality of decision-making at the board, CEO and management levels which in turn engages the monitoring cycle.

Again, there is no case of double counting the **[AudIndMon] (+)** and **[BrdIndMon] (+)** variables. While the independence component *drivers* of **[AudIndMon] (+)** and **[BrdIndMon] (+)** are retained as the above studies would urge, an additional driver on account of the frequency or number of meetings is added. Thus, this relational effect path is hypothesised to have a stronger effect than the **[AudIndMon] (+)** and **[BrdIndMon] (+)** relational effect paths in isolation. So, assuming a constant proportion of independent directors on the board and audit committee, a company which increases the frequency of audit committee meetings is predicted to improve the quality of internal and external monitoring and audit and, in turn, the quality of board, CEO and management decision-making. This equates to a coverage/rating of +7/87.50 *rprox* for the **[AudIndFreq] (+)** variable in the Coverage Table (Table 3.1) and the Relational Proximity Table (Table 3.2).

9.2.1.1 Board and audit committee expertise

9.2.1.1.1 Accounting financial expertise relevant but possible disincentive effect As discussed in Chapter 8,[76] accounting expertise on the audit committee appears more likely than other types of financial expertise to reduce the likelihood of earnings manipulation. However, the presence of financial experts may lead to some detrimental ‘free rider’ effects on the monitoring function required on the part of other audit committee directors.

---

[75] See discussion in section 2.6.7 above.

[76] See discussion in sections 8.4–8.4.4 above.

Agrawal and Chadha also examine financial expertise of the audit committee. Again, contrary explanations occur. The authors explain that US requirements such as NYSE Final Rules s 303A.07(a),[77] assume that '[M]embers with no experience in accounting or finance are less likely to be able to detect problems in financial reporting'.[78] However, the authors warn that (again) the time dedicated to identifying accounting problems as well as a possible disincentive effect on non-financial committee members *could* have counter-productive effects as 'the presence of a member with financial expertise can lead other members to become less vigilant'.[79] The authors find, however, that the probability of earnings manipulation is reduced in 'companies whose boards or audit committees include an independent director *with financial expertise*'.[80]

In some studies, the *nature* of the financial expertise is the focus. For Carcello, Hollingsworth, Klein and Neal, the presence of accounting (but not other experience) financial expertise reduces earnings manipulation[81] as does the independence of the financial expert.[82] Importantly, and reinforcing a theme highlighted in Chapter 7,[83] the authors conclude that a beneficial combination of governance variables can substitute for financial expertise.[84] This study was among others later reviewed by Cunningham[85] who draws the same conclusion in relation to accounting expertise for audit committees which must be disclosed (or, if not present, explained)[86] consequent on reforms contained in SOX:

---

77 NYSE Final Rules, above n 51. See Commentary to section 303A.07, Audit Committee Additional Requirements, Rule (a).

78 Agrawal and Chadha, above n 48, 6.

79 Ibid.

80 Ibid, 4 (emphasis added).

81 J V Carcello, C W Hollingsworth, A Klein and T L Neal, 'Audit Committee Financial Expertise, Competing Corporate Governance Mechanisms, and Earnings Management' (February 2006), accessed 4 March 2015 at SSRN: http://ssrn.com/abstract=887512, 3.

82 Ibid.

83 See the discussion of 'overall' governance and the 'gap-filling' function of governance variables in section 7.3.1.3–7.3.1.3.1 above.

84 Carcello, Hollingsworth, Klein and Neal, above n 81, 32.

85 Lawrence A Cunningham, 'Rediscovering Board Expertise: Legal Implications of the Empirical Literature', GWU Law School Public Law Research Paper No 363 (23 October 2007), accessed 4 March 2015 at SSRN: http://ssrn.com/abstract=1024261, 16–17.

86 PL 107-204, 2002 HR 3763, July 30, 2002, 116 Stat 745, available at http://www.sec.gov/about/laws/soa2002.pdf ('SOX'), section 407(a). 'Financial expert' is defined in paragraph (b). See also Cunningham, above n 85, 11.

> [g]estures in SOX signal a sharp, yet still inchoate, conception of expertise on audit committees to promote superior financial reporting. Empirical evidence suggests that this works—directors with *accounting expertise* on audit committees are associated with more faithful financial reporting.[87]

Thus, the implication of this is that *accounting expertise* (Monitoring & Audit Factor No 5) is required to effectively tackle the significant width and complexity of modern company accounting requirements and thus to improve the quality and integrity of the reporting function (Reporting Factor No 1). In turn, this enhances market monitoring of the company which enhances the company's own internal monitoring and, consequently, decision-making (Decision-making Factor No 7).

9.2.1.1.2 [AudAccEarn] (+)[88] and [AudFree] (−)[89] variables relational effect paths

[AUDACCEARN] (+): AUDIT COMMITTEE – ACCOUNTING EXPERTISE – EARNINGS MANIPULATION REDUCTION EFFECT In light of the above studies, the **[AudAccEarn] (+)** variable is ascribed a positive (+) directional marker to reflect a reduction effect on the probability of earnings manipulation. The relational effect path of **[AudAccEarn] (+)** is hypothesised to be identical to that of **[AudExpAcc] (+)**[90] (which is itself identical to **[AudCom] (+)**) but with the reduction effect targeted at the probability of earnings manipulation rather than firm value and/or operating performance. The starting point of all three variables, however, remains the same – Monitoring & Audit Factor No 5 (Internal and External/Audit Monitoring Quality). Thus, for example, if a company increased the accounting expertise on its audit committee, the relational approach predicts that there will be an enhancement in the quality of monitoring emanating from the audit committee and, consequently, a reduction in the likelihood of earnings manipulation. As seen in the **[AudExpAcc] (+)** variable[91] and the **[AudCom] (+)** variable,[92] Monitoring & Audit Factor No 5 has a reflexive (dual direction) interrelationship with Reporting Factor No 1 and Decision-making Factor No 7. Thus, the relational approach predicts an improvement in

---

87 Cunningham, above n 85, 32 (emphasis added).

88 Audit Committee – Accounting Expertise – Earnings Manipulation Reduction Effect.

89 Audit Committee – Non-Accounting Expertise – 'Free Rider' Effect.

90 Audit Committee – Financial Expertise (Accounting) – see discussion in section 8.4.4 above.

91 See discussion in section 8.4.4 above.

92 See discussion in section 8.4.2 above.

the transparency, timing and integrity of financial and other reports and an improvement in the quality of board, CEO and management decision-making consequent on an increase in the accounting expertise of the audit committee.

In the case of the **[AudExpAcc] (+)** variable,[93] the relational effect path was hypothesised to apply by isolating the interrelationships of only the accounting expertise factor and not the independence factor. The same reasoning applies in the case of **[AudAccEarn] (+)** giving rise again to an identical relational effect path. On this 'accounting only' view, the zone of effect of **[AudAccEarn] (+)** would extend to all governance factors except Stakeholders Factor No 6 and Responsibility Factor No 8. Importantly, like the **[AudCom] (+)** and **[AudExpAcc] (+)** variables, the single direction effect of Compliance Factor No 2 (Corporate Governance and Legal Compliance) is predicted to remain operative and strong on **[AudAccEarn] (+)** because of the significant guidance in governance codes relating to the functions of the audit committee.[94] This equates to a coverage/rating of +6/75.00 *rprox* in the Coverage Table (Table 3.1) and the Relational Proximity Table (Table 3.2).

[AUDFREE] (−): AUDIT COMMITTEE – NON-ACCOUNTING EXPERTISE – 'FREE RIDER' EFFECT The **[AudFree] (−)** variable seeks to represent the possible 'free rider' effect identified by Agrawal and Chadha above[95] and thus carries a negative (−) directional marker signifying an increase in the probability of earnings manipulation. Thus, the **[AudFree] (−)** variable's relational effect path is hypothesised to be identical to the relational effect path for **[AudAccEarn] (+)** but with a negative (−) directional marker. This equates to a coverage/rating of −6/75.00 *rprox* in the Coverage Table (Table 3.1) and the Relational Proximity Table (Table 3.2).

9.2.1.1.3 [DualEarn] (−)[96] variable relational effect path The review of the above studies suggests that the probability of earnings manipulation is increased by combination of the dual roles of CEO and Chairperson. Therefore, the **[DualEarn] (−)** variable is ascribed a negative (−) directional marker in the relational approach. The relational effect path for **[DualEarn] (−)** is hypothesised to extend to all eight governance factors except Compliance Factor No 2 in the same manner

---

93 See discussion in section 8.4.4 above.

94 See Table 6.2 in section 6.2.2 above.

95 See discussion in section 9.2.1.1.1 above.

96 Duality of CEO/Chair Positions – Probability of Earnings Manipulation.

as the **[DualTrade] (+/−)**[97] variable which, in turn, traced the pathway for **[BrdIndMon] (+)**[98] and **[BrdSkills] (+)**.[99]

The relational approach stated in sections 8.6.1–8.6.2 above that the 'crux' of the **[DualTrade] (+/−)** variable was – like the **[BrdIndMon] (+)** variable – the effect of independence (or lack thereof) on the reflexive relationship between Monitoring & Audit Factor No 5 and Decision-making Factor No 7. This reasoning similarly applies in the case of **[DualEarn] (−)** which equates to a coverage/rating of −7/87.50 *rprox* for this variable in the Coverage Table (Table 3.1) and the Relational Proximity Table (Table 3.2).

9.2.1.2 Summary of board and audit committee independence, time, expertise and duality factors

Thus, in summarising the preceding two sections, this analysis indicates that no firm conclusions can be made about the independence factor alone. However, the strong implication from the studies is that increases in the following factors, in combination with independence, may well reduce the likelihood of earnings manipulation:

- financial (particularly accounting) expertise of the audit committee – **[AudAccEarn] (+)**[100];
- time spent in review or number/regularity of audit committee meetings – **[AudIndFreq] (+)**[101]; and
- separation of the CEO and Chairperson functions – **[DualEarn] (−)**.[102]

Of course, these variables are not absolutes. For example, in the case of audit committee independence, the examination has noted above that the current US regime imposes an independence requirement on all audit committee members. But Klein on the one hand and Marrakchi Chtourou *et al* on the other disagree as to the effectiveness of a 100 per cent independent audit committee.[103] Here, the relational approach agrees with Klein that

---

97 Duality of CEO/Chair Positions – Monitoring and Decision-Quality 'Trade-off' – see discussion in sections 8.6.1–8.6.2 above.

98 See discussion in sections 7.3.2.1.1–7.3.2.1.2 above.

99 See discussion in section 7.3.1.2.1 above.

100 Audit Committee – Accounting Expertise – Earnings Manipulation Reduction Effect – see discussion in section 9.2.1.1.2 above.

101 Audit Committee – Independence in Combination with Frequency of Meeting – Reduction in Earnings Manipulation Effect – see discussion in section 9.2.1 above.

102 Duality of CEO/Chair Positions – Probability of Earnings Manipulation – see discussion in section 9.2.1.1.3 above.

103 Klein, above n 38, 25 and Marrakchi Chtourou, Bédard and Courteau, above n 55, 4. See discussion in section 9.2.1 above.

the audit committee should not entirely consist of independent directors. For the relational approach, this is on account of the hypothesised effects of the **[AudIndInfo] (−)** variable above.[104] There, it was noted that the relational effect path of the **[AudIndInfo] (−)** variable is hypothesised to equate to a coverage/rating of −4/50.00 *rprox* in the Coverage Table (Table 3.1) and the Relational Proximity Table (Table 3.2). This is identical to the **[BrdIndInfo] (−)**[105] variable in section 7.3.2.1.3 above. There is a reduction of the information flow to the audit committee in relation to 'firm-specific' and 'manager-specific' information as well as information asymmetry of outside audit committee members.[106]

In relation to the third factor – the time spent in review or regularity of meetings – while the general import of this factor is recognised, the consideration raised by Agrawal and Chadha above[107] in connection with the size and complexity of corporate operations and the consequent difficulty in identifying 'accounting irregularities' is a strong caveat. In other words, there is great difficulty in delineating a specific benchmark (for example, in relation to the minimum number of meetings) for this factor. The time spent in review or frequency of audit committee meetings will, it is hypothesised, in turn depend on a number of factors in addition to the sheer size or complexity factor – for example, the financial expertise of the audit committee members. Here, the role of the external audit is also critical.

9.2.2 Board and Audit Committee Size and Earnings Management

In this section, the relational approach identifies suggestions that the likelihood of earnings manipulation is reduced by reductions in board and audit committee size. In addition, there appears some consistency between these findings and those presented earlier relating to board effectiveness.[108]

Although outside the US, UK and Australia, in relation to board size and propensity for earnings management, Ching, Firth and Rui review Hong Kong companies and find that earnings manipulation is greater as board size increases.[109] The authors state that '[t]he results are

---

[104] See discussion in section 8.4.3 above.

[105] Board Independent: Executive Director Proportion – Information Flow and Decision Quality 'Trade-off'.

[106] See discussion in section 7.3.2.1.3 above.

[107] See discussion in section 9.2.1 above.

[108] See discussion in sections 8.2.1–8.2.2.2 above.

[109] K Ching, M Firth and O M Rui, 'Earnings Management, Corporate Governance and the Market Performance of Seasoned Equity Offerings' (September 2002), accessed 4 March 2015 at SSRN: http://ssrn.com/abstract=337880, 8.

consistent with Jensen's (1993) view that smaller boards provide more of a controlling function than do larger boards'.[110] As noted above, for Anderson, Deli and Gillan, increases in the independence of the board and audit committee and in the frequency of board and audit committee meetings increase the degree of information relating to the reports (as does division of the CEO and chairperson functions).[111] However, for the authors, the level of this degree is not increased by increasing the size of the board but is increased by a reduction in audit committee size.[112]

Although both pointing in favour of smaller rather than larger boards and audit committees, a concluded view cannot be formed in relation to this factor given the sample size. This is not surprising given the relational approach's view in relation to the governance effects of board size generally.[113] There, the relational approach was unable to predict any consistent or conclusive result in relation to the relationship between board size and firm operating performance and/or firm value beyond the intuitive appeal of arguments concerning a perceived negative relationship between board size (above a particular point) and board effectiveness. Both studies presented here point in the same direction (a reduction in size) with the result that there is probably more indicative weight attaching to this finding (and the relational approach puts it no higher than this).

Thus, for the reasons set out in sections 8.2.2–8.2.2.2 above, the relational effect path for the **[BrdCmEarn] (+/−)** variable is given a dual-direction marker (+/−) and has a zone of effect identical to the **[BrdCmSize] (+/−)** variable.[114] Here, as there, the issue goes (first, it is submitted) to Jensen's effectiveness of the coordination, communication and decision-making of the board, thus giving rise to a starting point of Decision-making Factor No 7. And this effectiveness issue is hypothesised to be identical for the **[BrdCmEarn] (+/−)** variable in relation to board and committee size and the likelihood of earnings manipulation. For example, in the case of the audit committee, increases in the size of this committee beyond the 'optimal' size are predicted to reduce the effectiveness of its coordination, communication and decision-making functions. Like the

---

[110] Ibid. The authors cite Michel C Jensen, 'The Modern Industrial Revolution, Exit, and the Failure of Internal Control Systems' (1993) 48 *Journal of Finance* 831–80.

[111] Anderson, Deli and Gillan, above n 65, 24.

[112] Ibid.

[113] See discussion in section 8.2.1–8.2.2.2 above.

[114] Board and Committee Size – see discussion in section 8.2.2.2 above.

[BrdCmSize] (+/−) variable, the optimal size will depend on the following intervening factors:

- compatibility of insider and outside shareholder interests;
- practicability of 'external verification' or monitoring;
- size of the firm;
- national/statutory governance code or regime requirements; and
- level of firm 'diversification'/complexity and debt.[115]

So both **[BrdCmSize] (+/−)** and **[BrdCmEarn] (+/−)** have a direction of effect which may be either positive or negative (+/−) depending upon the point for the 'optimal' number of directors for that particular firm. Thus, **[BrdCmEarn] (+/−)** affects all governance factors except Stakeholders Factor No 6 and Responsibility Factor No 8. Therefore, **[BrdCmEarn] (+/−)** has a coverage/rating of +/−6/75.00 *rprox* in the Coverage Table (Table 3.1) and the Relational Proximity Table (Table 3.2).

9.2.3 Review of Auditors, Non-Audit Services and Earnings Management

Chapter 5's examination of the Enron corporate collapse relating to the independence of auditors generally and, more specifically, the provision of non-audit services,[116] suggests that these services may undermine the independence of auditors and increase the likelihood of earnings manipulation. Here, the relational approach presents conflicting studies as to whether such a relation exists.

In Chapter 5's studies of the Enron corporate collapse (Autopsies of the Enron and Hastie Corporate Collapses Key Field No 2) which involved critical audit and auditor failure, a detailed study was undertaken in relation to both the following factors identified by commentators in the audit failure:

- independence[117]; and
- non-audit services.[118]

---

115 See discussion in section 8.2.2.2 above.

116 For a discussion of different approaches to the regulation of non-audit services, see OICU-IOSCO, Technical Committee and Emerging Markets Committee of the International Organization of Securities Commissions, *Survey on the Regulation of Non-Audit Services Provided by Auditors to Audited Companies*, March 2007, available at http://www.iosco.org/library/pubdocs/pdf/IOSCOPD241.pdf (accessed 4 March 2015).

117 See discussion in sections 5.2.4.1–5.2.4.2 above.

118 Ibid.

The principal governance variables related to the external or independent audit from Chapter 5 are examined below:

- **[ExtAudEarn] (+)**: External/Independent Audit Function: +7/87.50 *rprox* in section 9.2.3.3; and
- **[NonAuditS] (−)**: Non-Audit Services of External Auditor: −7/87.50 *rprox* in sections 9.2.3.2–3.

9.2.3.1 Review of independence, reputational constraints and auditor 'attachment' from the Enron corporate collapse

As noted in Chapter 5, for Coffee, independent auditors constitute, at least in theory, 'gatekeepers' who are also intended to reduce agency costs.[119] Risk of legal liability and damage to reputation should act as motivations for the auditor in performing its role.[120] Barton identified a large number of client defections from Andersen as the fallout from the Enron audit failure.[121] The relational approach then examined the relationship between auditor reputation and firm value. Callen and Morel found some loss in firm value because of the Andersen failure but these losses were less than expected.[122]

Coffee, in describing the possible causes of earnings manipulation, notes that one reason for 'audit failures' may be 'inherent limitations on the auditor's role or capacity'.[123] In such circumstances:

> generally accepted accounting principles empower corporate management to engage in earnings management by allocating them discretionary authority that the auditors cannot in effect reverse or challenge.[124]

---

[119] John C Coffee, 'The Acquiescent Gatekeeper: Reputational Intermediaries, Auditor Independence and the Governance of Accounting', Columbia Law and Economics Working Paper No 191 (May 2001), available at SSRN: http://ssrn.com/abstract=270944, 2.

[120] Ibid, 8.

[121] Jan Barton, 'Who Cares about Auditor Reputation?', available at SSRN: http://ssrn.com/abstract=436967, 22. See discussion in section 5.2.4.2 above.

[122] Jeffery L Callen and Mindy Morel, 'The Enron-Andersen Debacle: Do Equity Markets React to Auditor Reputation?', EFMA 2003 Helsinki Meetings (December 2002), available at SSRN: http://ssrn.com/abstract=341440, 11. See discussion in section 5.2.4.2 above.

[123] Coffee, above n 119, 5.

[124] Ibid (footnote omitted). The author cites P Rosenfeld, 'What Drives Earnings Management? Generally Accepted Accounting Principles' (2000) 190 *Journal of Accountancy* 106 (1 October 2000).

The implication here is that discretionary accounting principles which are not in the nature of mandatory rules for the treatment of accounting issues contribute to earnings manipulation.

Gillan and Martin[125] observed that the Andersen audit – where the firm undertook both the internal and external audit function – in effect required Andersen to review its own work with the consequent loss of independence.[126] Barrett was of the opinion that auditor 'attachment' – the pressure to give a clean audit opinion to retain existing business and foster new business – was already a problem for auditors.[127] He found that the Andersen 'integrated' audit strengthened the 'attachment' that Andersen already had with its client.[128] Barrett considered that the 'revolving door' practice whereby Enron hired many Andersen former employees contributed to a 'familiarity' between auditor and client with consequent uncritical acceptance of management assertions.[129]

Familiarity between auditor and client has been dealt with in Australia by the CLERP 9 reforms to the Corporations Act 2001.[130] Du Plessis *et al* describe the impetus for the CLERP 9 reforms as the collapses of Enron and WorldCom in the US and HIH Insurance Ltd in Australia[131] and undertake a detailed review of the CLERP 9 provisions relating to accounting and audit governance including the preceding Ramsay Report.[132] The CLERP 9 provisions include:

---

[125] See discussion in section 5.2.4.2 above.

[126] Stuart L Gillan and John D Martin, 'Financial Engineering, Corporate Governance, and the Collapse of Enron', U of Delaware Coll. of Bus. and Econ. Ctr. for Corp. Governance Working Paper No 2002-001 (November 2002), available at SSRN: http://ssrn.com/abstract=354040, 27.

[127] Matthew J Barrett, 'Enron and Andersen – What Went Wrong and Why Similar Audit Failures Could Happen Again', available at SSRN: http://ssrn.com/abstract=794831, 159. See discussion in section 5.2.4.2 above.

[128] Ibid, 160.

[129] Ibid, 161–2.

[130] Corporations Act 2001 (Cth). This Act is available at: http://www.austlii.edu.au/au/legis/cth/consol_act/ca2001172/index.html#s9 (accessed 4 March 2015).

[131] Jean Jacques du Plessis, Anil Hargovan and Mirko Bagaric, *Principles of Contemporary Corporate Governance*, 2nd edn, Cambridge: Cambridge University Press, 2011, pp 202–3.

[132] Ibid, chapter 8, especially sections 8.3–8.7 and Chapter 9. See Ian Ramsay, *Independence of Australian Company Auditors: Review of Current Australian Requirements and Proposals for Reform*, Report to the Minister for Financial Services and Regulation, Commonwealth of Australia, October 2001 (as printed in March 2002), accessed 4 March 2015 at http://archive.treasury.gov.au/contentitem.asp?ContentID=296.

- a general requirement for auditor independence – if a conflict of interest occurs and the auditor is aware that it exists, the auditor must take reasonable steps to ensure any conflict of interest ceases: s 324CA;[133]
- for this purpose, a conflict of interest situation means circumstances where the auditor is not capable of exercising objective and impartial judgement in relation to the conduct of the audit or where a reasonable person, with full knowledge of the relevant facts and circumstances would conclude the same – s 324CD;[134]
- a prohibition period of two years before an auditor can become an officer of the audit client if that person was a lead auditor or review auditor for the audit – s 324CJ;[135]
- a rotation period – if a person plays a significant role in the audit of a listed company for five successive financial years, the individual is not permitted to play a significant role in the audit for a later financial year unless the individual has not played a significant role in the audit for at least two successive financial years – s 324DA;[136] and
- in relation to non-audit services – the director's report for a listed company must include the details of amounts paid or payable for non-audit services, a statement whether the directors are satisfied that the provision of non-audit services by the auditor is compatible with the general standard of independence for auditors imposed by the Corporations Act and a statement of the directors' reasons for being satisfied that the non-audit services did not compromise the auditor independence requirements – s 300(11B).[137]

Given the last of these reforms, how do commentators treat non-audit services and the independence of the auditor?

9.2.3.2 Non-audit services

Again, a detailed examination in relation to non-audit services 'sanctioning' was undertaken in relation to the Enron corporate collapse.[138] Coffee, for one, found that the threat of removing non-audit services from the auditor

---

133 Corporations Act 2001, above n 130, s 324CA.
134 Ibid, s 324CD.
135 Ibid, s 324CJ.
136 Ibid, s 324DA.
137 Ibid, s 300(11B).
138 See discussion in section 5.2.4.2 above.

eroded the firm's reputational constraints.[139] The author also suggested that equity-based compensation for executives increased pressure on auditors to 'acquiesce in earnings management'.[140] Additional observations are now made here in relation to this factor.

In the case of non-audit services provided by accounting firms to their clients, Larcker and Richardson express the governance issue in terms of a decrease in independence owing to 'the risk of foregoing lucrative non-audit services'.[141] The authors found that provision of non-audit services is linked to accruals/earnings management for approximately 20 per cent of sample firms.[142] In respect of these sample firms, the authors identify their critical features to include:

- higher insider holdings;
- smaller board of directors (and audit committee); and
- lower percentage of independent board (and audit committee) members.[143]

Two of these factors – smaller boards and audit committees – pose a dilemma. These factors appear to be at odds with the findings noted above[144] that, while no concluded view can be reached, smaller boards and audit committees may reduce earnings manipulation. In the absence of further empirical evidence, it is possible that the other two features identified by Larcker and Richardson – higher inside equity ownership and lower board independence – may well have a more pronounced effect the smaller the relevant board or committee.

In a 2008 study in relation to non-audit services, Brown, Falaschetti and Orlando found that a negative relationship existed between non-audit

---

139 John C Coffee, 'Understanding Enron: It's About the Gatekeepers, Stupid', Columbia Law & Economics Working Paper No 207 (30 July, 2002), accessed 4 March 2015 at SSRN: http://ssrn.com/abstract=325240, 5–6 and 15–16.

140 Ibid, 18–19.

141 D F Larcker and S A Richardson, 'Corporate Governance, Fees for Non-audit Services and Accrual Choices' (April 2003), accessed 4 March 2015 at SSRN: http://ssrn.com/abstract=394441, 1.

142 Ibid, 25.

143 Ibid (format altered and bullet points added). For a discussion of the effects of banning non-audit services on financial reporting fraud, see Dain C Donelson, John M McInnis and Richard Mergenthaler, 'The Effect of Board Independence and Non-Audit Services on Financial Reporting Fraud' (29 August 2012), accessed 4 March 2015 at SSRN: http://ssrn.com/abstract=2138348.

144 See discussion in section 9.2.2 above.

services and earnings quality but that its effect was reduced by the effect of the market and, possibly, mandatory disclosure rules.[145]

Other studies find no such relationship as that identified by Larcker and Richardson or Brown *et al.* For Ruddock, Taylor and Taylor, increases in non-audit services do not 'on average' cause auditors to accept less conservative accounting.[146] Agrawal and Chadha, too, found that non-audit services were not related to the probability of earnings manipulation.[147] Thus, the results for the non-audit services factor are inconclusive in terms of earnings management. Despite this, detailed changes in relation to the provision of non-audit services were introduced by SOX[148] and consequent exchange listing rules such as the NYSE Final Rules.[149]

---

[145] James R Brown, Dino Falaschetti and Michael J Orlando, 'Auditor Independence and Earnings Quality: Evidence for Market Discipline vs. Sarbanes-Oxley Proscriptions', FSU College of Law, Law and Economics Paper No 07-33 (21 February 2008), accessed 4 March 2015 at SSRN: http://ssrn.com/abstract=940847, 1–2.

[146] C M S Ruddock, S J Taylor and S L Taylor, 'Non-Audit Services and Earnings Conservatism: Is Auditor Independence Impaired?' (April 2004), accessed 4 March 2015 at SSRN: http://ssrn.com/abstract=303343, 5 and 25.

[147] Agrawal and Chadha, above n 48, 4.

[148] SOX, above n 86, section 201 – Prohibition on external auditor for provision of non-audit services (as defined/listed) to issuer: Such services are defined to include:

(1) bookkeeping or other services related to the accounting records or financial statements of the audit client;
(2) financial information systems design and implementation;
. . .
(5) internal audit outsourcing services;
(6) management functions or human resources;
. . .
(8) legal services and expert services unrelated to the audit;. . .

Section 201 also provides that a firm may provide non-audit services, including tax services (excluding those listed above), only if the activity is approved in advance by the Audit Committee of the Issuer.

See also section 202 relating to preapproval – all auditing services and non-audit services provided to the Issuer by the auditor must be preapproved by the Audit Committee of the Issuer.

[149] NYSE Final Rules, above n 51, section 303A.07(b)(i)(A) Audit Committee Additional Requirements – 'The Audit Committee must have a written charter that addresses the Committee's purpose . . . to assist board oversight of the independent auditor's qualifications and independence'.

9.2.3.3 [ExtAudEarn] (+)[150] and [NonAuditS] (−)[151] variables relational effect paths

The **[ExtAudEarn] (+)** variable is a 'strong form' independence variable. The term 'strong form' seeks to express an independence status that is hypothesised to have a stronger monitoring effect than the independence factor present in the board and audit committee functions. The independence element on the board and audit committee comes from outside directors. But the independence element in **[ExtAudEarn] (+)** comes from a number of considerations. First is on account of the external auditor's familiarity with the financial operations and records of the company. Second is the mandatory status of the external audit in governance statutes like the Corporations Act.[152] Third is the significant guidance in relation to the external audit in governance codes.[153] Indeed, the independent/external audit was found to be a core feature of global and national listed governance codes combined.[154] Finally, the reputational constraints on the external auditor are hypothesised to have a significant effect.[155] Thus, the relational effect path of the **[ExtAudEarn] (+)** variable has a positive (+) directional marker that hypothesises a reduction in earnings management consequent on the external audit function.

Thus, the independence element in the **[ExtAudEarn] (+)** variable is hypothesised to have a stronger monitoring 'improvement' or 'enhancement' effect on Monitoring & Audit Factor No 5 (Internal and External/Audit Monitoring Quality) than **[BrdIndMon] (+)**[156] and **[AudIndMon] (+)**.[157] By contrast, the independence ingredient in these variables is outside-director-based which is hypothesised to be more open to management influence and less familiar with the company's financial affairs than the external auditor. For example, in the case of outside directors, the relational approach has hypothesised that there is a reduction in the flow of 'firm-specific' and 'manager-specific' information to the board

---

150 External/Independent Audit Function.

151 Non-Audit Services of External Auditor.

152 See, for example, Corporations Act 2001, above n 130, ss 301(1), 307, 307A, 307C, 308 and 309.

153 See Table 6.2, item 5.ii in section 6.2.2 above. See also discussion in section 6.2.3.1.5 above.

154 See discussion in section 6.8.1, item 5.ii above.

155 See discussion in section 5.2.4.2 above.

156 Board Independent Director: Executive Director Proportion – Monitoring Effect – see discussion in sections 7.3.2.1.1–7.3.2.1.2 above.

157 Audit Committee – Independence – Monitoring Effect – see discussion in sections 8.4.1–8.4.3 above.

and that outside directors have inferior information compared to inside directors.[158]

On this basis – and putting aside the strength of the effect – the zone of effect of the **[ExtAudEarn] (+)**[159] variable is hypothesised to extend to all governance factors except the overriding nature of Compliance Factor No 2 (as explained in section 2.6.2 above). Similarly to the **[BrdSkills] (+)** and **[BrdIndMon] (+)** variables, compliance with corporate governance and legal requirements on the company – which remain constant by the force of 'hard', 'soft' or 'hybrid' law[160] – is hypothesised not to be affected by the **[ExtAudEarn] (+)** variable. This gives rise to a coverage/rating of +7/87.50 *rprox* in the Coverage Table (Table 3.1) and the Relational Proximity Table (Table 3.2).

While not conclusive, to the extent that the above studies suggest that the independence of the external auditor is reduced in the direction of the inside management by the provision of non-audit services (even if tempered by 'market discipline' and 'disclosure mandates'), the direction of the relational effect path of the **[NonAuditS] (−)** variable will be negative (−) suggesting an increase in the probability of earnings management. Here, the predicted reduction in the independence ingredient leads to the hypothesis that the zone of effect of the **[NonAuditS] (−)** variable extends to all governance factors except Compliance Factor No 2 in the same manner – but opposite direction – as the **[ExtAudEarn] (+)**[161] variable above. **[ExtAudEarn] (+)** was, in turn, modelled on the **[BrdIndMon] (+)**[162] variable and the **[BrdSkills] (+)**[163] variable. This equates to a coverage/rating for the **[NonAuditS] (−)** variable of – 7/87.50 *rprox* in the Coverage Table (Table 3.1) and Relational Proximity Table (Table 3.2).

9.2.4 Summary and Conclusion of Empirical Studies Key Field No 4 in Chapter 10

Chapter 9 has examined the third set of studies in relation to the relational approach's over-arching purpose of the long-term efficiency and sustainability of the for-profit corporation. Instead of measures of firm operating performance and firm value, Chapter 9 has used as a proxy the

---

158 See discussion in section 7.3.2.1.3 above.

159 External/Independent Audit Function – see discussion in this section 9.2.3.3.

160 See discussion in section 6.1.3.1 above.

161 External/Independent Audit Function – see discussion in this section 9.2.3.3.

162 Board Independent Director: Executive Director Proportion – Monitoring Effect – see discussion in sections 7.3.2.1.1–7.3.2.1.2 above.

163 Board – Director Skills 'Mix' – see discussion in section 7.3.1.2.1 above.

probability of earnings manipulation or management. The chapter has presented relational effect paths for governance variables including the monitoring effect of the transparency and timing of reporting and the consequent reduction effect on the flow of information. Other governance variables examined include board and audit committee independence, time and financial expertise, duality in the CEO/chairperson roles and board and audit committee size effects on earnings management. The chapter reprised and expanded upon aspects of the Enron corporate collapse analysed in Chapter 5 to examine the earnings management effects of auditor independence, reputational constraints and auditor 'attachment' as well as the effects of non-audit services.

The following Chapter 10 examines the fourth and final part of the Empirical Studies Key Field No 4. Again, the relational approach reviews governance variables first introduced in Chapter 5's 'autopsies' of the Enron and Hastie corporate collapses. In particular, the chapter will examine the effects of firm-specific 'good' governance variables relating to executive, CEO and director compensation. Among these variables will be to examine the effects of director and management equity holdings, the level of director, CEO and executive compensation and the granting of short-term options to directors and executives.

10. Empirical studies Key Field No 4 (Part 4): 'Good' corporate governance and director, CEO and management compensation

10.1 OVERVIEW OF GOVERNANCE APPROACHES AND PURPOSE OF CHAPTER 10

The design, structure (including performance, incentives and shareholder 'say-on-pay'[1]) and development of director, CEO and management compensation was highlighted in the era of the GFC and continues today. The examination of the consequent effect on agency costs and firm governance of the compensation variable has been undertaken by commentators including, notably, Professor Bebchuk[2] and Professor Hill.[3]

In the relational approach, Chapter 10 highlights areas or studies of

---

[1] For a discussion of the US and Australian initiatives of advisory shareholder 'say-on-pay' legislation and its effect on firm value, see section 10.2.3.1 of this chapter 10.

[2] See, for example, Lucian Arye Bebchuk and Jesse M. Fried, 'Executive Compensation as an Agency Problem' (2003) 17 *Journal of Economic Perspectives* 71–92, accessed 5 March 2015 at SSRN: http://ssrn.com/abstract=364220; Lucian Arye Bebchuk and Yaniv Grinstein, 'Firm Expansion and CEO Pay', Harvard Law and Economics Discussion Paper No 533; Johnson School Research Paper No 27-06 (August 2007), accessed 5 March 2015 at SSRN: http://ssrn.com/abstract=838245 and Lucian A Bebchuk and Jesse M Fried, 'Paying for Long-Term Performance' (2010) 158 *University of Pennsylvania Law Review* 1915–59; Harvard Law and Economics Discussion Paper No 658 (1 December 2009), accessed 5 March 2015 at SSRN: http://ssrn.com/abstract=1535355.

[3] See, for example, Jennifer G Hill, 'Regulating Executive Remuneration: International Developments in the Post-Scandal Era' (2006) 3 *European Company Law* 64; Vanderbilt Law and Economics Research Paper No 06-06, accessed 5 March 2015 at SSRN: http://ssrn.com/abstract=887944 and Jennifer G Hill, 'New Trends in the Regulation of Executive Remuneration' in R P Austin and A Y Bilski (eds), *Directors In Troubled Times*, pp 100–23, Ross Parsons Centre of Commercial, Corporate and Taxation Law, 2009; Sydney Law School Research Paper No 10/22; Vanderbilt Law and Economics Research Paper No 10-05;

particular relevance to director, CEO and executive compensation and incentives in the context of the Enron corporate collapse discussed in Chapter 5. In Chapter 5, the compensation and incentives variables were examined by a review of aspects of the undermining of director independence[4] and the risk management[5] function by equity holdings and share options and the use of 'off-balance sheet' entities to mask debt and executive payments.[6] Attention will also refocus on the effect of CEO, executive and director compensation and incentives on the practice of earnings management[7] by Enron including the effects of short-term share options.[8]

10.1.1 The Governance Issue – The Director/CEO Compensation Levels Variable: [DirCEO$] (+/−)

The governance issue relating to director compensation is summarised by the International Organization of Securities Commissions ('IOSCO') in the following terms:

> [t]he actual level of compensation may be relevant to assure, on the one hand, that qualified candidates are attracted to the job, but also, on the other, to make sure that an excessive level of remuneration is not impairing board members' objectivity, *e.g.* by making them captive to the interests of those who play a significant role in the nomination (or re-nomination) of board members or determination of remuneration packages.[9]

The argument is, of course, also extended to CEO and executive compensation. Indeed Dent, in stating that the reality of corporate governance lies in 'CEO domination' rather than any other model, considers that the 'overwhelming' evidence is that 'most boards are passive, dominated by CEOs who exert their power in their own interests'.[10] Again, Dent gives

---

ECGI – Law Working Paper No 142/2010 (7 February 2010), accessed 5 March 2015 at SSRN: http://ssrn.com/abstract=1549429.

4 See discussion in section 5.2.2.1.1 above.

5 See discussion in section 5.2.2.1.2 above.

6 See discussion in section 5.2.3.1 above.

7 See discussion in section 5.2.3.2 above.

8 See discussion in section 5.2.3.2.1 above.

9 Technical Committee of the International Organisation of Securities Commissions (IOSCO) in consultation with the OECD, *Board Independence of Listed Companies, Final Report*, March 2007, accessed 5 March 2015 at http://www.iosco.org/library/pubdocs/pdf/IOSCOPD238.pdf ('IOSCO Report'), 26.

10 G W Dent, 'Academics in Wonderland: The Team Production and Director Primacy Models of Corporate Governance', Case Legal Studies Research

reasons including the CEO's role in recommending directors for board vacancies, the view that (purported) 'outside' directors who are themselves CEOs 'defer' to one another as a reciprocal practice and loyalty by outside directors to the person who nominated them.[11] Among the costs of this domination, for Dent, is excessive management compensation,[12] 'lavish' executive perquisites and 'design flaws' in executive pay.[13]

More recently in 2010, Frydman and Jenter examine CEO compensation and find the evidence consistent with two explanations – managerial power[14] and competitive forces[15] – but that neither provides a full explanation for the growth in CEO pay levels.[16] Despite Dent's views, Larcker and Tayan include among their 'Seven Myths of Corporate Governance' that US 'CEOs are systematically overpaid' and that 'There is No "Pay for Performance" in CEO Compensation'.[17]

10.1.2 Approaches to Governance of Compensation

How, then, is the governance aspect of compensation approached? Hill and Yablon investigate the governance consequences of 'positional conflict' and performance-based remuneration[18] and give an overview of three approaches to the issue:

Paper No 07-21 (June 2007), accessed 5 March 2015 at SSRN: http://ssrn.com/abstract=995186, 14 of 72 (footnote omitted).

[11] Ibid.

[12] For a discussion of US reforms in relation to executive compensation, see Kenneth M Rosen, 'Who Killed Katie Couric? And Other Tales From The World Of Executive Compensation Reform' (2008) 76 *Fordham Law Review* 2907, accessed 5 March 2015 at SSRN: http://ssrn.com/abstract=1125295.

[13] Dent, above n 10,15 of 72 (footnotes omitted).

[14] Carola Frydman and Dirk Jenter, 'CEO Compensation', Rock Center for Corporate Governance at Stanford University Working Paper No 77 (19 March 2010), accessed 5 March 2015 at SSRN: http://ssrn.com/abstract=1582232, 18.

[15] Ibid, 20–22.

[16] Ibid, 22.

[17] David F Larcker and Brian Tayan, 'Seven Myths of Corporate Governance', Rock Center for Corporate Governance at Stanford University Closer Look Series: Topics, Issues and Controversies in Corporate Governance No CGRP-16 (1 June 2011), accessed 5 March 2015 at SSRN: http://ssrn.com/abstract=1856869, 2–3. For the use of 'relative performance evaluation' awards (such as stock and cash) in executive compensation contracts, see J Carr Bettis, John M Bizjak, Jeffrey L Coles and Brian Young, 'The Presence, Value, and Incentive Properties of Relative Performance Evaluation in Executive Compensation Contracts' (February 8, 2014), accessed 23 April 2015 at SSRN: http://ssrn.com/abstract=2392861.

[18] Jennifer G Hill and C M Yablon, 'Corporate Governance and Executive Remuneration: Rediscovering Managerial Positional Conflict', Vanderbilt Law

> [t]he first of these is self-constraint (with judicial enforcement) via fiduciary duties.
> The second technique involves eliminating or controlling conflicts of interest through corporate governance techniques, such as the use of independent directors, remuneration committees and greater control by shareholders . . .
> The final way of dealing with the problem has been to accept the existence of managerial self-interest, but to try to align that self-interest with the interests of shareholders.[19]

Hill and Yablon point to the NYSE Final Rules[20] as an example of the second method.[21] The Rules require the board to be comprised of a 'majority' of independent directors to 'increase the quality of board oversight and lessen the possibility of damaging conflicts of interest'.[22] In addition, in the case of board subcommittees, the Rules prescribe for listed companies a 'compensation committee'[23] on which only independent directors may sit. A review of corporate governance codes in table-form, including these features, was presented in Chapter 6. For the third 'alignment' method, Hill and Yablon point to performance-based and option-based compensation for management.[24]

---

and Economics Research Paper No 03-02, accessed 5 March 2015 at SSRN: http://ssrn.com/abstract=375240.

19 Ibid, 13 (formatting altered). An examination of Hill and Yablon's first approach, directors' fiduciary duties, is beyond the scope of this first stage of the relational approach.

20 New York Stock Exchange, *Final NYSE Corporate Governance Rules* ('NYSE Final Rules'), approved by SEC 4 November 2003 (except s 303A.08) and 30 June 2003 (s 303A.08). The Rules (as amended from time to time) comprise section 303A.00 of the NYSE Listed Company Manual. See section 303A.00 Corporate Governance Standards (approved 25 November 2009), available at http://nysemanual.nyse.com/lcm/ (accessed 5 March 2015). Subsequent amendments have been made to:

- Section 303A.00 – Corporate Governance Standards (approved 22 August 2013)
- Section 303A.02 – Corporate Governance Standards (approved 11 January 2013)
- Section 303A.05 – Corporate Governance Standards (approved 11 January 2013)
- Section 303A.07 – Audit Committee Additional Requirements (approved 22 August 2013)

These Rule amendments are available at http://nysemanual.nyse.com/lcm/ (accessed 5 March 2015).

21 Hill and Yablon, above n 18, 14.

22 NYSE Final Rules, above n 20, s 303A.01 Independent Directors and Commentary.

23 NYSE Final Rules, above n 20, s 303A.05(a) Compensation Committee.

24 Hill and Yablon, above n 18, 15. For a discussion of the agent-principal theory in relation to CEO incentives, see Joseph Dunning, 'Agency Theory

Chapters 6[25] and 7[26] identified director independence as a 'core' or 'central' governance variable which is considered vital to the board's function of the monitoring of the CEO and management. The enhancement of (or reduction in) the monitoring of the CEO and management will be demonstrated to be an important end or intervening effect of the variables examined in this chapter. Thus, the principal governance variables identified in Table 2.1 relating to director independence, the level of director/CEO compensation and equity and option holdings are:

- **[AudIndMon] (+)** – Audit Committee – Independence – Monitoring Effect, +7/87.50 *rprox*;[27]
- **[DirCEO$] (+/−)** – Director/CEO Compensation Levels, +/−7/87.50 *rprox*;[28]
- **[AudShortOpts] (−)** – Audit Committee – Short Term Options Granted to Outside Directors – Reduction in Monitoring Effect, −7/87.50 *rprox*;[29]
- **[BrdIndMon] (+)** – Board Independent Director: Executive Director Proportion – Monitoring Effect, +7/87.50 *rprox*;[30]
- **[EqOptIncent] (+)** – Equity/Option Plans and Holdings of Directors/ Executives – Incentive/'Alignment' Effect (excludes short-term options), +7/87.50 *rprox*;[31]
- **[EqOptEntrch] (−)** – Equity/Option Plans and Holdings of Directors/ Executives – 'Entrenchment' Effect (excludes short-term options), −7/87.50 *rprox*;[32] and
- **[ShortTOpts] (−)** – Short-Term Option Holdings/Plans of Directors and Executives, −7/87.50 *rprox*.[33]

In Chapter 5, many commentators pointed to the undermining of director independence as central to the Enron collapse. Authors such as Branson identified 'outrageously high' directors' fees and consulting contracts for

---

and CEO Incentives' (23 January 2012), available at SSRN: http://ssrn.com/abstract=2034618.

25 See discussion in section 6.8.1 above.
26 See discussion in section 7.3.2.1 above.
27 See discussion in section 8.4.3 above.
28 See discussion in section 10.2.4 below.
29 See discussion in section 10.2.5.1 below.
30 See discussion in sections 7.3.2.1.1–7.3.2.1.2 above.
31 See discussion in section 10.2.4 below.
32 Ibid.
33 See discussion in section 10.2.5.1 below.

directors[34] as undermining director independence and thus the monitoring of management. An alternative – and more scrutinised – variable argued to undermine independence was the equity holdings and share options of supposedly outside independent directors.[35]

10.1.3 Alignment of Performance, Option Compensation and the Purpose of Chapter 10

This Chapter 10, in focusing on the risk of agency costs for outside shareholders, identifies and examines various governance effects which are perceived to flow from the 'alignment' method identified by Hill and Yablon.[36] The application of the relevant principles in the context of the Enron corporate collapse was examined in Chapter 5. Here, the corporate governance ramifications of director, CEO and executive compensation will be examined with respect to governance variables including:

- compensation effects on the level/quality of monitoring and firm value and operating performance;
- the possible connection between firm size and director/executive compensation; and
- compensation effects on governance through reputational constraints.

The chapter will conclude with a summary of the recurring themes and tensions in the governance effects of director, CEO and management compensation.

10.2 COMPENSATION, THE LEVEL/QUALITY OF MONITORING AND FIRM VALUE AND OPERATING PERFORMANCE

In this section, the relational approach examines the perceived governance effects in either direction of Hill and Yablon's 'alignment' method

---

[34] Douglas M Branson, 'Enron – When All Systems Fail: Creative Destruction or Roadmap to Corporate Governance Reform?' (2003) 48 *Villanova Law Review* 989; Villanova Law/Public Policy Research Paper No 2003-13, accessed 5 March 2015 at SSRN: http://ssrn.com/abstract=473205, 1003. See discussion in section 5.2.2.1 above.

[35] See discussion in sections 5.2.2.1–5.2.2.1.1 above.

[36] Hill and Yablon, above n 18, 13.

of compensation.[37] The level of director and CEO compensation levels is represented by the **[DirCEO$] (+/−)**[38] variable.

Looking ahead in the case of the proportion of equity held by inside directors and/or management, little can be predicted in terms of benefit for outside shareholders on account of two counterbalancing effects of this variable. The positive 'incentive alignment' effect is reflected in the **[EqOptIncent] (+)**[39] variable and the negative 'entrenchment' effect is represented by the **[EqOptEntrch] (−)**[40] variable.[41] In addition, the examination highlights a number of studies where granting options pursuant to management and/or director incentive schemes is found to increase the likelihood of earnings manipulation or 'management'.

10.2.1 Proportion of Insider/Management Equity Ownership – 'Incentive Alignment' Effect Countered by 'Entrenchment' Effect

Commentator autopsies of the Enron corporate collapse[42] led by Gillan and Martin pointed accusingly to deficiencies in the standard of monitoring of management as a result of both director share and option holdings[43] and the Enron compensation policy[44] itself. Gordon, too, identified the undermining of director independence as a monitoring variable as a result of substantial share ownership, share options and excessive director compensation 'since a director's sharp questioning of senior management may led (sic) to subtle pressures against his/her renomination'.[45]

---

37 See discussion in section 10.1.2 above.

38 Director/CEO Compensation Levels. See discussion in section 10.2.4 below.

39 Equity/Option Plans and Holdings of Directors/Executives – Incentive/'Alignment' Effect (excludes short-term options). See discussion in section 10.2.4 below.

40 Equity/Option Plans and Holdings of Directors/Executives – 'Entrenchment' Effect (excludes short-term options). See discussion in section 10.2.4 below.

41 The terms 'incentive alignment' effect and 'entrenchment' effect are taken from O Fuerst and S Kang, 'Corporate Governance, Expected Operating Performance, and Pricing', accessed 5 March 2015 at SSRN: http://ssrn.com/abstract=141357, 6–7.

42 See discussion in section 5.2.2.1.1 above.

43 Stuart L Gillan and John D Martin, 'Financial Engineering, Corporate Governance, and the Collapse of Enron', U of Delaware Coll. of Bus. and Econ. Ctr. for Corp. Governance Working Paper No 2002-001 (November 2002), accessed 5 March 2015 at SSRN: http://ssrn.com/abstract=354040, 23–4. See discussion in section 5.2.2.1.1 above.

44 Ibid, 24.

45 Jeffrey N Gordon, 'What Enron Means for the Management and Control of the Modern Business Corporation: Some Initial Reflections' (2002) 69 *University*

In the study by Fuerst and Kang above,[46] the authors also examined the degree of insider/management ownership of shares in an attempt to describe the effects of that ownership on the interests of outside shareholders. The authors rely on the work of Morck, Shleifer and Vishny to explain that, initially, such ownership assists to *align* the positions of insiders and outsiders, but that, after a certain point, increasing the size of management ownership may harm outsider interests.[47]

These two distinct effects find traction in the Enron context. There, Gordon also tells us that while share options may enhance the alignment of management and outside shareholder interests, 'they provide perverse managerial incentives'[48] with the result that:

> managers will be strongly tempted to produce the financial results the market 'expects' through manipulation of financial results.[49]

In a 2007 study, Kumar and Sivaramakrishnan similarly find the degree of board independence to have an 'ambiguous' effect[50] on firm value where board equity ownership exists.[51]

10.2.2 Studies Finding Positive Relationship Between Compensation and Firm Value and/or Operating Performance for [DirCEO$] (+/−)

In favour of the relationship, Daines, Nair and Kornhauser examine the relationship between CEO compensation and skill level as measured by firm performance – 'in perpetuating good firm performance and

---

of Chicago Law Review 1233 (Summer 2002), accessed 5 March 2015 at SSRN: http://ssrn.com/abstract=305343, 12. See discussion in section 5.2.2.1.1 above.

[46] See discussion in section 7.3.2.1.5 above.

[47] Fuerst and Kang, above n 41, 6–7 (emphasis added). The authors cite R Morck, A Shleifer and R W Vishny, 'Management Ownership and Corporate Performance: An Empirical Analysis' (1988) 20 *Journal of Financial Economics* 293–316.

[48] Jeffrey N Gordon, 'Governance Failures of the Enron Board and the New Information Order of Sarbanes-Oxley', Columbia Law and Economics Working Paper No 216; Harvard Law and Economics Discussion Paper No 416 (March 2003), accessed 5 March 2015 at SSRN: http://ssrn.com/abstract=391363, 5. See discussion in section 5.2.2.1.1 above.

[49] Ibid.

[50] Praveen Kumar and Shiva Sivaramakrishnan, 'Who Monitors the Monitor? The Effect of Board Independence on Executive Compensation and Firm Value' (16 January 2007), accessed 5 March 2015 at SSRN: http://ssrn.com/abstract=988543, 23.

[51] Ibid.

in reversing or turning around poor firm performance'.[52] The authors find important evidence linking CEO pay to firm performance, but this requires two preconditions – that the compensation be performance-based and that block-holder monitoring exist.[53] Hanlon, Rajgopal and Shevlin similarly find a significant positive correlation between the granting of share options to executives and future firm operating performance, a result the authors considered to be 'consistent with the incentive alignment perspective'.[54]

In a 2007 study by Bhagat and Bolton,[55] the shareholding of directors was one variable that 'is significantly positively correlated with better contemporaneous and subsequent *operating* performance'.[56] The director shareholding governance variable was also positively related to 'disciplinary management turnover' in times of poor performance.[57]

Bhagat and, this time, Carey and Elson investigate the relationship between firm performance and outside director shareholdings.[58] The authors found an association (not necessarily causative) between substantial director shareholdings and improved performance.[59] Important for the relational approach's purposes in this section relating to the level of monitoring, the authors conclude that there is a 'probable correlation' between substantial director shareholdings and improvements in the oversight of management.[60]

Finally, Perry investigates the relationship between the incentive compensation of independent directors, board monitoring of management

---

52 R Daines, V B Nair and L A Kornhauser, 'The Good, the Bad and the Lucky: CEO Pay and Skill', Univ of Pennsylvania Institute for Law and Economics, Research Paper Series (August 2005), accessed 5 March 2015 at SSRN: http://ssrn.com/abstract=622223, 4 and 27.

53 Ibid, 27.

54 M Hanlon, S Rajgopal and T J Shevlin, 'Are Executive Stock Options Associated with Future Earnings?', JAE Boston Conference, October 2002 (20 December 2002), accessed 5 March 2015 at SSRN: http://ssrn.com/abstract=318101, 41.

55 See discussion in section 7.3.1.2 above.

56 Sanjai Bhagat and Brian Bolton, 'Corporate Governance and Firm Performance' (June 2007), accessed 5 March 2015 at SSRN: http://ssrn.com/abstract=1017342, 5 (emphasis in original).

57 Ibid, 6.

58 Sanjai Bhagat, Dennis C Carey and Charles M Elson, 'Director Ownership, Corporate Performance, and Management Turnover' (31 December 1998), accessed 5 March 2015 at SSRN: http://ssrn.com/abstract=134488, 15–16.

59 Ibid, 15.

60 Ibid, 16.

and CEO turnover.[61] The author finds that where independent directors are entitled to 'incentive compensation', monitoring of the board (measured by the probability of 'CEO turnover') increases as firm performance falls.[62] The author, in concluding that equity-incentive plans align board and shareholder interests, observes that 'the likelihood of a firm adopting a stock-based incentive plan for directors is positively related to the fraction of independent directors on the board and institutional ownership'.[63] That Perry should conclude that monitoring quality was linked to independent director incentives is, of course, no surprise given the discussion in Chapter 7. In this respect Fernandes, in a study further described in the next section, concludes that:

> [t]hese results suggest that to foster the board of directors' effective monitoring role, special attention needs to be paid to the role, quality and integrity of their non-executive directors. In particular, their real independence should be guaranteed.[64]

Thus, for Perry and Fernandes, the independence of directors is an important precondition in equity incentive compensation.

10.2.3 Studies Finding No or Negative Relationship Between Compensation and Firm Value and/or Operating Performance for [DirCEO$] (+/−)

Despite the preceding observation, the perceived link between executive compensation and firm value and/or operating profit is rejected by the study by Fernandes. For Fernandes, who investigates the relationship between firm performance, independence of the board and executive compensation in Portugal,[65] the level of compensation is linked to firm size but not firm performance[66] and increases in the proportion of non-executive directors increase compensation levels.[67] While concerned with

---

[61] T Perry, 'Incentive Compensation for Outside Directors and CEO Turnover', presented at Tuck-JFE Contemporary Corporate Governance Conference (June 2000), available at SSRN: http://ssrn.com/abstract=236033.

[62] Ibid, 2 and 24.

[63] Ibid, 24.

[64] Nuno G Fernandes, 'Board Compensation and Firm Performance: The Role of "Independent" Board Members' (December 2005), ECGI – Finance Working Paper No 104/2005, accessed 5 March 2015 at SSRN: http://ssrn.com/abstract=830244, 2. See also 17.

[65] Ibid.

[66] Ibid, 2 and 17.

[67] Ibid.

firm value rather than operating performance, Brick, Palia and Wang find no relationship between firm value and the level of CEO compensation.[68]

In a 2007 study, however, Cremers, Bebchuk and Peyer find a negative relationship between 'CEO centrality' and firm value.[69] The authors define 'CEO centrality' as the relative importance of the CEO in the corporation's upper management. This is measured by the 'CEO's pay slice' or 'CPS' being the percentage of the total compensation of the top five executives paid to the CEO.[70] The authors give various explanations for the negative relationship between CEO centrality and firm value but, in 'governance' terms of the agency costs identified in Chapter 4, they suggest the possibility that this points to agency problems.[71]

The authors also describe other results which 'might reflect governance problems' including those relating to acquisition decisions.[72] Thus, high CPS appears to be harmful to the long-term efficiency and sustainability of the corporation in the case of acquisitions.

In another study,[73] also concerned with CPS, the authors find that CPS 'has been increasing over the past decade' and that high CPS is also indicative of weaker shareholder protection, higher management entrenchment and CEO/chairperson duality.[74] Conversely, CPS falls with increases in 'insiders' on the Board.

10.2.3.1 Say-on-Pay shareholder voting

The 'Say-on-Pay' legislative initiative in the United States 'does not limit executive compensation but requires a non-binding shareholder vote on it' and the Australian position, known as the 'two-strikes approach' is similar but with an important qualification.[75] The Australian Say-On-Pay

---

[68] Ivan E Brick, Darius Palia and Chia-Jane Wang, "Simultaneous Estimation of CEO Compensation, Leverage, and Board Characteristics on Firm Value", unpublished working paper, AFA 2006 Boston Meetings Paper (March 2005), 5.

[69] Martijn Cremers, Lucian Arye Bebchuk, and Urs C Peyer, 'CEO Centrality', Harvard Law and Economics Discussion Paper No 601 (December 2007, Revised May 2008), accessed 5 March 2015 at SSRN: http://ssrn.com/abstract=1030107, 1. See discussion in section 7.3.2.1.1 above.

[70] Ibid, 1.

[71] Ibid, 2.

[72] Ibid, 3.

[73] Lucian Arye Bebchuk, Martijn Cremers and Urs C Peyer, 'Pay Distribution in the Top Executive Team', Harvard Law and Economics Discussion Paper No 574 (February 2007), available at SSRN: http://ssrn.com/abstract=964303.

[74] Ibid, 2.

[75] See Jie Cai and Ralph A Walkling, 'Shareholders' Say on Pay: Does it Create Value?', Drexel College of Business Research Paper No 2008-06 (February 2008), accessed 5 March 2015 at SSRN: http://ssrn.com/abstract=1030925, 3.

regime is also an advisory/non-binding shareholder vote on the company's 'remuneration report'. The directors' report for listed companies must include the matters set out in section 300A of the Corporations Act 2001.[76] The matters in subsection (1) of section 300A must be included in the directors' report under the heading 'remuneration report': section 300A(1A). At a listed company's Annual General Meeting (AGM), a resolution that the remuneration report be adopted must be put to the vote: section 250R(2). The vote on the resolution is advisory only and does not bind the directors or the company: section 250R(3).

The Corporations Act was amended by the Corporations Amendment (Improving Accountability on Director and Executive Remuneration) Act 2011 (Cth) to provide for a voting procedure relating to the remuneration report. If an advisory shareholder vote on the remuneration report receives 25 per cent of the vote against adoption of the report, then the notice of the AGM to members the following year must state this and state that a 'spill resolution' for the re-election of directors will be put at the AGM: section 249L(2). At this later AGM, if the vote on the adoption of the remuneration report again receives 25 per cent of the vote against the adoption of the resolution, then section 250V will apply: section 250U. Under section 250V, a 'spill resolution' must be put at the later AGM that another meeting of members must be held within 90 days (the 'spill meeting') and that all the company's directors cease to hold office immediately before the end of the spill meeting: section 250V(1). If the spill resolution is passed (that is, by a simple majority), then the spill meeting must be held within 90 days: section 250W(2). If the company does not hold the spill meeting within 90 days, then each person who

---

The Australian 'two-strikes approach' was adopted from recommendations of the Productivity Commission. See Australian Government, Productivity Commission, *Executive Remuneration in Australia*, Productivity Commission Inquiry Report No 49, 19 December 2009. See especially, section 9.3, 'Elevating the consequences of a significant "no" vote', pp 294–301 and section 11, 'The reform package', Box 11.2, preliminary Discussion Draft Recommendation No 15, available at http://http://www.pc.gov.au/inquiries/completed/executive-remuneration/report/executive-remuneration-report.pdf (accessed 5 March 2015).

For the background to amendments to the Corporations Act relating to disclosure and reporting of executive remuneration, see Australian Government, Corporations and Markets Advisory Committee (CAMAC), Executive Remuneration, Report, April 2011, accessed 5 March 2015 at http://www.camac.gov.au/camac/camac.nsf/byHeadline/PDFFinal+Reports+2011/$file/Executive_remuneration_report_April11.pdf.

[76] Corporations Act 2001 (Cth) accessed 5 March 2015 at http://www.austlii.edu.au/au/legis/cth/consol_act/ca2001172/.

is a director at the end of the 90 days commits a strict liability offence: sections 250W(5)–(6).

There is some suggestion that the two-strikes procedure could be used by shareholders dissatisfied with performance or governance issues apart from remuneration matters. The first company to experience the two-strikes procedure in Australia was Penrice Soda Holdings Limited. It received two strikes against its remuneration report even though senior executives had not received compensation increases for over two years.[77] The company's chairman, David Trebeck, instead alluded that the vote was directed towards the company's falling profitability, increasing debt and recent losses.[78] At the same general meeting, the shareholders voted against the re-election of one of the non-executive directors, John Hirst.[79] The company announced a restructuring one day before the spill meeting in January 2013 which included an up-coming closure of one of the company's chemical facilities that would be replaced by importing cheaper soda ash for its operations.[80] The company's largest shareholder, London City Equities (LCE), nominated three directors for the spill meeting.[81]

Despite this, other commentators have rejected the idea that the two-strikes policy will act generally as the 'lightning rod' for shareholder dissatisfaction that the chairman had suggested stating that 'the average vote for incumbent directors facing re-election was 95 per cent'.[82] In the end, the chairman and another non-executive director, Andrew Fletcher, were re-elected, each receiving about 78 per cent of the vote.[83] The three

---

[77] Paul Garvey, 'Penrice investors strike again on pay', *The Australian*, 31 October 2012 accessed 5 March 2015 at http://www.theaustralian.com.au/business/companies/penrice-investors-strice-again-on-pay/story-fn91v9q3-1226507014689.

[78] Ibid.

[79] Sally Rose, 'Second strike not about remuneration says Penrice chair', *Australian Financial Review*, 1 November 2012, accessed 5 March 2015 at http://www.afr.com/f/free/markets/capital/cfo/second_strike_not_about_remuneration_uabR7LX3UapdG8LFsO2CqM.

[80] Damon Kitney, 'Penrice chair stares down strike force', *The Australian*, January 24, 2013, accessed 5 March 2015 at http://www.theaustralian.com.au/business/companies/penrice-chair-stares-down-strike-force/story-fn91v9q3-122656041 3992.

[81] Ibid.

[82] Adele Ferguson, 'Two strikes restore fizz for investors', *Sydney Morning Herald*, 25 January 2013, accessed 5 March 2015 at http://www.smh.com.au/business/two-strikes-restore-fizz-for-investors-20130124-2d9mn.html.

[83] Philip Wen, 'Axe two-strikes rule, Penrice directors say', *Sydney Morning Herald*, 25 January 2013, accessed 5 March 2015 at http://www.smh.com.au/business/axe-twostrikes-rule-penrice-directors-say-20130125-2dbam.html.

LCE-nominated candidates failed to be elected, each receiving approximately 25 per cent of the vote on the (separate) resolutions for their election.[84]

Is Say-on-Pay voting an effective governance tool? Cai and Walkling identify the opposing camps on the effectiveness of Say-on-Pay voting:

> [p]roponents argue that the bill will increase shareholder democracy and align owner-manager interests. Opponents argue it will usurp power that is best left to the management and boards of specific firms.[85]

Indeed, the relational approach describes below that the governance outcome for Say-on-Pay regimes may vary depending on factors such as:

- the level of CEO compensation;
- the degree of entrenchment of the management; and
- the form of the Say-on-Pay regime relating to whether the vote is advisory, unconditionally binding or only conditionally binding.

In their primary experiment, Cai and Walkling found that there was improvement in firm value for firms with abnormally high CEO compensation.[86] Thus, on this view, the effective sphere of operation of Say-on-Pay regimes is limited to firms with a compensation regime which is already displaying governance problems as described in the following paragraph. However, Cai and Walkling divide the results according to the level of firm governance with no effect expected on highly entrenched managements.[87] This view would again exclude from the effective sphere of operation Say-on-Pay regimes where they are needed most.

Larcker, Ormazabal and Taylor examined market reaction to regulation initiatives relating to executive pay (including 'Say-on-Pay')

---

[84] Ibid.

[85] Cai and Walkling, above n 75, 36. For recent support of shareholder voting in relation to Say-on-Pay, see Paul H Edelman, Randall S Thomas and Robert B Thompson, 'Shareholder Voting in an Age of Intermediary Capitalism' (2014) *Southern California Law Review*, forthcoming; European Corporate Governance Institute (ECGI) – Law Working Paper No 246/2014; Vanderbilt Law and Economics Research Paper No 14-9 (27 August 2014), accessed 5 March 2015 at SSRN: http://ssrn.com/abstract=2401746.

[86] Cai and Walkling, above n 75, 36.

[87] Ibid.

and found an 'insignificant reaction'.[88] However, the authors then found 'that capping or regulating executive pay will result in less efficient contracts and negatively affect shareholder wealth in these firms'.[89]

As noted above, 'Say-on-Pay' in its US form comprises a 'non-binding' or 'advisory' vote by shareholders in relation to the company's executive pay programme.[90] Citing the preceding study by Larcker, Ormazabal and Taylor, Larcker and (this time) Tayan conclude in a 2011 paper that Say-on-Pay may likely harm firm value.[91] Indeed, Bainbridge echoes the words of Roberta Romano to label the 2010 Dodd-Frank US Say-on-Pay provisions as 'quack corporate governance' in a highly critical review.[92]

While the above relates to US-style 'advisory' or 'non-binding' Say-on-Pay shareholder voting, other studies have sought to model different

---

[88] David F Larcker, Gaizka Ormazabal and Daniel J Taylor, 'The Market Reaction to Corporate Governance Regulation', (2011) 101(2) *Journal of Financial Economics* 431–448, 433; Rock Center for Corporate Governance at Stanford University Working Paper Series No 82 (October 14, 2010).

[89] Ibid.

[90] Larcker and Tayan, above n 17, 3.

[91] Ibid, 4 (footnote omitted). See also James F Cotter, Alan R Palmiter and Randall S Thomas, 'The First Year of "Say on Pay" Under Dodd-Frank: An Empirical Analysis and Look Forward' (2013) 81(3) *George Washington Law Review* 967; Vanderbilt Law and Economics Research Paper No. 12-32; Wake Forest Univ Legal Studies Paper No. 2220259, (February 17, 2013), accessed 23 April 2015 at SSRN: http://ssrn.com/abstract=2162957; Randall S Thomas and Christoph Van der Elst, 'The International Scope of Say on Pay', ECGI – Law Working Paper No. #227; Vanderbilt Law and Economics Research Paper No.13-22 (September 2013), accessed 23 April 2015 at SSRN: http://ssrn.com/abstract=2307510 and Randall S Thomas and Christoph Van der Elst, "Say on Pay Around the World", Vanderbilt Law and Economics Research Paper 14-10. (January 20, 2014), accessed 23 April 2015 at SSRN: http://ssrn.com/abstract=2401761.

[92] Stephen M Bainbridge, 'Dodd-Frank: Quack Federal Corporate Governance Round II', UCLA School of Law, Law-Econ Research Paper No 10-12 (7 September 2010), accessed 5 March 2015 at SSRN: http://ssrn.com/abstract=1673575, 35. For an overview of the seven principal provisions of the Dodd-Frank Act, see Stephen M Bainbridge, 'The Corporate Governance Provisions of Dodd-Frank', UCLA School of Law, Law-Econ Research Paper No 10-14 (27 October 2010), accessed 5 March 2015 at SSRN: http://ssrn.com/abstract=1698898. See also John C Coffee, 'The Political Economy of Dodd-Frank: Why Financial Reform Tends to be Frustrated and Systemic Risk Perpetuated' (2012) 97 *Cornell Law Review* 1019; Columbia Law and Economics Working Paper No 414 (9 January 2012), accessed 5 March 2015 at SSRN: http://ssrn.com/abstract=1982128.

Say-on-Pay regimes. Göx, Imhof and Kunz[93] distinguish between three scenarios. First is the advisory/non-binding shareholder vote.[94] The second form is unconditionally binding 'where shareholders can reject the CEO's bonus regardless of the project's performance'.[95] The third form is conditional 'where shareholders vote on the bonus proposal only in case of poor performance while having no say on the bonus in case of project success'.[96] The authors find that *advisory* voting does not reduce executive compensation levels. By contrast, *unconditionally* binding shareholder voting does reduce such remuneration – but with a negative effect on firm profit.[97]

Göx, Imhof and Kunz found that *conditionally* binding voting avoided these problems.[98] Thus, for the authors, *conditionally* binding voting – dependent on performance or project success – both reduces executive compensation in times of poor performance and avoids distorting CEO investment incentives.

10.2.3.2 Independence and the level of CEO compensation

It was observed above that, for Fernandes, increases in the proportion of non-executive directors increase executive compensation levels in Portugal.[99] What is the state of this relationship in Anglo-American corporate governance?

The link between CEO compensation levels and independence of the Board was examined recently by Guthrie, Sokolowsky and Wan.[100] The authors examine an earlier 2009 study by Chhaochharia and Grinstein relating to compliance with majority board independence requirements.[101] Guthrie *et al* argue that Chhaochharia and Grinstein's results are not applicable to publicly-traded firms *in general* on account of two 'outliers'

---

93 Robert F Göx, Frédéric Imhof and Alexis H Kunz, '"Say on Pay" Design and its Repercussion on CEO Investment Incentives, Compensation, and Firm Profit' (13 April 2010), available at SSRN: http://ssrn.com/abstract=1588682.

94 Ibid, 21.

95 Ibid.

96 Ibid.

97 Ibid, 22.

98 Ibid.

99 See discussion in section 10.2.3 above.

100 Katherine Guthrie, Jan Sokolowsky and Kam-Ming Wan, 'CEO Compensation and Board Structure Revisited' (2012) 67(3) *Journal of Finance* 1149–68 (18 September 2010), accessed 5 March 2015 at SSRN: http://ssrn.com/abstract=1680476.

101 Ibid, 2.

in the sample of CEO compensation which 'unduly impact' the results.[102] Guthrie *et al* conclude that independence on the compensation committee increases CEO pay but not independence on the board itself. Further, this result appears to require the precondition of strong monitors – such as block-holders.[103]

In section 10.2.2 above, evidence linking CEO pay to firm performance required two preconditions, one of which was also such block-holder monitoring (the other was performance-based compensation). Whether Apple and Fossil should have been excluded from the original sample by Chhaochharia and Grinstein has spawned some debate between the competing authors.[104] And Guthrie *et al* have suggested alternative explanations for their 2010 findings. For the first explanation, executive or inside directors with better information monitor the CEO more closely which reduces the level of CEO pay. By contrast, independent directors with inferior information and less effective monitoring judge the CEO less harshly than their inside counterparts leading to CEO pay increases.[105]

10.2.4 Summary of Studies and Relational Effect Paths for [DirCEO$] (+/−), [EqOptIncent] (+)[106] and [EqOptEntrch] (−)[107]

Thus, the overall impression of the studies examined is that only very guarded conclusions can be drawn here. First, a number of studies find no relationship between director and CEO/executive pay levels (represented by the **[DirCEO$] (+/−)** variable) and firm value and/or operating performance. If a causative relation exists between the CEO/executive pay levels variable and firm value, then, according to the 2007 study by Cremers,

---

102 Ibid, 3. These 'outliers' were said to be Steve Jobs of Apple and Kosta Kartsotis of Fossil. See 8–12.

103 Ibid, 19–20.

104 See, for example, Katherine Guthrie, Jan Sokolowsky and Kam-Ming Wan, 'CEO Compensation and Board Structure – Rejoinder' (18 April 2012 and posted 16 June 2012), accessed 5 March 2015 at SSRN: http://ssrn.com/abstract=2084630.

105 Katherine Guthrie, Jan Sokolowsky and Kam-Ming Wan, 'CEO Compensation and Board Structure Revisited – Addendum' (27 March 2012 and revised 20 March 2013), accessed 5 March 2015 at SSRN: http://ssrn.com/abstract=2074895, 2 and 7.

106 Equity/Option Plans and Holdings of Directors/Executives – Incentive/'Alignment' Effect (excludes short-term options).

107 Equity/Option Plans and Holdings of Directors/Executives – 'Entrenchment' Effect (excludes short-term options).

Bebchuk and Peyer described in section 10.2.3, it may well be negative. A significant number of studies examined found a positive relationship between director and CEO/executive pay levels and firm value and/or operating performance. However, this positive relationship may be heavily qualified by at least three pre-conditions.

First, putting a number of studies together, the relationship between director and CEO/executive pay levels and firm value and/or operating performance may well rely on the existence of independent directors and some sort of incentive-based payment, whether by way of performance-based payments, equity or options. In addition, one of the studies also requires the simultaneous operation of 'block-holder monitoring', a condition which may well be difficult to expect in a widely-dispersed shareholding company as explained in Chapter 8.[108] Nonetheless, this may be achievable where a sufficiently 'active' institutional or other large shareholder exists.

Not surprisingly, perhaps all that can be plausibly said at this time is that the dividing line between the 'incentive alignment' and 'entrenchment' effects identified by Fuerst and Kang will be a matter of degree always depending on the individual characteristics of the relevant firm, its ownership structure and the behaviour of its manager-owners themselves. In such cases, the question of the strength of the national shareholder protection/governance regime becomes relevant, in this case operating in the reverse direction than previously discussed[109] and compensating for perceived gaps in the firm-specific governance measures. In these circumstances of divided studies, the relational approach will assess the 'incentive alignment' effect and, conversely, the 'entrenchment' effect of director equity and option holdings (excluding short-term options) separately.

It follows then that the relational effect path of governance factors[110] for **[EqOptIncent] (+)**[111] is positive (+) with the starting point of Alignment Factor No 3 (Alignment of Management and Shareholder Interests[112]). Therefore, the relational effect path is the same as that of the Shareholder-Primacy Model 'Umbrella' (or 'guiding principle') in Figure 2.5[113] with the

---

108 See discussion in sections 8.5–8.5.2 above.

109 See discussion in section 7.3.1.3.1 above.

110 See the construction of the eight governance factors in sections 2.6.1–2.6.8 above.

111 Equity/Option Plans and Holdings of Directors/Executives – Incentive/'Alignment' Effect (excludes short-term options).

112 See discussion in section 2.6.3 above.

113 Ibid.

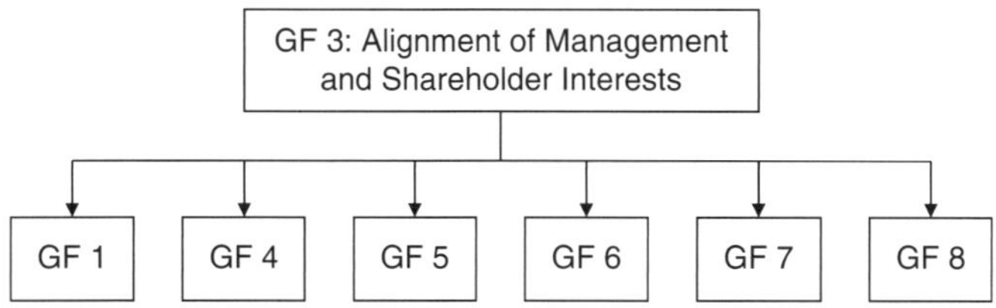

Figure 10.1 [EqOptIncent] (+) variable relational effect path

exception of the exclusion of the overriding requirements of Compliance Factor No 2 (Corporate Governance and Legal Compliance[114]).

Here, Alignment Factor No 3 is the 'umbrella' or 'guiding principle' over all other governance factors except Compliance Factor No 2 which is excluded as discussed below. Therefore, there is a direct one-directional link between Alignment Factor No 3 and Monitoring & Audit Factor No 5 (Internal and External/Audit Monitoring Quality). Thus, for example, governance variables which lead to improvements in the alignment of shareholder and management interests are hypothesised to consequently enhance the quality of monitoring on behalf of shareholders.

Alignment Factor No 3 and Monitoring & Audit Factor No 5 have an alternative link in which each of these governance factors has a connecting and reflexive relationship through Decision-making Factor No 7 (Quality of Board, CEO and Management Decision-Making). This is depicted in Figure 2.6's Shareholder-Primacy Interrelationship Scheme. But the one-directional link from Alignment Factor No 3 to Monitoring & Audit Factor No 5 is the more direct.

As in the case of the **[BrdSkills] (+)**[115] and **[BrdIndMon] (+)**[116] variables, the zone of effect for **[EqOptIncent] (+)** excludes the overriding nature of Compliance Factor No 2. Again by example – and similarly to those variables – the provisions of corporate law statutes and governance codes which govern share and option incentive schemes for the CEO/executives and directors cannot be altered by the equity or option decisions or actions of the company or board. Indeed, Compliance Factor No 2 performs in part a 'gap-filling' function for gaps in firm-level governance variables.[117]

---

[114] See discussion in section 2.6.2 above.

[115] Board – Director Skills 'Mix'. See discussion in section 7.3.1.2.1 above.

[116] Board Independent Director: Executive Director Proportion – Monitoring Effect. See discussion in sections 7.3.2.1.1–7.3.2.1.2 above.

[117] See discussion in section 7.3.1.3.1 above.

Thus, **[EqOptIncent] (+)** is ascribed a coverage/rating of +7/87.50 *rprox* in the Coverage Table (Table 3.1) and the Relational Proximity Table (Table 3.2).

[EqOptEntrch] (−) Relational Effect Path – Equity/Option Plans and Holdings of Directors/Executives – 'Entrenchment' Effect (excludes short term options) Conversely, at the level of director and CEO/executive equity ownership where the 'entrenchment' effect is operative (that is, in conjunction with but dominating the 'alignment' effect), the relational effect path of the **[EqOptEntrch] (−)**[118] variable is negative following the same relational effect path as its positive counterpart. Thus, there is still a direct one-directional link between Alignment Factor No 3 (Alignment of Management and Shareholder Interests) and Monitoring & Audit Factor No 5 (Internal and External/Audit Monitoring Quality). But, for example, and conversely to the **[EqOptIncent] (+)** variable, this governance variable is hypothesised to lead to reductions in the alignment of shareholder and management interests and to consequently reduce the quality of monitoring on behalf of shareholders.

This gives rise to a coverage/rating of −7/87.50 *rprox* for the **[EqOptEntrch] (−)** variable in the Coverage Table (Table 3.1) and the Relational Proximity Table (Table 3.2).

[DirCEO$] (+/−) Relational Effect Path – Director/CEO Compensation Levels Finally, the relational approach has examined conflicting studies for the operation of the level of director and CEO compensation (**[DirCEO$] (+/−)**) and firm value and operating performance.

The operation of this governance variable will depend on the 'incentive alignment' and 'entrenchment' effects identified by Fuerst and Kang.[119] Thus, the behaviour of the **[DirCEO$] (+/−)** variable may be positive or negative depending on the behaviour and strength of the **[EqOptIncent] (+)** and **[EqOptEntrch] (−)** variables (and which dominates over the other) acting in opposition to each other at any time.

This gives rise to a 'dual direction' marker for the **[DirCEO$] (+/−)** variable with an identical relational effect path to both **[EqOptIncent] (+)** and **[EqOptEntrch] (−)**. This gives rise to a coverage/rating of +/−7/87.50 *rprox* for the **[DirCEO$] (+/−)** variable in the Coverage Table (Table 3.1) and the Relational Proximity Table (Table 3.2).

---

[118] Equity/Option Plans and Holdings of Directors/Executives – 'Entrenchment' Effect (excludes short-term options).

[119] See discussion in section 10.2.1 above.

10.2.4.1 The nature and operation of the compensation committee – [CompCom] (+/−)

Here, the hypothesis is that the levels and structure of the **[DirCEO$] (+/−)**, **[EqOptIncent] (+)** and **[EqOptEntrch] (−)** governance variables are themselves dependent on the operation and structure of the **[CompCom] (+/−)**[120] variable. This is because the composition and levels of director, CEO and executive compensation flows (at least internally) from decision-making within the compensation committee. For example, in the 2010 study by Guthrie *et al* above, the authors found that increasing the independence of the compensation committee increases CEO pay (on the precondition of the presence of strong monitors).[121]

Therefore, the **[CompCom] (+/−)** variable has a dual direction marker (+/−) as the composition and levels of director, CEO and executive compensation – and therefore the balancing point between Fuerst and Kang's 'alignment' and 'entrenchment' effects of that compensation – will be affected positively or negatively by the operation of this variable.

This gives rise to a 'dual direction' marker for the **[CompCom] (+/−)** variable with an identical relational effect path to **[EqOptIncent] (+)**, **[EqOptEntrch] (−)** and (from the previous section) **[DirCEO$] (+/−)**. This gives rise to a coverage/rating of +/−7/87.50 *rprox* for the **[CompCom] (+/−)** variable in the Coverage Table (Table 3.1) and Relational Proximity Table (Table 3.2).

10.2.5 Short-Term Options and the Risk of Earnings Manipulation

The principal governance variables identified in Table 2.1 relating equity and option holdings are:

- **[AudShortOpts] (−)** – Audit Committee – Short Term Options Granted to Outside Directors – Reduction in Monitoring Effect, −7/87.50 *rprox*;[122]
- **[EqOptIncent] (+)** – Equity/Option Plans and Holdings of Directors/ Executives – Incentive/'Alignment' Effect (excludes short-term options), +7/87.50 *rprox*;[123]
- **[EqOptEntrch] (−)** – Equity/Option Plans and Holdings of Directors/ Executives – 'Entrenchment' Effect (excludes short-term options), −7/87.50 *rprox*;[124] and

---

120 Compensation Committee – Presence, Operation and Frequency.
121 See discussion in section 10.2.3.2 above.
122 See discussion in section 10.2.5.1 below.
123 See discussion in section 10.2.4 above.
124 See discussion in section 10.2.4 above.

- **[ShortTOpts] (−)** – Short-Term Option Holdings/Plans of Directors and Executives, −7/87.50 *rprox.*[125]

In the Enron context,[126] commentators pointed to the short-term focus of share options as a factor contributing to significant levels of earnings manipulation. Recalling that discussion, Bratton observed that options lead managers to pursue 'high risk strategies'.[127]

And other similar views abound. Gordon suggests[128] that the granting of short-term options may have increased fraudulent practices and risk-taking by executives to increase the share price[129] and Gillan and Martin similarly emphasise the short-term option problem.[130]

Confirming the Enron collapse analysis, for Marrakchi Chtourou, Bédard and Courteau, the risk of earnings misstatement increases with short-term options granted to outside audit committee directors[131] thus inhibiting the function of such directors to monitor financial statement integrity.[132] Similarly, for Tehranian, Cornett, Marcus and Saunders,[133] option incentive plans increase earnings manipulation (but not performance).[134]

Indeed, the risks posed by the granting of options, particularly short-term ones, are recognised by the International Organization of Securities Commissions ('IOSCO') in its Final Report, *Board Independence of Listed Companies*:

> [s]ome forms of compensation (e.g. stock options), if not properly designed, may shorten the planning horizon of board members and weaken their

---

125 See discussion in section 10.2.5.1 below.

126 See discussion in section 5.2.3.2.1 above.

127 William W Bratton, 'Enron and the Dark Side of Shareholder Value' (2001–2002) 76 *Tulane Law Review* 1275 (May 2002), accessed 5 March 2015 at SSRN: http://ssrn.com/abstract=301475, 49. See discussion in section 5.2.3.2.1 above.

128 See discussion in section 5.2.3.2.1 above.

129 Gordon, above n 45, 15–16.

130 See discussion in section 5.2.3.2.1 above.

131 S Marrakchi Chtourou, J Bédard and L Courteau, 'Corporate Governance and Earnings Management' (21 April 2001), accessed 5 March 2015 at SSRN: http://ssrn.com/abstract=275053, 4.

132 Ibid, 27.

133 H Tehranian, M M Cornett, A J Marcus and A Saunders, 'Earnings Management, Corporate Governance, and True Financial Performance' (January 2006), accessed 5 March 2015 at SSRN: http://ssrn.com/abstract=886142, 1–6 and 18–19.

134 Ibid, 1–2, 5 and 18–19.

> incentive to monitor rigorously potential managerial bias in favour of short term gains, earnings management or, in extreme cases, outright fraud.[135]

Thus, the IOSCO view of short-term options is consistent with those of the commentators presented here.

An analysis of the practice of 'backdating' options is beyond the scope of this first stage of the relational approach but received wide consideration from the commentators, particularly Professors Bebchuk, Grinstein and Peyer.[136]

10.2.5.1 [AudShortOpts] (−)[137] and [ShortTOpts] (−)[138] relational effect paths

The crux of the **[AudShortOpts] (−)** and **[ShortTOpts] (−)** variables in the studies above and the IOSCO Report is an increased risk of earnings misstatement due to short term options granted to independent directors on the audit committee or the board itself which, it is argued, reduces the quality of the internal monitoring function. Thus both variables are ascribed a negative (−) directional marker.

The relational approach has described the 'incentive alignment' effect and 'entrenchment' effects identified by Fuerst and Kang in relation to the issue of short-term options to directors.[139] For the reasons set out in section 10.2.1 above, the relational effect paths for **[AudShortOpts] (−)** and **[ShortTOpts] (−)** are identical to that of both **[EqOptIncent] (+)** and **[EqOptEntrch] (−)** with the starting point of Alignment Factor No 3

---

135 IOSCO Report, above n 9, 26.

136 Lucian A Bebchuk, Yaniv Grinstein and Urs Peyer, 'Lucky CEOs' (2010) 65(6) *Journal of Finance* 2363–401 (published as 'Lucky CEOs and Lucky Directors'); Harvard Law and Economics Discussion Paper No 566 (2006), accessed 5 March 2015 at SSRN: http://ssrn.com/abstract=945392; Lucian A Bebchuk, Yaniv Grinstein and Urs Peyer, 'Lucky CEOs and Lucky Directors' (2010) 65(6) *Journal of Finance* 2363–2401; Johnson School Research Paper Series No 39-09; CELS 2009 4th Annual Conference on Empirical Legal Studies Paper (15 May 2009), accessed 5 March 2015 at SSRN: http://ssrn.com/abstract=1405316 and Lucian A Bebchuk, Yaniv Grinstein and Urs Peyer, 'Lucky Directors' (2010) 65(6) *Journal of Finance* 2363–401 (published as 'Lucky CEOs and Lucky Directors'); Harvard Law and Economics Discussion Paper No 573 (2006), accessed 5 March 2015 at SSRN: http://ssrn.com/abstract=952239.

137 Audit Committee – Short Term Options Granted to Outside Directors – Reduction in Monitoring Effect.

138 Short-Term Option Holdings/Plans of Directors and Executives.

139 See discussion in section 10.2.1 above.

(Alignment of Management and Shareholder Interests). Therefore, the relational effect paths for **[AudShortOpts] (−)** and **[ShortTOpts] (−)** are the same as that of the **[EqOptIncent] (+)**[140] variable in Figure 10.1 above. There, Alignment Factor No 3 (Alignment of Management and Shareholder Interests) is the 'umbrella' or 'guiding principle' over the other governance factors with the exception of the overriding nature of Compliance Factor No 2 (Corporate Governance and Legal Compliance). Again, Compliance Factor No 2 is excluded from the relational effect path because it remains constant and is not affected by the option-granting decisions or actions of the company or board. Thus, Compliance Factor No 2 performs in part a 'gap-filling' function for gaps in firm-level governance variables.[141]

This gives rise to a coverage/rating of −7/87.50 in the Coverage Table (Table 3.1) and the Relational Proximity Table (Table 3.2) for both **[AudShortOpts] (−)** and **[ShortTOpts] (−)**.

10.2.6 Possible Connection Between Director and CEO Compensation Level

Several studies discussed in sections 10.2.1–10.2.3 above sought to determine whether any causative relationship exists between the level of director compensation (in the form of equity and/or options) and the quality of director monitoring of management. While some support was found for this proposition in the studies – and this is reflected in the **[EqOptIncent] (+)** relational effect path in section 10.2.4 – it was not by any means universal. However, some greater support can be found for the proposition that director and CEO compensation levels are linked as follows in this section 10.2.6.

Is director compensation linked to the difficulty of monitoring the firm and therefore CEO compensation?

In this respect, Brick, Palmon and Wald, after noting that supervision of management[142] is a key function of the board, hypothesise 'that director compensation is related to the difficulty of monitoring the firm' and

140 Equity/Option Plans and Holdings of Directors/Executives – Incentive/'Alignment' Effect (excludes short-term options).

141 See discussion in section 7.3.1.3.1 above.

142 For a discussion of the 'trade-off' consequences for management and the flow of information to the board in the case of the board's functions of monitoring as opposed to advising management, see Renee B Adams, 'The Dual Role of Corporate Boards as Advisors and Monitors of Management: Theory and Evidence' (previously titled 'The Dual Role of Corporate Boards as Advisors and

therefore also related to CEO compensation.[143] Thus, the authors find a positive relationship between director and CEO compensations.[144] Seeking to determine whether this relationship is due to 'unobserved firm complexity' as opposed to 'cronyism', the authors find a negative relationship between firm performance and excess director compensation[145] leading them to adopt the latter explanation.[146]

For Evans and Evans, the shareholdings of non-executive directors operate as a 'restraint' on CEO compensation levels.[147] In addition, and consistent with the findings of Brick *et al*, Evans and Evans find that increases in non-executive director compensation are linked to increases in the CEO compensation level.[148]

10.3 POSSIBLE CONNECTION BETWEEN FIRM SIZE AND DIRECTOR/EXECUTIVE COMPENSATION

There is also some suggestion that the level of compensation (in one study by Lee, for outside directors and, in the other by Fernandes, for executives) is linked to firm size. The study by Fernandes further suggests a positive link between executive pay and the proportion of non-executive directors on the board.

As noted earlier in Chapter 8, one of the factors affecting the size of the board is likely to be firm size.[149] As Lee explains:

> [t]he larger size [of firms] makes the earning of firms more sensitive to the board quality, so that the larger sized firms pay more to outside directors. Also, the big firms give more reputation values (generated by the performance of the firm) to board members. Conclusively, the large size makes

---

Monitors of Management') (November 2001), accessed 5 March 2015 at SSRN: http://ssrn.com/abstract=241581.

143 I E Brick, O Palmon and J K Wald, 'CEO Compensation, Director Compensation, and Firm Performance: Evidence of Cronyism' (1 May 2002), accessed 5 March 2015 at SSRN: http://ssrn.com/abstract=303574, 2.

144 Ibid.

145 Ibid, 3.

146 Ibid, 2–3.

147 Robert T Evans and John P Evans, 'The Influence of Non-Executive Director Control and Rewards on CEO Remuneration: Australian Evidence', EFMA 2002 London Meetings (March 12, 2001), accessed 5 March 2015 at SSRN: http://ssrn.com/abstract=263050, 7 and 15–16.

148 Ibid.

149 See discussion in sections 8.2.1–8.2.2.2 above.

> board positions more attractive to the talented candidates for outside directors.[150]

Accordingly, there is support for the proposition that there is a positive relationship between firm size and outside director compensation levels.

Support for this possible 'firm size: compensation' relationship is also found by Fernandes, who investigates the relationship between firm performance, independence of the board and executive compensation in Portugal.[151] For Fernandes, the level of compensation is linked to firm size but not firm performance[152] and increases in the proportion of non-executive directors increase compensation levels.[153]

Michaud and Gai investigate in 2009 the relationship between firm performance and CEO compensation finding that firm size (determined by sales) is a determinant of CEO compensation and that firm performance does not affect CEO compensation.[154] The authors explain the result by reference to the reason that, as firm size increases, the 'pool of talent' capable of managing the firm is reduced and that this smaller pool has greater power to increase its compensation claims.[155]

More recently in 2011, Mehran, Morrison and Shapiro examine governance lessons learned from the GFC.[156] The authors observe in relation to executive pay that:

> [t]he level of executive pay in a nonfinancial firm is generally related to the size of the firm's assets (market value of equity or book value), its asset complexity, and the industry structure and competition. Leverage has an insignificant effect

---

150 C Lee, 'Where Do the Talented People Work as Outside Directors?', CAEPR Working Paper No 2007-006 (14 August 2007), accessed 5 March 2015 at SSRN: http://ssrn.com/abstract=988119, 3.

151 Fernandes, above n 64.

152 Ibid, 2 and 17.

153 Ibid.

154 Dennis Wright Michaud and Yunwei Gai, 'CEO Compensation and Firm Performance' (20 December 2009), accessed 5 March 2015 at SSRN: http://ssrn.com/abstract=1531673, 50.

155 Ibid. For an analysis and criticism of the use of 'external' or 'peer' benchmarking in the setting of CEO compensation levels (including the argument that it is necessary for executive retention), see Charles M Elson, and Craig K Ferrere, 'Executive Superstars, Peer Groups and Over-Compensation – Cause, Effect and Solution' (7 August 2012), accessed 5 March 2015 at SSRN: http://ssrn.com/abstract=2125979.

156 Hamid Mehran, Alan D Morrison and Joel D Shapiro, 'Corporate Governance and Banks: What Have We Learned from the Financial Crisis?', Federal Reserve Bank of New York Staff Report No 502 (1 June 2011), accessed 5 March 2015 at SSRN: http://ssrn.com/abstract=1880009.

> on pay, and, on average, firms judiciously choose their leverage for its effects on their credit ratings and potential costs of distress.[157]

Accordingly, for the authors, factors affecting executive pay in the GFC include firm size and complexity but not leverage.

10.4 COMPENSATION, GOVERNANCE AND REPUTATIONAL CONSTRAINTS

10.4.1 Reputational Constraints on Compensation are Dependent on Disclosure and Transparency

In Chapter 4, it was explained that important governance mechanisms in the agency theory component of the shareholder and stakeholder models of the firm are the market for corporate control and, complementing this, reputational constraints on directors.[158] There is some suggestion in one of the studies reviewed in the relational approach that such constraints, acting on the board, also place downward pressure on managerial compensation.

In this respect, Singh investigates the role of executive compensation as an incentive and indicator of governance quality.[159] The author explains that:

> [t]he compensation decisions a firm's board of directors [makes] sends a potentially strong signal about the independence of the board from management.[160]

In this way, the author concludes that reputational constraints limit the level of executive remuneration, the operation of these constraints being dependent on the existence of well-known governance variables – disclosure standards and transparent reporting.[161] By contrast, for Singh, 'gaps in the reporting requirements'[162] may lead to rent-extraction by managers including '. . . less transparent forms of pay, such as perks'.[163] Thus, for example, comprehensive disclosure requirements relating to executive

---

157 Ibid, 5 (footnote omitted).

158 See discussion in section 4.2.2 above.

159 R Singh, 'Board Independence and the Design of Executive Compensation' (September 2006), EFA 2005 Moscow Meetings Paper, accessed 5 March 2015 at SSRN: http://ssrn.com/abstract=673741, 1.

160 Ibid.

161 Ibid, 20.

162 Ibid.

163 Ibid.

remuneration in the form of cash, equity and options but with comparatively less disclosure requirements relating to perquisites will, based on the agency costs theory, encourage claims for the latter. This is because agency theory tells us that inside managers will exploit their information advantage (information asymmetry) over dispersed shareholders to increase their wealth.[164]

Separate governance variables are ascribed to the 'disclosure standards' (**[ReputDiscl] (+)**[165]) and 'transparent reporting' (**[ReputRep] (+)**[166]) aspects of the reputational constraints identified by Singh. These concepts or facets – hypothesised to be acting downwards on Compensation Factor No 4 (Board, CEO and Management Compensation and Incentives) – operate in the same manner as the **[TransTimeMon] (+)**[167] variable depicted in Figure 9.1 above.

As noted in section 9.1.2.1, the **[TransTimeMon] (+)** variable's relational effect path is hypothesised to begin with Reporting Factor No 1 (Transparency, Timing and Integrity of Financial and Other Reports) itself as the 'driver' of this zone of effect. A 'chain' of reflexive relationships then directly link Reporting Factor No 1, Monitoring & Audit Factor No 5 (Internal and External/Audit Monitoring Quality), Decision-making Factor No 7 (Quality of Board, CEO and Management Decision-making) and culminating in Compensation Factor No 4 (Board, CEO and Management Compensation and Incentives). Being reflexive, this chain exerts influence in the opposite direction as well. So, for example, this chain works in the reverse. The nature and level of a firm's board, CEO and executive compensation (Compensation Factor No 4) is hypothesised to affect the quality of the decision-making of those organs (Decision-making Factor No 7). This then has consequential effect on the quality of monitoring (Monitoring & Audit Factor No 5) and, thus, the quality of the reporting function (Reporting Factor No 1).

Therefore, the **[ReputDiscl] (+)** and **[ReputRep] (+)** variables are each hypothesised to affect all governance factors. This equates to a coverage/rating of +8/100.00 *rprox* in the Coverage Table (Table 3.1) and the Relational Proximity Table (Table 3.2) for both the **[ReputDiscl] (+)** and **[ReputRep] (+)** variables.

---

164 Evans and Evans, above n 147, 3–4. See discussion in sections 4.2.3–4.2.3.1 above.

165 Reputational Constraints – 'Disclosure Standards'.

166 Reputational Constraints – 'Transparent Reporting'.

167 Transparency and Timing of Reporting – Monitoring Effect.

10.5 CONCLUDING REMARKS ON THE RECURRING THEMES AND TENSIONS IN EXECUTIVE, CEO AND DIRECTOR COMPENSATION

Chapter 10 has examined the fourth and final part of the studies forming the Empirical Studies Key Field No 4 by examining perceived links between executive, CEO and director compensation and measures of firm value, operating performance and the probability of earnings manipulation. Other perceived links included firm size and reputational constraints and links between the CEO and director compensation levels *inter se*. The different forms of compensation have included performance-based and/or equity-based compensation and options (including short-term options).

10.5.1 The Compensation 'Trade-off'

The review in Chapter 10 suggests that director and management equity ownership has a 'trade-off' effect on the corporation between – on the one hand – the 'incentive alignment' effect and – on the other – the 'entrenchment' effect observed by Fuerst and Kang.[168]

Translating this to the Relational Proximity Table (Table 3.2), **[EqOptIncent] (+)**[169] and **[EqOptEntrch] (−)**[170] each have a coverage/rating of 7/87.50 *rprox* as described in section 10.2.4 above – the former positive and the latter negative. This indicates the strong (and opposite) hypothetical effects of these two governance variables. The strength (or otherwise) of the national shareholder protection scheme is hypothesised to be relevant in finding the balancing point in this trade-off reflected in a coverage/rating of +8/100.00 *rprox* for the positive effects of the **[NationGov] (+)**[171] variable.

---

168 See discussion in section 10.2.1 above.

169 Equity/Option Plans and Holdings of Directors/Executives – Incentive/'Alignment' Effect (excludes short-term options) – see discussion in section 10.2.4 above.

170 Equity/Option Plans and Holdings of Directors/Executives – 'Entrenchment' Effect (excludes short-term options) – see discussion in section 10.2.4 above.

171 National Governance/Shareholder Protection Regime – see discussion in section 7.3.1.3.2 above.

10.5.2 Compensation and the Level/Quality of Monitoring

There was some support for a causative link between increases in the level of director compensation (**[DirCEO$] (+/−)**[172]) and an increase in the quality of monitoring of management. But this seems to require that:

(i) the directors be independent (see previously the **[BrdIndMon] (+)**[173] variable which has a coverage/rating of +7/87.50 *rprox*);[174]
(ii) the compensation be incentive-based (including the **[EqOptIncent] (+)**[175] and **[EqOptEntrch] (−)**[176] variables from the previous section); and/or
(iii) (alternatively or additionally) that those directors have 'substantial' equity holdings (again, **[EqOptIncent] (+)** and **[EqOptEntrch] (−)**).

Instead, there is more persuasive support in section 10.2.6 above for the proposition that director and CEO compensation levels are linked, although this may require the directors to be independent.

10.5.3 Firm Operating Performance and Firm Value

Again in relation to **[DirCEO$] (+/−)**,[177] the effect of this variable is both positive (+) and negative (−) at a coverage/rating of +/−7/87.50 indicating an inconclusive relationship on account of conflicting studies in sections 10.2.2–10.2.3. Some studies find *no* relationship between CEO/executive pay levels and firm performance and/or firm value. If a causative relation exists between CEO/executive pay levels and firm value, it may well be negative according to Cremers, Bebchuk and Peyer.[178]

---

172 Director/CEO Compensation Levels has a coverage/rating of +/−7/87.50 *rprox* – see discussion in section 10.2.4 above.

173 Board Independent Director: Executive Director Proportion – Monitoring Effect.

174 See discussion in sections 7.3.2.1.1–7.3.2.1.2 above.

175 Equity/Option Plans and Holdings of Directors/Executives – Incentive/'Alignment' Effect (excludes short-term options) – see discussion in section 10.2.4 above.

176 Equity/Option Plans and Holdings of Directors/Executives – 'Entrenchment' Effect (excludes short-term options) – see discussion in section 10.2.4 above.

177 Director/CEO Compensation Levels has a coverage/rating of +/−7/87.50 *rprox* – see discussion in section 10.2.4 above.

178 Cremers, Bebchuk and Peyer, above n 69. See discussion in section 10.2.3 above.

The review suggests that *if* a positive relationship is to be found between CEO/executive pay levels and firm operating performance, it is heavily qualified. This relies on, at the least:

(i) existence of an incentive-based payment that is, performance-based payments (Daines, Nair and Kornhauser[179]) or options (Hanlon, Rajgopal and Shevlin[180]) – the **[EqOptIncent] (+)**[181] and **[EqOptEntrch] (−)**[182] variables; and
(ii) simultaneous operation of 'block-holder' monitoring (Daines, Nair and Kornhauser[183]) – the **[BlockMon] (+)**[184] and **[BlockCosts] (−)**[185] variables.

The relational approach concluded this examination by hypothesising that the behaviour of the **[DirCEO$] (+/−)** variable may be positive or negative depending on the behaviour and strength of the **[EqOptIncent] (+)**[186] and **[EqOptEntrch] (−)**[187] variables acting in opposition to each other at any time. This gives rise to a 'dual direction' marker for **[DirCEO$] (+/−)** with an identical relational effect path to both **[EqOptIncent] (+)** and **[EqOptEntrch] (−)**. This equates to a coverage/rating of +/−7/87.50 *rprox* for the **[DirCEO$] (+/−)** variable in the Coverage Table (Table 3.1) and the Relational Proximity Table (Table 3.2).

10.5.4 Short-Term Options and Earnings Manipulation

The relational approach review in sections 10.2.5–10.2.5.1 reveals some cautionary findings that the risk of earnings misstatement increases with

---

179 See discussion in section 10.2.2 above.

180 Ibid.

181 Equity/Option Plans and Holdings of Directors/Executives – Incentive/'Alignment' Effect (excludes short-term options) – see discussion in section 10.2.4 above.

182 Equity/Option Plans and Holdings of Directors/Executives – 'Entrenchment' Effect (excludes short-term options) – see discussion in section 10.2.4 above.

183 See discussion in section 10.2.2 above.

184 Block Shareholding – Monitoring Effect – see discussion in sections 8.5.1–8.5.2 above.

185 Block Shareholding – Other Shareholder Agency Costs – see discussion in sections 8.5.1–8.5.2 above.

186 Equity/Option Plans and Holdings of Directors/Executives – Incentive/'Alignment' Effect (excludes short-term options) – see discussion in section 10.2.4 above.

187 Equity/Option Plans and Holdings of Directors/Executives – 'Entrenchment' Effect (excludes short-term options) – see discussion in section 10.2.4 above.

short-term options granted to outside audit committee directors (the **[AudShortOpts] (−)**[188] variable) thus inhibiting the function of such directors to monitor financial statement integrity (as suggested by Marrakchi Chtourou, Bédard and Courteau[189]).

There was further suggestion that option incentive plans (**[ShortTOpts] (−)**[190]) increase earnings manipulation but not performance (Tehranian, Cornett, Marcus and Saunders[191]). This caution finds a coverage/rating in the Coverage Table (Table 3.1) and Relational Proximity Table (Table 3.2) for both **[AudShortOpts] (−)** and **[ShortTOpts] (−)** of −7/87.50 *rprox*.[192]

These findings are also reflected in the findings of the commentator evaluations of the Enron corporate collapse in Chapter 5. There, commentators examined the role of share options, particularly those with a short-term structure, and bonus payments linked to share-price performance. It was hypothesised that these forms of CEO, executive and director compensation:

(i) increase the likelihood of the adoption of high-risk taking strategies by management (Bratton[193]);
(ii) increase the risk of 'aggressive accounting manipulations' to boost stock option values (Armour and McCahery[194]); and
(iii) increase the likelihood of fraud and risk-taking to increase the share price (Gordon[195]).

10.5.5 Firm Size, Independence and Director/Executive Compensation

There is some suggestion in section 10.3 that the level of compensation for outside directors (Lee) and/or executives (Fernandes) – the **[DirCEO$]**

---

[188] Audit Committee – Short Term Options Granted to Outside Directors – Reduction in Monitoring Effect – see discussion in section 10.2.5.1 above.

[189] See discussion in section 10.2.5 above.

[190] Short-Term Option Holdings/Plans of Directors and Executives – see discussion in section 10.2.5.1 above.

[191] See discussion in section 10.2.5 above.

[192] See discussion in section 10.2.5.1 above.

[193] See discussion in section 5.2.3.2.1 above.

[194] John Armour and Joseph A McCahery, 'After Enron: Improving Corporate Law and Modernising Securities Regulation in Europe and the US', Amsterdam Center for Law & Economics Working Paper No 2006-07 (June 2006), accessed 5 March 2015 at SSRN: http://ssrn.com/abstract=910205, 2. See discussion in section 5.2.3.2.1 above.

[195] See discussion in section 5.2.3.2.1 above.

(+/−)[196] variable – is linked to the intervening variable of firm size. Michaud and Gai, too, found that firm size (determined by sales) is a determinant of CEO compensation and that firm performance does not affect CEO compensation.[197] The authors suggest that increases in firm size reduce the 'pool of talent' able to manage that firm causing an increase in the price for CEOs.[198]

10.5.6 Compensation and Reputational Constraints

Singh suggests that reputational constraints limit the level of executive remuneration, the author adding that the operation of these constraints is dependent on the presence of 'disclosure standards' and 'transparent reporting'.[199] Following Singh, the relational approach ascribes separate governance variables to these pre-conditions. The **[ReputDiscl] (+)**[200] variable represents the 'disclosure standards' pre-condition and is ascribed the highest positive coverage/rating of +8/100.00 *rprox*. The 'transparent reporting' condition is represented by **[ReputRep] (+)**[201] and again is ascribed the highest positive coverage/rating of +8/100.00 *rprox*. These two governance variables – hypothesised to be acting downwards on compensation levels within Compensation Factor No 4 – operate in the same manner as the **[TransTimeMon] (+)**[202] governance variable depicted in Figure 9.1 above.

10.6 CONCLUSION OF EMPIRICAL STUDIES KEY FIELD NO 4

The operation of the director/CEO compensation variables (**[DirCEO$] (+/−)**, **[EqOptIncent] (+)** and **[EqOptEntrch] (−)**) and the short-term option variables (**[AudShortOpts] (−)** and **[ShortTOpts] (−)**) in the context of the Enron corporate collapse was undertaken in detail in Chapter 5 with

---

196 Director/CEO Compensation Levels has a coverage/rating of +/−7/87.50 *rprox* – see discussion in section 10.2.4 above.

197 Michaud and Gai, above n 154, 50.

198 Ibid. See discussion in section 10.3 above.

199 See discussion in section 10.4.1 above.

200 Reputational Constraints – 'Disclosure Standards' – see discussion in section 10.4.1 above.

201 Reputational Constraints – 'Transparent Reporting' – see discussion in section 10.4.1 above.

202 Transparency and Timing of Reporting – Monitoring Effect – see discussion in section 9.1.2.1 above.

the results supported by the analysis in this Chapter 10. The analysis in this Chapter 10 also concludes the analysis of the Empirical Studies Key Field No 4 – empirical and other studies of the effectiveness of corporate governance variables (including the strength of the national shareholder protection regime).

Within Chapters 7–10, the relational approach has identified, analysed and justified a relational effect path for each of the 39 governance variables first presented in Table 2.1. A summary of each relational effect path for these governance variables – including the number of governance factors affected and the direction of effect – was presented in the Coverage Table (Table 3.1) and the Relational Proximity Table (Table 3.2).

In the following Chapter 11, the relational approach presents concluding observations and analysis relating to the relational proximity of the governance variables and observations on the structure, explanatory power and limitations of the relational approach. Chapter 11 concludes the relational approach with suggested improvements and areas for further research.

11. Relational approach conclusions

Estimating the future effects of (publicly known) governance provisions (or governance characteristics correlated with them) is far from a straightforward matter and requires not only knowing the public information about the provisions but also plugging it into an appropriate structural model of the firms and their environment.

Lucian A Bebchuk, Alma Cohen and Charles C Y Wang[1]

11.1 RELATIONAL APPROACH CONCLUSIONS AND APPROACH OF CHAPTER 11

The relational approach has explained that many governance variables are mandated or enforced on a 'comply or explain' basis by the multitude of governance codes in operation today. For example, in the case of Australia's ASX 2014 Principles and Recommendations,[2] companies listed on the Australian Securities Exchange are, under ASX Listing Rules, required to disclose the extent of their compliance with the Principles and Recommendations.[3]

But this does *not* tell us the relative importance of each variable in avoiding or reducing agency costs and therefore enhancing firm value, profitability and, thus in the long-term, the sustainability of the corporation. The introductory quote from Bebchuk, Cohen and

[1] Lucian A Bebchuk, Alma Cohen and Charles C Y Wang, 'Learning and the Disappearing Association Between Governance and Returns' (2013) 108(2) *Journal of Financial Economics* 323–48; Harvard Law and Economics Discussion Paper No 667 (1 June 2011), accessed 5 March 2015 at SSRN: http://ssrn.com/abstract=1589731, 6.

[2] ASX Corporate Governance Council, Third Edition of the Principles and Recommendations were released on 27 March 2014 and (at p 7) took effect for a company's financial year commencing on or after July 1, 2014 ('ASX 2014 Principles and Recommendations'), accessed 5 March 2015 at http://www.asx.com.au/regulation/corporate-governance-council.htm.

[3] See Australian Securities Exchange, ASX Listing Rule 4.10.3, available at http://www.asx.com.au/documents/rules/Chapter04.pdf. See also ASX 2014 Principles and Recommendations, ibid, p 5.

Wang, too, provides some insight into difficulties posed for this process. Indeed, the authors remind us of the limitations of theoretical studies in this area:

> Because theoretical analysis can usually identify both positive and negative effects that such reforms could have and, in any event, cannot tell us much about the effects' magnitude, the sign and magnitude of a given reform's effect cannot be a priori precisely identified on theoretical grounds, leading researchers to make extensive use of events studies.[4]

While the theoretical studies referred to by Bebchuk, Cohen and Wang are said to have shortcomings in determining the sign (that is, the direction of effect) and the magnitude (that is, strength of effect) of a given reform, the relational approach adds to the field by demonstrating an approach for ascribing such a sign with greater certainty. The strength of the effect under the relational approach awaits empirical testing.

Nor is the relational approach affected by events which affect the value or performance of corporations or the value of their equities such as the Global Financial Crisis. By contrast, the relational approach can be used to compare the interrelationships between governance variables internal to the company in crisis and non-crisis periods to identify problems or breakdowns in relationships.

Relational Governance Determines the 'Efficient Zone' for a Variable

For regulators, policy-makers, law-reformers and corporate actors and their advisors, each governance variable represents an individual area of inquiry in a governance review of the corporation. The structure or operation of governance variables within the corporation can then be assessed by comparison to the way they *should* behave according to the relational approach and its normative relative proximity values. In the relational approach, deficiencies in the structure or operation of particular governance variables within the corporation place the corporation outside the 'efficient zone' for that variable. As the efficient zone of a governance variable reflects the relative agency cost value ascribed to that variable in the Relational Proximity Table (Table 3.2), a deficiency in the real-world structure or behaviour of such a variable has the efficiency- and sustainability-reducing effects reflected from that value.

In the physics of the behaviour of light, the angle of incidence equals the angle of reflection. In governance terms, the relational approach

---

[4] Bebchuk, Cohen and Wang, above n 1.

demonstrates that a real-world deficiency in the structure or operation of a governance variable within the corporation will reduce the efficiency and sustainability of the corporation by the relative value equivalent to the 'relational proximity rating' of that variable taken from the Relational Proximity Table (Table 3.2). As more deficiencies are detected in other governance variables, the relative risk of inefficiency and a reduction in the sustainability of the corporation magnifies by the aggregate relational proximity of those variables.

Specifically for regulators, policy-makers, law-reformers and corporate actors and their advisors, the relational approach can also thus be used to review and map the purpose, structure and operation of current governance variables in governance codes and schemes around the world and to assess reform proposals in the field.

11.2 KEY AIMS AND DEVELOPMENTS OF THE RELATIONAL APPROACH FROM CHAPTER 1

The approach of this chapter will be to present the elements of the relational approach which were developed as a response to the key goals or aims from Chapter 1.[5] These were to:

(1) introduce a new definition of corporate governance;
(2) create a simulated corporate governance environment which represents the 'real world' sphere of corporate governance;
(3) identify, describe and map diagrammatically the interrelationships, themes and factors underpinning this environment;
(4) create a comparative table or scheme system upon which to compare across sectors and over time the governance variables utilised in the major US, UK, Australian and global governance codes and schemes; and
(5) as an over-arching aim, to propose an approach or tool for regulators, policy-makers, law reformers and corporate actors to predict and measure the relative importance of governance variables in reducing (or increasing) agency costs and enhancing (or reducing) the long-term efficiency and sustainability of the for-profit firm.

As part of this, the conclusion will review these key elements of the relational approach and how they can be used in future to advance the understanding of corporate governance.

[5] See discussion in section 1.4 above.

Second will be to highlight those elements which have emerged from the analysis contained in the Key Fields as particularly significant for the relational approach.

11.2.1 To Introduce a New Definition of Corporate Governance

This is the three relational axes of good governance examined in Chapter 2.[6] This is the theoretical set of scales which weighs the objectives, behaviours and positional conflict of insiders such as the directors, CEO and management with traditional outsiders such as shareholders and other wider stakeholders. Reflecting the increasing influence of stakeholder theory – in the same way as Australia's ASX 2007–10 Revised Principles and 2014 Principles and Recommendations[7] – the three relational axes represent the competing claims on the governance framework of the national corporate governance or shareholder protection regime and, in turn, the governance systems of individual companies.

Unlike the original Cadbury Report definition,[8] the three relational axes reflect in more concrete terms the role of insiders in risk-taking and innovation but still maintain that Report's emphasis on monitoring/supervision of management and reporting to shareholders. The three relational axes, like the OECD Principles,[9] reflect the aim that the maximisation of the interests of stakeholders beyond the shareholders are important in the firm's long-term sustainability. Why has this approach been taken?

The three relational axes denote that the governance system of a company is not static. They are the continuing considerations which the directors must apply to decisions concerning the company's resources. The company's long-term efficiency and sustainability requires the continual weighing process of these axes and the maximisation of these considerations. How is this achieved?

---

6 See discussion in sections 2.3.1–2.3.3 above.

7 ASX Corporate Governance Council, *Corporate Governance Principles and Recommendations with 2010 Amendments*, June 2010 ('ASX 2007–10 Revised Principles'), accessed 5 March 2015 at http://www.asxgroup.com.au/corporate-governance-council.htm and ASX 2014 Principles and Recommendations, above n 2.

8 The Committee on the Financial Aspects of Corporate Governance, *Report of the Committee on the Financial Aspects of Corporate Governance*, London: Gee & Co Ltd, 1 December 1992 ('Cadbury Report'), Para 2.5.

9 Organisation for Economic Co-Operation and Development, *OECD Principles of Corporate Governance 2004*, 2004, OECD Publications Service, Paris ('OECD Principles'), Preamble, p 11. See http://www.oecd.org/document/49/0,3343,en_2649_34813_31530865_1_1_1_37439,00.html (accessed 5 March 2015).

The recurring themes and tensions underpinning corporate governance discourse – the eight governance factors – are weighed in this set of scales. Using empirical studies as a springboard, the results of the weighing process were calculated and presented for the reader. These are the two interrelationship schemes in Figure 2.6, reflecting the shareholder primacy environment and Figure 2.7, again – like the OECD – reflecting stakeholder theory. These schemes act as maps to guide the decision-making processes of the directors to enhance the firm's long-term efficiency and sustainability.

11.2.2 To Create a Simulated Corporate Governance Environment which Represents the 'Real World' Sphere of Corporate Governance

These are the four Key Fields introduced in Chapter 1[10] and comprising the largest components of the relational approach:

Key Field No 1:	Application of the Principal Theories of the Firm to the Relational Approach (Chapter 4)
Key Field No 2:	'Autopsies' of the Enron and Hastie Corporate Collapses (Chapter 5)
Key Field No 3:	Comparative Corporate Governance Codes (Chapter 6)[11]
Key Field No 4:	Empirical Studies on the Effectiveness of Governance Variables (Chapters 7–10)

In this way, the relational approach created a simulated corporate governance environment which represents the 'real world' sphere of corporate governance. This is represented by the four Key Fields and 39 governance variables to which the Fields give rise. As noted in section 1.3.2, the four Key Fields were selected on the basis of the number of works on the SSRN platform as a measure of impact. Thus, of immediate value for regulators, policy-makers, law-reformers and corporate actors and their advisors, the relational approach's simulated environment is very topical and current – in effect the 39 most-often considered governance variables in governance discourse.

Like any simulated or 'model' environment, the components of the environment must obey the 'laws of nature' of that environment. Thus, all the theoretical components of the relational approach – and how

---

10 See discussion in sections 1.3.2–1.3.2.4 above.

11 These were originally based on the OECD Principles, above n 9.

they 'fit' with each other – were demonstrated in the relational corporate governance framework in Figure 2.8. As explained there, all the components of the relational approach are ultimately drawn from the four Key Fields that form the base of the pyramid-like structure of the framework.

To maintain the explanatory and predictive power of the relational approach, it will be necessary to continuously track new studies in relation to each Key Field. And, while the size of this book has restricted the Key Fields to four in number, the relational approach's simulated environment may be expanded in future to more closely resemble the real world by adding Key Fields as they emerge. Possibilities flagged in Chapter 1 include non-profit corporations and governance, non-English-origin shareholder protection regimes and corporate social responsibility principles. Further Key Fields could involve (block-holder) shareholder activism, corporate culture effects and board diversity.

11.2.3 To Identify, Describe and Map Diagrammatically the Interrelationships, Themes and Factors Underpinning this Environment

This is the Weighing Mechanism of the relational approach. As noted above, this Mechanism is comprised of the three relational axes of good governance, the eight governance factors and the interrelationship schemes between these factors shown in Figures 2.6 and 2.7. These three components are combined to create a relational effect path for each governance variable. The starting point(s) of each relational effect path was demonstrated by the relational approach to be the empirical studies of the effectiveness of governance variables in Key Field No 4.

The relational approach demonstrated that the governance factors are the eight most significant or principal recurring aims, themes and tensions underlying or arising from the collective 'sphere' of corporate governance discourse:

Reporting Factor No 1:	Transparency, Timing and Integrity of Financial and Other Reports
Compliance Factor No 2:	Corporate Governance and Legal Compliance
Alignment Factor No 3:	Alignment of Management and Shareholder Interests
Compensation Factor No 4:	Board, CEO and Management Compensation and Incentives

Monitoring & Audit Factor No 5:	Internal and External/Audit Monitoring Quality
Stakeholders Factor No 6:	Identification, Participation and Protection of Stakeholder Interests
Decision-making Factor No 7:	Quality of Board, CEO and Management Decision-making
Responsibility Factor No 8:	Delineation and Disclosure of Powers, Duties and Lines of Responsibility.

The Weighing Mechanism was depicted in Figure 4.1. The relational approach demonstrated that the Weighing Mechanism is the theoretical representation of the voluntary 'obligations' comprising the nexus of contracts theory of the firm. The Weighing Mechanism undertakes a theoretical or hypothetical 'weighing' exercise to depict – descriptively and diagrammatically – the themes and considerations relevant to the competing or opposing interests of 'insiders' and 'outsiders' of the corporation. In short, the eight governance factors are 'weighed' in the three relational axes of good governance which acts like a set of scales to weigh the often competing aims or objectives (Objectives Axis No 1), behaviours (Behaviours Axis No 2) and interests (Positional Conflict Axis No 3) of 'insiders' and 'outsiders' of the corporation.

As noted above, the results of this weighing process are already calculated and presented for the reader – these are the two interrelationship schemes in Figures 2.6 (for the shareholder primacy model) and 2.7 (for the stakeholder model). These schemes are the two diagrams of *hypothesised or predicted interrelationships* between the eight governance factors. Thus, in turn, the interrelationship schemes represent the hypothesised or predicted interrelationships between the four Key Fields and the 39 governance variables to which the Fields give rise.

11.2.4 To Create a Comparative Table or Scheme System upon which to Compare Across Sectors and Over Time the Governance Variables Utilised in the Major US, UK, Australian and Global Governance Codes and Schemes

These are the relational approach's Governance Code Tables and Commonality Tables presented in Chapter 6.

Like the three relational axes, the Governance Code Tables again reflect the influence of the OECD Principles. The relational approach demonstrated that a comprehensive Governance Code Table can be constructed from elements of each of the global, US, UK and Australian sectors. The Tables compared the governance variables utilised in the major global and Anglo-American Governance Codes in operation today – including the OECD Principles, the NYSE Final Rules, the FRC's UK Corporate Governance Code 2014 and the ASX 2014 Principles and Recommendations.[12] Such a Table can be applied to determine the scope and nature of any governance code including, in the future, non-common-law origin countries.

On account of its comprehensive listing of governance variables, the Governance Code Table will be a useful comparative tool for regulators, policy-makers and law reformers in the area. In this respect, the relational approach has demonstrated that a Governance Code Table such as that presented in Chapter 6 can be used to track the degree of harmonisation or convergence in governance codes including, again, those of non-common-law origin countries. In this way, refinements or additions to governance codes over time can be assessed.

Flowing from the convergence aspect of the Governance Code Tables are the Commonality Tables. The relational approach presented a Commonality Table to list the recurring governance variables within a sector and across sectors. Thus, the relational approach has produced a Commonality Table for the global sector (Table 6.3) and each of the sectors of the US (Table 6.5) and UK (Table 6.7).[13]

---

[12] See OECD Principles, above n 9; ASX 2014 Principles and Recommendations, above n 2; Financial Reporting Council (FRC), *The UK Corporate Governance Code*, September 2014, London, accessed 5 March 2015 at http://www.frc.org.uk/ ('UK Corporate Governance Code 2014') and New York Stock Exchange, *Final NYSE Corporate Governance Rules* ('NYSE Final Rules'), approved by SEC 4 November 2003 (except s 303A.08) and 30 June 2003 (s 303A.08). The Rules (as amended from time to time) comprise section 303A.00 of the NYSE Listed Company Manual. See section 303A.00 Corporate Governance Standards (approved 25 November 2009), available at http://nysemanual.nyse.com/lcm/ (accessed 5 March 2015). Subsequent amendments have been made to:

- Section 303A.00 – Corporate Governance Standards (approved 22 August 2013)
- Section 303A.02 – Corporate Governance Standards (approved 11 January 2013)
- Section 303A.05 – Corporate Governance Standards (approved 11 January 2013)
- Section 303A.07 – Audit Committee Additional Requirements (approved 22 August 2013)

These Rule amendments are available at http://nysemanual.nyse.com/lcm/ (accessed 3 March 2015).

[13] No Commonality Table is presented for the Australian sector as explained in section 6.6.1 above.

Again to display the convergence aspect, the relational approach presented a Commonality Table to compare the US, UK and Australian listed corporate governance codes – those codes currently in operation and backed with an enforcement or disclosure regime stemming from the listing rules of the relevant stock or securities exchanges.[14] Again, refinements and additions to governance codes can be tracked and assessed.

The relational approach concluded the examination of the commonality of governance variables by presenting a 'core' set of governance variables from the global and national listed sectors combined. These were:

- timely/regular disclosure of information (item 2.iii);
- questions and voting in meetings (item 2.iv);
- interested or conflicted director disclosure (items 3.v and 6.iv.e);
- employee/management/director incentive and participation schemes (item 4.iv);
- timely disclosure of material information including remuneration policies (item 5.i.b);
- independent/external audit (item 5.ii);
- quality and integrity of information (item 5.iii);
- board functions and independence – compliance with statutory and legal duties on organisation/directors (item 6.i);
- principal board responsibilities – corporate governance compliance (item 6.iv.b);
- principal board responsibilities – selection and monitoring of key management (item 6.iv.c);
- principal board responsibilities – fair and open election of directors (item 6.iv.d);
- principal board responsibilities – interested director or management conflicts or transactions (item 6.iv.e);
- principal board responsibilities – reporting, audit, financial/operational control, risk management and internal audit (item 6.iv.f);
- independence from management – non-executive/independent directors (item 6.v.a); and
- independence from management – responsibilities of board sub-committees delineated and disclosed (item 6.v.b).

The relational approach demonstrated through commonality the significance of these governance variables in for-profit governance code discourse and for the relational approach in the identification, design

---

[14] See Commonality Table 6.9 and discussion in section 6.7.1 above.

and articulation of the three relational axes of good governance[15] and the governance factors.[16]

11.2.5 As an Over-arching Aim, to Propose an Approach or Tool for Regulators, Policy-Makers, Law Reformers and Corporate Actors to Predict, Measure and Enhance the Relative Importance of Governance Variables inter se in Reducing (or Increasing) Agency Costs and Enhancing (or Reducing) the Long-Term Efficiency and Sustainability of the For-Profit Firm

This is the relational approach itself. It was introduced and defined in Chapter 1 as the examination and evaluation of the *interrelationships* between individual governance structures, mechanisms, processes and protocols (that is, governance variables) that seek to minimise or avoid (or, contrastingly, increase) agency costs between economic actors 'inside' and 'outside' the for-profit corporation. The relational approach explained that the approach gives rise to the theoretical Weighing Mechanism of the relational approach – the three relational axes of good governance, the eight governance factors and the two interrelationship schemes. The interrelationship schemes identify the number of governance factors affected by a governance variable and the direction of effect. The schemes are used in conjunction with the empirical studies in Chapters 7–10 to construct a relational effect path for that governance variable. These empirical studies provide the starting point for the relational effect path.

The *rationale* of relational corporate governance is that the interrelationships between governance variables and their effects (whether positive or negative) on such agency costs affect the long-term efficiency and survival/sustainability of the firm. If these interrelationships can be better understood, then the relational approach *hypothesises or predicts* that the relative importance of governance variables *inter se* in reducing (or increasing) these agency costs and enhancing (or reducing) shareholder welfare (measured by proxies for shareholder wealth such as firm cost of capital, firm value/share price and firm operating performance) can be determined or predicted with better confidence. The hypothesised or predicted effects on these agency cost and shareholder welfare measures, in turn, permits determinations and predictions to be made in relation to the long-term efficiency and survival/sustainability of the corporation.

The Coverage Table (Table 3.1) is the first of two operational tables

---

[15] See discussion in sections 2.3.1–2.3.3 above.

[16] See discussion in sections 2.6.1–2.6.8 above.

of the relational approach. The relational effect path of each governance variable describes a *predicted or hypothesised interrelationship* directly or indirectly between each governance variable and one or more of the eight governance factors (the recurring themes and tensions underlying corporate governance). The description of, and results displayed for, each relational effect path are summarised in this Coverage Table. The summarised results are known as that governance variable's 'coverage'. This coverage is the number of governance factors affected, and the direction of effect (positive or negative), by each governance variable. The maximum coverage is +/−8 units. The results of the coverage of a governance variable are set out in the Coverage Table (Table 3.1).

The Relational Proximity Table (Table 3.2) is the ultimate operational table and represents the results of the relational corporate governance approach. The coverage measure is converted into the 'relational proximity rating' of that governance variable in the Relational Proximity Table. This rating is a *proportion* expressed as a number on a scale from 0 to a maximum of +/−100.00 units known as ***rprox***. The Relational Proximity Table 'groups' governance variables in descending order of relative importance in reducing (or increasing) agency costs and enhancing (or reducing) the long-term efficiency and survival/sustainability of the firm.

Having presented the relational approach's conclusions for its key research questions, the chapter now turns to highlight elements of the Key Fields as particularly significant for the relational approach.

11.3 THE APPLICATION OF THE PRINCIPAL THEORIES OF THE FIRM TO THE RELATIONAL APPROACH

For regulators, policy-makers, law-reformers and corporate actors, this book has demonstrated that the relational approach to governance variables adds explanatory power to the principal theories of the firm, in particular agency theory, the shareholder primacy model and the director-primacy model of corporate governance. To reflect the critical role of information asymmetry in agency theory, the relational approach's governance factors are designed to reduce (or at least reflect) this informational problem.

And this informational problem is demonstrated by the relational approach's analysis of the Enron collapse in Key Field No 2 (for example, 'phantom' profits and off-balance sheet entities[17]) and the 'core' features

[17] See discussion in section 5.2.1.1 above.

of governance codes in Key Field No 3 listed above from section 6.8.1. Not surprisingly, then, the Coverage Table (Table 3.1) and Relational Proximity Table (Table 3.2) accord the highest governance variable coverage and relational proximity ratings (and therefore highest relative importance in reducing agency costs) to governance variables similarly designed to reduce this informational problem.

The relational approach also demonstrated that the market for corporate control is essential to nexus theory.[18] To reflect this significance, governance variables which are components of the market for corporate control have relatively higher governance variable coverage and relational proximity ratings. Indeed, no component of the market for corporate control has a lower coverage/rating (ignoring the direction) than 8/100.00 *rprox* which reflects the relational approach's degree of alignment with the nexus of contracts theory. As noted above, the Weighing Mechanism of the relational approach is a theoretical representation of nexus theory.

As a practical example, the relational approach demonstrated that staggered board elections and other anti-takeover mechanisms – by virtue of constituting a shareholder welfare-reducing term of the nexus of contracts – reduce firm value and, consequently, firm sustainability.[19] Such mechanisms reduce the effectiveness of the market for corporate control as a market-efficiency sanction and are thus ascribed the maximum negative relational proximity of −8/100.00 *rprox*.

11.4 CONCLUDING REMARKS FOR 'OVERALL' GOVERNANCE AND BOARD FACTORS I AND II

11.4.1 'Overall' or 'Multi-Variable' Governance

The relational approach demonstrates the central or prominent operation of board and director-related variables in the governance mix as well as the external audit function. In this respect, the relational approach concludes that the combinations or groupings of governance variables which affect firm value and/or firm performance are board and committee size, a high level of attendance at board meetings, director independence and the proportion of executive directors and the presence and operation (including frequency of meeting) of board committees – in particular the audit,

[18] See discussion in section 4.2.2 above.

[19] See discussion in sections 8.3–8.3.1.1 above.

nominating and compensation committees. The mix must also contain the equity (including option) compensation and/or holdings of directors and executives, the board skills 'mix', the external/independent audit function, annual review of the board and outside/external board advisors. The mix is completed by the annual election of all directors (instead of staggered board elections), the absence of other anti-takeover mechanisms, block-holding and activism variables and the outside board positions held by independent directors.

11.4.2 Board Factors I – 'Independence' and Proportion of Non-Executive/Independent Directors

In the case of the director independence variable, an elegant case is argued that some of the perceived benefits may include enhanced acquisition decisions and monitoring and a greater likelihood of dismissal of the CEO after poor performance.[20] Despite the inconclusive support for this variable in empirical studies at this time, the relational approach demonstrated that the *real push* for independence in corporate governance discourse stems from the governance codes in Key Field No 3. There, the relational approach concluded that the key features of global and national listed governance codes included 'board functions and independence – compliance with statutory and legal duties on organisation/directors', 'independence from management – non-executive/independent directors' and 'independence from management – responsibilities of board sub-committees delineated and disclosed'.[21]

And the relational approach demonstrated that these features flowed from corporate collapses of the time. The Enron corporate collapse highlighted the undermining of the director independence factor on the grounds of 'outrageously high' director and consulting contracts for directors[22] as well as share and option holdings which caused problems in monitoring.[23] Potential conflicts of interest also arose on the risk

---

[20] See discussion in section 7.3.2.1.1 above.

[21] See the discussion in section 6.8.1 above.

[22] Douglas M Branson, 'Enron – When All Systems Fail: Creative Destruction or Roadmap to Corporate Governance Reform?' (2003) 48 *Villanova Law Review* 989; Villanova Law/Public Policy Research Paper No 2003-13, accessed 5 March 2015 at SSRN: http://ssrn.com/abstract=473205, 1003. See discussion in section 5.2.2.1 above.

[23] Stuart L Gillan and John D Martin, 'Financial Engineering, Corporate Governance, and the Collapse of Enron', U of Delaware Coll. of Bus. and Econ. Ctr. for Corp. Governance Working Paper No 2002-001 (November 2002),

management committee on account of options paid to directors.[24] The Enron collapse also highlighted loss of director independence through board member familiarity, deference to inside directors[25] and the regular attendance of the Chairman and (separate) CEO at the executive, finance and audit committees.[26]

In the case of the perceived positive link between the independence variable and firm operating performance and/or firm value, the relational approach demonstrated that the results of empirical studies are conflicting with many of the studies examined finding no such relation. The relational approach concluded, however, that intervening variables for director independence include the relative importance of the CEO,[27] the size of the board and the level of equity holdings for the CEO, management and both 'inside' and independent directors.[28]

11.4.3 Board Factors II – Board Size

In relation to the second slate of individual board factors examined by the relational approach, the board size factor appears to be itself affected by a wide range of other intervening factors. The size of the board will be affected by national statutory or governance code requirements. In addition, the size of the board will be larger the wider the gap between insider and outsider interests, the more difficult the practicability of external monitoring, the larger the firm's operations or size and the greater the firm's diversity and/or complexity and debt level.[29] However, no consistent or conclusive result could be confidently predicted in relation to the relationship between board size and firm operating performance and/or firm value.[30]

---

available at SSRN: http://ssrn.com/abstract=354040, 23–24 (footnotes omitted). See discussion in section 5.2.2.1.1 above.

[24] See discussion in section 5.2.2.1.2 above.

[25] See discussion in section 5.2.2.2 above.

[26] Gillan and Martin, above n 23, 25.

[27] Martijn Cremers, Lucian Bebchuk and Urs Peyer, 'CEO Centrality', Harvard Law and Economics Discussion Paper No 601 (December 2007, Revised May 2008), available at SSRN: http://ssrn.com/abstract=1030107, 1 and 3. See discussion in section 7.3.2.1.1 above.

[28] See discussion in sections 7.3.2.1.5–7.3.2.1.7 above.

[29] See discussion in sections 8.2.1–8.2.2.2 above.

[30] See discussion in section 8.2.2.1 above.

11.4.4 Audit Sub-Committee – Presence, Independence and Expertise

The perceived link between audit sub-committee independence and firm value and/or operating performance remains, at this time, a matter of debate. Again, the relational approach demonstrates the significance of this committee as flowing from governance codes in Key Field No 3. The relational approach there demonstrated 'independence from management – responsibilities of board sub-committees delineated and disclosed' as a key feature of international and national listed corporate governance codes.[31]

The relational approach demonstrated that a positive link likely exists between audit committee financial expertise and firm value and/or operating performance on account of perceived improvements in the quality of monitoring. It is likely that *accounting* expertise will be most significant again on monitoring quality grounds given the complexity of modern company accounting and reporting requirements.[32]

11.4.5 Independence and Earnings Management

The relational approach demonstrated that, alone, the independence factor is of inconclusive explanatory power in minimising earnings manipulation.[33] However, an increase in the independence factor appears to be critical in reducing earnings manipulation *when combined with* increases in the time spent in review (or the number of audit committee meetings), increases in the financial expertise of the relevant directors/committee and separation of the CEO and chairperson functions.[34] The relational approach confirmed the discussion in the previous section by demonstrating that *accounting* expertise is more likely than other types of financial expertise to reduce the likelihood of earnings manipulation. However, the presence of financial experts may lead to some 'free rider' negative effects on the quality of monitoring by other directors on the audit committee.[35]

11.4.6 Executive, CEO and Director Compensation

Chapter 10 examined the fourth and final part of the empirical studies Key Field No 4 by examining perceived links between executive, CEO and

---

[31] See discussion in section 6.8.1 above.
[32] See discussion in section 9.2.1.1.1 above.
[33] See discussion in section 9.2.1.2 above.
[34] Ibid.
[35] See discussion in section 9.2.1.1.2 above.

director compensation and measures of firm value, operating performance and the probability of earnings manipulation.

Other perceived links included firm size and reputational constraints and links between the CEO and director compensation levels *inter se*. The different forms of compensation have included incentive-based equity compensation and options (including short-term options). The relatively recent phenomenon of shareholder 'Say-on-Pay' statutes was also examined for governance effects.

The significance and debate relating to optimal executive, CEO and director compensation will be on-going. This is demonstrated by the presence as 'core' features of governance codes of 'employee/management/director incentive and participation schemes' and the 'timely disclosure of material information including remuneration policies'.[36]

11.4.6.1 Substantial director shareholdings and independence

There was some support among empirical studies for a link between increases in the level of director shareholdings and firm operating performance. In this respect, some studies found that substantial director shareholdings were associated with increased operating performance,[37] 'disciplinary management turnover' in times of poor performance[38] and improvements in the oversight of management. The independence element is also likely to be a significant requirement here. Where *independent* directors are entitled to 'incentive compensation', monitoring of the board (measured by the probability of 'CEO turnover') increases as firm performance falls.[39]

11.4.6.2 CEO/executive compensation and firm operating performance/value

Some studies find *no* relationship between CEO/executive pay levels and firm performance and/or firm value.[40] If a causative relation exists between

---

[36] See discussion in section 6.8.1 above.

[37] Sanjai Bhagat and Brian Bolton, 'Corporate Governance and Firm Performance' (June 2007), accessed 5 March 2015 at SSRN: http://ssrn.com/abstract=1017342, 5. See discussion in section 10.2.2 above.

[38] Ibid, 6.

[39] T Perry, 'Incentive Compensation for Outside Directors and CEO Turnover', presented at Tuck-JFE Contemporary Corporate Governance Conference (June 2000), accessed 5 March 2015 at SSRN: http://ssrn.com/abstract=236033, 2 and 24.

[40] See, for example, Ivan E Brick, Darius Palia and Chia-Jane Wang, 'Simultaneous Estimation of CEO Compensation, Leverage, and Board

CEO/executive pay levels and firm value, it may well be negative.[41] The relational approach demonstrates that, *if* a positive relationship is to be found between CEO/executive pay levels and firm operating performance, it is heavily qualified relying on, at the least, existence of an incentive-based payment (that is, performance-based payments[42] or options[43]) and the simultaneous operation of 'block-holder' monitoring.[44]

11.4.6.3 Short-term options and earnings manipulation

In Chapter 10, cautionary findings were presented that the risk of earnings misstatement increases with short-term options granted to outside audit committee directors inhibiting the function of such directors to monitor financial statement integrity.[45] In addition, option incentive plans may well increase earnings manipulation but not performance.[46]

These findings are also reflected in the findings of the commentator evaluations of the Enron collapse in Chapter 5. There, commentators examined the role of share options, particularly those with a short-term structure, and bonus payments linked to share-price performance. The relational approach there demonstrated that these forms of CEO, executive and director compensation increase the likelihood of the adoption of high risk-taking strategies by management,[47] increase the risk of

---

Characteristics on Firm Value', unpublished working paper, AFA 2006 Boston Meetings Paper (March 2005), 5. See discussion in section 10.2.3 above.

[41] Cremers, Bebchuk and Peyer, above n 27, 1. See discussion in sections 10.2.3 and 10.2.4 above.

[42] R Daines, V B Nair and L A Kornhauser, 'The Good, the Bad and the Lucky: CEO Pay and Skill', Univ of Pennsylvania Institute for Law and Economics, Research Paper Series (August 2005), accessed 5 March 2015 at SSRN: http://ssrn.com/abstract=622223, 4 and 27. See discussion in sections 10.2.2 and 10.2.4 above.

[43] M Hanlon, S Rajgopal and T J Shevlin, 'Are Executive Stock Options Associated with Future Earnings?', JAE Boston Conference, October 2002 (20 December 2002), accessed 5 March 2015 at SSRN: http://ssrn.com/abstract=318101, 41. See discussion in sections 10.2.2 and 10.2.4 above.

[44] Daines, Nair and Kornhauser, above n 42, 27. See discussion in sections 10.2.2 and 10.2.4 above.

[45] S Marrakchi Chtourou, J Bédard and L Courteau, 'Corporate Governance and Earnings Management' (April 21, 2001), accessed 5 March 2015 at SSRN: http://ssrn.com/abstract=275053, 4 and 27. See discussion in section 10.2.5 above.

[46] H Tehranian, M M Cornett, A J Marcus and A Saunders, 'Earnings Management, Corporate Governance, and True Financial Performance' (January 2006), accessed 5 March 2015 at SSRN: http://ssrn.com/abstract=886142, 1–6 and 18–19. See also 1–2, 5 and 18–19. See discussion in section 10.2.5 above.

[47] William W Bratton, 'Enron and the Dark Side of Shareholder Value' (2001–2002) 76 *Tulane Law Review* 1275 (May 2002), accessed 5 March 2015 at SSRN: http://ssrn.com/abstract=301475, 49. See discussion in section 5.2.3.2.1 above.

'aggressive accounting manipulations' to boost stock option values[48] and increase the likelihood of fraud and risk-taking to increase the share price.[49]

11.5 OBSERVATIONS ON THE EXPLANATORY POWER OF THE RELATIONAL APPROACH AND FUTURE RESEARCH

The relational approach flagged earlier in this chapter improvement in the explanatory power of the relational approach through expansion of the Key Fields.

In this penultimate section of the relational approach, an improvement to the relational approach is suggested consequent on future large-scale empirical testing.

The 'Mode' of the Relational Approach

In Chapter 2,[50] the relational approach demonstrated that, in the relational approach's shareholder-primacy mode, Alignment Factor No 3 (Alignment of Board, CEO, Management and Shareholder Interests) acts as an 'umbrella' or 'guiding' principle over governance factors with the exception of Compliance Factor No 2 (Corporate Governance and Legal Compliance). This would include Stakeholders Factor No 6 (Identification, Participation and Protection of Stakeholder Interests). Where, however, the relational approach is in stakeholder mode as presented in Figure 2.7, shareholder interests do not necessarily rank above those of other non-shareholder-stakeholders and so Alignment Factor No 3 will not dominate over Stakeholders Factor No 6.[51]

An alternative approach to determine or set the mode of the relational

---

48 John Armour and Joseph A McCahery, 'After Enron: Improving Corporate Law and Modernising Securities Regulation in Europe and the US', Amsterdam Center for Law & Economics Working Paper No 2006-07 (June 2006), accessed 5 March 2015 at SSRN: http://ssrn.com/abstract=910205, 2. See discussion in section 5.2.3.2.1 above.

49 Jeffrey N Gordon, 'What Enron Means for the Management and Control of the Modern Business Corporation: Some Initial Reflections' (2002) 69 *University of Chicago Law Review* 1233 (Summer 2002), accessed 5 March 2015 at SSRN: http://ssrn.com/abstract=305343, 15–16. See discussion in section 5.2.3.2.1 above.

50 See discussion in section 2.7.1 and Shareholder Primacy Interrelationship Scheme Figure 2.6 above.

51 See discussion in section 2.7.1 and Figure 2.7 above.

approach would be to have, as the only ‘umbrella’ principle ranking above other governance factors, Compliance Factor No 2. Theoretically, this would represent the ‘neutral mode’ of the relational approach. Where the relational approach is to reflect, again theoretically, shareholder primacy mode, an *additional weighting* would be accorded to Alignment Factor No 3 in the Coverage Table (Table 3.1) and (consequently) the Relational Proximity Table (Table 3.2).

The precise additional weighting to be accorded to Alignment Factor No 3 in such a case would be determined by further empirical investigation. In the case of stakeholder mode, both Alignment Factor No 3 and Stakeholders Factor No 6 would be accorded the relevant additional weighting (which may not necessarily be equivalent) in the Coverage Table and the Relational Proximity Table.

Multiple Relational Effect Paths

Of course, a large number of interrelationships or interactions between governance variables – both direct and indirect – can be conceived and constructed from the interrelationship schemes. Again due to considerations of size, this first stage of the relational approach has presented a single relational effect path for each governance variable. This is hypothesised to be the most direct pathway or zone of effect of governance factors based on the starting point which was determined by the empirical studies in Key Field No 4.

In future stages of the relational approach based on empirical testing, it will be possible to devise multiple relational effect paths for the same governance variable. This means not just the most direct pathway but others revealed in these empirical studies. These paths will not necessarily take in as many or the same governance factors. Additionally, the order in which the governance factors are affected may affect the strength of the effect. This will enhance the explanatory and predictive power of the relational approach as the relational proximity rating of a governance variable will reflect the sum total (or, perhaps, a multiple) of its multiple pathways.

11.6 CONCLUDING REMARKS FOR THE RELATIONAL APPROACH

The relational approach has presented a new unifying theme to complement and enhance the explanatory power of the existing principal ‘law and economics’ theories and models of the firm. The relational corporate governance approach is akin to a ‘governance version’ of the Human

Genome Project. It has evaluated and mapped on a 'first principles' basis the nature, operation, effect and, consequently, the relative importance of 39 of the myriad of corporate governance variables which arise in international and national corporate governance best practice and discourse. The relational approach is primarily orientated to the Anglo-American model of corporate governance but with the capacity for – in the future – ultimate comparative relevance to 'continental' systems.

Relational corporate governance is the construction of various theoretical components and operational tables to weigh competing interests which (in their simplest form) primarily involve those 'inside' the corporation (directors, CEO and management) and those 'outside' (shareholders, employees, lenders and other external stakeholders such as regulators and social interests).

To make hypotheses in relation to the relative importance of individual governance variables in enhancing or reducing the long-term efficiency and sustainability of the corporation, the relational approach has constructed a Weighing Mechanism comprised of three theoretical components. First, the three relational axes of good governance act like a set of scales to theoretically 'weigh' the competing objectives, behaviours and positional conflict of those 'inside' the corporation and those 'outside'. Second, the relational approach identified a set of eight governance factors which are the eight most common or recurring themes in this approach's 'landscape' or representation of the real-world sphere of corporate governance. Third, the relational approach constructed two interrelationship schemes or diagrams of the hypothesised interrelationships between these governance factors. To do so, the relational approach analysed four Key Fields of corporate governance research – the pre-eminent theories of the firm, Enron corporate collapse literature, international and national governance codes and empirical studies of the effectiveness of governance variables in affecting shareholder-wealth measures.

The interrelationship schemes identify the effects (positive, negative or both) of the governance variables on the 'enhancement' or 'diminution' of the themes represented in each governance factor. In many cases, the views of authors and commentators as to the effect of the governance variables on shareholder-wealth measures are conflicting or limited in scope to less than the full number of governance factors. In such cases, the relational approach has reconciled or extended these studies using the interrelationship schemes to determine the hypothetical or normative effects of the governance variables on the relevant governance factors and to find the starting point of the relational effect paths.

The number and direction of the governance factors affected by a governance variable comprises the coverage of that governance variable.

This is in turn converted to a proportion known as that governance variable's relational proximity rating or *rprox*. This rating reflects the relative importance of the individual governance variables in affecting (positively or negatively) agency costs and enhancing or reducing the long-term efficiency and sustainability of the Anglo-American for-profit corporation.

This book has demonstrated that the relational approach may be used as a tool to complement and enhance the explanatory power of the existing principal 'law and economics' theories and models of the firm, to map the effectiveness of corporate governance variables in use in corporate governance codes around the world and to assess reform proposals in the field. It is proposed that, in the future, the relational approach will be econometrically and computer modelled and empirically tested. Over time, the components comprised in the relational corporate governance framework – in particular, those at the base of its pyramid structure and referred to as Key Fields – may thus be expanded to approximate in more detail the sphere of corporate governance best practice and discourse.

Appendix 1: Glossary of governance variables

Column 2 of this Glossary contains the names of the 39 corporate governance and management mechanisms, structures, processes and protocols examined by the relational approach and known as 'governance variables'. As is the practice in many 'multi-variable' studies, the governance variables are abbreviated in alphabetical order in Column 3. For ease of identification, the relevant abbreviations will appear in square parentheses '[ ]' throughout the book.

The nature, operation and effect of the individual governance variables is examined in detail in Key Field No 4 – Empirical Studies of the Effectiveness of Governance Variables in Chapters 7–10. Column 5 contains the reference in the relational approach to the discussion of the relevant 'relational effect path' of that governance variable.

Table A.1 Glossary of governance variables

1. No.	2. Governance Variable	3. Abbreviation (Alphabetical)	4. Description	5. Relational Effect Path
1.	Audit Committee – Accounting Expertise – Earnings Manipulation Reduction Effect	**AudAccEarn** (+)	The presence of one or more audit committee members with financial expertise of an *accounting* nature *vis-à-vis* other forms of financial expertise. This variable measures the predicted reduction or fall in earnings manipulation or management as a result of that accounting expertise.	**9.2.1.1.2**
2.	Audit Committee – Presence, Operation and Frequency	**AudCom** (+)	The basic matters pertaining to the audit committee of the board of directors. These include principally its (usually mandated) existence, basic structure, performance of its functions and responsibilities and number of meetings or time in review.	**8.4.2**
3.	Audit Committee – Financial Expertise (Accounting)	**AudExpAcc** (+)	The presence of one or more audit committee members with financial expertise of an *accounting* nature *vis-à-vis* other forms of financial expertise. This variable measures the predicted increase in firm value and operating performance as a result of that accounting expertise.	**8.4.4**
4.	Audit Committee – Non-Accounting Expertise – 'Free Rider' Effect	**AudFree** (−)	The presence of one or more audit committee members *without* accounting expertise. This variable tests whether such members 'free-ride' or become 'less vigilant'[1] because of reliance on other committee members – that is, the suggestion that non-accounting members may lack the necessary expertise to understand complex accounting issues and may rely excessively on 'accounting-expertise'	**9.2.1.1.2**

Table A.1 (continued)

1. No.	2. Governance Variable	3. Abbreviation (Alphabetical)	4. Description	5. Relational Effect Path
			members to carry out the monitoring function of the committee without adding sufficient additional skills, knowledge or monitoring capacity.	**9.2.1.1.2**
5.	Audit Committee – Independence in Combination with Frequency of Meeting – Reduction in Earnings Manipulation Effect	**AudIndFreq** (+)	This variable represents the effect, in combination with the independence of the audit committee, of the time spent in review or the number of audit committee meetings. This variable measures the predicted reduction or fall in earnings manipulation or management as a result of that time in review and audit committee meetings.	**9.2.1**
6.	Audit Committee – Independence – Information Flow and Decision Quality 'Trade-off'	**AudIndInfo** **(−)**	The number or proportion of audit committee members who are outside or independent directors. Similar to the **[BrdIndInfo] (−)** variable, this variable tests whether there is a *reduction* in the volume or quality of information flowing to the audit committee as a result of a possible reluctance by management to fully and frankly disclose material to independent directors with a consequent *reduction* in the quality of decision-making by the committee and, in turn, the quality of monitoring by the board of the CEO and management.	**8.4.3**

7.	Audit Committee – Independence – Monitoring Effect	**AudIndMon** (+)	The number or proportion of audit committee members who are outside or independent directors. This variable tests whether there is an improvement in the monitoring by the audit committee of the CEO and management as a consequence of the presence of outside or independent directors on the audit committee.	**8.4.3**
8.	Audit Committee – Short Term Options Granted to Outside Directors – Reduction in Monitoring Effect	**AudShortOpts** (−)	This variable relates to the level or amount of compensation granted to outside or independent directors who are on the audit committee in the form of short-term options. The variable tests the relationship (if any) between the nature and levels of this compensation and matters such as agency costs, the quality of decision-making, monitoring of the CEO and management and the manipulation or management of earnings.	**10.2.5.1**
9.	Block Shareholding – Other Shareholder Agency Costs	**BlockCosts** (−)	The presence of 'block' shareholders or 'block-holders' with shareholdings of more than 5%. This variable tests whether such block-holdings cause an increase in agency costs to other small widely-dispersed shareholders.	**8.5.1–8.5.2**
10.	Block Shareholding – Monitoring Effect	**BlockMon** (+)	The presence of 'block' shareholders or 'block-holders' with shareholdings of more than 5%. This variable tests whether such block-holdings cause an improvement in the monitoring of management with a consequent reduction in agency costs to other small widely-dispersed shareholders and improvement in firm operating performance or value.	**8.5.1–8.5.2**

Table A.1 (continued)

1. No.	2. Governance Variable	3. Abbreviation (Alphabetical)	4. Description	5. Relational Effect Path
11.	Board – Attendance Level (High)	**BrdAttend** (+)	A high attendance level of directors at board meetings. The variable tests whether an increase in attendance enhances the quality of the monitoring of the CEO and management by the board with a consequential improvement in decision-making.	**7.3.2.1.2**
12.	Board and Committee (Non-Audit) Size – Earnings Manipulation Effect	**BrdCmEarn** (+/−)	This variable tests whether the likelihood of earnings manipulation is affected by changes in the size of the board and committees (other than the audit committee).	**9.2.2**
13.	Board and Committee Size	**BrdCmSize** (+/−)	The number of members of the board and committees (other than the audit committee) including the structural determinants of this size and the consequences on the effectiveness of the monitoring capacity and decision-making quality of the board and these committees consequent on changes in its/their size.	**8.2.2.2**
14.	Board Independent Director: Executive Director Proportion – Information Flow and Decision Quality 'Trade-off'	**BrdIndInfo** (−)	The number or proportion of board members who are outside or independent directors. This variable tests whether there is a *reduction* in the volume or quality of information flowing to the board as a result of a possible reluctance by management to fully and frankly disclose material to independent directors with a consequent *reduction* in the quality of decision-making by the board and, in turn, the quality of monitoring by the board of the CEO and management.	**7.3.2.1.3**

15.	Board Independent Director: Executive Director Proportion – Monitoring Effect	**BrdIndMon** (+)	The number or proportion of board members who are outside or independent directors. This variable tests whether there is an improvement in the monitoring of the CEO and management as a consequence of the presence of outside or independent directors on the board.	**7.3.2.1.1– 7.3.2.1.2**
16.	Board – Annual Review	**BrdReview** (+)	An evaluation of the performance of the board, directors and committees in relation to their relevant functions and duties against relevant benchmarks or measures such as those contained in governance codes.	**7.3.2.1.2**
17.	Board – Director Skills 'Mix'	**BrdSkills** (+)	The nature and combination of the different skills, experience and competencies of individual board members for the purposes of effectively carrying out the board's functions including the quality of decision-making, strategic planning, corporate governance compliance, monitoring of the CEO and key management, reporting/ disclosure, audit, financial and operational control, risk management and recognition of stakeholder interests including corporate social responsibility and ethical decision-making.	**7.3.1.2.1**
18.	Compensation Committee – Presence, Operation and Frequency	**CompCom** (+/−)	The basic matters pertaining to the compensation committee of the board of directors. These include principally its existence, basic structure, performance of its functions and responsibilities and number of meetings.	**10.2.4.1**
19.	Director/CEO Compensation Levels	**DirCEO$** (+/−)	This variable relates to the level or amount of director and CEO compensation, the interrelationship (if any) between these levels and the consequences for matters such as the quality of decision-making, monitoring of management and the manipulation or management of earnings. This variable does *not* include the equity or option holdings and plans for directors, CEO and executives. These are tested under the '**EqOpt**'-prefix variables below.	**10.2.4**

Table A.1 (continued)

1. No.	2. Governance Variable	3. Abbreviation (Alphabetical)	4. Description	5. Relational Effect Path
20.	Duality of CEO/Chair Positions – CEO Dismissal Probability	**DualDismiss** (−)	The holding of the roles of CEO and chairperson of the board at the same time by a person. This variable tests the likelihood of the CEO being dismissed particularly for poor performance by the company in such circumstances.	**8.6.3**
21.	Duality of CEO/Chair Positions – Probability of Earnings Manipulation	**DualEarn** (−)	The holding of the roles of CEO and chairperson of the board at the same time by a person. This variable tests the likelihood of earnings manipulation or management consequent on combining these roles.	**9.2.1.1.3**
22.	Duality of CEO/Chair Positions – Effect on Strategic Decision-making	**DualStrat** (−)	The holding of the roles of CEO and chairperson of the board at the same time by a person. This variable tests whether participation in strategic decision-making by directors is reduced consequent on combining these roles.	**8.6.3**
23.	Duality of CEO/Chair Positions – Monitoring and Decision-Quality 'Trade-off'	**DualTrade** (+/−)	The holding of the roles of CEO and chairperson of the board at the same time by a person. This variable tests whether such circumstances cause or contribute to a 'trade-off' between enhancements in the quality of board decision-making due to the bringing of 'inside' or firm-specific knowledge on the one hand and reductions in the quality of the board's monitoring of the CEO and management on the other.	**8.6.1–8.6.2**

24.	Equity/Option Plans and Holdings of Directors/Executives – Incentive/'Alignment' Effect (excludes short-term options)	**EqOptIncent** (+)	This variable relates to the level or amount of director, CEO and executive compensation in the form of equity or option plans and holdings (excluding short-term options). The variable tests the relationship (if any) between the nature and levels of this compensation and matters such as the quality of decision-making, monitoring of management and the manipulation or management of earnings. In particular, the variable tests whether the nature and level of such compensation may 'align' the interests of the 'inside' directors, CEO and executives with 'outside' widely-dispersed shareholders with consequent reductions in agency costs for those shareholders and improvements in firm performance and value.	**10.2.4**
25.	Equity/Option Plans and Holdings of Directors/Executives – 'Entrenchment' Effect (excludes short-term options)	**EqOptEntrch** (−)	This variable is closely related to the previous **[EqOptIncent]** (+) variable but seeks to test the opposite effect. In particular, the variable tests whether, instead or at the same time as any alignment of 'insider' and 'outsider' interests tested by the previous variable, the nature and levels of such compensation 'entrench' relevant directors, CEO and executives. The consequences of such entrenchment may increase agency costs for 'outside' widely-dispersed shareholders due to such directors, CEO and executives engaging in management misconduct (such as 'shirking', empire-building, overcompensation and over-consumption of 'perks'[2]) and other value-reducing behaviours.	**10.2.4**
26.	External/Independent Audit Function	**ExtAudEarn** (+)	The (usually mandated) requirement of an external or independent audit of the corporation's financial	**9.2.3.3**

Table A.1 (continued)

1. No.	2. Governance Variable	3. Abbreviation (Alphabetical)	4. Description	5. Relational Effect Path
			statements. This variable tests the effect of external audit on the practice of earnings manipulation by the company's board, CEO or management.	
27.	National Governance/ Shareholder Protection Regime	**NationGov** (+)	The strength or otherwise of the national shareholder protection regime as a result of the statutory and regulatory regime in which the corporation operates. Many such studies examine whether the strength of the shareholder protection regime affects firm performance and/or value and whether better protection is afforded by common law or English-origin countries on the one hand and code or civil law countries on the other.	**7.3.1.3.2**
28.	Nominating Committee – Presence, Operation and Frequency	**NomCom** (+/−)	The basic matters pertaining to the nominating committee of the board of directors. These include principally its existence, basic structure, performance of its functions and responsibilities and number of meetings.	**7.3.1.2.2**
29.	Nominating Committee – Independence Proportion	**NomInd** (+)	This variable tests for the effects of the number or proportion of members of the nominating committee who are outside or independent directors.	**7.3.1.2.2**
30.	Non-Audit Services of External Auditor	**NonAuditS** (−)	This variable tests whether the provision of non-audit services by the firm conducting the company's annual external audit reduces the independence of the auditor and the consequences (if any) for earnings manipulation or management and restatements.	**9.2.3.2–9.2.3.3**

31.	Other Anti-Takeover Mechanisms (excludes staggered board elections)	**OtherATMs** (−)	The effect of anti-takeover mechanisms (other than staggered board elections) on the (argued) disciplining and management replacement effects of the market for corporate control with the effect that management may become 'entrenched'. The consequences of such entrenchment may increase agency costs for 'outside' widely-dispersed shareholders due to the directors, CEO and/or executives engaging in management misconduct (such as 'shirking', empire-building, overcompensation and over-consumption of 'perks'[3]) and other value-reducing behaviours.	**8.3.1.1**
32.	Outside Board Positions of Independent Directors	**OutBrdPos** (−)	The number of board positions on other companies and organisations held by the independent or outside directors. This variable tests whether there is a reduction in the quality of monitoring of the CEO and management by such directors or whether such directors 'shirk' responsibilities such as serving on committees.	**8.2.3.1**
33.	Outside/External Board Advisers	**OutBrdAdv** (+)	Whether the board or its committees engage outside or independent advisers, experts or consultants to advise the board in relation to particular financial, operational, risk management and other matters requiring the relevant expertise and the effects of such a practice.	**7.3.2.1.2**
34.	Reputational Constraints – 'Disclosure Standards'	**ReputDiscl** (+)	'Reputational constraints' are consequences[4] and signals to inside and outside markets for decision agents[5] for individual directors, CEOs and managers relating to the performance of those 'insider' actors that assist or	**10.4.1**

Table A.1 (continued)

1. No.	2. Governance Variable	3. Abbreviation (Alphabetical)	4. Description	5. Relational Effect Path
			accompany the (argued) disciplining and replacement effects of the market for corporate control. Such reputational constraints are argued to act to restrict or dissuade directors, CEOs and managers from engaging in management misconduct and like value-reducing behaviours as well as constraining the level of executive compensation.[6] The operation of such constraints is argued to be partly dependent on appropriate and adequate 'disclosure standards' existing in (and set by) the relevant statutory and regulatory regime.[7]	
35.	Reputational Constraints – 'Transparent Reporting'	**ReputRep** (+)	As for the preceding **[ReputDiscl]** (+) variable, the operation of reputational constraints is argued to be partly dependent on circumstances and governance variables affecting 'transparent reporting'.[8]	**10.4.1**
36.	Staggered Board Elections	**StagBrdElect** (−)	The effect of staggered board elections (an anti-takeover mechanism) in which only a proportion of directors (that is, less than the full board) is open to re-election at a particular annual meeting of shareholders. In particular, the effects of such elections on the (argued) disciplining and management replacement effects of the market for corporate control with the effect that management may become 'entrenched'. The consequences of such entrenchment may increase agency costs for 'outside'	**8.3.1.1**

			widely-dispersed shareholders due to the directors, CEO and/or executives engaging in management misconduct (such as 'shirking', empire-building, overcompensation and over-consumption of 'perks'[9]) and other value-reducing behaviours.	
37.	Short-Term Option Holdings/Plans of Directors and Executives	**ShortTOpts** (−)	This variable is related to the **[EqOptIncent] (+)** and **[EqOptEntrch] (−)** variables both of which *exclude* a consideration of short-term options. This variable relates to the level or amount of director, CEO and executive compensation in the form of short-term options. The variable tests the relationship (if any) between the nature and levels of this compensation and matters such as agency costs, the quality of decision-making, monitoring of the CEO and management and the manipulation or management of earnings.	**10.2.5.1**
38.	Transparency and Timing of Reporting – Monitoring Effect	**TransTimeMon** (+)	This variable tests the principal aim of reporting – the reduction of agency costs associated with problems of 'information asymmetry'[10] between insiders such as the directors, CEO and management and 'outside' widely-dispersed shareholders. In particular, the variable examines the effects of improvements in the transparency, integrity and timing of financial and other reports on enhancing the monitoring of the CEO and management.	**9.1.2.1**
39.	Transparency and Timing of Reporting – Information Flow Reduction Effect	**TransTimeRedn** (−)	This variable examines the opposite effect of the preceding **[TransTimeMon] (+)** variable. It tests whether, instead of or at the same time as any (argued) improvements in the monitoring of management consequent on	**9.1.2.1**

Table A.1 (continued)

1. No.	2. Governance Variable	3. Abbreviation (Alphabetical)	4. Description	5. Relational Effect Path
			improvements in the transparency and timing of reporting, there may be an increase in agency costs for outside widely-dispersed shareholders due to (again argued) negative effects on the quality of information flow from management to the board with consequential reductions in the quality of decision-making and monitoring of the CEO and management.	

Notes:

1. See Anup Agrawal and Sahiba Chadha, 'Corporate Governance and Accounting Scandals', (September 2004), AFA 2004 San Diego Meetings, accessed 5 March 2015 at SSRN: http://ssrn.com/abstract=595138, 6.
2. Hollis Ashbaugh-Skaife, Daniel W Collins and Ryan LaFond, 'Corporate Governance and the Cost of Equity Capital', December 2004, accessed 5 March 2015 at SSRN: http://ssrn.com/abstract=639681, 1.
3. Ibid.
4. Lawrence A Cunningham, 'Behavioural Finance and Investor Governance' (2002) 59 *Washington & Lee Law Review* 767, accessed 5 March 2015 at SSRN: http://ssrn.com/abstract=255778, 3.
5. Eugene F Fama and Michael C Jensen, 'Separation of Ownership and Control' in Michael C Jensen, *Foundations Of Organizational Strategy*, Cambridge, MA: Harvard University Press, 1998, and (1983) 26 *Journal of Law and Economics* 301–26, accessed 5 March 2015 at SSRN: http://ssrn.com/abstract=94034, 19.
6. Ravi Singh, 'Board Independence and the Design of Executive Compensation', (September 2006), EFA 2005 Moscow Meetings Paper, accessed 5 March 2015 at SSRN: http://ssrn.com/abstract=673741, 1.
7. Ibid, 20.
8. Ibid.
9. Ashbaugh-Skaife, Collins and LaFond, above n 2.
10. Robert T Evans and John P Evans, 'The Influence of Non-Executive Director Control and Rewards on CEO Remuneration: Australian Evidence', EFMA 2002 London Meetings, accessed 5 March 2015 at SSRN: http://ssrn.com/abstract=263050, pp 3–4, 1

Appendix 2: Glossary of relational approach terms and components

This Glossary is an introduction – intended for ongoing reference by the reader – to the principal theoretical and operational terms and components of the relational corporate governance approach. The theoretical components of the relational approach are introduced and constructed in chapters 1–2. The operational results are displayed in the Coverage Table (Table 3.1) and the Relational Proximity Table (Table 3.2).

The relational approach is built from an artificial environment that simulates the real-world sphere of corporate governance and is comprised of the four Key Fields:

1. Application of the principal theories of the firm to the relational approach (chapter 4)
2. 'Autopsies' of the Enron and Hastie corporate collapses (chapter 5)
3. Comparative corporate governance codes (chapter 6)
4. Empirical studies of the effectiveness of governance variables (chapters 7–10)

In this Glossary, terms appearing in **bold** type in the definition or explanation section are themselves defined elsewhere in this Glossary.

Table A.2 Glossary of relational corporate governance approach terms and components

Term	Definition or Explanation
Behaviours Axis No. 2	**Behaviours Axis No. 2:** 'entrepreneurism' and 'innovation' (risk-taking) are balanced against risk management, 'control' and 'accountability' (responsibility). See the **Three Relational Axes of Good Governance** and the **Weighing Mechanism**.
Commonality	The process of identifying the 'core' or 'central' features of a number of **Governance Codes** within a sector (global, US, UK and Australia) and across sectors by the recurrence of **Governance Variables** in those Codes. See sections 6.1.1–6.1.2 above.
Commonality Table	The list of recurring **Governance Variables** within a sector (global, US, UK and Australia) and across sectors. See Table 6.3 (global), Table 6.5 (US) and Table 6.7 (UK). There is no Commonality Table for the Australian sector – see section 6.6.1 above.
'Coverage' of a Governance Variable	The number and identity of the **Governance Factors** affected by a **Governance Variable** and the direction of the effect. This is displayed in the **relational effect path** of a Governance Variable and summarised in the **Coverage Table (Table 3.1)**.
Coverage Table (Table 3.1)	This is the first of two operational tables of the relational corporate governance approach presented in this book. The **relational effect path** of each **Governance Variable** describes what the relational approach submits is a *predicted or hypothesised interrelationship* directly or indirectly between each **Governance Variable** and one or more of the eight **Governance Factors** (the recurring themes and tensions underlying corporate governance). The description of, and results displayed for, each **relational effect path** are summarised in this **Coverage Table (Table 3.1)**. The summarised results are known as that Governance Variable's **'Coverage'**. This Coverage is the number of Governance Factors affected, and the direction of effect (positive or negative), by each Governance Variable. The results of the Coverage of a Governance Variable set out in the **Coverage Table (Table 3.1)** are then converted into a numerical rating (known as the **Relational Proximity Rating** or ***rprox*** of a Governance Variable) in the **Relational Proximity Table (Table 3.2)**.
Enron corporate collapse	See **Key Field No. 2** (chapter 5).

Governance Codes	The international (OECD, ICGN and CACG) and national (US, UK and Australian) corporate governance codes, statutes, schemes and directives of best practice listed in Table 6.1 that mandate, prescribe or recommend (as the case may be) the adoption of **Governance Variables** by a corporation. See **Key Field No. 3** in chapter 6. The 'core' or 'central' features of these codes are described in section 6.8.1 above.
Governance Code Table	This is a comparative table or scheme used to compare across sectors and over time the **Governance Variables** utilised in the major International/cross-border (OECD, ICGN and CACG) and US, UK and Australian **Governance Codes**. A Governance Code Table for each of these sectors is contained in chapter 6.
Governance Factors	These Governance Factors are themes the relational approach submits are the eight most significant or principal recurring aims, themes and tensions underlying or arising from the collective 'sphere' of the four **Key Fields** – (1) the application of the principal theories of the firm to the relational approach; (2) 'autopsies' of the Enron and Hastie corporate collapses; (3) comparative corporate **Governance Codes** and (4) empirical studies of the effectiveness of Governance Variables. See section 2.1 above for the eight Governance Factors which are constructed in sections 2.6.1–2.6.8 above: • Reporting Factor No. 1 • Compliance Factor No. 2 • Alignment Factor No. 3 • Compensation Factor No. 4 • Monitoring & Audit Factor No. 5 • Stakeholders Factor No. 6 • Decision-making Factor No. 7 • Responsibility Factor No. 8 The eight Governance Factors form part of the **Weighing Mechanism** of the relational approach. See section 2.1 and section 4.2 above.

Table A.2 (continued)

Term	Definition or Explanation
Governance Variables	The governance and management structures, mechanisms, processes and protocols which are employed by a corporation to punish or deter management misconduct, to align the interests of corporate 'insiders' such as the directors, CEO and management with 'outsiders' such as widely-dispersed shareholders and to otherwise reduce agency costs and other shareholder value-reducing managerial behaviour or actions. In the real-world sphere of corporate governance, **Governance Variables** may be found in the multitude of international and national **Governance Codes** operating in the world today (Chapter 6). The 39 Governance Variables examined in this first stage of the relational approach are set out in Table 2.1 above. They are described in **Table A.1 of Appendix 1, *Glossary of Governance Variables***. Empirical and other studies relating to the effectiveness of these Variables are examined in chapters 7–10.
Interrelationship Schemes	These are the two (2) diagrams of *hypothesised or predicted interrelationships* between the eight **Governance Factors**. Thus, in turn, the Interrelationship Schemes represent the hypothesised or predicted interrelationships between the four **Key Fields** and the 39 **Governance Variables** to which the Fields give rise. There are two Scheme diagrams. The first represents the hypothesised or predicted interrelationships between the **Governance Factors** (and thus the **Governance Variables**) under the rubric of the shareholder primacy model of corporate governance and its associated shareholder wealth-maximisation principle. See **Shareholder Primacy Interrelationship Scheme** in Figure 2.6 above. The second Interrelationship Scheme represents these interrelationships under the 'stakeholder' model. See **Stakeholder Model Interrelationship Scheme** in Figure 2.7 above. The Interrelationship Schemes identify the number of Governance Factors affected by a Governance Variable and the direction of effect. The Schemes are used in conjunction with the empirical studies in chapters 7–10 to construct a **relational effect path** for that Governance Variable.

Key Fields	Four ‘fields’ or ‘areas’ of inquiry or examination which the relational approach submits are the four most significant or principal in terms of the volume of studies on the Social Science Research Network or SSRN database (see http://www.ssrn.com accessed 23 April 2015) and impact in the sphere of corporate governance best practice study and discourse. See section 1.3.2 above. The four **Key Fields** comprise: **1**. The application of the principal theories of the firm to the relational approach (chapter 4); **2**. ‘Autopsies’ of the Enron and Hastie corporate collapses (chapter 5); **3**. Comparative corporate **Governance Codes** (chapter 6); and **4**. Empirical studies of the effectiveness of **Governance Variables** (chapters 7–10). The **Key Fields** form the base of the pyramid-like structure of the relational approach known as the **Relational Corporate Governance Framework**. See Figure 2.8 above. Thus, all theoretical and operational components of the relational approach are ultimately drawn from the four **Key Fields**.
Key Field No. 1	The application of the principal and currently pre-eminent theories and models of the firm to the relational approach. These comprise the ‘nexus of contracts’, ‘agency’ (costs) theory, the ‘shareholder’ primacy model and its associated shareholder wealth-maximisation principle, the ‘stakeholder’ model and the ‘director primacy’ model of corporate governance. See chapter 4.
Key Field No. 2	‘Autopsies’ of the Enron and Hastie Group corporate collapses. This is comprised of literature and studies relating to the Enron corporate collapse which seek to catalogue relevant **Governance Variable** *failings* surrounding that collapse. The Enron corporate collapse is compared to the collapse of the Hastie Group detailed in the Administrators’ Report under section 439A of the *Corporations Act*. See chapter 5.
Key Field No. 3	Comparative Corporate **Governance Codes**. The international (OECD, ICGN and CACG) and national (US, UK and Australian) corporate **Governance Codes**, statutes, schemes and directives of best practice listed in Table 6.1 above. See chapter 6.

Table A.2 (continued)

Term	Definition or Explanation
Key Field No. 4	Empirical field studies of the effectiveness of **Governance Variables** in reducing (increasing) agency costs and enhancing (reducing) the long-term efficiency and survival/sustainability of the for-profit corporation. These aims are usually measured by proxies for shareholder wealth including the firm cost of capital, firm value/share price, firm operating performance and the likelihood of earnings manipulation or 'management'. This Field includes studies of the strength of the national shareholder protection regime. This Field comprises the largest of the **Key Fields** and is examined in detail in chapters 7–10.
Objectives Axis No. 1	**Objectives Axis No. 1:** the freedom of a company's management to pursue (profit-maximising) objectives (value enhancement) at one end is balanced against the interests of the shareholders (owners) in monitoring management's performance (performance assessment and reporting) and seeing that a company's resources are not dissipated (value preservation); See the **Three Relational Axes of Good Governance** and the **Weighing Mechanism**.
Positional Conflict Axis No. 3	**Positional Conflict Axis No. 3:** the interests of those 'within' the company such as the board, CEO and management (internal stakeholders) are balanced against the interests of those 'outside' the company such as shareholders, employees, lenders, suppliers, government legislators and regulators and social interests including the environment and the general public (external stakeholders). See the **Three Relational Axes of Good Governance** and the **Weighing Mechanism**.
Relational Corporate Governance Approach	This is the approach introduced in this book and defined in chapter 1 as the examination and evaluation of the *interrelationships* between individual governance structures, mechanisms, processes and protocols (**Governance Variables**) that seek to minimise or avoid (or, contrastingly, increase) agency costs between economic actors 'inside' and 'outside' the for-profit corporation. This concept is further examined in chapters 2 and 4 as giving rise to the theoretical **Weighing**

	Mechanism of the relational approach – the **Three Relational Axes of Good Governance**, the eight **Governance Factors** and the two **Interrelationship Schemes**. The Interrelationship Schemes identify the number of Governance Factors affected by a Governance Variable and the direction of effect. The Schemes are used in conjunction with the empirical studies in chapters 7–10 to construct a **relational effect path** for that Governance Variable.
Relational Corporate Governance Framework	This is the diagram in Figure 2.8 above which brings together all the theoretical components of the **Relational Corporate Governance Approach**.
Relational Proximity Rating or *rprox*	A numerical rating scale from 0.00 to a maximum of +/− 100.00 units abbreviated as ***rprox***. This is displayed in the **Relational Proximity Table (Table 3.2)**. The **Relational Proximity Rating** or ***rprox*** is determined by converting the **'Coverage'** of a **Governance Variable** from the **Coverage Table (Table 3.1)**. This Rating may be positive (+) or negative (–). A positive rating represents a *hypothesis or prediction* by the relational approach that the relevant Governance Variable *reduces* agency costs and *enhances* the long-term efficiency and survival/sustainability of the firm as determined by proxies for shareholder welfare/wealth such as firm cost of capital, firm value/share price, firm operating performance and the likelihood of earnings manipulation or 'management'. A negative rating represents the opposite effect on these measures. Thus, the Relational Proximity Rating represents the relative importance (also referred to as 'centrality') of that Governance Variable (*vis-à-vis* other Governance Variables) in reducing (or increasing) agency costs and enhancing (or reducing) the long-term efficiency and survival/sustainability of the firm. In the Relational Proximity Table (Table 3.2), Governance Variables are depicted in descending order in groupings of identical hypothesised or predicted relative importance.
Relational Proximity Table (Table 3.2)	This is the ultimate operational table of the book and represents the results of the **relational corporate governance approach**. The penultimate table, the **Coverage Table (Table 3.1)**, illustrates the identity and number of the eight **Governance Factors** (the recurring themes and tensions underlying corporate governance)

Table A.2 (continued)

Term	Definition or Explanation
	affected or influenced by each **Governance Variable** and the direction (positive or negative) of that effect – this result is known as the **'Coverage'** of that Governance Variable. This Coverage measure is then converted into the **Relational Proximity Rating** of that Governance Variable in the **Relational Proximity Table (Table 3.2)**. This Rating is a *proportion* expressed as a number on a scale from 0 to a maximum of +/− 100.00 units known as ***rprox***. The Relational Proximity Table 'groups' Governance Variables in descending order of **relative importance** in reducing (or increasing) agency costs and enhancing (or reducing) the long-term efficiency and **survival/ sustainability** of the firm.
Relative importance of a Governance Variable	See **Relational Proximity Rating** *or* ***rprox***.
Shareholder Primacy Interrelationship Scheme	See **Interrelationship Schemes** and Figure 2.6 above.
Stakeholder Model Interrelationship Scheme	See **Interrelationship Schemes** and Figure 2.7 above.
survival or sustainability of the firm	This concept is represented by 'proxy' or 'substitute' measures for (usually) shareholder welfare or wealth such as, most commonly, firm cost of capital, firm operating performance and firm value/ share price (see chapters 7, 8 and 10). The concept is also measured by the likelihood of earnings manipulation or 'management' (see chapter 9). If these proxy measures can be maintained, improved and optimised over the long-run time-frame then, all other things being equal, the corporation will continue as a 'going concern' or financially viable entity.

Three Relational Axes of Good Governance	This is the first of three components of the theoretical **Weighing Mechanism** of the relational approach. See sections 2.3.1–2.3.3 above. The **Three Relational Axes of Good Governance** act like a 'set of scales' to theoretically weigh the aims/objectives (Objectives Axis No. 1), behaviours (Behaviours Axis No. 2) and interests (Positional Conflict Axis No. 3) of 'insiders' and 'outsiders' of the corporation and is defined as follows: **Objectives Axis No. 1:** the freedom of a company's management to pursue (profit-maximising) objectives (value enhancement) at one end is balanced against the interests of the shareholders (owners) in monitoring management's performance (performance assessment and reporting) and seeing that a company's resources are not dissipated (value preservation); **Behaviours Axis No. 2:** "entrepreneurism" and "innovation" (risk-taking) are balanced against risk management, "control" and "accountability" (responsibility); and **Positional Conflict Axis No. 3:** the interests of those 'within' the company such as the board, CEO and management (internal stakeholders) are balanced against the interests of those 'outside' the company such as shareholders, employees, lenders, suppliers, government legislators and regulators and social interests including the environment and the general public (external stakeholders) The recurring themes and tensions underpinning corporate governance discourse and depicted in the eight **Governance Factors** are weighed in the Three Relational Axes of Good Governance. See sections 2.1 and 4.2. above. The results of this weighing process are already calculated and presented for the reader – these are the two **Interrelationship Schemes** in Figures 2.6 and 2.7. See section 2.1 above.

Table A.2 (continued)

Term	Definition or Explanation
Weighing Mechanism	The Weighing Mechanism of the relational approach is a theoretical component comprised of three parts - the **Three Relational Axes of Good Governance**, the eight **Governance Factors** and the two **Interrelationship Schemes**. It is depicted in Figure 4.1 and is submitted to be the theoretical representation of the intersection of the voluntary 'obligations' comprising the nexus of contracts theory of the firm. The Weighing Mechanism undertakes a theoretical or hypothetical 'weighing' exercise to depict – descriptively and diagrammatically – the themes and considerations relevant to the competing or opposing interests of 'insiders' and 'outsiders' of the corporation. The eight Governance Factors are 'weighed' in the Three Relational Axes of Good Governance which acts like a set of scales to weigh the often competing aims or objectives (**Objectives Axis No. 1**), behaviours (**Behaviours Axis No. 2**) and interests (**Positional Conflict Axis No. 3**) of 'insiders' and 'outsiders' of the corporation. The results of this weighing process are already calculated and presented for the reader – these are the two Interrelationship Schemes in Figure 2.6 (for the shareholder primacy model) and Figure 2.7 (for the stakeholder model). These Schemes are the two diagrams of *hypothesised or predicted interrelationships* between the eight Governance Factors. Thus, in turn, the Interrelationship Schemes represent the hypothesised or predicted interrelationships between the four **Key Fields** and the 39 **Governance Variables** to which the Fields give rise. See sections 2.1 and 4.2 above.

Bibliography

KEY FIELD NO 1 – THE APPLICATION OF THE PRINCIPAL THEORIES OF THE FIRM TO THE RELATIONAL APPROACH

Ashbaugh-Skaife, Hollis, Collins, Daniel W and LaFond, Ryan, 'Corporate Governance and the Cost of Equity Capital' (December 2004), accessed 3 March 2015 at SSRN: http://ssrn.com/abstract=639681.

Awrey, Dan, Blair, William and Kershaw, David, 'Between Law and Markets: Is There a Role for Culture and Ethics in Financial Regulation?', LSE Legal Studies Working Paper No 14/2012 (October 5, 2012), accessed 3 March 2015 at SSRN: http://ssrn.com/abstract=2157588.

Bainbridge, Stephen M, 'In Defense of the Shareholder Wealth Maximization Norm: A Reply to Professor Green' (1993) 50 *Washington & Lee Law Review* 1423, accessed 3 March 2015 at SSRN: http://ssrn.com/abstract=303780.

Bainbridge, Stephen M, 'The Board of Directors as Nexus of Contracts: A Critique of Gulati, Klein & Zolt's "Connected Contracts" Model', UCLA, School of Law Research Paper No 02-05 (January 2002), accessed 3 March 2015 at SSRN: http://ssrn.com/abstract=299743.

Bainbridge, Stephen M, 'Director Primacy: The Means and Ends of Corporate Governance', UCLA, School of Law Research Paper No. 02-06 (February 2002), accessed 3 March 2015 at SSRN: http://ssrn.com/abstract=300860.

Bainbridge, Stephen M, 'Why a Board? Group Decisionmaking in Corporate Governance' (2002) 55 *Vanderbilt Law Review* 1–55, accessed 3 March 2015 at SSRN: http://ssrn.com/abstract=266683.

Bainbridge, Stephen M, 'The Geography of Revlon-Land' (2013) 81 *Fordham Law Review*, Forthcoming; UCLA School of Law, Law-Econ Research Paper No 12-13 (July 23, 2012), available at SSRN: http://ssrn.com/abstract=2115769.

Bainbridge, Stephen M, 'Preserving Director Primacy by Managing Shareholder Interventions', *Research Handbook on Shareholder Power and Activism*, Forthcoming; UCLA School of Law, Law-Econ. Research

Paper No. 13-09 (August 27, 2013), available at SSRN: http://ssrn.com/abstract=2298415.

Bainbridge, Stephen M and Henderson, M Todd, 'Boards-R-Us: Reconceptualizing Corporate Boards', University of Chicago Coase-Sandor Institute for Law & Economics Research Paper No. 646; UCLA School of Law, Law-Econ Research Paper No. 13-11 (July 10, 2013), available at SSRN: http://ssrn.com/abstract=2291065.

Baird, Douglas and Henderson, M Todd, 'Other People's Money' (2008) 60 *Stanford Law Review* 1309, Symposium Issue, 2008, available at SSRN: http://ssrn.com/abstract=1017615.

Bebchuk, Lucian A and Roe, Mark J, 'A Theory of Path Dependence in Corporate Ownership and Governance' (1999) 52 *Stanford Law Review* 127–170, accessed 24 April 2015 at SSRN: http://ssrn.com/abstract=202748.

Berle, Adolph A and Means, Gardiner C, *The Modern Corporation and Private Property*, New York, NY: The Macmillan Company, 1932.

Bovens, Mark, 'Analysing and Assessing Accountability: A Conceptual Framework' (2007) 13(4) *European Law Journal* 447–468, available at SSRN: http://ssrn.com/abstract=992006.

Bratton, William W, 'The "Nexus Of Contracts" Corporation: A Critical Appraisal' (1989) 74 *Cornell L Rev* 407.

Bratton, William W, "Berle and Means Reconsidered at the Century's Turn" (2001) 26(3) *Journal of Corporation Law* 737–770, accessed 24 April 2015 at SSRN: http://ssrn.com/abstract=291081, especially pp 753–759.

Capasso, Arturo, 'Stakeholder Theory and Corporate Governance: The Role of Intangible Assets', accessed 3 March 2015 at SSRN: http://ssrn.com/abstract=610661.

Charreaux, Gerard J and Desbrieres, Philippe, 'Corporate Governance: Stakeholder Value versus Shareholder Value' (1998) 1(2) *Revue Finance Contrôle Stratégie* 57–88 (June 1998), accessed 3 March 2015 at SSRN: http://ssrn.com/abstract=262902.

Charreaux, Gerard, J, 'Corporate Governance Theories: From Micro Theories to National Systems Theories' (January 2004), Universite de Bourgogne Fargo Working Paper No 1040101, accessed 3 March 2015 at SSRN: http://ssrn.com/abstract=486522.

Cheffins, Brian R, 'Does Law Matter?: The Separation of Ownership and Control in the United Kingdom', September 2000, ERSC Centre for Business Research, University of Cambridge, Working Paper No. 172, available at SSRN: http://ssrn.com/abstract=245560.

Cheffins, Brian R, 'The History of Corporate Governance', *Oxford Handbook Of Corporate Governance*, Mike Wright, Donald Siegel,

Kevin Keasey and Igor Filatotchev, eds., Oxford University Press, 2013; University of Cambridge Faculty of Law Research Paper No. 54/2011; ECGI – Law Working Paper No. 184/2012, (December 1, 2011), accessed 24 April 2015 at SSRN: http://ssrn.com/abstract=1975404.

Cheffins, Brian R, 'The History of Modern U.S. Corporate Governance: Introduction', *Edward Elgar's Corporate Governance in the New Global Economy Series*, 2011; University of Cambridge Faculty of Law Research Paper No. 29/2012, accessed 24 April 2015 at SSRN: http://ssrn.com/abstract=2192151.

Chilosi, Alberto and Damiani, Mirella, 'Stakeholders vs. Shareholders in Corporate Governance' (20 March 2007), accessed 3 March 2015 at SSRN: http://ssrn.com/abstract=975293.

Chilosi, Alberto and Damiani, Mirella, 'Stakeholders vs. Shareholders in Corporate Governance' (2007) 4(4) *The ICFAI Journal of Corporate Governance* 7–45, available at SSRN: http://ssrn.com/abstract=1046881.

Claessens, Stijn and Burcin Yurtoglu, Besim, 'Corporate Governance in Emerging Markets: A Survey' (15 January 2012), accessed 3 March 2015 at SSRN: http://ssrn.com/abstract=1988880.

Columbia Law School, *Symposium on Contractual Freedom in Corporate Law*, 9 and 10 December 1988 published at (1989) 89 *Colum L Rev* 1395.

Cunningham, Lawrence A, 'Behavioral Finance and Investor Governance' (2002) 59 *Washington & Lee Law Review* 767, accessed 3 March 2015 at SSRN: http://ssrn.com/abstract=255778.

Dent Jr, George W, 'Academics in Wonderland: The Team Production and Director Primacy Models of Corporate Governance', Case Legal Studies Research Paper No 07-21 (June 2007), accessed 3 March 2015 at SSRN: http://ssrn.com/abstract=995186.

Easterbrook, Frank H and Fischel, Daniel R, 'The Corporate Contract' (1989) 89 *Colum L Rev* 1416.

Evans, Robert T and Evans, John P, 'The Influence of Non-Executive Director Control and Rewards on CEO Remuneration: Australian Evidence', EFMA 2002 London Meetings, accessed 3 March 2015 at SSRN: http://ssrn.com/abstract=263050.

Fama, Eugene F and Jensen, Michael C, 'Separation of Ownership and Control' in Michael C Jensen, *Foundations of Organizational Strategy*, Cambridge, MA: Harvard University Press, 1998 and (1983) 26 *Journal of Law and Economics* 301–26, accessed 3 March 2015 at SSRN: http://ssrn.com/abstract=94034.

Fama, Eugene F, Jensen, Michael C, Fisher, Lawrence and Roll, Richard, 'The Adjustment of Stock Prices to New Information' (1969) 10 *International Economic Review* 1–22, accessed 24 April 2015 at SSRN: http://ssrn.com/abstract=321524.

Hart, O, 'An Economist's Perspective On The Theory Of The Firm' (1989) 89 *Colum L Rev* 1757.

Hermalin, Benjamin E and Weisbach, Michael S, 'A Framework for Assessing Corporate Governance Reform' (6 February 2006), accessed 3 March 2015 at SSRN: http://ssrn.com/abstract=881581.

Hill, Jennifer G, 'The Shifting Balance of Power between Shareholders and the Board: News Corp's Exodus to Delaware and Other Antipodean Tales' (January 2008), Sydney Law School Research Paper No 08/20, accessed 3 March 2015 at SSRN: http://ssrn.com/abstract=1086477.

Hill, Jennifer G, 'The Rising Tension between Shareholder and Director Power in the Common Law World' (2010) 18 *Corporate Governance: An International Review* 344–359; Sydney Law School Research Paper No. 10/34; Vanderbilt Law and Economics Research Paper No. 10-11; ECGI – Law Working Paper No. 152/2010 (March 30, 2010), accessed 24 April 2015 at SSRN: http://ssrn.com/abstract=1582258.

Jensen, Michael C and Meckling, William H, 'Theory of the Firm: Managerial Behavior, Agency Costs and Ownership Structure' in Michael C. Jensen, *A Theory of the Firm: Governance, Residual Claims and Organizational Forms*, Cambridge, MA: Harvard University Press, December 2000; (1976) 3(4) *Journal of Financial Economics*, accessed 3 March 2015 at SSRN: http://ssrn.com/abstract=94043.

Jensen, Michael C, 'Value Maximization, Stakeholder Theory, and the Corporate Objective Function' in J. Andriof, *et al* (eds), *Unfolding Stakeholder Thinking*, Sheffield: Greenleaf Publishing, 2002. Also published in (2001) 14(3) *Journal of Applied Corporate Finance* 8–21; (2001) 7 *European Financial Management* 297–317 and in M. Beer and N. Norhia (eds), *Breaking the Code of Change*, Cambridge, MA: Harvard Business School Press, 2000 (October 2001), accessed 3 March 2015 at SSRN: http://ssrn.com/abstract=220671.

Jensen, Michael C and Ruback, R S, 'The Market for Corporate-Control – the Scientific Evidence' (1983) 11(1–4) *Journal of Financial Economics* 5–50.

Joerg, Petra, Loderer, Claudio F, Roth, Lukas and Waelchli, Urs, 'Shareholder Value: Principles, Declarations, and Actions', ECGI – Finance Working Paper No 95/2005 (5 August 2008), accessed 3 March 2015 at SSRN: http://ssrn.com/abstract=1099936.

Jones, Meredith A, Marshall, Shelley D, Mitchell, Richard James and Ramsay, Ian, 'Company Directors' Views Regarding Stakeholders', Univ of Melbourne Legal Studies Research Paper No 270 (October 2007), accessed 3 March 2015 at SSRN: http://ssrn.com/abstract=1023259.

Joo, Thomas Wuil, 'Theories and Models of Corporate Governance' in H. Kent Baker, Ronald Anderson (eds), *Corporate Governance: A*

Synthesis Of Theory, Research, And Practice, Hoboken, NJ: John Wiley & Sons, 2010; UC Davis Legal Studies Research Paper No 213, accessed 3 March 2015 at SSRN: http://ssrn.com/abstract=1543397.

Keay, Andrew R, 'Moving Towards Stakeholderism? Constituency Statutes, Enlightened Shareholder Value and All That: Much Ado About Little?' (4 January 2010), accessed 3 March 2015 at SSRN: http://ssrn.com/abstract=1530990.

Keay, Andrew R, 'Stakeholder Theory in Corporate Law: Has It Got What It Takes?' (4 January 2010), accessed 3 March 2015 at SSRN: http://ssrn.com/abstract=1531065.

Langevoort, Donald C, 'Theories, Assumptions and Securities Regulation: Market Efficiency Revisited' (1992) 140 *U Pa L Rev* 85.

Licht, Amir N, 'The Maximands of Corporate Governance: A Theory of Values and Cognitive Style' (November 2003), ECGI – Law Working Paper No 16/2003, accessed 3 March 2015 at SSRN: http://ssrn.com/abstract=469801 and (2004) 29(3) *Delaware Journal of Corporate Law* 649–746, accessed 3 March 2015 at SSRN: http://ssrn.com/abstract=764025.

Maher, Maria and Andersson, Thomas, 'Corporate Governance: Effects on Firm Performance and Economic Growth' (February 2000), accessed 3 March 2015 at SSRN: http://ssrn.com/abstract=218490.

Manne, H G, 'Mergers and the Market for Corporate-Control' (1965) 73(2) *Journal of Political Economy*, 110–20.

Millon, David, 'Radical Shareholder Primacy' (2014) 10(4) *University of St. Thomas Law Journal* 1013; Washington & Lee Legal Studies Paper No. 2014-17, (July 28, 2014), accessed 23 April 2015 at SSRN: http://ssrn.com/abstract=2473189.

O'Kelley, Charles R T, 'Berle and the Entrepreneur' (2010) 33(4) *Seattle University Law Review* 1141, accessed 24 April 2015 at SSRN: http://ssrn.com/abstract=1579220.

O'Kelley, Charles R T, 'Coase, Knight, and the Nexus-of-Contracts Theory of the Firm: A Reflection on Reification, Reality, and the Corporation as Entrepreneur Surrogate' (2011–2012) 35(4) *Seattle University Law Review* 1247–1270, (March 6, 2012), accessed 23 April 2015 at SSRN: http://ssrn.com/abstract=2017237.

Rhee, Robert J, 'Corporate Ethics, Agency, and the Theory of the Firm' (2008) 3(2) *Journal of Business & Technology Law* 1101, accessed 3 March 2015 at SSRN: http://ssrn.com/abstract=1083478.

Riley, C A, 'Contracting Out of Company Law: Section 459 of the Companies Act 1985 and the Role of the Courts' (1992) 55 *Modern Law Rev* 782.

Roe, Mark J, 'Political Preconditions To Separating Ownership from Corporate Control' (2000) 53 *Stanford Law Review* 539, accessed 3 March 2015 at SSRN: http://ssrn.com/abstract=165143.

Roe, Mark J, 'The Inevitable Instability of American Corporate Governance', Harvard Law and Economics Discussion Paper No 493, September 2004, accessed 3 March 2015 at SSRN: http://ssrn.com/abstract=615561.

Roe, Mark J, 'The Institutions of Corporate Governance', Harvard Law and Economics Discussion Paper No 488 (August 2004) (Revised 17 March 2008), accessed 3 March 2015 at SSRN: http://ssrn.com/abstract=612362.

Singh, Ravi, 'Board Independence and the Design of Executive Compensation', EFA 2005 Moscow Meetings Paper; Harvard NOM Working Paper No 673741 (September 2006), accessed 3 March 2015 at SSRN: http://ssrn.com/abstract=673741, 1.

Stapleton, Jane, 'Duty of Care and Economic Loss: A Wider Agenda' (1991) 107 *Law Quarterly Review* 249, 255.

Stout, Lynn A, 'Why We Should Stop Teaching Dodge v. Ford' (September 2007), UCLA School of Law, Law-Econ Research Paper No. 07-11, accessed 3 February 2015 at SSRN: http://ssrn.com/abstract=1013744.

Strine, Leo E and Laster, Travis J, 'The Siren Song of Unlimited Contractual Freedom', Harvard Law School John M. Olin Center Discussion Paper No. 789, (August 1, 2014), accessed 23 April 2015 at SSRN: http://ssrn.com/abstract=2481039.

Turnbull, Shann, 'Why Unitary Boards Are Not Best Practice: A Case for Compound Boards', November 2000, accessed 3 March 2015 at SSRN: http://ssrn.com/abstract=253803, 2.

Zeitoun, Hossam and Osterloh, Margit, 'Firm Governance and the Role of Top Management' (April 23, 2008), available at SSRN: http://ssrn.com/abstract=1124397.

KEY FIELD NO 2 – AUTOPSIES OF THE ENRON AND HASTIE CORPORATE COLLAPSES

Armour, John and McCahery, Joseph A, 'After Enron: Improving Corporate Law and Modernising Securities Regulation in Europe and the US', Amsterdam Center for Law & Economics Working Paper No 2006-07 (June 2006), accessed 3 March 2015 at SSRN: http://ssrn.com/abstract=910205.

Bainbridge, Stephen M, 'The Tournament at the Intersection of Business and Legal Ethics' (2003–2004) 1(2) *University of St. Thomas Law Journal* 909–24, accessed 3 March 2015 at SSRN: http://ssrn.com/abstract=429304.

Bainbridge, Stephen M, 'Corporate Lawyers as Gatekeepers' in Bainbridge, Stephen M, *Corporate Governance After The Financial*

Crisis, Oxford: Oxford University Press, 2012; UCLA School of Law, Law-Econ Research Paper No 12-03 (6 January 2012), available at SSRN: http://ssrn.com/abstract=1980975.

Baird, Douglas G and Rasmussen, Robert K, 'Four (or Five) Easy Lessons From Enron' (2002) 55 *Vanderbilt Law Review* 102, accessed 3 March 2015 at SSRN: http://ssrn.com/abstract=358442.

Ball, Ray, 'Market and Political/Regulatory Perspectives on the Recent Accounting Scandals' (2008) 47(2) *Journal of Accounting Research* 277–323 (May 2009), accessed 3 March 2015 at SSRN: http://ssrn.com/abstract=1272804.

Barrett, Matthew J, 'Enron and Andersen – What Went Wrong and Why Similar Audit Failures Could Happen Again', accessed 3 March 2015 at SSRN: http://ssrn.com/abstract=794831.

Barton, Jan, 'Who Cares about Auditor Reputation?', accessed 3 March 2015 at SSRN: http://ssrn.com/abstract=436967.

Black, Julia, 'Paradoxes and Failures: "New Governance" Techniques and the Financial Crisis' (2012) 75(6) *Modern Law Review* 1037–1063.

Blanchard, Danielle and Dionne, Georges, 'Risk Management and Corporate Governance', HEC Montreal Risk Management Chair Working Paper No 03-04 (September 2003), accessed 3 March 2015 at SSRN: http://ssrn.com/abstract=441482.

Branson, Douglas M, 'Enron – When All Systems Fail: Creative Destruction or Roadmap to Corporate Governance Reform?' (2003) 48 *Villanova Law Review* 989; Villanova Law/Public Policy Research Paper No 2003-13, accessed 3 March 2015 at SSRN: http://ssrn.com/abstract=473205.

Bratton, William W, 'Enron and the Dark Side of Shareholder Value' (2001–2002) 76 *Tulane Law Review* 1275 (May 2002), accessed 3 March 2015 at SSRN: http://ssrn.com/abstract=301475, 7–8.

Brickey, Kathleen F, 'Andersen's Fall from Grace' (2004) 81 *Washington University Law Quarterly* 917, accessed 3 March 2015 at SSRN: http://ssrn.com/abstract=508462.

Callen, Jeffery L and Morel, Mindy, 'The Enron-Andersen Debacle: Do Equity Markets React to Auditor Reputation?', EFMA 2003 Helsinki Meetings (December 2002), accessed 3 March 2015 at SSRN: http://ssrn.com/abstract=341440.

Catanach, Anthony H and Rhoades, Shelley C, 'Enron: A Financial Reporting Failure?' (2003) 48(4) *Villanova Law Review* 1057, 2003, accessed 3 March 2015 at SSRN: http://ssrn.com/abstract=418920.

Chang, Chingfu, Chi, Wuchun and Liu, Chiawen, 'Client Characteristics and Auditor Switch in an Audit Failure' (20 April 2003), accessed 3 March 2015 at SSRN: http://ssrn.com/abstract=403700.

Coffee, John C, 'Understanding Enron: It's About the Gatekeepers, Stupid', Columbia Law & Economics Working Paper No 207 (30 July 2002), accessed 3 March 2015 at SSRN: http://ssrn.com/abstract=325240.

Coffee, John C, 'A Theory of Corporate Scandals: Why the U.S. and Europe Differ', Columbia Law and Economics Working Paper No 274 (March 2005), accessed 3 March 2015 at SSRN: http://ssrn.com/abstract=694581.

Cremers, Martijn, Bebchuk, Lucian A and Peyer, Urs, 'CEO Centrality', Harvard Law and Economics Discussion Paper No 601 (December 2007, Revised May 2008), accessed 3 March 2015 at SSRN: http://ssrn.com/abstract=1030107.

Cunningham, Lawrence A, 'Sharing Accounting's Burden: Business Lawyers in Enron's Dark Shadows' (2002) 57(4) *Business Lawyer (ABA)* 1421–62, accessed 3 March 2015 at SSRN: http://ssrn.com/abstract=307978.

Cunningham, Lawrence A, 'Berkshire Beyond Buffett: The Enduring Value of Values (Chapter 8)', GWU Law School Public Law Research Paper No. 2014-45; GWU Legal Studies Research Paper No. 2014-45, (2014), accessed 23 April 2015 at SSRN: http://ssrn.com/abstract=2488476.

Dent, George W, 'Academics in Wonderland: The Team Production and Director Primacy Models of Corporate Governance', Case Legal Studies Research Paper No 07-21 (June 2007), accessed 3 March 2015 at SSRN: http://ssrn.com/abstract=995186.

de Zwart, Francesco, 'Enron and Hastie: What Can We Learn' (2014) 29 *Australian Journal of Corporate Law* 169–211.

Dharan, Bala G and Bufkins, William R, 'Red Flags in Enron's Reporting of Revenues & Key Financial Measures' (23 July 2008), accessed 3 March 2015 at SSRN: http://ssrn.com/abstract=1172222.

Dionne, Georges, Chun, Olfa Maalaoui and Triki, Thouraya, 'Risk Management and Corporate Governance: The Importance of Independence and Financial Knowledge', (February 2013), accessed 24 April 2015 at SSRN: http://ssrn.com/abstract=2020987.

Eisenberg, Theodore and Macey, Jonathon R, 'Was Arthur Andersen Different? An Empirical Examination of Major Accounting Firms' Audits of Large Clients', Cornell Legal Studies Research Paper No 04-03; Yale Law & Economics Research Paper No 287 (November 12, 2003), accessed 3 March 2015 at SSRN: http://ssrn.com/abstract=468761.

Fama, Eugene F and Jensen, Michael C, 'Separation of Ownership and Control' in Michael C Jensen, *Foundations Of Organizational Strategy*, Cambridge, MA: Harvard University Press, 1998 and (1983) 26 *Journal of Law and Economics* 301–26, accessed 3 March 2015 at SSRN: http://ssrn.com/abstract=94034.

Felton, James and Kim, Jongchai, 'Warnings from the Enron Message Board' (2002) 11(3) *Journal of Investing* 29–52, accessed 3 March 2015 at SSRN: http://ssrn.com/abstract=918519.

Fleischer, Victor, 'Enron's Dirty Little Secret: Waiting for the Other Shoe to Drop' (2002) 94(8) *Tax Notes*, accessed 3 March 2015 at SSRN: http://ssrn.com/abstract=301911.

Free, Clinton Wallace and Macintosh, Norman B, 'Management Control Practice and Culture at Enron: The Untold Story' (8 August 2006), available at SSRN: http://ssrn.com/abstract=873636.

Fuerst, O and Kang, S, 'Corporate Governance, Expected Operating Performance, and Pricing', accessed 3 March 2015 at SSRN: http://ssrn.com/abstract=141357.

Gillan, Stuart L and Martin, John D, 'Financial Engineering, Corporate Governance, and the Collapse of Enron', U of Delaware Coll. of Bus. and Econ. Ctr. for Corp. Governance Working Paper No. 2002-001 (November 2002), accessed 3 March 2015 at SSRN: http://ssrn.com/abstract=354040.

Gillan, Stuart L and Martin, John D, 'Corporate Governance Post-Enron: Effective Reforms, or Closing the Stable Door?' (21 March 2007), accessed 3 March 2015 at SSRN: http://ssrn.com/abstract=977585.

Gordon, Jeffrey N, 'What Enron Means for the Management and Control of the Modern Business Corporation: Some Initial Reflections' (2002) 69 *University of Chicago Law Review* 1233 (Summer 2002), accessed 3 March 2015 at SSRN: http://ssrn.com/abstract=305343.

Gordon, Jeffrey N, 'Governance Failures of the Enron Board and the New Information Order of Sarbanes-Oxley', Columbia Law and Economics Working Paper No 216; Harvard Law and Economics Discussion Paper No 416 (March 2003), accessed 3 March 2015 at SSRN: http://ssrn.com/abstract=391363.

Hill, Jennifer G, 'Regulating Executive Remuneration: International Developments in the Post-Scandal Era' (2006) 3 *European Company Law* 64; Vanderbilt Law and Economics Research Paper No 06-06, accessed 3 March 2015 at SSRN: http://ssrn.com/abstract=887944

Hill, Jennifer G, 'Why Did Australia Fare So Well in the Global Financial Crisis?' *The Regulatory Aftermath Of The Global Financial Crisis*, E Ferran, N Moloney, J G Hill and J C Coffee, Jr, Cambridge University Press, 2012, pp 203–300; Sydney Law School Research Paper No. 12/35, (May 20, 2012), accessed 23 April 2015 at SSRN: http://ssrn.com/abstract=2063267.

Jensen, Michael C, 'The Agency Cost of Overvalued Equity and the Current State of Corporate Finance' (2004) 10(4) *European Financial Management* 549–565, accessed 23 April 2015 at SSRN: http://ssrn.com/abstract=560961.

Jensen, Michael C, 'Agency Costs of Overvalued Equity', ECGI – Finance Working Paper No 39/2004; Harvard Business School NOM Working Paper No 04-26; (2005) 34(1) *Financial Management* 5–19 (March 2005), accessed 3 March 2015 at SSRN: http://ssrn.com/abstract=480421.

Kroger, John R, 'Enron, Fraud and Securities Reform: An Enron Prosecutor's Perspective' (2005) 76(1) *University of Colorado Law Review* 57–138 (December 2004), accessed 3 March 2015 at SSRN: http://ssrn.com/abstract=537542.

Larcker, David F, Larcker, Sarah M and Tayan, Brian, 'Lululemon: A Sheer Debacle in Risk Management', Rock Center for Corporate Governance at Stanford University Closer Look Series: Topics, Issues and Controversies in Corporate Governance and Leadership No. CGRP-41; Stanford University Graduate School of Business Research Paper No. 14-21, (June 17, 2014), accessed 23 April 2015 at SSRN: http://ssrn.com/abstract=2455983.

Larcker, David F and Tayan, Brian, 'Corporate Governance According to Charles T. Munger', Rock Center for Corporate Governance at Stanford University Closer Look Series: Topics, Issues and Controversies in Corporate Governance and Leadership No. CGRP-38, (March 3, 2014), accessed 23 April 2015 at SSRN: http://ssrn.com/abstract=2404077.

Licht, Amir N, 'Culture and Law in Corporate Governance', European Corporate Governance Institute (ECGI) – Law Working Paper No. 247/2014, (March 6, 2014), accessed 23 April 2015 at SSRN: http://ssrn.com/abstract=2405538.

McCahery, Joseph A and Vermeulen, Erik P M, 'Six Components of Corporate Governance That Cannot Be Ignored', Lex Research Topics in Corporate Law & Economics Working Paper No. 2014-2; European Corporate Governance Institute (ECGI) – Law Working Paper No. 248/2014; Tilburg Law School Research Paper No. 08/2014, (March 9, 2014), accessed 23 April 2015 at SSRN: http://ssrn.com/abstract=2406565.

Morck, R, Shleifer, A and Vishny, R W, 'Management Ownership and Corporate Performance: An Empirical Analysis' (1988) 20 *Journal of Financial Economics* 293–316.

Popadak, Jillian A, 'A Corporate Culture Channel: How Increased Shareholder Governance Reduces Firm Value', (October 25, 2013), accessed 24 April 2015 at SSRN: http://ssrn.com/abstract=2345384.

PPB Advisory, *Hastie Group Limited and Specific Subsidiaries, Report by Joint and Several Administrators Pursuant to Section 439A of the Corporations Act 2001*, 21 January 2013, accessed 3 March 2015 at http://www.ppbadvisory.com/creditor-information/v/281/hastie-group/2nd-creditor-meeting (*'Administrators' Report'*).

Rapoport, Nancy B, 'Enron, Titanic, and The Perfect Storm' (2003) 71 *Fordham Law Review* 1373, accessed 3 March 2015 at SSRN: http://ssrn.com/abstract=498122.

Roe, Mark J, 'The Inevitable Instability of American Corporate Governance', Harvard Law and Economics Discussion Paper No 493 (September 2004), accessed 3 March 2015 at SSRN: http://ssrn.com/abstract=615561.

Rosen, Robert Eli, 'Risk Management and Corporate Governance: The Case of Enron' (2003) 35 *Connecticut Law Review* 1157, accessed 3 March 2015 at SSRN: http://ssrn.com/abstract=468168.

Samanta, Navajyoti and Das, Tirthankar, 'Role of Auditors in Corporate Governance' (October 11, 2009), accessed 3 March 2015 at SSRN: http://ssrn.com/abstract=1487050.

Schwarcz, Steven L, 'Rethinking the Disclosure Paradigm in a World of Complexity' (2004) *University of Illinois Law Review* 1; Duke Law School, Public Law Research Paper No 34, accessed 3 March 2015 at SSRN: http://ssrn.com/abstract=336685.

Sharfman, Bernard S and Toll, Steven J, 'Dysfunctional Deference and Board Composition: Lessons from Enron' (2008) 103 *Northwestern University Law Review Colloquy* 153–62, 2008, accessed 3 March 2015 at SSRN: http://ssrn.com/abstract=1160302.

Vakkur, Nicholas V, McAfee, R Preston and Kipperman, Fred, 'The Unintended Effects of the Sarbanes Oxley Act of 2002' (2009) 22(1) *Research in Accounting Regulation* 18–28 (17 February 2009) accessed 3 March 2015 at SSRN: http://ssrn.com/abstract=1345475.

Van der Elst, Christoph, 'The Risks of Corporate Legal Principles of Risk Management', ECGI – Law Working Paper No. 160/2010; Tilburg Law School Research Paper No. 013/2010, (June 10, 2010), accessed 24 April 2015 at SSRN: http://ssrn.com/abstract=1623526.

Van der Elst, Christoph, 'The Risk Management Duties of the Board of Directors', Financial Law Institute Working Paper Series 2013-02, (April 22, 2013), accessed 24 April 2015 at SSRN: http://ssrn.com/abstract=2267502.

Vasudev, P M and Watson, Susan, 'Corporate Governance after the Financial Crisis' in P M Vasudev and Susan Watson, eds, *Corporate Governance After The Financial Crisis*, Edward Elgar Ltd, 2012, accessed 23 April 2015 at SSRN: http://ssrn.com/abstract=209076.

Weisbach, Michael S and Hermalin, Benjamin E, 'Boards of Directors as an Endogenously Determined Institution: A Survey of the Economic Literature' (15 June 2000), available at SSRN: http://ssrn.com/abstract=233111.

KEY FIELD NO 3 – COMPARATIVE CORPORATE GOVERNANCE CODES

Bainbridge, Stephen M, 'In Defense of the Shareholder Wealth Maximization Norm: A Reply to Professor Green' (1993) 50 *Washington & Lee Law Review* 1423, accessed 3 March 2015 at SSRN: http://ssrn.com/abstract=303780.

Baums, Theodor and Scott, Kenneth E, 'Taking Shareholder Protection Seriously? Corporate Governance in the United States and Germany' (2005) 53 *American Journal of Comparative Law* 31, accessed 3 March 2015 at SSRN: http://ssrn.com/abstract=473185

Berndt, Markus, 'Global Differences in Corporate Governance Systems – Theory and Implications for Reforms' (November 2000), Harvard Law and Economics Discussion Paper No 303, accessed 3 March 2015 at SSRN: http://ssrn.com/abstract=255886.

Black, Julia, 'Decentring Regulation: Understanding the Role of Regulation and Self-Regulation in a "Post-Regulatory" World' (2001) 54 *Current Legal Problems* 103.

Black, Julia, 'Paradoxes and Failures: "New Governance" Techniques and the Financial Crisis' (2012) 75(6) *Modern Law Review* 1037–63.

Blair, Margaret M, 'Post-Enron Reflections on Comparative Corporate Governance' (6 June 2002), Georgetown Law and Economics Research Paper No 316663, accessed 3 March 2015 at SSRN: http://ssrn.com/abstract=316663.

Böckli, Peter, Davies, Paul L, Ferran, Eilis, Ferrarini, Guido A, Garrido Garcia, José M, Hopt, Klaus J, Pietrancosta, Alain, Pistor, Katharina, Roth, Markus, Skog, Rolf, Soltysinski, Stanislaw, Winter, Jaap W and Wymeersch, Eddy, 'Making Corporate Governance Codes More Effective: A Response to the European Commission's Action Plan of December 2012' (11 December 2013), accessed 3 March 2015 at SSRN: http://ssrn.com/abstract=2366273.

Braendle, Udo C and Noll, Juergen, 'On the Convergence of National Corporate Governance Systems' (August 2005), accessed 3 March 2015 at SSRN: http://ssrn.com/abstract=506522.

Branson, Douglas, 'The Very Uncertain Prospect of "Global" Convergence in Corporate Governance' (2001) 34 *Cornell International Law Journal* 321, accessed 3 March 2015 at SSRN: http://ssrn.com/abstract=244742.

Clark, Robert C, 'Corporate Governance Changes in the Wake of the Sarbanes-Oxley Act: A Morality Tale for Policymakers Too' (5 December 2005), Harvard Law and Economics Discussion Paper No 525, accessed 3 March 2015 at SSRN: http://ssrn.com/abstract=808244.

Coffee, John C, 'Racing Towards the Top?: The Impact of Cross-Listings and Stock Market Competition on International Corporate Governance' (30 May 2002), Columbia Law and Economics Working Paper No 205, accessed 3 March 2015 at SSRN: http://ssrn.com/abstract=315840.

Coffee, John C, 'The Future as History: The Prospects for Global Convergence in Corporate Governance and Its Implications' (February 1999), Columbia Law School Center for Law and Economic Studies Working Paper No 144, accessed 3 March 2015 at SSRN: http://ssrn.com/abstract=142833.

Coffee, John C, 'A Theory of Corporate Scandals: Why the U.S. and Europe Differ' (March 2005), Columbia Law and Economics Working Paper No 274, accessed 3 March 2015 at SSRN: http://ssrn.com/abstract=694581.

Cunningham, Lawrence A, 'Commonalities and Prescriptions in the Vertical Dimension of Global Corporate Governance' (1999) 84 *Cornell Law Review* 1133, accessed 3 March 2015 at SSRN: http://ssrn.com/abstract=244665.

Davies, Paul L, and Hopt, Klaus J, 'Boards in Europe – Accountability and Convergence' (2013) 61 *American Journal of Comparative Law* 301–75; ECGI – Law Working Paper No 205/2013; Oxford Legal Studies Research Paper No 40/2013 (1 April 2013), accessed 3 March 2015 at SSRN: http://ssrn.com/abstract=2212272.

de Zwart, Francesco (90% author) and Gilligan, George, 'Comparative Corporate Governance Schemes and their Relevance for the Sporting Sector', Monash University Department of Business Law and Taxation, Working Paper No 16 (November 2008), accessed 3 March 2015 at http://ssrn.com.abstract=1295682.

de Zwart, Francesco (95% author) and Gilligan, George, 'Sustainable Governance in Sporting Organisations' in Rodriguez, Placido, Kesenne, Stefan and Dietl, Helmut (eds), *Social Responsibility and Sustainability in Sports*, Oviedo: Ediciones de la Universidad de Oviedo, 2009.

du Plessis, Jean Jacques, Hargovan, Anil and Bagaric, Mirko, *Principles of Contemporary Corporate Governance*, 2nd edn, Cambridge: Cambridge University Press, 2011.

Gerner-Beuerle, Carsten, 'Determinants of Corporate Governance Codes', LSE Legal Studies Working Paper No 5/2014 (10 February 2014), available at SSRN: http://ssrn.com/abstract=2346673.

Gordon, Jeffrey N, 'An International Relations Perspective on the Convergence of Corporate Governance: German Shareholder Capitalism and the European Union, 1990–2000' (February 2003), ECGI – Finance Research Paper Series, accessed 3 March 2015 at SSRN: http://ssrn.com/abstract=374620.

Grantham, Ross, 'Corporate Governance Codes in Australia and

New Zealand: Propriety and Prosperity' (2004) 23 *The University of Queensland Law Journal* 218.

Hansmann, Henry and Kraakman, Reinier, 'Reflections on the End of History for Corporate Law' in Rasheed, Abdul and Yoshikawa, Toru (eds), *Convergence of Corporate Governance: Promise and Prospects*, Basingstoke: Palgrave-Macmillan, 2012; Yale Law & Economics Research Paper No 449 (15 August 2011), accessed 3 March 2015 at SSRN: http://ssrn.com/abstract=2095419.

Hill, Jennifer G, 'Regulatory Responses to Global Corporate Scandals' (2005) 32 *Wisconsin International Law Journal* 367; Sydney Law School Research Paper No 06/35, accessed 3 March 2015 at SSRN: http://ssrn.com/abstract=886104.

Hill, Jennifer G, 'Evolving "Rules of the Game" in Corporate Governance Reform' (July 2007), Sydney Law School Research Paper No 07/47, accessed 3 March 2015 at SSRN: http://ssrn.com/abstract=1000085.

Keay, Andrew R, 'Accountability and the Corporate Governance Framework: From Cadbury to the UK Corporate Governance Code' (31 August 2012), accessed 3 March 2015 at SSRN: http://ssrn.com/abstract=214317.

Scott, Colin, 'Regulation in the Age of Governance: the Rise of the Post-Regulatory State', Chapter 7 in Jordana, Jacint and Levi-Faur, David (eds), *The Politics of Regulation: Institutions and Regulatory Reforms for the Age of Governance*, Cheltenham, UK and Northampton. MA, USA: Edward Elgar, 2005.

KEY FIELD NO 4 – EMPIRICAL STUDIES ON THE EFFECTIVENESS OF GOVERNANCE VARIABLES

Abbott, L J, Parker, S and Peters, G F, 'Audit Committee Characteristics and Financial Misstatement: A Study of the Efficacy of Certain Blue Ribbon Committee Recommendations' (March 2002), accessed 5 March 2015 at SSRN: http://ssrn.com/abstract=319125.

Adams, Renee B, 'The Dual Role of Corporate Boards as Advisors and Monitors of Management: Theory and Evidence', previously titled 'The Dual Role of Corporate Boards as Advisors and Monitors of Management', accessed 5 March 2015 at SSRN: http://ssrn.com/abstract=241581.

Adams, Renee B and Ferreira, Daniel, 'A Theory of Friendly Boards' (2007) 62(1) *Journal of Finance* 217–50, accessed 5 March 2015 at SSRN: http://ssrn.com/abstract=866625.

Adams, Renee B and Mehran, H, 'Corporate Performance, Board Structure and its Determinants in the Banking Industry', EFA 2005 Moscow Meetings (8 August 2005), accessed 5 March 2015 at SSRN: http://ssrn.com/abstract=302593.

Aggarwal, Reena, Erel, I, Stulz, R M and Williamson, R G, 'Do U.S. Firms Have the Best Corporate Governance? A Cross-Country Examination of the Relation Between Corporate Governance and Shareholder Wealth', Fisher College of Business Working Paper No 2006-03-006 (2006), accessed 5 March 2015 at SSRN: http://ssrn.com/abstract=954169.

Aggarwal, Reena, Saffi, Pedro A C and Sturgess, Jason, 'The Role of Institutional Investors in Voting: Evidence from the Securities Lending Market', AFA 2013 San Diego Meetings Paper (July 7, 2012), available at SSRN: http://ssrn.com/abstract=2023480.

Agrawal, Anup and Chadha, S, 'Corporate Governance and Accounting Scandals', AFA 2004 San Diego Meetings (September 2004), accessed 5 March 2015 at SSRN: http://ssrn.com/abstract=595138.

Agrawal, Anup and Knoeber, Charles R, 'Corporate Governance and Firm Performance', in Christopher R Thomas, William F Shughart II (eds), *Oxford Handbook In Managerial Economics*, Oxford: Oxford University Press, 2012 (15 March 2012), accessed 5 March 2015 at SSRN: http://ssrn.com/abstract=2024764.

Ammann, Manuel, Oesch, David and Schmid, Markus M, 'Corporate Governance and Firm Value: International Evidence' (3 November 2010), accessed 5 March 2015 at SSRN: http://ssrn.com/abstract=1692222.

Anderson, K L, Deli, D N and Gillan, S L, 'Boards of Directors, Audit Committees, and the Information Content of Earnings', Weinberg Center for Corporate Governance Working Paper No 2003-04 (September 2003), accessed 5 March 2015 at SSRN: http://ssrn.com/abstract=444241.

Armour, John and Cheffins, Brian R, 'The Rise and Fall (?) of Shareholder Activism by Hedge Funds', ECGI – Law Working Paper No 136/2009 (1 September 2009), accessed 5 March 2015 at SSRN: http://ssrn.com/abstract=1489336.

Armour, John, Deakin, Simon, Sarkar, Prabirjit, Siems, Mathias and Singh, Ajit, 'Shareholder Protection and Stock Market Development: An Empirical Test of the Legal Origins Hypothesis', University of Cambridge, CBR Working Paper, (February 2008), accessed 23 April 2015 at SSRN: http://ssrn.com/abstract=1094355.

Armour, John and McCahery, Joseph A, 'After Enron: Improving Corporate Law and Modernising Securities Regulation in Europe and the US', Amsterdam Center for Law & Economics Working Paper No 2006-07 (June 2006), accessed 5 March 2015 at SSRN: http://ssrn.com/abstract=910205.

Ashbaugh-Skaife, H, Collins, D W and LaFond, R, 'Corporate Governance and the Cost of Equity Capital' (December 2004), accessed 5 March 2015 at SSRN: http://ssrn.com/abstract=639681.

Bainbridge, Stephen M, 'The Creeping Federalization of Corporate Law' (2003) 26(1) *Regulation* 32–39, Spring 2003, accessed 5 March 2015 at SSRN: http://ssrn.com/abstract=389403.

Bainbridge, Stephen M, 'Dodd-Frank: Quack Federal Corporate Governance Round II', UCLA School of Law, Law-Econ Research Paper No 10-12 (7 September 2010), accessed 5 March 2015 at SSRN: http://ssrn.com/abstract=1673575.

Bainbridge, Stephen M, 'The Corporate Governance Provisions of Dodd-Frank', UCLA School of Law, Law-Econ Research Paper No 10-14 (27 October 2010), accessed 5 March 2015 at SSRN: http://ssrn.com/abstract=1698898.

Barrett, Matthew J, 'Enron and Andersen – What Went Wrong and Why Similar Audit Failures Could Happen Again', accessed 5 March 2015 at SSRN: http://ssrn.com/abstract=794831.

Barros Kimbro, Marinilka and Xu, Danielle, 'Shareholders Have a Say on Executive Compensation: Evidence from Say-on-Pay in the United States' (April 1, 2013), accessed 23 April 2015 at SSRN: http://ssrn.com/abstract=2209936.

Barton, Jan, 'Who Cares about Auditor Reputation?', accessed 5 March 2015 at SSRN: http://ssrn.com/abstract=436967.

Beasley, M S and S E Salterio, 'The Relationship Between Board Characteristics and Voluntary Improvements in Audit Committee Composition and Experience' (28 February 2001), accessed 5 March 2015 at SSRN: http://ssrn.com/abstract=272590, 2.

Bebchuk, Lucian A, 'The Myth that Insulating Boards Serves Long-Term Value' (2013) 113 *Columbia Law Review*, 1637–94; Harvard Law and Economics Discussion Paper No 755 (1 September 2013), accessed 5 March 2015 at SSRN: http://ssrn.com/abstract=2248111.

Bebchuk, Lucian A, Brav, Alon, Jackson, Robert J and Jiang, Wei, 'Pre-Disclosure Accumulations by Activist Investors: Evidence and Policy', (2013) 39 *Journal of Corporation Law*, Forthcoming; Columbia Business School Research Paper No. 13-33, (April 1, 2013), accessed 23 April 2015 at SSRN: http://ssrn.com/abstract=2258083.

Bebchuk, Lucian A, Brav, Alon and Jiang, Wei, 'The Long-Term Effects of Hedge Fund Activism', Columbia Business School Research Paper No. 13-66, (July 9, 2013), accessed 23 April 2015 at SSRN: http://ssrn.com/abstract=2291577.

Bebchuk, Lucian A and Cohen, A, 'The Costs of Entrenched Boards' (2005) 78 *Journal of Financial Economics* 409–33; Harvard Law and

Economics Discussion Paper No 478, accessed 5 March 2015 at SSRN: http://ssrn.com/abstract=556987, 1.

Bebchuk, Lucian A, Coates IV, J C and Subramanian, G, 'The Trouble with Staggered Boards: A Reply to Georgeson's John Wilcox' (2003) 11(2) *Corporate Governance Advisor* 17–19, accessed 5 March 2015 at SSRN: http://ssrn.com/abstract=384980.

Bebchuk, Lucian A, Cohen, Alma and Ferrell, Allen, 'What Matters in Corporate Governance?' (September 1, 2004); (2009) 22(2) *Review of Financial Studies* 783–827 (February 2009); Harvard Law School John M. Olin Center Discussion Paper No 491 (2004), accessed 5 March 2015 at SSRN: http://ssrn.com/abstract=593423.

Bebchuk, Lucian A, Cohen, Alma and Wang, Charles C Y, 'Golden Parachutes and the Wealth of Shareholders', Harvard Law and Economics Discussion Paper No 683 (1 December 2010), accessed 5 March 2015 at SSRN: http://ssrn.com/abstract=1718488.

Bebchuk, Lucian A, Cohen, Alma and Wang, Charles C, 'Staggered Boards and the Wealth of Shareholders: Evidence from Two Natural Experiments', Harvard Law and Economics Discussion Paper No 697 (June 1, 2010 and revised July 2011), accessed 5 March 2015 at SSRN: http://ssrn.com/abstract=1706806.

Bebchuk, Lucian A, Cohen, Alma and Wang, Charles C Y, 'Learning and the Disappearing Association Between Governance and Returns' (2013) 108(2) *Journal of Financial Economics* 323–48; Harvard Law and Economics Discussion Paper No 667 (1 June 2011), accessed 5 March 2015 at SSRN: http://ssrn.com/abstract=1589731.

Bebchuk, Lucian A, Cremers, Martijn and Peyer, Urs C, 'Pay Distribution in the Top Executive Team', Harvard Law and Economics Discussion Paper No 574 (February 2007), accessed 5 March 2015 at SSRN: http://ssrn.com/abstract=964303.

Bebchuk, Lucian A and Fried, Jesse M, 'Executive Compensation as an Agency Problem' (2003) 17 *Journal of Economic Perspectives* 71–92, accessed 5 March 2015 at SSRN: http://ssrn.com/abstract=364220.

Bebchuk, Lucian A and Fried, Jesse M, 'Paying for Long-Term Performance' (2010) 158 *University of Pennsylvania Law Review* 1915–59; Harvard Law and Economics Discussion Paper No 658 (1 December 2009), accessed 5 March 2015 at SSRN: http://ssrn.com/abstract=1535355.

Bebchuk, Lucian A and Grinstein, Y, 'Firm Expansion and CEO Pay', Harvard Law and Economics Discussion Paper No 533; Johnson School Research Paper No 27-06 (August 2007), accessed 5 March 2015 at SSRN: http://ssrn.com/abstract=838245.

Bebchuk, Lucian A, Grinstein, Yaniv and Peyer, Urs C, 'Lucky CEOs',

Harvard Law and Economics Discussion Paper No 566 (November 2006), accessed 5 March 2015 at SSRN: http://ssrn.com/abstract=945392.

Bebchuk, Lucian A, Grinstein, Yaniv and Peyer, Urs, 'Lucky Directors' (2010) 65(6) *Journal of Finance* 2363–401 (published as 'Lucky CEOs and Lucky Directors'); Harvard Law and Economics Discussion Paper No 573 (2006), accessed 5 March 2015 at SSRN: http://ssrn.com/abstract=952239.

Bebchuk, Lucian A, Grinstein, Yaniv and Peyer, Urs C, 'Lucky CEOs and Lucky Directors' (2010) 65(6) *Journal of Finance* 2363–401; Johnson School Research Paper Series No 39-09; CELS 2009 4th Annual Conference on Empirical Legal Studies Paper (15 May 2009), accessed 5 March 2015 at SSRN: http://ssrn.com/abstract=1405316.

Bebchuk, Lucian A and Jackson, Robert J Jr, 'The Law and Economics of Blockholder Disclosure', Harvard Law and Economics Discussion Paper No. 702; (2012) 2(1) *Harvard Business Law Review* 39; Harvard Law and Economics Discussion Paper No. 702; Columbia Law and Economics Research Paper No. 405, (July 12, 2011), accessed 23 April 2015 at SSRN: http://ssrn.com/abstract=1884226.

Bebchuk, Lucian A and Jackson, Robert J, 'Toward a Constitutional Review of the Poison Pill' (2014) 114 *Columbia Law Review* 1549–94; Harvard Law School John M. Olin Center Discussion Paper No 772; Columbia Public Law Research Paper No 14-386 (September 2014), accessed 5 March 2015 at SSRN: http://ssrn.com/abstract=2401098.

Bebchuk, Lucian A and Weisbach, Michael S, 'The State of Corporate Governance Research', Fisher College of Business Working Paper No 2009-03-20; (2010) 23(3) *Review of Financial Studies* 939–61; Fisher College of Business Working Paper No 2009-03-20; Charles A. Dice WP 2009-21; Harvard Law and Economics Discussion Paper No 652 (17 November 2009), accessed 5 March 2015 at SSRN: http://ssrn.com/abstract=1508146.

Berle, Adolph A and Means, Gardiner C, *The Modern Corporation and Private Property*, New York, NY: The Macmillan Company, 1932.

Bettis, J Carr, Bizjak, John M, Coles, Jeffrey L and Young, Brian, 'The Presence, Value, and Incentive Properties of Relative Performance Evaluation in Executive Compensation Contracts', (February 8, 2014), accessed 23 April 2015 at SSRN: http://ssrn.com/abstract=2392861.

Beyer, Anne, Larcker, David F and Tayan, Brian, 'Does the Composition of a Company's Shareholder Base Really Matter?', Rock Center for Corporate Governance at Stanford University Closer Look Series: Topics, Issues and Controversies in Corporate Governance and Leadership No. CGRP-42, (July 31, 2014), accessed 23 April 2015 at SSRN: http://ssrn.com/abstract=2474792.

Bhagat, Sanjai and Black, Bernard S, 'The Non-Correlation Between Board Independence and Long-Term Firm Performance' (2002) 27 *Journal of Corporation Law* 231–73, accessed 5 March 2015 at SSRN: http://ssrn.com/abstract=133808, 233.

Bhagat, Sanjai and Bolton, Brian J, 'Corporate Governance and Firm Performance' (June 2007), accessed 5 March 2015 at SSRN: http://ssrn.com/abstract=1017342.

Bhagat, Sanjai, Bolton, Brian J and Romano, Roberta, 'The Promise and Peril of Corporate Governance Indices', ECGI – Law Working Paper No 89/2007 (7 October 2007), accessed 5 March 2015 at SSRN: http://ssrn.com/abstract=1019921.

Bhagat, Sanjai, Carey, Dennis C and Elson, Charles M, 'Director Ownership, Corporate Performance, and Management Turnover' (31 December 1998), accessed 5 March 2015 at SSRN: http://ssrn.com/abstract=134488.

Black, Bernard S, 'Shareholder Activism and Corporate Governance in the United States', as published in *The New Palgrave Dictionary of Economics and the Law*, Basingstoke: Palgrave-Macmillan, 1998, Vol 3, pp 459–65, accessed 5 March 2015 at SSRN: http://ssrn.com/abstract=45100.

Black, Bernard S and Kim, Woochan, 'The Effect of Board Structure on Firm Value in an Emerging Market: IV, DiD, and Time Series Evidence from Korea', Finance Working Paper No 179/2007 (June 2007), accessed 5 March 2015 at: http://ssrn.com/abstract=968287.

Branson, Douglas M, 'Enron, 'When All Systems Fail: Creative Destruction or Roadmap to Corporate Governance Reform?' (2003) 48 *Villanova Law Review* 989; Villanova Law/Public Policy Research Paper No 2003-13, accessed 5 March 2015 at SSRN: http://ssrn.com/abstract=473205, 1003.

Bratton, William W, 'Enron and the Dark Side of Shareholder Value' (2001–2002) 76 *Tulane Law Review* 1275 (May 2002), accessed 5 March 2015 at SSRN: http://ssrn.com/abstract=301475.

Bratton, William W and McCahery, John A, 'Comparative Corporate Governance and the Theory of the Firm: The Case Against Global Cross Reference' (1999) 38(2) *Columbia Journal of Transnational Law* 213, accessed 5 March 2015 at SSRN: http://ssrn.com/abstract=205455.

Brick, I E, Palia, D and Wang, C-J, 'Simultaneous Estimation of CEO Compensation, Leverage, and Board Characteristics on Firm Value', AFA 2006 Boston Meetings Paper (March 2005), accessed 5 March 2015 at SSRN: http://ssrn.com/abstract=687487, 5.

Brick, I E, Palmon, O and Wald, K J, 'CEO Compensation, Director Compensation, and Firm Performance: Evidence of Cronyism'

(1 May 2002), accessed 5 March 2015 at SSRN: http://ssrn.com/abstract=303574.

Bris, A and Cabolis, C, 'Corporate Governance Convergence by Contract: Evidence from Cross-Border Mergers', Yale ICF Working Paper No 02-32 (September 2002), accessed 5 March 2015 at SSRN: http://ssrn.com/abstract=321101.

Brown, James R, Falaschetti, Dino and Orlando, Michael J, 'Auditor Independence and Earnings Quality: Evidence for Market Discipline vs. Sarbanes-Oxley Proscriptions', FSU College of Law, Law and Economics Paper No. 07-33 (21 February 2008), accessed 5 March 2015 at SSRN: http://ssrn.com/abstract=940847.

Brown, L D and Caylor, M L, 'Corporate Governance and Firm Performance' (7 December 2004), accessed 5 March 2015 at SSRN: http://ssrn.com/abstract=586423.

Brown, L D and Caylor, M L, 'Corporate Governance and Firm Valuation' (20 December 2005), accessed 5 March 2015 at SSRN: http://ssrn.com/abstract=754484.

Brown, L D and Caylor, M L, 'Corporate Governance and Firm Operating Performance' (7 December 2006), accessed 5 March 2015 at SSRN: http://ssrn.com/abstract=814205.

Bruno, V and Claessens, Stijn, 'Corporate Governance and Regulation: Can There Be Too Much of a Good Thing?' (1 March 2007), World Bank Policy Research Working Paper No 4140, accessed 5 March 2015 at SSRN: http://ssrn.com/abstract=964802.

Bryan, D M, Liu, C and Tiras, S L, 'The Influence of Independent and Effective Audit Committees on Earnings Quality' (6 January 2004), accessed 5 March 2015 at SSRN: http://ssrn.com/abstract=488082.

Buckland, R, 'UK Company Board Structures and Corporate Performance: A Cohort Study of 1990s IPOs in the UK', EFMA 2001 Lugano Meetings; Aberdeen Accountancy, Finance & Mgmt Working Paper 01-01 (2001), accessed 5 March 2015 at SSRN: http://ssrn.com/abstract=269807.

Cai, Jie and Walkling, Ralph A, 'Shareholders' Say on Pay: Does it Create Value?', Drexel College of Business Research Paper No 2008-06 (February 2008), accessed 5 March 2015 at SSRN: http://ssrn.com/abstract=1030925.

Callen, Jeffery L and Morel, Mindy, 'The Enron-Andersen Debacle: Do Equity Markets React to Auditor Reputation?', EFMA 2003 Helsinki Meetings (December 2002), accessed 5 March 2015 at SSRN: http://ssrn.com/abstract=341440.

Carcello, J V, Hollingsworth, C W, Klein, A and Neal, T L, 'Audit Committee Financial Expertise, Competing Corporate Governance

Mechanisms, and Earnings Management' (February 2006), available at SSRN: http://ssrn.com/abstract=887512.

Chapple, Larelle, Ferguson, Colin and Kang, Diana, 'Corporate Governance and Misappropriation' (15 June 2007), accessed 5 March 2015 at SSRN: http://ssrn.com/abstract=1011936.

Cheffins, Brian R, Bank, Steven A and Wells, Harwell, 'Law and History by Numbers: Use, But with Care', ECGI – Law Working Paper No. 230/2013; University of Cambridge Faculty of Law Research Paper No. 50/2013; UCLA School of Law, Law-Econ Research Paper 13-21; Temple University Legal Studies Research Paper No. 2013-47, (October 28, 2013), accessed 23 April 2015 at SSRN: http://ssrn.com/abstract=2348654.

Cheffins, Brian R, Black, Bernard S and Klausner, Michael D, 'Outside Directors, Liability Risk and Corporate Governance: A Comparative Analysis (English Version)', ECGI – Law Working Paper No 48, accessed 23 April 2015 at SSRN: http://ssrn.com/abstract=800584.

Chhaochharia, Vidhi and Grinstein, Y, 'Corporate Governance and Firm Value: The Impact of the 2002 Governance Rules' (March 2007), Johnson School Research Paper Series No 23-06, accessed 5 March 2015 at SSRN: http://ssrn.com/abstract=556990.

Ching, K, Firth, M and Rui, O M, 'Earnings Management, Corporate Governance and the Market Performance of Seasoned Equity Offerings' (September 2002), accessed 5 March 2015 at SSRN: http://ssrn.com/abstract=337880.

Coffee, John C, 'The Acquiescent Gatekeeper: Reputational Intermediaries, Auditor Independence and the Governance of Accounting', Columbia Law and Economics Working Paper No 191 (May 2001), accessed 5 March 2015 at SSRN: http://ssrn.com/abstract=270944.

Coffee, John C, 'Understanding Enron: It's About the Gatekeepers, Stupid', Columbia Law & Economics Working Paper No 207 (30 July 2002), accessed 5 March 2015 at SSRN: http://ssrn.com/abstract=325240.

Coffee, John C, 'The Political Economy of Dodd-Frank: Why Financial Reform Tends to be Frustrated and Systemic Risk Perpetuated' (2012) 97 *Cornell Law Review* 1019; Columbia Law and Economics Working Paper No 414 (9 January 2012), accessed 5 March 2015 at SSRN: http://ssrn.com/abstract=1982128.

Cohen, Alma and Wang, Charles C Y, 'How Do Staggered Boards Affect Shareholder Value? Evidence from a Natural Experiment' (2013) *Journal of Financial Economics*, Forthcoming; Harvard Business School Accounting & Management Unit Working Paper No. 13-068,

(July 3, 2013), accessed 23 April 2015 at SSRN: http://ssrn.com/abstract=2141410.

Coles, L J, Daniel, N D and Naveen, L, 'Boards: Does One Size Fit All?' (February 2005), accessed 5 March 2015 at SSRN: http://ssrn.com/abstract=665746.

Cotter, James F, Palmiter, Alan R and Thomas, Randall S, 'The First Year of "Say on Pay" Under Dodd-Frank: An Empirical Analysis and Look Forward' (2013) 81(3) *George Washington Law Review* 967; Vanderbilt Law and Economics Research Paper No. 12-32; Wake Forest Univ Legal Studies Paper No. 2220259, (February 17, 2013), accessed 23 April 2015 at SSRN: http://ssrn.com/abstract=2162957.

Cremers, Martijn, Bebchuk, Lucian A and Peyer, Urs, 'CEO Centrality', Harvard Law and Economics Discussion Paper No 601 (December 2007, Revised May 2008), accessed 5 March 2015 at SSRN: http://ssrn.com/abstract=1030107.

Cremers, K J M and Nair, V B, 'Governance Mechanisms and Equity Prices', Yale ICF Working Paper No 03-15; NYU, Center for Law and Business Research Paper No 03-09; AFA 2004 San Diego Meetings (August 2003), accessed 5 March 2015 at SSRN: http://ssrn.com/abstract=412140.

Cuñat, Vincente, Gine, Mireia and Guadalupe, Maria, 'The Vote is Cast: The Effect of Corporate Governance on Shareholder Value' (17 February 2010), accessed 5 March 2015 at SSRN: http://ssrn.com/abstract=1555961.

Cunningham, Lawrence A, 'Behavioral Finance and Investor Governance' (2002) 59 *Washington & Lee Law Review* 767, accessed 5 March 2015 at SSRN: http://ssrn.com/abstract=255778.

Cunningham, Lawrence A, 'Rediscovering Board Expertise: Legal Implications of the Empirical Literature', GWU Law School Public Law Research Paper No 363 (23 October 2007), accessed 5 March 2015 at SSRN: http://ssrn.com/abstract=1024261.

Daines, R, Nair, V B and Kornhauser, L A, 'The Good, the Bad and the Lucky: CEO Pay and Skill', Univ of Pennsylvania Institute for Law and Economics, Research Paper Series (August 2005), accessed 5 March 2015 at SSRN: http://ssrn.com/abstract=622223.

Dallas, Lynne, 'Short-Termism, the Financial Crisis, and Corporate Governance' (2011) 37 *Journal of Corporation Law* 264; San Diego Legal Studies Paper No 12-078 (16 February 2012), accessed 5 March 2015 at SSRN: http://ssrn.com/abstract=2006556.

DeFond, M L, Hann, R N and Hu, X, 'Does the Market Value Financial Expertise on Audit Committees of Boards of Directors?', Leventhal School of Accounting, University of Southern California, Los Angeles,

California 90089-1421 (January 2004), accessed 5 March 2015 at SSRN: http://ssrn.com/abstract=498822.

Dent, George W, 'Academics in Wonderland: The Team Production and Director Primacy Models of Corporate Governance' (June 2007), Case Legal Studies Research Paper No 07-21, accessed 5 March 2015 at SSRN: http://ssrn.com/abstract=995186.

Dichev, Ilia D, Graham, John R, Harvey, Campbell R and Rajgopal, Shivaram, 'A Guide to Earnings Quality' (October 30, 2013), accessed 23 April 2015 at SSRN: http://ssrn.com/abstract=2347428.

Dichev, Ilia D, Graham, John R, Harvey, Campbell R and Rajgopal, Shivaram, 'The Misrepresentation of Earnings' (September 12, 2014), accessed 23 April 2015 at SSRN: http://ssrn.com/abstract=2376408.

Dionne, Georges and Triki, Thouraya, 'Risk Management and Corporate Governance: The Importance of Independence and Financial Knowledge for the Board and the Audit Committee' (28 March 2005 posted 14 January 2012), accessed 5 March 2015 at SSRN: http://ssrn.com/abstract=686470.

Donelson, Dain C, McInnis, John M and Mergenthaler, Richard, 'The Effect of Board Independence and Non-Audit Services on Financial Reporting Fraud' (29 August 2012), accessed 5 March 2015 at SSRN: http://ssrn.com/abstract=2138348.

Duchin, Ran, Matsusaka, John G and Ozbas, Oguzhan, 'When Are Outside Directors Effective?', USC CLEO Research Paper No C07-13 (February 2008), accessed 5 March 2015 at SSRN: http://ssrn.com/abstract=1026488.

Dunning, Joseph IV, 'Agency Theory and CEO Incentives' (23 January 2012), accessed 5 March 2015 at SSRN: http://ssrn.com/abstract=2034618.

du Plessis, Jean Jacques, Hargovan, Anil and Bagaric, Mirko, *Principles of Contemporary Corporate Governance*, 2nd edn, Cambridge: Cambridge University Press, 2011.

Dybvig, Philip H and Warachka, Mitch, 'Tobin's q Does Not Measure Firm Performance: Theory, Empirics, and Alternative Measures' (10 September 2012), accessed 5 March 2015 at SSRN: http://ssrn.com/abstract=1562444.

Edelman, H, Thomas, Randall S and Thompson, Robert B, 'Shareholder Voting in an Age of Intermediary Capitalism' (2014) *Southern California Law Review*, forthcoming; European Corporate Governance Institute (ECGI) – Law Working Paper No 246/2014; Vanderbilt Law and Economics Research Paper No 14-9 (27 August 2014), accessed 5 March 2015 at SSRN: http://ssrn.com/abstract=2401746.

Edmans, Alex, 'Blockholders and Corporate Governance', ECGI

– Finance Working Paper No. 385, (October 11, 2013), accessed 23 April 2015 at SSRN: http://ssrn.com/abstract=2285781.

Elbadry, Ahmed, Gounopoulos, Dimitrios and Skinner, Frank S, ‘Governance Quality and Information Asymmetry’, *Financial Markets, Institutions and Instruments*, forthcoming, (January 3, 2014), accessed 23 April 2015 at SSRN: http://ssrn.com/abstract=2373902.

Elson, Charles M and Ferrere, Craig K, ‘Executive Superstars, Peer Groups and Over-Compensation – Cause, Effect and Solution’ (7 August 2012), accessed 5 March 2015 at SSRN: http://ssrn.com/abstract=2125979.

Erkens, David H, Hung, Mingyi and Matos, Pedro P, ‘Corporate Governance in the 2007–2008 Financial Crisis: Evidence from Financial Institutions Worldwide’ (2012) 18(2) *Journal of Corporate Finance* 389–411 (15 January 2012), accessed 5 March 2015 at SSRN: http://ssrn.com/abstract=1397685.

Evans, Robert T and Evans, John P, ‘The Influence of Non-Executive Director Control and Rewards on CEO Remuneration: Australian Evidence’, EFMA 2002 London Meetings (12 March 2001), accessed 5 March 2015 at SSRN: http://ssrn.com/abstract=263050.

Fama, Eugene F, ‘Agency Problems and the Theory of the Firm’ (1980) 88 *Journal of Political Economy* 134–45.

Fama, Eugene F and Jensen, Michael C, ‘Separation of Ownership and Control’ in Michael C Jensen, *Foundations Of Organizational Strategy*, Cambridge, MA: Harvard University Press, 1998 and (1983) 26 *Journal of Law and Economics* 301–49, accessed 5 March 2015 at SSRN: http://ssrn.com/abstract=94034.

Fama, Eugene F, Jensen, Michael C, Fisher, Lawrence and Roll, Richard, ‘The Adjustment of Stock Prices to New Information’ (1969) 10 *International Economic Review* 1–22, accessed 5 March 2015 at SSRN: http://ssrn.com/abstract=321524.

Farber, D B, ‘Restoring Trust After Fraud: Does Corporate Governance Matter?’ (4 October 2004), accessed 5 March 2015 at SSRN: http://ssrn.com/abstract=485403.

Fernandes, Nuno G, ‘Board Compensation and Firm Performance: The Role of “Independent” Board Members’ (December 2005), ECGI – Finance Working Paper No 104/2005, accessed 5 March 2015 at SSRN: http://ssrn.com/abstract=830244.

Fich, E M and Shivdasani, A, ‘Are Busy Boards Effective Monitors?’, ECGI – Finance Working Paper No 55/2004; AFA 2005 Philadelphia Meetings (October 2004), accessed 5 March 2015 at SSRN: http://ssrn.com/abstract=607364.

Fogel, Kathy, Ma, Liping and Morck, Randall, ‘Powerful Independent Directors’, European Corporate Governance Institute (ECGI) – Finance

Working Paper No. 404/2014, (January 9, 2014), accessed 23 April 2015 at SSRN: http://ssrn.com/abstract=2377106.

Frydman, Carola and Jenter, Dirk, 'CEO Compensation', Rock Center for Corporate Governance at Stanford University Working Paper No 77 (19 March 2010), accessed 5 March 2015 at SSRN: http://ssrn.com/abstract=1582232.

Fuerst, O and Kang, S, 'Corporate Governance, Expected Operating Performance, and Pricing', accessed 5 March 2015 at SSRN: http://ssrn.com/abstract=141357.

Gillan, Stuart L and Starks, L T, 'Corporate Governance, Corporate Ownership, and the Role of Institutional Investors: A Global Perspective', Weinberg Center for Corporate Governance Working Paper No 2003-01 (August 2003), accessed 5 March 2015 at SSRN: http://ssrn.com/abstract=439500.

Gillan, Stuart L and Martin, John D, 'Financial Engineering, Corporate Governance, and the Collapse of Enron', U of Delaware Coll. of Bus. and Econ. Ctr. for Corp. Governance Working Paper No 2002-001 (November 2002), accessed 5 March 2015 at SSRN: http://ssrn.com/abstract=354040.

Gilson, Ronald J and Gordon, Jeffrey N, 'Agency Capitalism: Further Implications of Equity Intermediation', European Corporate Governance Institute (ECGI) – Law Working Paper No. 239/2014; Stanford Law and Economics Olin Working Paper No. 456; Columbia Law and Economics Working Paper No. 461, (February 1, 2014), accessed 23 April 2015 at SSRN: http://ssrn.com/abstract=2359690.

Goldman Sachs JBWere (Gray, A, analyst), Research Report, *Good Corporate Governance = Good Investment Returns, A strong result from governance investment strategies again for FY06*, June 2006, available at www.gsjbw.com. Source: Corporate Governance International, subscriber letter, 16 June 2006 and attachments (copy on file with author).

Gompers, P A, Ishii, J L and Metrick, A, 'Corporate Governance and Equity Prices' (2003) 118(1) *Quarterly Journal of Economics* 107–55, February 2003, accessed 5 March 2015 at SSRN: http://ssrn.com/abstract=278920.

Gordon, Jeffrey N, 'What Enron Means for the Management and Control of the Modern Business Corporation: Some Initial Reflections' (2002) 69 *University of Chicago Law Review* 1233 (Summer 2002), accessed 5 March 2015 at SSRN: http://ssrn.com/abstract=305343.

Gordon, Jeffrey N, 'Governance Failures of the Enron Board and the New Information Order of Sarbanes-Oxley', Columbia Law and Economics Working Paper No 216; Harvard Law and Economics Discussion Paper No. 416 (March 2003), accessed 5 March 2015 at SSRN: http://ssrn.com/abstract=391363.

Gordon, Jeffrey N, 'Independent Directors and Stock Market Prices: The New Corporate Governance Paradigm', ECGI – Law Working Paper No 74/2006, (August 2006), accessed 23 April 2015 at SSRN: http://ssrn.com/abstract=928100.

Gordon, Jeffrey N, 'The Rise of Independent Directors in the United States, 1950–2005: Of Shareholder Value and Stock Market Prices' (2007) 59 *Stanford Law Review* 1465, accessed 23 April 2015 at SSRN: http://ssrn.com/abstract=1086397.

Göx, Robert F, Imhof, Frédéric and Kunz, Alexis, 'Say on Pay Design and its Repercussion on CEO Investment Incentives, Compensation, and Firm Profit' (13 April 2010), accessed 5 March 2015 at SSRN: http://ssrn.com/abstract=1588682.

Goyal, V K and Park, C W, 'Board Leadership Structure and CEO Turnover' (July 2001), accessed 5 March 2015 at SSRN: http://ssrn.com/abstract=224055.

Gugler, K P, Mueller, D C and Yurtoglu, B B, 'Corporate Governance and the Returns on Investment', EFA 2002 Berlin Meetings Presented Paper; ECGI – Finance Working Paper No 06/2003 (January 2003), accessed 5 March 2015 at SSRN: http://ssrn.com/abstract=299520.

Guthrie, Katherine, Sokolowsky, Jan and Wan, Kam-Ming, 'CEO Compensation and Board Structure Revisited' (2012) 67(3) *Journal of Finance* 1149–68 (18 September 2010), accessed 5 March 2015 at SSRN: http://ssrn.com/abstract=1680476.

Guthrie, Katherine, Sokolowsky, Jan and Wan, Kam-Ming, 'CEO Compensation and Board Structure – Rejoinder' (18 April 2012 and posted 16 June 2012), accessed 5 March 2015 at SSRN: http://ssrn.com/abstract=2084630.

Guthrie, Katherine, Sokolowsky, Jan and Wan, Kam-Ming, 'CEO Compensation and Board Structure Revisited – Addendum' (27 March 2012 and revised 20 March 2013), accessed 5 March 2015 at SSRN: http://ssrn.com/abstract=2074895.

Hackman, J R, ed., *Groups That Work*, San Francisco, CA: Jossey-Bass, 1990.

Hanlon, M, Rajgopal, S and Shevlin, T J, 'Are Executive Stock Options Associated with Future Earnings?', JAE Boston Conference, October 2002 (20 December 2002), accessed 5 March 2015 at SSRN: http://ssrn.com/abstract=318101.

Hermalin, Benjamin E, 'Firm Value and Corporate Governance: Does the Former Determine the Latter?' (2 January 2008), accessed 5 March 2015 at SSRN: http://ssrn.com/abstract=1080090.

Hermalin, Benjamin E and Weisbach, Michael S, 'Boards of Directors as an Endogenously Determined Institution: A Survey of the Economic Literature' (2003) 9(1) *FRBNY Economic Policy Review* 7–26.

Hermalin, Benjamin E and Weisbach, Michael S, 'Transparency and Corporate Governance' (21 January 2007), accessed 5 March 2015 at SSRN: http://ssrn.com/abstract=958628.

Hermalin, Benjamin E and Weisbach, Michael J, 'Understanding Corporate Governance Through Learning Models of Managerial Competence', Fisher College of Business Working Paper No. 2014-03-04, (March 27, 2014), accessed 23 April 2015 at SSRN: http://ssrn.com/abstract=2417278.

Hill, Jennifer G, 'Regulatory Responses to Global Corporate Scandals' (2005) 23 *Wisconsin International Law Journal* 367, accessed 5 March 2015 at SSRN: http://ssrn.com/abstract=886104.

Hill, Jennifer G, 'Regulating Executive Remuneration: International Developments in the Post-Scandal Era' (2006) 3 *European Company Law* 64; Vanderbilt Law and Economics Research Paper No 06-06, accessed 5 March 2015 at SSRN: http://ssrn.com/abstract=887944.

Hill, Jennifer G, 'New Trends in the Regulation of Executive Remuneration' in R P Austin and A Y Bilski (eds), *Directors In Troubled Times*, pp 100–23, Ross Parsons Centre of Commercial, Corporate and Taxation Law, 2009; Sydney Law School Research Paper No 10/22; Vanderbilt Law and Economics Research Paper No 10-05; ECGI – Law Working Paper No 142/2010 (7 February 2010), accessed 5 March 2015 at SSRN: http://ssrn.com/abstract=1549429.

Hill, Jennifer G and Yablon, Charles M, 'Corporate Governance and Executive Remuneration: Rediscovering Managerial Positional Conflict', Vanderbilt Law and Economics Research Paper No 03-02, accessed 5 March 2015 at SSRN: http://ssrn.com/abstract=375240.

Hsu, Hwa-Hsien and Wu, Yu-Hsuan, 'Board Composition, Audit Committee Structure, "Grey Directors" and the Incidences of Corporate Failure in the UK' Finance and Corporate Governance Conference 2010 Paper (10 December 2009), accessed 5 March 2015 at SSRN: http://ssrn.com/abstract=1532997.

Hutchinson, M R, 'An Analysis of the Association Between Firms' Investment Opportunities, Board Composition, and Firm Performance', accessed 5 March 2015 at SSRN: http://ssrn.com/abstract=295483.

Jensen, Michael C, 'The Modern Industrial Revolution, Exit, and The Failure of Internal Control Systems' (1993) 48(3) *Journal of Finance* 831–80.

Jensen, Michael C, 'The Agency Cost of Overvalued Equity and the Current State of Corporate Finance', Harvard NOM Working Paper No 04-26, accessed 5 March 2015 at SSRN: http://ssrn.com/abstract=560961.

Jensen, Michael C, 'Agency Costs of Overvalued Equity', Harvard NOM Working Paper No 04-26; ECGI – Finance Working Paper No 39/2004 (March 2005), accessed 5 March 2015 at SSRN: http://ssrn.com/abstract=480421.

Jiraporn, Pornsit, Davidson III, Wallace N, Ning, Yixi and DaDalt, Peter J, 'Too Busy to Show Up? An Analysis of Directors' Absences' (21 January 2008), accessed 5 March 2015 at SSRN: http://ssrn.com/abstract=1254642.

Katelouzou, Dionysia, 'Worldwide Hedge Fund Activism: Dimensions and Legal Determinants' (2014) *University of Pennsylvania Journal of Business Law*, forthcoming; King's College London Law School Research Paper No. 2014-8, (September 22, 2014), accessed 23 April 2015 at SSRN: http://ssrn.com/abstract=2357547.

Kimbro, Marinilka and Xu, Danielle, 'Shareholders Have a Say on Executive Compensation: Evidence from Say-on-Pay in the United States' (April 1, 2013) available at SSRN: http://ssrn.com/abstract=2209936.

Klapper, L F and Love, I, 'Corporate Governance, Investor Protection and Performance in Emerging Markets' (March 2002), World Bank Policy Research Working Paper No 2818, accessed 5 March 2015 at SSRN: http://ssrn.com/abstract=303979.

Klein, A, 'Audit, Committee, Board of Director Characteristics, and Earnings Management', New York University School Of Law, NYU Center for Law and Economics, Law & Economics Research Paper Series, Working Paper No 06-42 (October 2006), accessed 5 March 2015 at SSRN: http://papers.ssrn.com/paper.taf?abstract_id=246674.

Kumar, Praveen and Sivaramakrishnan, Shiva, 'Who Monitors the Monitor? The Effect of Board Independence on Executive Compensation and Firm Value' (16 January 2007), accessed 5 March 2015 at SSRN: http://ssrn.com/abstract=988543.

Langevoort, Donald C, 'Theories, Assumptions and Securities Regulation: Market Efficiency Revisited' (1992) 140 *U Pa L Rev* 85.

La Porta, Rafael, Lopez-de-Silanes, Florencio, Shleifer, Andrei and Vishny, R W, *Law and Finance*, NBER Working Paper No 5661 (July 1996).

La Porta, Rafael, Lopez-de-Silanes, Florencio, Shleifer, Andrei and Vishny, R W, 'Investor Protection and Corporate Governance' (June 1999), accessed 5 March 2015 at SSRN: http://ssrn.com/abstract=183908.

La Porta, Rafael, Lopez-de-Silanes, Florencio and Shleifer, Andrei, 'The Economic Consequences of Legal Origins' (2008) 46(2) *Journal of Economic Literature* 285–332, accessed 5 March 2015 at SSRN: http://ssrn.com/abstract=1028081.

Larcker, David F, Ormazabal, Gaizka and Taylor, Daniel J, 'The Market Reaction to Corporate Governance Regulation' (2011) 101(2)

Journal of Financial Economics 431–48; Rock Center for Corporate Governance at Stanford University Working Paper Series No 82 (14 October 2010), accessed 5 March 2015 at SSRN: http://ssrn.com/abstract=165033.

Larcker, David F and Richardson, S A, 'Corporate Governance, Fees for Non-audit Services and Accrual Choices' (April 2003), accessed 5 March 2015 at SSRN: http://ssrn.com/abstract=394441.

Larcker, David F, Richardson, S A and Tuna, A I, 'How Important is Corporate Governance?' (May 2005), accessed 5 March 2015 at SSRN: http://ssrn.com/abstract=595821.

Larcker, David F, So, Eric C and Wang, Charles C Y, 'Boardroom Centrality and Firm Performance', Rock Center for Corporate Governance at Stanford University Working Paper No 84 (17 August 2012), accessed 5 March 2015 at SSRN: http://ssrn.com/abstract=1651407.

Larcker, David F and Tayan, Brian, 'Seven Myths of Corporate Governance', Rock Center for Corporate Governance at Stanford University Closer Look Series: Topics, Issues and Controversies in Corporate Governance No CGRP-16 (1 June 2011), accessed 5 March 2015 at SSRN: http://ssrn.com/abstract=1856869.

Lasfer, M and Faccio, M, 'Managerial Ownership, Board Structure and Firm Value: The UK Evidence', Cass Business School Research Paper (30 August 1999), accessed 5 March 2015 at SSRN: http://ssrn.com/abstract=179008.

Lee, C, 'Where Do the Talented People Work as Outside Directors?', CAEPR Working Paper No 2007-006 (14 August 2007), accessed 5 March 2015 at SSRN: http://ssrn.com/abstract=988119.

Lehn, K, Patro, S and Zhao, M, 'Determinants of the Size and Structure of Corporate Boards: 1935–2000' (November 2003), accessed 5 March 2015 at SSRN: http://ssrn.com/abstract=470675.

Linck, J S, Netter, J M and Yang, T, 'The Determinants of Board Structure' (23 March 2007), accessed 5 March 2015 at SSRN: http://ssrn.com/abstract=729935.

Mak, Y T and Kusnadi, K, 'Size Really Matters: Further Evidence on the Negative Relationship Between Board Size and Firm Value', NUS Business School Working Paper (March 2002), accessed 5 March 2015 at SSRN: http://ssrn.com/abstract=303505.

Marrakchi Chtourou, S, Bédard, J and Courteau, L, 'Corporate Governance and Earnings Management' (21 April 2001), accessed 5 March 2015 at SSRN: http://ssrn.com/abstract=275053.

Masulis, Ronald W, Wang, Cong and Xie, Fei, 'Corporate Governance and Acquirer Returns', ECGI – Finance Working Paper No 116/2006, accessed 5 March 2015 at SSRN: http://ssrn.com/abstract=697501.

McCahery, Joseph A, Starks, Laura T and Sautner, Zacharias, 'Behind the Scenes: The Corporate Governance Preferences of Institutional Investors' AFA 2011 Denver Meetings Paper; Tilburg Law School Research Paper No 010/2010 (13 December 2010), accessed 5 March 2015 at SSRN: http://ssrn.com/abstract=1571046.

Mehran, Hamid, Morrison, Alan D and Shapiro, Joel D, 'Corporate Governance and Banks: What Have We Learned from the Financial Crisis?', Federal Reserve Bank of New York Staff Report No. 502 (1 June 2011), accessed 5 March 2015 at SSRN: http://ssrn.com/abstract=1880009.

Michaud, Dennis Wright and Gai, Yunwei, 'CEO Compensation and Firm Performance' (20 December 2009), accessed 5 March 2015 at SSRN: http://ssrn.com/abstract=1531673.

Morck, R, 'Behavioral Finance in Corporate Governance – Independent Directors and Non-Executive Chairs', Harvard Institute of Economic Research Discussion Paper No 2037 (May 2004), accessed 5 March 2015 at SSRN: http://ssrn.com/abstract=527723.

Morck, R, Shleifer, A and Vishny, R W, 'Management Ownership and Corporate Performance: An Empirical Analysis' (1988) 20 *Journal of Financial Economics* 293–316.

Ng, Anthony, Gul, Ferdinand and Mensah, Yaw, 'Managerial Entrenchment and Value-Relevance of Earnings During the Pre- and Post-Sarbanes Oxley Periods' (September 2007), accessed 5 March 2015 at SSRN: http://ssrn.com/abstract=1012746.

Nosworthy, Beth, Symes, Christopher F and Le Mire, Suzanne, 'Expertise is the New Game? Obligations on Corporate Managers in Solvent and Insolvent Companies', Working Paper for Conference, *Corporate Law – Progressive Possibilities*, Australian National University (ANU), 3–5 February 2013, 19 of 28 (footnotes omitted) (copy on file with author).

Patel, S A and Dallas, G S, 'Transparency and Disclosure: Overview of Methodology and Study Results – United States' (16 October 2002), accessed 5 March 2015 at SSRN: http://ssrn.com/abstract=422800.

Peasnell, Ken V, Pope, Peter F and Young, Steven, 'Board Monitoring and Earnings Management: Do Outside Directors Influence Abnormal Accruals?' (October 2000), accessed 5 March 2015 at SSRN: http://ssrn.com/abstract=249557.

Perry, T, 'Incentive Compensation for Outside Directors and CEO Turnover', presented at Tuck-JFE Contemporary Corporate Governance Conference (June 2000), accessed 5 March 2015 at SSRN: http://ssrn.com/abstract=236033.

Pritchard, Adam C, Ferris, Stephen P and Jagannathan, Murali, 'Too Busy to Mind the Business? Monitoring by Directors with Multiple Board

Appointments', University of Michigan Law School, Working Paper No 99-013; CORI Working Paper No 2001-02 (June 2002), accessed 5 March 2015 at SSRN: http://ssrn.com/abstract=167288.

Raheja, Charu G, 'Determinants of Board Size and Composition: A Theory of Corporate Boards' (2005) 40(2) *Journal of Financial and Quantitative Analysis* 283–306, accessed 5 March 2015 at SSRN: http://ssrn.com/abstract=522542, 4.

Roe, Mark J, 'Corporate Short-Termism – In the Boardroom and in the Courtroom' (2013) 68 *Business Lawyer* 977; ECGI – Law Working Paper No. 210; Harvard Public Law Working Paper No. 13-18, (August 1, 2013) accessed 23 April 2015 at SSRN: http://ssrn.com/abstract=2239132.

Rose, Paul and Sharfman, Bernard S, 'Shareholder Activism as a Corrective Mechanism in Corporate Governance', Ohio State Public Law Working Paper No. 225, (September 11, 2013), accessed 23 April 2015 at SSRN: http://ssrn.com/abstract=2324151.

Rosen, Kenneth M, 'Who Killed Katie Couric? And Other Tales From The World Of Executive Compensation Reform' (2008) 76 *Fordham Law Review* 2907, available at SSRN: http://ssrn.com/abstract=1125295.

Rosenfeld, P, 'What Drives Earnings Management? Generally Accepted Accounting Principles' (2000) 190 *Journal of Accountancy* 106 (1 October 2000).

Ruddock, C M S, Taylor, S J and Taylor, S L, 'Non-Audit Services and Earnings Conservatism: Is Auditor Independence Impaired?' (April 2004), accessed 5 March 2015 at SSRN: http://ssrn.com/abstract=303343.

Ruigrok, W, Peck, S I and Keller, H, 'Board Characteristics and Involvement in Strategic Decision Making: Evidence from Swiss Companies' (2006) 43(5) *Journal of Management Studies* 1201–26, accessed 5 March 2015 at SSRN: http://ssrn.com/abstract=910636.

Shleifer, A and Vishny, R, 'A Survey of Corporate Governance' (1997) 52(2) *Journal of Finance* 737–83.

Singh, R, 'Board Independence and the Design of Executive Compensation' (September 2006), EFA 2005 Moscow Meetings Paper, accessed 5 March 2015 at SSRN: http://ssrn.com/abstract=673741.

Smith, M, 'Audit Committee Effectiveness: Did the Blue Ribbon Committee Recommendations Make a Difference?' (2006) 3(2) *International Journal of Accounting, Auditing and Performance Evaluation* 240–51, accessed 5 March 2015 at SSRN: http://ssrn.com/abstract=1001531.

Tehranian, H, Cornett, M M, Marcus, A J and Saunders, A, 'Earnings Management, Corporate Governance, and True Financial Performance' (January 2006), accessed 5 March 2015 at SSRN: http://ssrn.com/abstract=886142.

Thomas, Randall S and Van der Elst, Christoph, 'Say on Pay Around the World', Vanderbilt Law and Economics Research Paper 14-10. (January 20, 2014), accessed 23 April 2015 at SSRN: http://ssrn.com/abstract=2401761.

Turnbull, Shann, 'Why Unitary Boards Are Not Best Practice: A Case for Compound Boards' (November 2000), available at SSRN: http://ssrn.com/abstract=253803.

Vishwanath, Tara and Kaufmann, Daniel, 'Towards Transparency in Finance and Governance' (September 1999), accessed 5 March 2015 at SSRN: http://ssrn.com/abstract=258978.

Weil, R L, Coates, D J and Marais, M L, 'Audit Committee Financial Literacy: A Work in Progress', CRSP Working Paper No 605 (11 March 2005), accessed 5 March 2015 at SSRN: http://ssrn.com/abstract=680281.

Weir, C, Laing, D and McKnight, P J, 'An Empirical Analysis of the Impact of Corporate Governance Mechanisms on the Performance of UK Firms', accessed 5 March 2015 at SSRN: http://ssrn.com/abstract=286440.

Weisbach, M S and Hermalin, Benjamin E, 'Boards of Directors as an Endogenously Determined Institution: A Survey of the Economic Literature' (15 June 2000), accessed 5 March 2015 at SSRN: http://ssrn.com/abstract=233111.

Wessels, Roberto E and Wansbeek, Tom, 'What is the Relation (If Any) between a Firm's Corporate Governance Arrangements and its Financial Performance?', CESifo Working Paper Series No. 4599, (January 31, 2014), accessed 23 April 2015 at SSRN: http://ssrn.com/abstract=2393995.

Xie, B, Davidson III, W N and DaDalt, P J, 'Earnings Management and Corporate Governance: The Roles of the Board and the Audit Committee' (5 July 2001), accessed 5 March 2015 at SSRN: http://ssrn.com/abstract=304195.

Index